DYSLEXIA IN ADOLESCENCE

Dyslexia in Adolescence: Global Perspectives presents international case studies on the psychosocial development and academic progress of adolescents with dyslexia to enhance understanding of adjustment factors, outcomes and support. The continuation of a qualitative longitudinal research project that focused on children between ten and twelve years of age, this volume revisits them between ages fourteen and sixteen. Through semi-structured interviews, personal narratives and other assessments, these case studies relate the trials and tribulations associated with the development of adolescents with dyslexia from around the world and the challenges that parents face in supporting their children.

Peggy L. Anderson, Ph.D., is Professor of Special Education in the School of Education at Metropolitan State University of Denver, Colorado, USA.

Regine Meier-Hedde, M.Ed., is a dyslexia therapist based in Hamburg, Germany.

DYSLEXIA IN ADOLESCENCE

Global Perspectives

*Edited by Peggy L. Anderson
and Regine Meier-Hedde*

NEW YORK AND LONDON

First published 2017
by Routledge
711 Third Avenue, New York, NY 10017

and by Routledge
2 Park Square, Milton Park, Abingdon, Oxon, OX14 4RN

Routledge is an imprint of the Taylor & Francis Group, an informa business

© 2017 Taylor & Francis

The right of Peggy L. Anderson and Regine Meier-Hedde to be identified as the authors of the editorial material, and of the authors for their individual chapters, has been asserted in accordance with sections 77 and 78 of the Copyright, Designs and Patents Act 1988.

All rights reserved. No part of this book may be reprinted or reproduced or utilised in any form or by any electronic, mechanical, or other means, now known or hereafter invented, including photocopying and recording, or in any information storage or retrieval system, without permission in writing from the publishers.

Trademark notice: Product or corporate names may be trademarks or registered trademarks, and are used only for identification and explanation without intent to infringe.

Library of Congress Cataloging in Publication Data
A catalog record for this book has been requested

ISBN: 978-1-138-64452-6 (hbk)
ISBN: 978-1-138-64453-3 (pbk)
ISBN: 978-1-315-62876-9 (ebk)

Typeset in Bembo and Stone Sans
by Florence Production Ltd, Stoodleigh, Devon, UK

This book is dedicated to the remarkable mothers of these adolescents with dyslexia who are truly the unsung heroes of this story as they work tirelessly, never giving up, to ensure that their children will realize all of their hopes and dreams.

CONTENTS

List of Tables ix

1 Dyslexia in Adolescence 1
  Peggy L. Anderson and Regine Meier-Hedde

2 Introduction to the Study 15
  Peggy L. Anderson and Regine Meier-Hedde

3 Johan, a Case Study of a Swedish Adolescent with Dyslexia 33
  Eva Wennås Brante

4 Gwyn, a Case Study of an Australian Adolescent with Dyslexia 50
  Christina E. van Kraayenoord

5 Ka-ho, a Case Study of a Chinese Adolescent with Dyslexia 68
  Steven S. W. Chu and Kevin K. H. Chung

6 Xavi, a Case Study of a Spanish Adolescent with Dyslexia 87
  Rosa María González Seijas

7 Percy, a Case Study of an Indian Adolescent with Dyslexia 101
  Sunil Karande and Rukhshana F. Sholapurwala

8 Alon, a Case Study of an Israeli Adolescent with Dyslexia 121
  Talya Gur

9 João, a Case Study of a Brazilian Adolescent with Dyslexia 139
    Giseli Donadon Germano and Simone Aparecida Capellini

10 Vicente, a Case Study of a Chilean Adolescent with Dyslexia 152
    Arturo Pinto Guevara and María Pomés

11 Jankó, a Case Study of a Hungarian Adolescent with Dyslexia 167
    Éva Gyarmathy

12 Valeriy, a Case Study of a Russian Adolescent with Dyslexia 180
    Olga Inshakova

13 Jacob, a Case Study of a Canadian Adolescent with Dyslexia 192
    Brenda Linn, Barbara Bobrow, and Ronald W. Stringer

14 Christian, a Case Study of a German Adolescent with Dyslexia 210
    Regine Meier-Hedde

15 Jim, a Case Study of an American Adolescent with Dyslexia 227
    Peggy L. Anderson

16 Cross-Case Analysis and Reflections 245
    Peggy L. Anderson and Regine Meier-Hedde

Contributor Biographies *284*
Index *289*

LIST OF TABLES

16.1 Evaluation of Success Attributes for Adolescents with Dyslexia   246
16.2 Total Scores for Self-Efficacy Questionnaire for Children   261
16.3 Adolescents' Evaluation of Reading Skill Improvement and
      Support Received   264
16.4 Reading Challenges and Solutions   267

1
DYSLEXIA IN ADOLESCENCE

Peggy L. Anderson and Regine Meier-Hedde

Understanding Dyslexia

Well over a century ago, Rudolph Berlin, a German ophthalmologist, coined the term *dyslexia* and described the unusual case of six adult patients with normal language skills who had lost their ability to read (Anderson & Meier-Hedde, 2001). Much later, this condition would come to be understood as *acquired* dyslexia as opposed to *developmental* dyslexia, which is the variant associated with children and adolescents. Today dyslexia continues to be one of the most enigmatic conditions known. That obviously bright children, often with above average intelligence, fail to learn to read as expected is a conundrum to the children themselves, their parents and their teachers. These children will become adolescents and adults who develop competency in other areas of education, vocation and life in general, but the ability to decode and comprehend print to any degree of efficiency, and to actually enjoy reading, may forever elude them.

Discrepant views and definitions of dyslexia frequently overwhelm parents and teachers to the point of frustration, leading many to debate the value and practicality of the label. In fact, Elliott and Grigorenko (2014) have devoted an entire book to questioning the theoretical construct of dyslexia, concluding that the use of this term should be discontinued because of its lack of scientific precision and validity. Before addressing some of these problems associated with defining dyslexia, it seems prudent to identify areas for which there is some accord. Although seemingly reductionist, there appear to be two major characteristics of dyslexia definitions that garner the most support and agreement: the neurological etiology and the discrepancy between the child's reading level and cognitive potential, sometimes referred to as unevenness in development. The latter is particularly important as historically children with dyslexia have often been treated as "slow" or intellectually incapable of typical achievement, which was sometimes used as a defense for ignoring their needs in the classroom.

Many countries have definitions of dyslexia, some of these are official, meaning they are issued from a government office, and others are unofficial, but widely accepted. There are also numerous countries that do not have their own national definitions, but have borrowed them from other countries. This overlapping of official and unofficial definitions and sharing across countries may have increased awareness of the condition, but has done little to clarify the term. In the United States, the influential International Dyslexia Association (IDA) uses the following definition subsequently adopted by the National Institute of Child Health and Human Development (NICHD), many states, and other countries:

> Dyslexia is a specific learning disability that is neurobiological in origin. It is characterized by difficulties with accurate and/or fluent word recognition and by poor spelling and decoding abilities. These difficulties typically result from a deficit in the phonological component of language that is often unexpected in relation to other cognitive abilities and the provision of effective classroom instruction. Secondary consequences may include problems in reading comprehension and reduced reading experience that can impede growth of vocabulary and background knowledge.
> (Lyon, Shaywitz & Shaywitz, 2003, p. 2)

It is important to note that this IDA definition is not the official definition of the U.S. government as dyslexia is considered to be one example of a *specific learning disability* (SLD) covered by the Individuals with Disabilities Act (IDEA), the educational entitlement legislation that guarantees services for school aged children with disabilities. This category is similar to that of other countries including Australia, Canada, China (Hong Kong) and the United Kingdom that use the term *specific learning difficulties* of which dyslexia is an example. In the United States this relationship between dyslexia and SLD causes some confusion as parents who have had their children privately tested and diagnosed with dyslexia are astonished when the schools refuse to provide services because the evaluation criteria have not met certain State guidelines (e.g., achievement is not significantly depressed to meet requirements for educational treatment). To further complicate the situation, some school district administrators and teachers who do not understand the relationship of dyslexia to the federal category of specific learning disabilities have been known to counsel parents that their schools do not recognize, diagnose or treat dyslexia. Such misinformation is baffling because dyslexia is named in IDEA as an example of a specific learning disability, but there is widespread ignorance surrounding this point, so much so that the United States Department of Education (Yudin, 2015) recently issued a federal guidance letter to officially inform all public schools that it is appropriate to use the term dyslexia "to describe and address the child's unique, identified needs through evaluation, eligibility, and IEP (Individualized Education Program) documents." Further, the federal guidance missive encouraged all "States to review their policies, procedures, and practices to ensure that they do not prohibit the use of the terms dyslexia, dyscalculia, and dysgraphia in evaluations, eligibility, and IEP documents." It is too soon to tell what effect that this federal directive will have, but hopefully schools in the United States will be more knowledgeable about dyslexia and more responsive to parents.

The IDA definition of dyslexia emphasizes "deficits in phonological components of language" as the cause of dyslexia, which is common to definitions of other English speaking countries as well as those with alphabetic languages. From this perspective, a dyslexic individual has difficulties reading and spelling because of a lack of capacity to associate spoken sounds with the written, which may account for the preponderance of dyslexia cases. Certainly the decoding theory of dyslexia has had the widest influence, but more current research has taken a broader look at reasons for difficulties with reading and spelling that are not consistent with cognitive abilities (Fletcher, Lyon, Fuchs & Barnes, 2007). Reading is a complex process of decoding, fluency and comprehension. Every component also relies on visual processing. Problems of reversing letters and words, missing parts of words or sentences, skipping lines of text or reading from right to left and other visual processing difficulties have a pronounced effect on decoding and fluency, in turn impeding comprehension. Neuro-psychological research supports the effects of certain aspects of visual processing on reading, particularly visual processing speed (Stenneken et al., 2011). Indeed the issue of processing speed has been a prominent finding in dyslexia research for a number of years (Ackerman & Dykman, 1996), but now researchers are starting to ask questions about the specific influence of speed on decoding. For example, how can measures of decoding determine contributions of both speed and accuracy to assess functioning in this area? (Morlini, Stella & Scorza, 2013). Research continues to be divided on the causes of dyslexia and how these explain different problems we see in dyslexic children. It is possible that further investigation will reveal support for particular factors related to reading subtypes, which will have important implications for intervention. However, at present, a more open-minded approach to dyslexia is warranted as it seems improbable that a single deficit in one particular area is an adequate explanation for all cases (Snowling & Hulme, 2012).

A final issue that confounds understanding of dyslexia is the use of synonymous or related terminology with different or similar meanings intended. For example, in the United States, there is some ambiguity between the terms *reading disability* and *dyslexia*; however, it is our understanding that in practice the two terms are used synonymously. Siegel (2003), in fact, perceives this to be the case for the entire continent of North America, which seems reasonable based on our experience. As previously mentioned, the term *reading difficulties* is used similarly to *reading disabilities* and *dyslexia* in other countries. In an effort to bring some clarity to this terminology, Elliott and Grigorenko (2014) suggested it would be preferable to use the term *reading disability* for decoding problems as a straightforward assessment could confirm such a condition and then other assessments and labels could be assigned for related difficulties (e.g., fluency, accuracy, spelling). While it may be true, as they suggested, that this type of classification would guide intervention, this could just as easily be accomplished by using *dyslexia* as the overarching label and adding subskill difficulties in the same manner. We agree with Riddick's (2010) perspective that the term *reading disability* focuses on the deficit model whereas *dyslexia* usually has a more positive connotation and can be construed as a learning difference instead of a disability, which seems preferable.

Academic Development and Implications

Early intervention is critical in preventing the effects of dyslexia from increasing as grade level advances. Unfortunately, most of these children are not provided with effective remediation sufficiently early at the intensity and duration required to avoid the deleterious effects of a wide gap between potential and reading level. All too often, children who are reading below level in first grade will remain poor readers with a 90% chance of having reading deficits in high school, usually with reading skills at sixth grade level or lower (Shaywitz et al., 1999). Longitudinal studies across different languages with more consistent orthographies than English have verified that poor reading in first and second grades is predictive of poor reading in eighth grade and beyond (Landerl & Wimmer, 2008; Tressoldi, Stella & Faggella, 2001). Most dyslexia professionals recommend systematic and explicit approaches to teaching language structure with an emphasis on phonics, but there is considerable debate regarding which programs or methods will achieve maximum results. The National Reading Panel (NICHD, 2000) specified that "systematic phonics programs are significantly more effective than non-phonics programs" (p. 93), but as Torgesen et al. (2001) noted, various programs do not appear to differ in their effectiveness.

The Rose Report (2009) recommended the adoption of the exclusive use of synthetic phonics for dyslexic students in the United Kingdom even though this has caused dissension among some researchers and educators who do not believe that this method is preferable if it excludes text-level reading until phonics are firmly established (Wyse & Goswami, 2008; Wyse & Styles, 2007). The Orton-Gillingham remedial method has achieved wide popularity as a "best-practice" in the remediation of dyslexia in spite of the fact that research provides little support for the effectiveness of this program over others for dyslexic individuals (Ritchey & Goeke, 2007; Turner, 2008; Vaughn & Linan-Thompson, 2003). Nevertheless, special education teachers who have experience with Orton-Gillingham and other multisensory phonological approaches such as the Wilson Reading Method (Wilson, 1996) may be able to unlock greater potential to make gains in reading because of their strong commitments to these programs. These multisensory remedial strategies, although developed in the United States, have also been successfully adapted for use with other countries, such as Singapore (Lim & Oei,

2015), and languages, including Arabic (Hazoury, Oweini & Bahous, 2009). To be certain, teachers need to be armed with a variety of teaching methods to address the student's unique learning style and preferences while strengthening phonological skills (Snowling & Hulme, 2011). Students with deficits in sound symbol association benefit from strengthening phonological skills. Snowling and Hulme (2011) advocate explicit training in phoneme awareness and have reported evidence that phonological approaches, while optimal in early grades, are also effective for adolescents. Lovett, Lacerenza and Borden (2000) provided evidence on the efficacy of the PHAST Decoding Program that incorporates strategies to improve decoding, word identification, fluency and reading comprehension skills, which has been a method found to be effective with both younger children and adolescents. Intensive remediation is also a necessary component to working with adolescents who continue to struggle with reading (Torgesen et al., 2001). Even though research has provided sufficient evidence of the benefits of basic skill instruction in adolescence, these recommendations are routinely ignored as schools continue to operate on the erroneous assumption that assistive technology and accommodations are sufficient for their needs.

Until third or fourth grade, children are learning to read, but after that they are reading to learn. Consequently, a reading deficit may affect virtually all other subject areas including math, where word problems take on greater importance. The bottom line: dyslexic students often lack basic reading skills when they enter high school. Without these skills, they are vulnerable to academic failure, negative outcomes and a less-than-successful transition to the demands of further education, career and other realities of adulthood (Reiff & Ofiesh, 2016). Given that 70% of secondary students with learning disabilities comprehend text below basic levels (Cortiella & Horowitz, 2014), reading skill instruction should continue well beyond elementary school in order to lay the foundation for success in high school and after. However, with the demands of content classes and pressure to meet graduation standards, secondary school teachers usually do not feel they have the time, skills or inclination to incorporate reading instruction into their academic courses. Students with dyslexia will not fare much better in any special education or remedial classes that might be offered as these teachers will likely be providing instruction in compensatory strategies to help students succeed in content courses and devoting scant time to teaching reading (Ofiesh, 2010). Without knowing how to read, write and understand basic math effectively, dyslexic students in high school are at great risk of academic (and social/psychological) failure with a greater probability of dropping out of high school (Cortiella & Horowtiz, 2014; Newman, Wagner, Cameto, Knokey & Shaver, 2010).

Many general and even special educators have a limited understanding of specific approaches for dyslexia, particularly at the secondary level of instruction. Thus, schools that are committed to extending reading instruction to adolescents sometimes turn to assistive technology reading programs that can offer support with the use of software programs that are more cost effective than one to one or small group remediation. Software-based reading programs, such as Mindplay's Virtual Reading Coach, Houghton Mifflin Harcourt's READ 180 and Taylor Associates' Reading Plus are examples of user-friendly technology programs that can be effective for teachers who do not have in-depth experience with reading intervention programs. An effective approach that general educators can implement is Peer-Assisted Learning Strategies (PALS) where stronger readers work with weaker students several times per week in the classroom (Fuchs & Fuchs, 2005). In any event, a one-size-fits all approach cannot address the variations of dyslexia (Coyne et al., 2013). Individualized approaches are the bedrock of working with students with special needs. Instruction should address the unique needs of each adolescent and capitalize on strengths and facilitate compensating for weaknesses.

Compensatory Learning Strategies

When students have difficulty with basic skills, they may struggle in virtually any content class. However, researchers have determined that specific learning strategies including content enhancement routines can be key to successful compensation at the secondary level (Deshler, 2005; Swanson & Deshler, 2003). Learning strategies are a core group of strategies that are designed to help adolescents with learning disabilities learn how to solve problems independently by thinking about how to organize and explore complex content. Content enhancement routines are examples of evidence-based learning strategies that assist teachers in presenting content in organizational frameworks that will facilitate comprehension, critical thinking, retention and application. These strategies range from simple concept maps that serve as advance organizers to more elaborate strategies, such as concept anchoring routines. Content area achievement can be greatly bolstered when adolescents with dyslexia are taught these strategies, provided with sufficient guided practice and supported with generalization exercises (Scanlon, Deshler & Schumaker, 1996; Schumaker & Deshler, 1992). Using these techniques, dyslexic students develop cognitive skills that can be applied in a variety of ways across the curriculum. Unfortunately, this happens infrequently as strategy instruction is not commonplace in the secondary curriculum because few content area teachers are familiar with these strategies. As Deshler (2005) suggested, even though we have discovered how to be successful with older students with academic problems, we are not applying this knowledge consistently in the classroom to support adolescent achievement.

Executive function, closely related to metacognition, is a critical component for effectively utilizing learning strategies (Jansiewicz, 2008). Popularly conceptualized as "thinking about thinking," metacognition is associated with utilizing the awareness of thinking to make decisions and follow through behaviorally. This can involve verbal mediation to organize thoughts, remain focused, evaluate solutions or next steps and reflect on whether a goal has been accomplished. The effect of reading without good comprehension has particular significance when students reach high school. Curriculum and instruction rely on the ability to understand the meaning of the written text. Especially relevant to dyslexia, proficient readers tend to use a greater degree of executive function than poor readers (Roth, 2008). A reader with efficient metacognitive skills will stop reading if something is incongruous and either reflect on the meaning or go back through the text to ascertain where the mistake was made. This allows the reader to select main ideas in the text (Kirby, Slivestri, Allingham, Parrila & La Fave, 2008). When reading is not fluid, students may find that they are too distracted to hone in on the overall monitoring of their thought processes connected to comprehension. A dyslexic reader, who is already using significant processing power on decoding, may lose interest in the text, which is only intensified with limited use of executive function. The results of Kirby's study showed that dyslexic students use time management strategies and study aids but they don't apply strategies for identifying main ideas and test taking. These findings suggest that helping dyslexic readers build skills in executive function and metacognition may help them improve reading and writing (Fidler & Everatt, 2012).

Assistive technology offers a variety of compensatory strategies for dyslexic secondary students. Raskind and Stanberry (2015) have identified a plethora of readily available and often inexpensive software including: graphic organizers and outlining systems; writing programs providing both linear (e.g., outlining) and nonlinear methods (e.g., webs); behavior prompts to remind students to stay on task; speech recognition programs; and word prediction programs. Additionally, virtually any computer contains a range of assistive technologies from screen readers to spelling and grammar checks. Some schools also provide students with literacy problems with digital textbooks, which is enormously beneficial. As with almost any technology, these approaches are useful to all students.

Not all dyslexic secondary students fail to keep up with the general curriculum. Many have learned to compensate, largely on their own. They have managed to utilize and be recognized for the strengths and intellectual acumen they possess. Many of these students have also been fortunate to have had specialized reading and writing instruction in elementary and middle schools. Others have had the financial ability to attend private schools for students with dyslexia and learning disabilities. With this assistance, more adolescents will attend and succeed at university level and go on to satisfying careers.

Characteristics of Dyslexic Adolescents

Adolescent development is a phenomenon that has been described in numerous ways. Early in the 20th century, psychologist Stanley Hall (1907) borrowed a term from a 19th century German literary movement, *Sturm und Drang* (storm and stress), to describe the powerful dynamics of adolescence. It is often a time of rebellion, of pushing back, of ups and downs. From the perspective of a psychologist such as Erik Erikson (1959), adolescence is a search for identity. It involves the beginning of a tentative psychological separation from parents. There is a need for independence, yet dependence on parents remains. Teenagers tend to group together to form a bonded identity as they simultaneously struggle to find their personal identity. Establishing peer relationships helps transition from dependence on parents to independence. In a sense, adolescents are usually in a constant state of internal (and external) conflict, hence *Sturm und Drang*. Of course, adaption to adolescence covers a spectrum, from unmanageable discord to positive adjustment unencumbered by the types of struggles mentioned above (Reiff & Ofiesh, 2016). Equally important, as adolescents emerge into young adulthood, they search for loving relationships with other people, often in terms of a partner. Success leads to strong relationships, while failure results in loneliness and isolation.

Adult developmental theory lends an additional perspective to working with adolescents with dyslexia. The search for identity tends to rattle self-confidence and self-esteem. Adolescents hit highs and lows as they move on to early adulthood. It is not unusual for these highs and lows to come in rapid succession. Most teenagers are somewhere in the middle of this spectrum; few would argue that it is a time replete with drama and histrionics, usually resolved as the adolescent continues to mature. Dyslexic adolescents live in a world where their difficulties in language intersect with the challenges of adolescent development. Although dyslexic students also make progress in reading, they barely ever catch up with their peers (Shaywitz, Morris, & Shaywitz, 2008). As these children enter the adolescent phase of their lives, they have lived with their learning disorder for quite some time. Many dyslexic children feel incompetent, embarrassed and inferior early in their education. If not addressed, these feelings continue into adolescence and adulthood. Reading difficulties are reportedly linked to both internalizing and externalizing factors (Maughan, Rowe, Loeber & Stouthamer-Loeber, 2006; Mugnaini, Lassi, La Malfa & Albertini, 2009). Many adolescents with dyslexia experience anxiety, depression and aggression that interfere with progress or complicate the condition (Dahle & Knivsberg, 2014; Eissa, 2010). Students often externalize their sense of inadequacy and exhibit a phenomenon known as learned helplessness (Peterson, Maier & Seligman, 1995). They do not see the point of trying when it only leads to failure.

The self-esteem issues of normal adolescence are amplified when a teenager struggles in school and carries this emotional baggage. Many adults with dyslexia remember being somewhat of a loner, certainly not material for the high school in-crowd (Reiff, Gerber & Ginsberg, 1997). Being relegated to the fringe is especially painful when one is focused on self-identity and forming relationships. Difficulty forming peer relationships may build unusual dependence on the relationship with parents. Children and adolescents with literacy difficulties face a higher risk of developing anxiety and separation disorders (Carroll, Maughan, Goodman & Meltzer, 2005). However, Jensen and Nutt (2015) provided a much more positive perspective on adolescent development as they contend that many changes in adolescence represent neurological maturation. The teenage years can also be a time when self-awareness is increased, specific talents emerge and strengths are identified.

Social and Emotional Issues

As noted, adolescence is socially and emotionally challenging for virtually all students, but learning disabilities such as dyslexia may exacerbate these issues (Bryan, 2005). Not all dyslexic adolescents have significant social/emotional and relationship difficulties. Many see themselves as competent, whole individuals. They take pride in their talents, creativity and ability to cope or even overcome their reading and writing challenges. Their dyslexic characteristics have meant that they have to do things differently. If the result is being more detail oriented, using a variety of resources to meet educational challenges and developing unusual but highly effective learning strategies, then they are effectively using their dyslexia to their advantage. However, this type of reframing may have a developmental component where such self-actualization is much more likely to occur in adulthood rather than adolescence (Reiff et al., 1997). Consequently, addressing the social and emotional needs of dyslexic adolescents may not only make school more comfortable, but help prepare them for the transition to adulthood.

Social and emotional competence is a prerequisite for realizing a meaningful and satisfying adulthood. Helping dyslexic adolescents to develop a strong self-concept, solid self-esteem, resilience and confidence in their ability to take on challenges is equally if not more important than teaching and learning academic and educational skills (Goldberg, Higgins, Raskind & Herman, 2003; Spekman, Goldberg & Herman, 1993). Social competence is not innate; it can be learned and applied. Positive emotional attributes can also be acquired (Raskind, Goldberg, Higgins & Herman, 2002; Reiff et al., 1997). Consequently, teachers and parents need to focus on this task. Parents, teachers and mentors play a significant role in emotional, behavioral and school related adjustment of adolescents with disabilities (Pham & Murray, 2016). The task is challenging, even more so when it involves letting go of negative self-perceptions and behaviors and replacing them with positive ones.

In school settings where many teachers are not knowledgeable about this condition, students with dyslexia may be considered slow, incapable or lazy. This is especially true for perceptions of secondary content education teachers (Wadlington, Wadlington & Hancock, 2009). Low self-esteem and ineffective social skills are natural reactions to ongoing failure in school and negative experiences with educators and peers (Edwards, 1994; Riddick, 2010). School failure sends a message that the child or adolescent is not competent, even incomplete. The reactions to this message are varied. It becomes difficult to trust teachers, other adults and even peers who consistently send negative messages. Learned helplessness becomes an understandable response when children do not believe they can succeed. In order to deflect negative perceptions, some students adopt "masks" where they take on roles such as class clown, trouble-maker, or victim (Smith, 1989).

Many teachers do not incorporate teaching and building social skills into their instruction. Parents need to advocate for introducing this component into the curriculum and explain that integrating social skills instruction need not require major changes in teaching style. For example, most teachers use small and cooperative group instruction. Monitoring the process of group interaction provides valuable opportunities for feedback on interpersonal skills. Students with social skills deficits often do or say something inappropriate, do not ingratiate themselves smoothly into conversations, misread nonverbal communication or become unwarrantedly defensive. Very often students have no idea that their social interaction is causing breakdowns in the group process, often leading to a distancing or marginalizing by other students. Supportive intervention may turn these sorts of negative social dynamics into teachable moments. It would be disingenuous to suggest that occasional feedback from a teacher will "fix" deeply ingrained social skills deficits. Nevertheless, simple recognition of these difficulties builds the student's awareness of the importance of appropriate social skills. Putting the focus on ways the student can achieve desired goals becomes less about criticism and more about learning useful behaviors.

Successful Outcomes

The way individuals with dyslexia think can actually be an asset in achieving success. Eide and Eide (2012) chronicled the lives of many successful individuals with dyslexia finding that the same processes that interfere with reading letters and numbers can allow for extraordinary capabilities that those without dyslexia often do not have. Malcolm Gladwell (2015) even promotes the idea of dyslexia as a "desirable difficulty." It makes reading and writing frustrating, but, at the same time, may force dyslexic individuals to develop better listening and creative problem-solving skills. Additionally, dyslexia may be a right brain advantage in an increasingly right-brain world of technology.

In a 20-year longitudinal study using both quantitative and qualitative data, Raskind, Goldberg, Higgins and Herman (2002) explored successful outcomes and identified six attributes (self-awareness, proactivity, perseverance, emotional stability, appropriate goal setting, presence and use of support systems). In addition, research has determined self-advocacy to be a critical component for success (Lock & Layton, 2001; Rosetti & Henderson, 2013). Effective self-advocacy depends on self-awareness as students need to understand their strengths and weaknesses in order to advocate for accommodations in school (and beyond). With these attributes, dyslexic students are more likely to have success and to participate in their general education classes (Carter, Prater & Dyches, 2009). If secondary students with dyslexia fail to become self-advocates, they will be unlikely to build a sense of control and personal autonomy, particularly when they enter the world beyond school. Although teachers and parents need to advocate for these adolescents, they will not be the ones to navigate the adult years. The goal of entering adulthood is increased independence.

References

Ackerman, P. T., & Dykman, R. A. (1996). The speed factor and learning disabilities: The toll of slowness in adolescents. *Dyslexia, 2*, 1–21.

Anderson, P. L., & Meier-Hedde, R. (2001). Early case reports of dyslexia in the United States and Europe. *Journal of Learning Disabilities, 34*, 9–21. doi:10.1177/00222194010 3400102

Bryan, T. (2005). Science-based advances in the social domain of learning disabilities. *Learning Disability Quarterly, 28*, 119–121. doi:10.2307/1593608

Carroll, J. M., Maughan, B., Goodman, R., & Meltzer, H. (2005). Literacy difficulties and psychiatric disorders: Evidence for comorbidity. *Journal of Child Psychology and Psychiatry, 46*(5), 524–532. doi:10.1111/j.1469–7610.2004.00366.x

Carter, N., Prater, M. A., & Dyches, T. T. (2009). *What every teacher should know about making accommodations and adaptations for students with mild to moderate disabilities*. Upper Saddle River, NJ: Pearson.

Cortiella, C., & Horowitz, S. H. (2014). *The state of learning disabilities: Facts, trends and emerging issues*. New York: National Center for Learning Disabilities.

Coyne, M. D., Simmons, D. C., Simmons, L. E., Hagan-Burke, S., Kwok, O., Kim, M., . . . Rawlinson, D. M. (2013). Adjusting beginning reading intervention based on student performance: An experimental evaluation. *Exceptional Children, 80*, 25–44. doi:10.1177/ 001440291308000101

Dahle, A. E., & Knivsberg, A. M. (2014). Internalizing, externalizing and attention problems in dyslexia. *Scandinavian Journal of Disability Research, 16*, 179–193. doi:10.1080/1501 7419.2013.781953

Deshler, D. D. (2005). Adolescents with learning disabilities: Unique challenges and reasons for hope. *Learning Disability Quarterly, 28*, 122–124.

Edwards, J. (1994). *The scars of dyslexia*. London: Cassell.

Eide, B. L., & Eide, F. F. (2012). *The dyslexia advantage: Unlocking the hidden potential of the dyslexic brain*. New York: Penguin.

Eissa, M. (2010). Behavioral and emotional problems associated with dyslexia. *Current Psychiatry, 17*(1), 39–47.

Elliott, J. G., & Grigorenko, E. L. (2014). *The dyslexia debate*. New York: Cambridge University Press.

Erikson, E. H. (1959). *Identity and the life cycle*. Madison, CT: International Universities Press.

Fidler, R., & Everatt, J. (2012). Reading comprehension in adult students with dyslexia. In N. Brunswick (Ed.), *Supporting dyslexic adults in higher education and the workplace* (pp. 91–100). Chichester, UK: John Wiley.

Fletcher, J. M., Lyon, G. R., Fuchs, L. S., & Barnes, M. A. (2007). *Learning disabilities: From identification to intervention*. New York: Guilford Press.

Fuchs, D., & Fuchs, L. S. (2005). Peer-assisted learning strategies: Promoting word recognition, fluency, and reading comprehension in young children. *Journal of Special Education, 39*, 34–44. doi: 10.1177/00224669050390010401

Gladwell, M. (2015). *David and Goliath: Underdogs, misfits, and the art of battling giant*. New York: Little, Brown & Company.

Goldberg, R. J., Higgins, E. L., Raskind, M. H., & Herman, K. L. (2003). Predictors of success in individuals with learning disabilities: A qualitative analysis of a 20-year longitudinal study. *Learning Disabilities Research & Practice, 18*, 222–236. doi:10.1111/1540-5826.00077

Hall, G. S. (1907). *Adolescence – its psychology and its relations to physiology, anthropology, sociology, sex, crime, and religion*. New York: D. Appleton.

Hazoury, K. H., Oweini, A. A., & Bahous, R. (2009). A multisensory approach to teach Arabic decoding to students with dyslexia. *Learning Disabilities: A Contemporary Journal, 7*, 1–20.

Jansiewicz, E. M. (2008). *The relationship between executive functions and metacognitive strategy learning and application*. Dissertation, Georgia State University. Retrieved from http://scholarworks.gsu.edu/psych_diss/42

Jensen, F. E., & Nutt, A. E. (2015). *The teenage brain: A neuroscientist's survival guide to raising adolescents and young adults*. New York: Harper.

Kirby, J. R., Slivestri, R., Allingham, B. H., Parrila, R., & La Fave, C. B. (2008). Learning strategies and study approaches of postsecondary students with dyslexia. *Journal of Learning Disabilities, 41*, 85–96.

Landerl, K., & Wimmer, H. (2008). Development of word reading: Fluency and spelling in a consistent orthography: An 8-year follow-up. *Journal of Educational Psychology, 100*, 150–161. doi:10.1037/0022-0663.100.1.150

Lim, L., & Oei, A. C. (2015). Reading and spelling gains following one year of Orton-Gillingham intervention in Singaporean students with dyslexia. *British Journal of Special Education, 42*, 374–389. doi:10.1111/1467-8578.12104

Lock, R. H., & Layton, C. A. (2001). Succeeding in postsecondary education through self advocacy. *Teaching Exceptional Children, 34*, 66–71. doi:10.1177/004005990103400210

Lovett, M. W., Lacerenza, L., & Borden, S. L. (2000). Putting struggling readers on the PHAST track: A program to integrate phonological and strategy-based remedial reading instruction and maximize outcomes. *Journal of Learning Disabilities, 33*, 458–476. doi:10.1177/002221940003300507

Lyon, G. R., Shaywitz, S. E., & Shaywitz, B. A. (2003). A definition of dyslexia. *Annals of Dyslexia, 53*, 1–14. doi:10.1007/s11881–003–0001–9

Maughan, B., Rowe, R., Loeber, R., & Stouthamer-Loeber, M. (2006). Reading problems and depressed mood. *Journal of Abnormal Child Psychology, 31*, 219–229.

Morlini, I., Stella, G., & Scorza, M. (2013). Assessing decoding ability: The role of speed and accuracy and a new composite indicator to measure decoding skill in elementary grades. *Journal of Learning Disabilities, 48*, 176–195. doi:10.1177/0022219413495298

Mugnaini, D., Lassi, S., La Malfa, G., & Albertini, G. (2009). Internalizing correlates of dyslexia. *World Journal of Pediatrics, 5*, 255–264. doi:10.1007/s12519-009-0049-7

National Institute of Child Health and Human Development. (2000). *Report of the National Reading Panel. Teaching children to read: An evidence-based assessment of the scientific research literature on reading and its implications for reading instruction* (NIH Publication No. 00–4769). Washington, DC: U.S. Government Printing Office.

Newman, L., Wagner, M., Cameto, R., Knokey, A. M., & Shaver, D. (2010). *Comparisons across time of the outcomes of youth with disabilities up to 4 years after high school.* A Report of Findings from the National Longitudinal Transition Study (NLTS) and the National Longitudinal Transition Study-2 (NLTS2) (NCSER 20103008). Menlo Park, CA: SRI International.

Ofiesh, N. (2010). *MASSive: A multifaceted approach to school success for individuals with learning differences.* Retrieved from www.nicoleofiesh.com

Peterson, C., Maier, S. F., & Seligman, M. E. (1995). *Learned helplessness: A theory for the age of personal control.* New York: Routledge.

Pham, Y. K., & Murray, C. (2016). Social relationships among adolescents with disabilities: Unique and cumulative associations with adjustment. *Exceptional Children, 82*, 234–250. doi:10.1177/0014402915585491

Raskind, M. H., Goldberg, R. J., Higgins, E. L., & Herman, K. L. (1999). Patterns of change and predictors of success in individuals with learning disabilities: Results from a twenty-year longitudinal study. *Learning Disabilities Research and Practice, 14* (1), 35–49.

Raskind, M. H., Goldberg, R. J., Higgins, E. L., & Herman, K. L. (2002). Teaching "life success" to students with LD: Lessons learned from a 20-year study. *Intervention in School and Clinic, 37*, 201–208. doi:10.1177/105345120203700402

Raskind, M., & Stanberry, K. (2015). *Assistive technology for kids with LD: An overview.* Retrieved from www.greatschools.org

Reiff, H. B., Gerber, P. J., & Ginsberg, R. (1997). *Exceeding expectations: Successful adults with learning disabilities.* Austin, TX: PRO-ED.

Reiff, H. B., & Ofiesh, N. S. (2016). *Teaching for the lifespan: Successfully transitioning students with learning differences to adulthood.* Thousand Oaks, CA: Corwin.

Riddick, B. (2010) *Living with dyslexia.* Abingdon, UK: Routledge.

Ritchey, K. D., & Goeke, J. L. (2007). Orton-Gillingham and Orton-Gillingham-based reading instruction: A review of the literature. *The Journal of Special Education, 40*, 171–183.

Rose, J. (2009). *Identifying and teaching children and young people with dyslexia and literacy difficulties* (The Rose Report). Nottingham, UK: DCSF Publications.

Rosetti, C. W., & Henderson, S. J. (2013). Lived experiences of adolescents with learning disabilities. *The Qualitative Report, 18*, 1–17.

Roth, L. S. (2008). *Comprehension monitoring, cognitive resources and reading disability.* Unpublished doctoral dissertation. University of Denver, CO.

Scanlon, D., Deshler, D. D., & Schumaker, J. B. (1996). Can a strategy be taught and learned in secondary inclusive classrooms? *Learning Disabilities Research & Practice, 11*, 41–57.

Schumaker, J. B., & Deshler, D. D. (1992). Validation of learning strategy interventions for students with learning disabilities: Results of a programmatic research effort. In B. Y. L. Wong (Ed.), *Contemporary intervention research in learning disabilities* (pp. 22–46). New York: Springer.

Shaywitz, S. E., Fletcher, J. M., Holahan, J. M., Schneider, A. E., Marchione, K. E., Stuebing, K., . . . Shaywitz, B. A. (1999). Persistence of dyslexia: The Connecticut longitudinal study at adolescence. *Pediatrics, 104*, 1351–1359.

Shaywitz, S. E., Morris, R., & Shaywitz, B. A. (2008) The education of dyslexic children from childhood to young adulthood. *Annual Review of Psychology, 59*, 451–475. doi:10.1146/annurev.psych.59.103006.093633

Siegel, L. S. (2003). Basic cognitive processes and reading disabilities. In H. L. Swanson, K. R. Harris, & S. Graham (Eds.), *Handbook of learning disabilities* (pp. 158–181). New York: Guilford Press.

Smith, S. L. (1989). The masks students wear. *Instructor, 98*, 27–32.

Snowling, M. E., & Hulme, C. (2011). Evidence-based interventions for reading and language difficulties: Creating a virtuous circle. *British Journal of Educational Psychology, 81*, 1–23. doi:10.1111/j.2044-8279.2010.02014

Snowling, M. E., & Hulme, C. (2012). Annual research review: The nature and classification of reading disorders—commentary on proposals for DSM-5. *Journal of Child Psychology and Psychiatry, 53*, 593–607.

Spekman, N. J., Goldberg, R. J., & Herman, K. (1993). An exploration of risk and resilience in the lives of individuals with learning disabilities. *Learning Disabilities Research and Practice, 8*, 11–18.

Stenneken, P., Egetemeir, J., Schulte-Körne, G., Müller, H., Schneider, W., & Finke, K. (2011). Slow perceptual processing at the core of developmental dyslexia: A parameter-based assessment of visual attention. *Neuropsychologia, 49*, 3454–3465. doi:10.1016/j

Swanson, H. L., & Deshler, D. (2003). Instructing adolescents with learning disabilities: Converting a meta-analysis to practice. *Journal of Learning Disabilities, 36*, 124–135.

Torgesen, J. K., Alexander, A. W., Wagner, R. K., Rashotte, C. A., Voeller, K. S., & Conway, T. (2001). Intensive remedial instruction for children with severe reading disabilities: Immediate and long-term outcomes from two instructional approaches. *Journal of Learning Disabilities 34*, 33–58. doi:10.1177/002221940103400104

Tressoldi, P. E., Stella, G., & Faggella, M. (2001). The development of reading speed in Italians with dyslexia: A longitudinal study. *Journal of Learning Disabilities, 34*, 67–78. doi:10.1177/002221940103400503

Turner, H. M. (2008). This systematic review empirically documents that the effectiveness of Orton-Gillingham and Orton-Gillingham-based reading instruction remains to be determined. *Evidence-Based Communication Assessment and Intervention, 2*, 67–69. doi:10.1080/17489530802037564

Vaughn, S., & Linan-Thompson, S. (2003). What is special about special education for students with learning disabilities? *The Journal of Special Education, 37*, 140–147.

Wadlington, E., Wadlington, P., & Hancock, R. (2009, April). *Teacher temperament: Impact on teaching style and students.* Annual Conference of the Association for Childhood Education International, Chicago, IL.

Wilson, B. (1996). *Wilson reading system, instructor manual* (3rd ed.). Willbury, MA: Wilson Language Training Corporation.

Wyse, D., & Goswami, U. (2008). Synthetic phonics and the teaching of reading. *British Educational Research Journal, 34*, 691–710. doi:10.1080/01411920802268912

Wyse, D., & Styles, M. (2007). Synthetic phonics and the teaching of reading: The debate surrounding England's 'Rose Report.' *Literacy, 41*, 35–42. doi:10.1111/j.1467-9345.2007.00455.x

Yudin, M. (October 23, 2015). United States Department of Education Office of Special Education and Rehabilitative Services Dyslexia Guidance Letter. Retrieved from https://www2.ed.gov/policy/speced/guid/idea/memosdcltrs/guidance-on-dyslexia-10-2015.pdf

2
INTRODUCTION TO THE STUDY

Peggy L. Anderson and Regine Meier-Hedde

Researchers as Listeners

Qualitative methods breathe life into research, allowing investigators to focus on people and to understand their lived experiences through their unique interpretive lenses. While social science researchers might disagree over the selection of particular methodologies, most would concur that there is great value in listening to those individuals we study. For educational researchers, these individuals are the children and their families who bravely tell us their stories and relate their personal feelings, presumably because they understand that these experiences are meaningful and the telling can make a difference for themselves as well as others. Without this intimate knowledge, we have only a distanced view of children's lived experiences distorted by "the narrowness of numbers" that comes to us through quantitative studies (Graue & Walsh, 1998). While we respect what seems to be a torrential data stream that is the mainstay of academic research, we sometimes feel like children and families become lost in these numbers. The importance of listening to others cannot be overestimated as it is critical to understanding human motivations, relationships and adaptations. Since the United Nations Convention on the Rights of the Child (1990) passed the 54 articles calling attention to children's rights, listening to the voices of children "has become a powerful and pervasive mantra for activists and policy makers world wide" (James, 2007, p. 261). These articles speak to the importance of respecting children's voices in many different contexts including school settings. For, as Hart (2002) noted, educators who encourage children to voice their opinions and participate in decision making are strengthening their confidence and evolving capacity to effect change. Implicit in this premise is the suggestion that there may be limited usefulness to promoting educational therapies, specific types of instruction and other interventions without consulting the consumers of these products (i.e., the children who will benefit or fail to benefit from these services). We spend a lot of time and effort *doing things* to children for purposes of remediation without ever even asking their opinions about these interventions. This is particularly true for children who have learning differences, such as dyslexia, or disabilities. Historically, we have not been good listeners for this group of children who have sometimes been marginalized as a result of their learning differences. This has been the case for those with severe disabilities (Kelly, 2007; Whitehurst, 2006) as well as those with reading disabilities (Raskind, Margalit & Higgins, 2006). After all, children and their parents do not typically set research agendas so their opportunity to share their personal perspectives is limited (Riddick, 2010). Thus, it should not be surprising that Mastropieri and her colleagues (2009) discovered that qualitative studies, where this sharing would primarily be reported, accounted for 6% or less of all special education research in the most prominent journals, which falls far short of what is needed to shed light on the unique needs of children with learning differences. Primary sources of data, such as interviews and case studies, have robust potential to support children's rights and lend credibility to their views, promoting autonomy and competency.

Case Study Approach

One of the most powerful qualitative research methods for studying children is the case study, which holds a time-honored position of respect in the fields of education, medicine and psychology. Our introduction to dyslexia and the unique characteristics of this condition came to us through medical case studies. One of the first published reports of an adolescent with dyslexia was recounted by the English physician Pringle Morgan (1896) in his case of Percy, a very bright 14-year-old boy who in spite of persistent efforts was unable to read. After seven years of tutoring and schooling, he could identify all of the letters, but could only spell one-syllable words and misspelled his own name. The paradoxical nature of this case is highlighted by the words of Percy's schoolmaster who had taught him for some years and declared, "He would be the smartest lad in school if the instruction were entirely oral" (p. 1378). Intellectual capability with depressed literacy is the hallmark of dyslexia. Although we do not know what became of Percy and his school achievement, the case report of his reading problem indelibly changed perceptions of this condition and marked the beginning of new research efforts. For the 50 years following this initial report of Percy's plight, there was a proliferation of these medical case reports that continued throughout Europe and expanded to the United States in the early 1900s (Anderson & Meier-Hedde, 2001). Although the Europeans were the first to document reading disabilities in case reports, Americans soon began to make up for lost time by extending efforts to educational aspects of dyslexia and publishing case study collections based on the work of pioneers such as Fernald, Monroe and Orton (see Hallahan & Mercer, 2002). Considering the estimable contribution of these early case studies, it would be difficult to argue they are less worthy than quantitative studies. There is enormous significance in the fact that these first reports provided the foundation for our current knowledge base of dyslexia, which underscores the value of single cases in the acquisition of new scientific knowledge.

While earlier social science research texts failed to provide consideration to the case study as a formal method (Yin, 2009), in the past 20 years, there has been a gradual movement toward acceptance of case study methodology and general recanting of previous criticism by experts now turned advocates of this research method (Flyvbjerg, 2011). Eysenck (1976) is an example of a notable former critic turned advocate of the case study approach. In spite of the growing recognition of its legitimacy, still there exists considerable confusion about this method of research in reference to other variants of qualitative investigations. Cresswell's (2013) explication of similar types of qualitative research gives some clarity to characteristics of the case study approach. He discussed the shared characteristics of grounded theory, narrative study, phenomenology, ethnography and case study approaches as well as factors that differentiate these qualitative methods. Grounded theory is a research strategy which involves the development of a theory on the basis of actions of the participants/issues studied; a theory emerges or is grounded in the data. In narrative research, the investigators collect and study the stories of a subject, retelling these and arranging them in chronological order to capture the individual's life. Phenomenology is intended to research a group of participants and describe the meaning of these individuals who have shared a lived experience, focusing on the commonality of that experience. Creswell noted that while ethnographies and case studies also have similar characteristics, case studies are "bounded" systems (i.e., each case is one bounded system) that are studied through the in-depth collection of data from multiple sources whereas ethnographies are studies of culture rather than specific problems of an individual or entity. Although Creswell's explanation is very informative and highlights specific characteristics that differentiate these methods, Merriam and Tisdell (2016) noted that in practice researchers also combine these methods in unique ways depending upon the goals of the researcher and study. For example, case study research can be ethnographic in nature if specific cases are studied to understand a cultural group or case study research can be implemented in a grounded theory design if the goal is to develop theories based on the study of the individuals who are the cases.

There also seems to be ambiguity regarding specific types of case studies and misperceptions surrounding the interpretation of this research. According to Stake (1995), if the case study research focuses on a single case for purposes of learning more about the uniqueness of that specific case, it is referred to as an *intrinsic case study*, but if a single case study is studied for purposes of a general understanding of a problem or issue, it can be referred to as an *instrumental case*, while a *collective case study* includes multiple cases that can lead to theory generation and generalization. Regardless of the type of case used in the research, the product of the case analysis is a written report that describes the details of the bounded case. The objective of the analysis and the written report is to provide a deeper understanding of the case by finding the best story (Stake, 1995). The collection and interpretation of case information constitute the qualitative study. These are necessary and sufficient to satisfy qualitative research conditions.

In case study research, the data is the story and the report tells that story. The threads of data are the intricate details that are the parts of the story, uncovered through the commonly accepted data gathering tools of interviews, records and artifacts, while the data analysis is the direct interpretation, both of which are integral to the nature of case study research (Merriam & Tisdell, 2016; Stake, 1995; Yin, 2009). In fact, the basic distinction between qualitative and quantitative research is that the former uses words as data while the latter uses numbers and statistical analysis (Braun & Clarke, 2013). There is no requirement to report numerical data analyzed through statistical manipulations in case study research. And those who are looking for the results of a treatment approach are confusing case study research with single subject design, two methods that share some characteristics but are distinctly different forms of research, as the latter is usually considered to be quantitative because numerical data are collected on repeated measurements, including a baseline phase and a treatment phase, and graphing of data for analysis (Nestor & Schutt, 2015; Shaughnessy, Zechmeister & Zechmeister, 2015).

Unfortunately, as Hodgetts and Stolte (2012) cautioned, sometimes attempts to publish case study research are met with criticisms of researcher bias and a lack of statistical generalization, which stem from the assumption that large representative samples are the gold standard for research. Clearly in social sciences, there is a bias toward large scale quantitative studies that use statistical analysis (Chima, 2005); however, as case study researchers we would suggest that generalization and quantification of data may be part and parcel of the case study approach for some investigations such as case study collections, but they are not specific criteria and should be viewed as optional for this empirical method of observation (Yin, 2009). For as Stake (1995) so aptly suggested:

> The real business of case study is particularization, not generalization. We take a particular case and come to know it well, not primarily as to how it is different from others, but what it is, what it does. There is emphasis on uniqueness, and that implies knowledge of others that the case is different from, but the first emphasis is on understanding the case itself.
> (p. 80)

Flyvbjerg (2011) contends that a major criterion for assessing the contribution of case study research hinges on whether it adds to the scientific knowledge base of a particular discipline as opposed to whether the outcome can be generalized. While quantitative studies can often yield results that are generalizable, they are not without limitations. For example, statistical analysis can identify that certain variables have predictive value, but they cannot inform us about how these variables influence a child's life (Goldberg, Higgins, Raskind & Herman, 2003) whereas qualitative research possesses this potential. To have the greatest impact, educational research that focuses on children with learning differences should strive to be authentic, multifaceted, intimate and holistic to cast light on the complexity of the condition that will ultimately inform parents, specialists and teachers in an effort to help the child (Bicehouse, 2012), which is what this dyslexia study aimed to accomplish. The current international investigation selected the case study method because it gave us the best opportunity to listen closely to the perspectives of these adolescents and their mothers with the hope of creating accurate personal stories to reflect the reality of their existence.

The Study Design

Study Objective and Research Questions

This study is the second part of a longitudinal research project that continued to explore the lived experiences of children with dyslexia using a constructivist paradigm (Hatch, 2002) that sought to uncover realities of the child, mother and researcher. A collective case study approach (Stake, 1995), sometimes referred to as a multiple-case design with a cross-case analysis (Yin, 2009), was implemented to study the lives of these children. To the best of our knowledge, prior to our case research that provided the results of Phase I of the study (see Anderson & Meier-Hedde, 2011 for complete results), there had never been a study that focused on the individual stories of children with dyslexia from around the world nor had such a collection of experiences ever been published. The current study was also unique as it was a longitudinal research project, which is relatively rare in the study of dyslexia. Given the problems with funding, subject attrition, researcher attrition and missing data, the logic of such an undertaking has been questioned (Raskind, Gerber, Goldberg, Higgins & Herman, 1998) even though most are in agreement that longitudinal research "remains an under-used but powerful tool in understanding the development of individuals with learning disabilities" (McKinney, 1994, p. 203). In contrast, outcome studies, to be differentiated from longitudinal research, have been undertaken and published with much greater frequency as it is easier to conduct retrospective research than to follow individuals over time. A key point of distinction between outcome and longitudinal studies concerns the minimum requirement for the latter of two data points (periods of time) for which information has been collected from the same individuals, a design that is commonly implemented in psychology to study developmental trajectories of individuals over time (Morling, 2015; Nestor & Schutt, 2015).

In case study research, it is essential for investigators to develop questions as an important prerequisite for this type of qualitative investigation (Hancock &

Algozzine, 2006; Stake, 1995), with "how" and "why" questions being the most preferable (Yin, 2009). Braun and Clarke (2013) have suggested that there should actually be three types of questions: (1) research questions focused on "finding out," (2) questions for participants to answer to generate data, and (3) questions that researchers ask of the data in order to answer the initial research questions. The objective of both Phase I and Phase II of this longitudinal study was to raise the general research question of how dyslexia had influenced the lives of these children and their families to be answered through the shared experiences of these children and their mothers. Phase I of the study focused on earlier experiences (10 to 12 years of age), which entailed collecting and interpreting medical and developmental data (birth, health and developmental histories), educational history (school achievement, dyslexia diagnosis and treatment), and social/emotional perspectives (child and mother perceptions of experiences). This first phase of the study emphasized factors leading up to the diagnosis of dyslexia and issues involving the child's school underachievement, such as recognition of differences in relation to peers, presence or absence of instructional support and perceptions of self as well as the mother's perceptions of the influence of the condition on the child and the family. Early school problems and adjustment to these during the middle childhood period were examined in depth. In Phase II of the study, there was a shift to the period of middle adolescence and further adjustment that would accompany this later period of development. This extension of study emphasized the adjustment experiences of individuals with dyslexia as opposed to the early recognition of this condition. One of the premises of this longitudinal study is that the condition of dyslexia will affect development variously throughout an individual's life span. It has been suggested that dyslexics have special strengths (Ehardt, 2009; Everatt, Steffert & Smythe, 1999) that could actually enhance the quality of life (Davis, 2010), while others have concluded that individuals with dyslexia will not fare as well as those without reading problems (Cortiella & Horowitz, 2014; Maughan, 1995; McLaughlin, Speirs & Shenassa, 2014). With regard to research centering specifically on adolescents, results have been mixed. Edwards (1994) found that the students she interviewed had experiences that lowered feelings of self-esteem and resulted in humiliation due to maltreatment in school, a finding also documented by other researchers (McNulty, 2003; Riddick, 2010). Yet, some studies have found that perceptions of well-being become more positive as age and grade level advance (Ingesson, 2007; Rosetti & Henderson, 2013) with diminishing stress associated with the condition (Raskind, Goldberg, Higgins & Herman, 1999), suggesting that the most taxing experiences may be confined to the early school years when the child first becomes aware of the reading problem and experiences great difficulty with academic demands (Anderson & Meier-Hedde, 2011). It seems completely possible that the reading problems imposed by the condition of dyslexia increase the complexity of achieving developmental tasks, resulting in a unique set of challenges and outcomes that accompany various stages of maturation.

The aim of this study was to obtain an understanding of how these adolescents were adjusting to the experience of living with dyslexia. Knowing that research has painted different pictures of dyslexia in adolescence, both positive and negative, we chose to develop our research protocol on the basis of a multifaceted model that would consider academic achievement, self-efficacy, success markers, hopefulness and motivation as well as general adjustment. In addition, we wanted to continue to study the influence of dyslexia on the mother and family. We developed semi-structured interviews and selected measures that would enhance understanding of these adolescents with dyslexia and address the following questions:

1. How are these adolescents adjusting to increasing school and life demands?
2. How are these adolescents developing socially and emotionally as they face the challenges of secondary school?
3. How are these adolescents academically progressing as they move from elementary to secondary school?
4. How does the condition of dyslexia influence mothers' life experiences?

Participants

There were two groups of participants in this study: the adolescents with dyslexia and their mothers. From the 17 children between the ages of 10 and 12 in the original study (Phase I) (Anderson & Meier-Hedde, 2011), 13 adolescents between the ages of 14 and 16 and their mothers continued in the current study (Phase II), which was a four-year-follow-up. The 23% attrition for Phase II is slightly less than expected in longitudinal research and was due to death, illness and personal problems of the representative researchers from the respective countries who had collected data and participated in Phase I of the study. The adolescents in this study were all males, which has been typical of previous dyslexia case study research that has favored males over females (Edwards, 1994; Riddick, 2010) reflecting the overrepresentation of boys identified with this condition. Another reason that males were targeted for this study was related to the international perspective of the research; possible sociocultural differences between males and females in various countries would complicate the interpretation of case data as there are vast differences in achievement expectations for males and females related to cultural variation. Thus, the variable of gender was controlled by including only males.

Although the sample for the current study included children from the lower socioeconomic class (e.g., one family could not afford child care, which necessitated sending the boy to live with relatives for many years) and the upper class (e.g., one child had a chauffeur to drive him to tutoring classes), the majority of cases are from the middle class. There was no attempt to control for the socioeconomic status of participants in this study. Previously, at least in the United States, reading disabilities (i.e., learning disabilities) were associated with middle class socioeconomic status (Sleeter, 1987); however, newer research has demonstrated that there is now greater representation of all socioeconomic classes in this category (Cortiella & Horowitz, 2014).

Participant selection for this research was based on age, gender and dyslexia diagnosis as verified by the researcher from that particular country. Across the globe there is scant consensus for labeling children with reading problems unconnected to low potential. Elliott and Grigorenko (2014) noted that "somewhat paradoxically, defining dyslexia is seemingly both very easy and very difficult" (p. 5) as most professionals agree that the definition should focus on particular difficulties evidenced by struggling readers, yet the field has been unable to produce a definition for operationalizing the condition. Perhaps the heterogeneity of children with dyslexia and the complexity of reading preclude a unifying conceptualization of reading disorders (Wolf & Bowers, 1999). For the purposes of this study dyslexia is a condition involving unexpected reading underachievement in light of average to above average cognitive potential. As this research project aimed to connect children by studying the common thread of reading failure, it was considered unnecessary to impose arbitrary diagnostic criteria that would likely be culturally biased. It was a necessary and sufficient condition that these dyslexia experts from their respective countries identified the participants as having this condition.

Selection of Researchers

The 13 researchers who collected and interpreted case study data for Phase II were the same individuals who participated in Phase I of this study with the exception of the researcher from Sweden, who was replaced because of retirement; continuation of researcher participation provided remarkable consistency in data collection. The principal investigators served as researchers for their respective countries (i.e., the United States and Germany) with the 11 additional researchers collecting data from the adolescents and mothers in their respective countries. As previously indicated, the attrition of participants was regrettable; however, in retrospect, the initial number of countries selected was perhaps overly ambitious considering the language differences and the distances that separated the principal investigators from the researchers and countries they represented. Thus, the study became more practical and manageable in Phase II with four fewer countries represented. Country selection was influenced by several factors including the desire to provide the widest global coverage. Consideration was also given to areas of the world that have a higher prevalence of dyslexia and more research, which is why there was more representation of European and English speaking countries. The major criterion for selecting researchers from the respective countries was that these individuals had a record of research and publication in the area of dyslexia. A secondary optional criterion was that the individuals had published in the area of social and emotional aspects of dyslexia but, given the fact that this area of study is not well represented in the literature, only approximately half of the investigators had this type of background.

Instrumentation

The Assessment Protocol included five sources of data: semi-structured interviews (adolescent and mother interviews), two scales (Academic and Emotional) of the Self-Efficacy Questionnaire for Children (SEQ-C) (Muris, 2001), the Achievement Goal Disposition Survey (adapted from Hayamizu & Weiner, 1991) and the Children's Hope Scale (Snyder et al., 1997). The adolescent and parent interviews were specifically developed for this study and pilot tested along with the additional instrumentation prior to establishing the final materials for the protocol. With regard to the adolescent and mother interviews, several references were consulted to determine how to optimally approach adolescents and parents in semi-structured interview situations. There is actually very little literature to guide researchers to develop and carry out interviews specifically for adolescents. Most of the work devoted to adolescents focuses on the technique of motivational interviewing associated with drug abuse (Naar-King & Suarez, 2011). However, we found Faux, Walsh and Deatrick's (1988) guidelines for intensive interviewing of adolescents to be beneficial. Although not focused on adolescents, we also found the work of Graue and Walsh (1998) to be extremely helpful in providing the background knowledge for generating reliable interview data, constructing a data record and interpreting that data within the context of the child's world. Additionally, Ryan and Dundon's (2008) work provided beneficial guidance in their research that focused on the key stages of the development of rapport in case study interviewing.

Adolescent's Interview

The semi-structured adolescent's interview for this study was developed in part on the basis of the success attribute construct, which was the foundation for a longitudinal study conducted by the Frostig Center in Pasadena, California (Goldberg et al., 2003; Raskind et al., 1999; Spekman, Goldberg & Herman, 1992). This research identified a set of *success attributes* that differentiated a group of successful adults with learning disabilities from another group who did not experience success. The first part of the Frostig Center study, which initially identified the success attributes of self-awareness, proactivity, perseverance, goal setting, presence/use of effective support systems and emotional stability/coping was conducted ten years after the participants left high school (Spekman et al., 1992). Ten years after this initial study, there was a 20-year follow-up that sought to further investigate the identified success attributes in an attempt to discover themes that would elucidate these and identify changes that may have occurred over time (Goldberg et al., 2003; Raskind et al., 1999; Raskind, Goldberg, Higgins

& Herman, 2002). The literature on self-determination, motivation and goal-directedness is consistent with the success attribute theory of adjustment. Although we could not obtain access to the original Frostig Center study interview, we developed success attribute questions for our interview on the basis of the operationalized explanations of these attributes (Raskind et al., 1999) and recommendations for remediation of these specific components (Raskind et al., 2002) as well as the published success attribute curriculum (Frostig Center, 2009).

In addition to numerous questions that were developed on the basis of the success attribute construct, we sought to address factors that had been identified in Phase I of our international dyslexia study (Anderson & Meier-Hedde, 2011). These included a number of specific issues associated with reading (e.g., technology supports, motivation to improve, achievement gains, time devoted to reading and personal learning/reading strategies, etc.) to learn if these adolescents' reading had improved and, if so, what type of improvements had been observed and how these were achieved. The interview also investigated the adolescents' general perceptions of school including teachers, remediation programs, tutorial support and homework. Social and emotional development was addressed with questions about relationships, emotional stability and coping.

Mother's Interview

The mother's semi-structured interview was developed with parallel items that were included in the adolescent's interview for purposes of triangulation as well as other questions that focused specifically on the influence of dyslexia on the mother and family life. The results of Phase I of our study helped to guide the question development for the mother's interview. Major sections of this interview included perceptions of reading achievement and teacher support, school communication and support, health issues, socialization within the family and with peers and vocational aspirations. The current interview was designed to better understand how the mothers were personally coping with the current challenges of parenting an adolescent with dyslexia, how the current phase of development compared to the previous and how they envisioned the future when this child would leave home and go out into the world.

Self-Efficacy Questionnaire for Children

Two scales (Academic and Emotional) of the Self-Efficacy Questionnaire for Children (Muris, 2001) were administered with the goal of obtaining information about the adolescents' self-perceptions of competency. Self-efficacy, the belief in one's abilities and the understanding that outcomes can be changed by motivation and effort, is an important component in school success. Students who have an external locus of control are likely to believe that the outcome of events is outside of their control in contrast to those who have an internal locus of control. Thus, students who feel that they have some control over their school achievement are more likely to make an effort to improve their chances of success. Research has suggested there is a close connection between self-concept, self-attribution and self-efficacy beliefs (Marsh, 1984) and a relationship between self-efficacy and increased intrinsic motivation (Bong & Clark, 1999; Niehaus, Rudasill & Adelson, 2012). Some research has determined that students with learning disabilities score lower on measures of academic self-concept and academic self-efficacy when compared to typical peers (Tabassam & Grainger, 2002). So it is not surprising that adolescents with learning disabilities who have positive academic self-perceptions have been found to work harder and use more strategies than those who have negative academic perceptions (Meltzer et al., 2004).

Achievement Goal Disposition Survey

This is a survey that was used to understand motivation for learning in reference to three possible sources: social approval, learning mastery and attainment of specific goals. The survey is rooted in tenets of Dweck's (1986) model proposing two kinds of achievement goals: a learning goal (for those who pursue goals out of interest and desire to master tasks) and a performance goal (for those who want to prove they can outperform others). Dweck's construct suggested that students with the learning goal orientation view learning challenges as positive experiences to acquire a new skill, which may help them to persist with difficult tasks compared to those who are motivated by attempting to outperform others to avoid displaying incompetence that can lead to helplessness and anxiety after task failure. Hayamizu and Weiner (1991) developed a survey that adapted Dweck's theory to specifically measure learning mastery and two separate performance goal tendencies (teacher/parent approval and goal achievement). This survey was later revised further by other researchers who used the measure to study motivation in students with learning disabilities (Núñez et al., 2011). For the current study, we expanded Hayamizu and Weiner's survey to include 24 statements to be classified in three different motivational categories: social approval (e.g., "I study because I want to be praised by my teachers"), learning mastery/intellectual curiosity (e.g., "I study because I like to use my brain") and goal attainment (e.g., "I study because I want to be admitted to university"), which helped us to shed light on the adolescents' achievement motivation. This adaptation is consistent with the work of Harackiewicz, Barron, Pintrich, Elliot & Thrash (2002) that proposed a revision of goal theory, suggesting that performance goals can actually be highly adaptive in that performance and mastery orientations can coexist in a multitude of different ways related to achievement. We reasoned that analyzing learning motivation would assist us in identifying strengths and weaknesses in these adolescents.

Children's Hope Scale

The Children's Hope Scale (Snyder et al., 1997) was developed to measure positive/optimistic thinking in relation to the attainment of goals. Snyder (2002) perceived hope to be based on the trilogy of goals, pathways (planning) and goal-directed energy that is cognitively mediated. He noted that when individuals lack hope in their lives, it could be the result of some force that has destroyed hopeful thinking during childhood or that the individual has not been taught to think in a hopeful manner. Snyder suggested that all children will encounter stressful barriers to their goals, but how they think about themselves in relation to these barriers is an important contributory factor to hopefulness. According to Snyder, obstacles to goal pursuits will result in negative feelings and, conversely, the successful pursuit of goals will empower individuals and results in positive thinking. Adolescents with dyslexia have likely encountered many hurdles as they continued through childhood and strived to meet achievement requirements of schooling with the disadvantage of reading difficulties so it is not surprising that they have lower levels of hopefulness, which may be related to lower levels of effort (Lackaye & Margalit, 2006, 2008). The Children's Hope Scale has been found to be correlated with academic achievement (Snyder et al., 1997). Considering the increasing importance of motivation and goal setting for children with dyslexia as they move into adolescence, we regarded this to be a valuable area of investigation. The scale is a six-item index that asks children from ages 8 to 16 to evaluate themselves with reference to statements that address goal directed dispositions (e.g., "I can think of many ways to get the things in life that are most important to me"). Snyder and his colleagues (1997) were able to discriminate between children with high hopes and low hopes based on analysis of this measure.

Report Guide and Implementation of Protocol

All participants, materials and procedures for this study were submitted and approved by the institutional review board of the principal investigator's university. The researchers who participated in this study were provided with comprehensive instructions for protocol implementation, including explanations of materials and verbatim instructions for the adolescent and mother to provide the clearest explanation possible. The research report guide also included a model case study that was developed from the pilot testing. The interviews and the three measures (i.e., Self-Efficacy Questionnaire, Academic Goals Disposition and Children's Hope Scale) were translated into the native language of the researchers' countries and subsequently administered to the adolescents and mothers who were interviewed separately. The interviews for the adolescents were generally accomplished within 90 minutes while the mothers' interviews were longer, usually closer to two hours. Sometimes, the researchers returned for a second interview with the mothers to gather additional information. The researchers translated the interviews into English and developed narrative case study reports that were forwarded to the principal investigators for editorial review.

Data Analysis and Interpretation

The primary method of case study data analysis for this investigation was direct interpretation and categorical aggregation as explained by Stake (1995). Within this conceptualization and with reference to our study, direct interpretation analyzes the individual responses to interview questions and interprets them as discrete units whereas categorical aggregation focuses on the analysis of a collection of responses. We used both of these methods to answer our research questions with reference to each individual participant. Although our original questions were used as guideposts, we also allowed ourselves and our researchers the flexibility to pursue related questions as they arose. We concur with the view that qualitative researchers must learn to trust the research paradigm and be committed to the goals of the investigation but permit sufficient flexibility to allow questions to shift in a way that provides further direction for the study (Ely, 1991; Merriam & Tisdell, 2016). Of course, this is easier said than done when there are no statistical models to direct interpretations, leaving the researcher to rely on his/her knowledge base and instincts to develop an accurate report reflecting the reality that was constructed by the participants. Our thoughts on qualitative data interpretation are consistent with Merriam's (1998) belief that reality is not an "objective entity," but rather a derivation of multiple interpretations of reality. This is a daunting responsibility from start to finish, as qualitative researchers construct multiple realities of the case by interpreting the unique reality of individuals who are all interpreting the world from their personal perspectives (Hatch, 2002). Baxter and Jack (2008) referred to the process of case study analysis and interpretation as the deconstruction of data for the purpose of subsequent reconstruction of meaning. Thus, for the current study, researchers were charged with the task of studying all of the pieces of the stories with their intricacies and constructing an interpretive narrative reflecting the adolescents' experiences based on the perspectives of both the mother and the adolescent. In effect, there were three parties engaged in the interpretive experience as the adolescent and mother were describing their realities and the researchers were interpreting data with reference to their backgrounds and expertise in dyslexia. And, finally, the principal investigators provided a fourth explicatory layer as we sought to clarify these interpretations to develop the most compelling reports. As this was an international study involving 11 languages, much care was taken to avoid misperceptions related to linguistic and/or sociocultural differences. Sorting out misunderstandings that arose because of differences in educational/psychological/medical terminology, school system structure, assessment/treatment methods and other related aspects required careful consideration. In summarizing epistemological commitments to case study research, Yazan (2015) noted that researchers' views about belief in the project of inquiry and the production of knowledge must permeate "every step of the entire investigation process, from selection of the phenomenon of interest that is put under scrutiny to the way the ultimate report is composed" (p. 136).

The report guide and case study exemplar provided the organizational framework for interpretation of data collected. Researchers were required to organize their interpretations in a sequential report format so that all the important data related to the research questions would be included and analyzed. As mentioned above, researchers were free to report and analyze all data of interest, but they were required to include the data in the interpretive sections that were coordinated with the interviews and assessments. Section headings in the case reports were consistent, facilitating the location of information from case to case. The Case Commentary section of each case study provided the researchers with the opportunity to add professional and national perspectives to the interpretation.

A secondary interpretation of the data involved a cross-case analysis to provide another layer of interpretation to the study. The cross-case analysis involved two processes: cross-case synthesis (Yin, 2009) and categorical aggregation of data across cases (Stake, 1995). In the cross-case synthesis, each case was examined with reference to specific identified variables that were selected. As recommended by Yin, data tables were constructed to identify salient characteristics of these variables. For example, one variable that was investigated was reading achievement improvement in the four years since Phase I of the study as perceived by the adolescent and the mother, who were both asked to identify this improvement with a score of 1 to 5. They were also asked to explain why they thought reading had improved to this degree (or failed to improve). In the cross-case synthesis, both the numeric information and reasons were listed for all 13 adolescents, providing an overall pattern with the potential to lead to conclusions. Other data were coded according to relevant measurements pertaining to variables (e.g., the presence/absence of success attributes), the magnitude of the problem (e.g., reading difficulty, homework, etc.), types of support (technology, tutorial, remedial, etc.), motivation (to improve reading, to do well in school, etc.), achievement gains (in reading, in other subjects) and other interview sources of information as well as the measures of self-efficacy (Self-Efficacy Questionnaire for Children), hopefulness (Children's Hope Scale) and motivation to achieve (Achievement Goal Disposition Survey). Some of this data was reported in the form of numeric frequencies for the primary purpose of summarizing the study rather than promoting the generalization of results as this study should not be construed as sampling research because there is no evidence that these cases are representative. We have sought to avoid the reductionism associated with comparative quantitative investigations and preferred to emphasize the holistic portraits of these adolescents. Each case story is unique and should be regarded as such.

References

Anderson, P. L., & Meier-Hedde, R. (2001). Early case reports of dyslexia in the United States and Europe. *Journal of Learning Disabilities, 34,* 9–21. doi:10.1177/002221940103400102

Anderson, P. L., & Meier-Hedde, R. (Eds.). (2011). *International case studies of dyslexia.* New York: Routledge.

Baxter, P., & Jack, S. (2008). Qualitative case study methodology: Study design and implementation for novice researchers. *The Qualitative Report, 13,* 544–559. Retrieved from http://nsuworks.nova.edu/tqr/vol13/iss4/2

Bicehouse, V. L. (2012). The portraiture of Nick: Scene one the early years. *Journal of Case Studies in Education, 4,* 1–6.

Bong, M., & Clark, R. E. (1999). Comparison between self-concept and self-efficacy in academic motivation research. *Educational Psychologist, 34,* 139–153. doi:10.1207/s15326985ep3403_1

Braun, V., & Clarke, V. (2013). *Successful qualitative research: A practical guide for beginners.* Thousand Oaks, CA: Sage.

Chima, J. S. (2005). *What's the utility of the case-study method for social science research? A response to critiques from the qualitative/statistical perspective.* Paper presented at the annual meeting of the American Political Science Association, Washington, DC. Retrieved from http://www.allacademic.com/meta/p41952_index.html

Cortiella, C., & Horowitz, S. H. (2014). *The state of learning disabilities: Facts, trends and emerging issues.* New York: National Center for Learning Disabilities.

Creswell, J. W. (2013). *Qualitative inquiry and research design: Choosing among five approaches* (3rd ed.). Thousand Oaks, CA: Sage.

Davis, R. D. (2010). *The gift of dyslexia.* New York: Penguin.

Dweck, C. S. (1986). Motivational processes affecting learning. *American Psychologist, 41,* 1040–1048. doi:org/10.1037/0003-066X.41.10.1040

Edwards, J. (1994). *The scars of dyslexia.* London: Cassell.

Ehardt, K. (2009). Dyslexia, not disorder. *Dyslexia, 15*(4), 363–366. doi:10.1002/dys.379

Elliott, J. G., & Grigorenko, E. L. (2014). *The dyslexia debate.* New York: Cambridge University Press.

Ely, M. (1991). *Doing qualitative research: Circles within circles.* London: The Falmer Press.

Everatt, J., Steffert, B., & Smythe, I. (1999). An eye for the unusual: Creative thinking in dyslexics. *Dyslexia, 5*(1), 28–46. doi:10.1002/(SICI)1099-0909(199903)5:1<28::AID-DYS126>3.0.CO;2-K

Eysenck, H. J. (1976). Introduction. In H. J. Eysenck (Ed.), *Case studies in behaviour therapy* (pp. 1–15). London: Routledge.

Faux, S. A., Walsh, M., & Deatrick, J. A. (1988). Intensive interviewing with children and adolescents. *Western Journal of Nursing Research, 10,* 180–194. doi:10.1177/019394598801000206

Flyvbjerg, B. (2011). Case study. In N. R. Denzin & Y. S. Lincoln (Eds.), *The Sage handbook of qualitative research* (pp. 301–316). Thousand Oaks, CA: Sage.

Frostig Center (2009). *The 6 success factors for children with learning disabilities.* San Francisco, CA: Jossey-Bass.

Goldberg, R. J., Higgins, E. L., Raskind, M. H., & Herman, K. L. (2003). Predictors of success in individuals with learning disabilities: A qualitative analysis of a 20-year longitudinal study. *Learning Disabilities Research & Practice, 18,* 222–236. doi:10.1111/1540-5826.00077

Graue, M. E., & Walsh, D. J. (1998). *Studying children in context: Theories, methods, & ethics*. Thousand Oaks, CA: Sage.

Hallahan, D. P., & Mercer, C. D. (2002). Learning disabilities: Historical perspectives. In R. Bradley, L. Danielson, & D. P. Hallahan (Eds.), *Identification of learning disabilities: Research to practice* (pp. 1–68). Mahwah, NJ: Lawrence Erlbaum.

Hancock, D. R., & Algozzine, B. (2006). *Doing case study research: A practical guide for beginning researchers*. New York: Teachers College Press.

Harackiewicz, J. M., Barron, K. E., Pintrich, P. R., Elliot, A. J., & Thrash, T. M. (2002). Revision of achievement goal theory: Necessary and illuminating. *Journal of Educational Psychology, 94*, 638–645.

Hart, S. N. (2002). Making sure the child's voice is heard. *International Review of Education, 48*, 251–258.

Hatch, J. A. (2002). *Doing qualitative research in education settings*. Albany, NY: State University of New York Press.

Hayamizu, T., & Weiner, B. (1991). A test of Dweck's model of achievement goals as related to perceptions of ability. *Journal of Experimental Education, 59*, 226–234. doi:10.1080/00220973.1991.10806562

Hodgetts, D. J., & Stolte, O. E. (2012). Case-based research in community and social psychology: Introduction to the special issue. *Journal of Community & Applied Social Psychology, 22*, 379–389. doi:10.1002/casp.2124

Ingesson, S. G. (2007). Growing up with dyslexia: Interviews with teenagers and young adults. *School Psychology International, 28*, 574–591. doi:10.1177/0143034307085659

James, A. (2007). Giving voice to children's voices: Practices and problems, pitfalls and potentials. *American Anthropologist, 109*, 261–272. doi:10.1002/casp.2124

Kelly, B. (2007). Methodological issues for qualitative research with learning disabled children. *International Journal of Social Research Methodology, 10*, 21–35. doi:10.1080/13645570600655159

Lackaye, T. D., & Margalit, M. (2006). Comparisons of achievement, effort, and self-perceptions among students with learning disabilities and their peers from different achievement groups. *Journal of Learning Disabilities, 39*, 432–446. doi:10.1177/00222194060390050501

Lackaye, T., & Margalit, M. (2008). Self-efficacy, loneliness, effort, and hope: Developmental differences in the experiences of students with learning disabilities and their non-learning disabled peers at two age groups. *Learning Disabilities: A Contemporary Journal, 6*(2), 1–20.

Marsh, H. (1984). Relations among self-attribution, dimensions of self-concept, and academic achievements. *Journal of Educational Psychology, 76*, 1291–1308. doi:10.1037/0022-0663.76.6.1291

Mastropieri, M. A., Berkeley, S., McDuffie, K. A., Graff, H., Marshak, L., Conners, N. A., ... Cuenca-Sanchez, Y. (2009). What is published in the field of special education? An analysis of 11 prominent journals. *Exceptional Children, 76*, 95–109. doi:10.1177/001440290907600105

Maughan, B. (1995). Annotation: Long-term outcomes of developmental reading problems. *Journal of Child Psychology and Psychiatry, 36*, 357–371. doi:10.1111/j.1469-7610.1995.tb01296.x

McKinney, J.D. (1994). Methodological issues in longitudinal research on learning disabilities. In S. Vaughn & C. Bos (Eds.), *Research in learning disabilities* (pp. 202–230). New York: Springer-Verlag.

McLaughlin, M. J., Speirs, K. E., & Shenassa, E. D. (2014). Reading disability and adult attained education and income: Evidence from a 30-year longitudinal study of a population-based sample. *Journal of Learning Disabilities, 47,* 374–386. doi:10.1177/0022 219412458323

McNulty, R. (2003). Dyslexia and the life course. *Journal of Learning Disabilities, 36,* 363–381. doi:10.1177/00222194030360040701

Meltzer, L., Reddy, R., Pollica, L. S., Roditi, B., Sayer, J., & Theokas, C. (2004). Positive and negative self-perceptions: Is there a cyclical relationship between teachers' and students' perceptions of effort, strategy use, and academic performance? *Learning Disabilities Research & Practice, 19,* 33–44. doi:10.1111/j.1540-5826.2004.00087.x

Merriam, S. B. (1998). *Qualitative research and case study applications in education.* San Francisco, CA: Jossey-Bass.

Merriam, S. B., & Tisdell, E. J. (2016). *Qualitative research: A guide to design and implementation* (4th ed.). San Francisco, CA: Jossey-Bass.

Morgan, P. (1896). A case of congenital word blindness. *British Medical Journal, 2*(1871), 1378.

Morling, B. (2015). *Research methods in psychology: Evaluating a world of information* (2nd ed.). New York: W.W. Norton.

Muris, P. (2001). A brief questionnaire for measuring self-efficacy in youths. *Journal of Psychopathology and Behavioral Assessment, 23,* 145–149. doi:10.1023/A:1010961119608

Naar-King, S., & Suarez, M. (2011). *Motivational interviewing for adolescents and young adults.* New York: Guilford Press.

Nestor, P. G., & Schutt, R. K. (2015). *Research methods in psychology* (2nd ed.). Thousand Oaks, CA: Sage Publications, Inc.

Niehaus, K., Rudasill, K. M., & Adelson, J. L. (2012). Self-efficacy, intrinsic motivation, and academic outcome among Latino middle school students participating in an after-school program. *Hispanic Journal of Behavioral Sciences, 34,* 118–136. doi:10.1177/0739 986311424275

Núñez, J. C., González-Pienda, J. A., Rodríguez, C., Valle, A., Gonzalez-Cabanach, R., & Rosário, P. (2011). Multiple goals perspective in adolescent students with learning difficulties. *Learning Disability Quarterly, 34,* 273–286. doi:10.1177/0731948711421763

Raskind, M. H., Gerber, P. J., Goldberg, R. J., Higgins, E., & Herman, K. (1998). Longitudinal research in learning disabilities: Report on an international symposium. *Journal of Learning Disabilities, 31,* 266–277.

Raskind, M. H., Goldberg, R. J., Higgins, E. L., & Herman, K. L. (1999). Patterns of change and predictors of success in individuals with learning disabilities: Results from a twenty-year longitudinal study. *Learning Disabilities Research & Practice, 14,* 35–49.

Raskind, M. H., Goldberg, R. J., Higgins, E. L., & Herman, K. L. (2002). Teaching "life success" to students with LD: Lessons learned from a 20-year study. *Intervention in School and Clinic, 37,* 201–208.

Raskind, M. H., Margalit, M., & Higgins, E. L. (2006). "My LD": Children's voices on the internet. *Learning Disability Quarterly, 29,* 253–268. doi:10.2307/30035553

Riddick, B. (2010). *Living with dyslexia* (2nd ed.). Abingdon, UK: Routledge.

Rosetti, C. W., & Henderson, S. J. (2013). Lived experiences of adolescents with learning disabilities, *Qualitative Report, 18*(47), 1–17.

Ryan, P., & Dundon, T. (2008). Case research interviews: Eliciting superior quality data. *International Journal of Case Method Research & Application, XX*(4), 444–450.

Shaughnessy, J. J., Zechmeister, E. B., & Zechmeister, J. S. (2015). *Research methods in psychology* (10th ed.). New York: McGraw-Hill.

Sleeter, C. (1987). Why is there learning disabilities? A critical analysis of the birth of the field with its social context. In T. S. Popkewitz (Ed.), *The formation of school subjects: The struggle for creating an American institution* (pp. 210–237). London: Palmer Press. doi:10.2307/1511280

Snyder, C. R. (2002). Hope theory: Rainbows in the mind. *Psychological Inquiry, 13*, 249–275. doi:10.1207/S15327965PLI1304_01

Snyder, C. R., Hoza, B., Pelham, W. E., Rapoff, M., Ware L., Danovsky, M., . . . Stahl, K. J. (1997). The development and validation of the Children's Hope Scale. *Journal of Pediatric Psychology, 22*, 399–421.

Spekman, N. J., Goldberg, R. J., & Herman, K. L. (1992). Learning disabled children grow up: A search for factors related to success in the young adult years. *Learning Disabilities Research & Practice, 7*, 161–170.

Stake, R. E. (1995). *The art of case study research*. Thousand Oaks, CA: Sage.

Tabassam, W., & Grainger, J. (2002). Self-concept, attributional style and self-efficacy beliefs of students with learning disabilities with and without attention deficit hyperactivity disorder. *Learning Disability Quarterly, 25*(2), 141–151. doi:10.2307/1511280

Whitehurst, T. (2006). Liberating silent voices—perspectives of children with profound and complex learning needs on inclusion. *British Journal of Special Education, 35*, 55–61. doi:10.1111/j.1468-3156.2006.00405.x

Wolf, M., & Bowers, P. G. (1999). The double-deficit hypothesis for the developmental dyslexias. *Journal of Educational Psychology, 91*(3), 415–438. doi:10.1037/0022-0663.91.3.415

Yazan, B. (2015). Three approaches to case study methods in education: Yin, Merriam, and Stake. *The Qualitative Report, 20*(2), 134–152.

Yin, R. K. (2009). *Case study research: Design and methods* (4th ed.). Thousand Oaks, CA: Sage.

3
JOHAN, A CASE STUDY OF A SWEDISH ADOLESCENT WITH DYSLEXIA

Eva Wennås Brante

At the time of the second interview Johan was 16 years old. He described himself as good at listening and having a keen interest in social issues. He was diagnosed as dyslexic in third grade when he was 9 years old. Johan is very open about his dyslexia and has no problems sharing his experiences as a dyslexic student. Reading is important to Johan, as long as he can "read with my ears" as he described it; he is an avid reader of audio books. During the interview, he usually answered questions about reading with a counter question: "Do you mean by the ears or not?" He distinguishes between reading with the ears and the eyes, and gives different answers depending on the reading condition.

Background

Diagnosis and Treatment

A brief summary of Johan's dyslexia diagnosis as described by Ingesson (2011) in the first case study analysis includes the following content. Johan initially began having problems in his last year of kindergarten when school preparation activities were introduced in the curriculum. In first grade, it became obvious that he was struggling with beginning reading and writing skills, at which time he began to receive some remedial instruction. In the third grade, Johan was finally given a formal assessment for dyslexia. The Wechsler Intelligence Test for Children (WISC-III; Wechsler, 1999) revealed that Johan had normal cognitive potential (FSIQ of 107), but a significant discrepancy between verbal (VIQ of 116) and performance abilities (PIQ of 95). His score on the Raven's Matrices was above average (placement at the 65–70th percentile). Johan showed an extremely slow reading speed, which affected his reading comprehension and exhibited "all the signs of phonological difficulty that are specific to reading and writing difficulties associated with dyslexia" (Ingesson, p. 87). He also had problems with oral sequences because of impaired auditory working memory and slow rapid naming; the latter is considered to be an indicator of reading difficulties (Wolff, 2014).

After his diagnosis, Johan received support from special education teachers on a regular basis up to secondary school. He also obtained schoolbooks in audio format. Now, at the age of 16, he has begun a social science program in an upper secondary school, which prepares students for university studies. At the time of the current interview, Johan was half-way into his first semester and was coping without a special education teacher. He uses screen reading extensively as well as audio books to keep up with his studies.

The Swedish grading scale ranges from F (not passed) to A. To pass, a student must have at least an E. Even though upper secondary school is not mandatory in Sweden, the school is still obliged to support students who are at risk of failing. The Upper Secondary School Ordinance states in Chapter 9, §1 and §4 (*Regler för målstyrning* [Rules for governing] 2011) that under 'certain conditions' a student may take a course more than once or have the program adjusted or reduced. Having heard both the student's and the teacher's concerns, the principal decides whether or not the student is entitled to support. If a student is under 18 years old, the school has to discuss the matter with the parents according to Chapter 9, §5 (*Regler för målstyrning* [Rules for governing] 2011). However, Johan expresses no wish for more support than the audio format of school books as well as the other assistive technology supports with which the school provides him.

Family and Home Life

Johan lives in Lund, a city in the south of Sweden, with his parents, an 18-year-old sister and a 10-year-old brother. Both his siblings and their father have dyslexia. Johan and his younger brother share a room in the family apartment, which causes some fighting as Johan can get quite annoyed with his brother. According to his mother, her three children each display a unique attitude toward dyslexia and school achievement. Johan's sister has high ambitions, studies a lot and does well in school. Johan is more relaxed: he wants to pass, but not necessarily with distinction. His brother has recently been diagnosed and has some sleeping problems related to his troubles in school.

Johan's mother believes him to have an amiable personality and described him as "a source of joy and a person who can light up a room." Unfortunately, he does not take part in family life as much as he did when he was younger and his mother misses his presence. His good sense of humor entertained the family. When he spends time with them, his mother is pleased. The family enjoys outdoor life as well as taking short trips to nearby hostels where they spend the night and explore the neighborhood. His mother hinted that this was more common before the two elder children entered their teens.

At home, Johan has to do some chores such as emptying the dishwasher and keeping his room tidy. The family has a system where they collect "crosses" on a piece of paper. If one of the children does a ten-minutes-chore (e.g., tidying up shoes and jackets in the hallway), a cross is marked on the paper. The crosses do not generate any money, but with a certain number of crosses, the family does something nice together.

Medical and Psychological Aspects

During middle school, Johan broke his legs and arms several times as he was highly active and somewhat impulsive. For example, he had certain rather unusual ideas, such as "Let's see what happens if I throw myself off this wall," which did not always end well. This is no longer a problem as he is calmer now. He does not use any medication and has no health problems.

In general, Johan has a relaxed personality; his mother says that he believes "what will be will be." The only thing his mother mentions as possibly health related is that Johan occasionally has difficulties going to sleep. She is not sure if it is connected to his thoughts about school or spending too much time in front of the computer. However, in relation to this she mentions that he suffered from nightmares when he was younger, and he also talks in his sleep. It is very hard to wake him up in the mornings. The mother sums it up with the statement that "nights are eventful for him."

Johan has no additional diagnoses, but his mother thinks that he also has attention problems. He gets easily distracted if there are several activities going on around him. Organizing and keeping focus are also difficult for Johan. He forgets to bring things home and to take them back to school. Recently, the father found him by the computer at one o'clock in the morning, checking something school-related he had forgotten about. One thing he has never left behind is his personal laptop, which he uses frequently in school.

Educational Perspectives

Reading Achievement and Progress

Johan's reading has not been tested since his diagnosis in third grade. The mother, when thinking back, said that it was remarkable that no testing had been administered since then. As Johan has almost all his learning materials in audio-format, the mother found it hard to determine how much his reading had improved, but she finally said that his reading ability now would probably be a 3 on a 5-point scale (with 5 indicating the most improvement). Johan thought his reading had improved since fourth grade as then he said that his reading ability was a 2 on a 5-point-scale, and now he thought it was between 3 and 4. He said he reads faster today, even though it is still an effort. His mother's opinion was that Johan has found other ways to comprehend the written language than to read with his eyes, thus he has no interest in reading practice. He reads "with his ears" every day, up to two hours, but nearly nothing in print format. If a form needs to be filled out or spelling checked in a text message, he may ask for his mother's assistance. Reading printed books, where pages are actually turned, is a very rare reading experience for him. Johan talked a lot about reading and pointed out several times that as long he can read with his ears, he has no problems with reading. However, when the audio books are absent, he finds reading tedious and "so much slower."

Johan is well aware that his parents have played a huge role in his achievement. He said:

> Mum has made me read books, which have made me a better reader, and they [both parents] had me sit with a lot of mathematic books so I became better in that, too. When I had English words to learn they helped me with that as well.

A goal for Johan and his mother has been that he should be able to read the Swedish subtitles to English movies. This is challenging for Johan as it takes his attention away from what happens on the screen. It is still an effort to read subtitles quickly enough as he noted, "The text on the TV takes longer to read, so you may not be able to focus as much on what happens on the screen." On the other hand, Johan stated that understanding spoken English is no longer a problem. Nowadays when he watches an English movie on DVD he just listens and understands. His English comprehension has improved a lot; he even listens to English books.

During what in Sweden is called the middle school period (grades 4, 5 and 6), Johan and his classmates unfortunately had new teachers almost every semester, which affected his school achievement. The parents had to learn how to handle arrangements concerning his dyslexia during this difficult time. The parade of different teachers and all the new demands put a strain on the family, resulting in stress and conflict. The emotional turmoil from these experiences during this period has stayed with his mother. Even if things are different now and run more smoothly, the memories of these troublesome years keep haunting her, as she said:

> Grade 4 to 6 was the toughest period. And we are still caught in that feeling, as it was the platform from which we learnt to handle Johan's dyslexia, and we carry some really bad experiences from that time, things that also became hard for Johan. And one of those things, the worst one, was the changing of teachers, which happened at least each semester during these grades.

During that period his mother found it overwhelming to tell one new teacher after another about Johan's problems and how to handle them. Although she wanted to wait a while each time before telling the new teacher all about Johan, not to single him out from the beginning, she also wanted assistance for him as soon as possible. At one point, she asked one of the new teachers "How are things going?" The teacher answered "Splendid! He is reading, turning the pages of his book." His mother felt her stomach turn over and told the teacher that he really had to check if Johan was reading or not. When he got back to her, he said, "I was wrong. Your child is not reading, but he has learnt to leaf through a book at a normal pace." Through this incident, his mother came to realize that she could not let his school have sole responsibility for his education; she had to be in charge. She was constantly on guard in order to make sure Johan got what he needed or was entitled to receive. Her main concern has been and still is that Johan should have the same possibilities in life as other children. At the time of the interview, her third child is in the same school with the same problem, but things are different as she feels that the school now acknowledges her insight into dyslexia.

After sixth grade, when transferring to secondary school, there was a parental conference she still remembers. The teacher said that "Johan is terrific boy, so nice and friendly, but as a school we have not done our homework. We, teachers and other staff, have not been able to meet Johan's needs." This was a huge acknowledgment for his mother. Even if it did not change anything, it was a relief to hear it. A similar incident occurred when Johan finished ninth grade. All students in the ninth grade were lined up and when the headmaster came to Johan, he stopped, said his name and wished him good luck with everything, which was gratifying to Johan and his mother.

Students in Sweden move to secondary school after sixth grade. Secondary schools are commonly organized with lockers in halls where students keep their books. Students must keep track of their schedule, find the right books and go to the designated classroom on time. This was a very hard world for Johan, who has always struggled with organization. The special education teacher in grades 4–6 used to help him remember which homework to bring home. This support disappeared when he moved to secondary school. Sometimes his mother had to go to school to get the books Johan had forgotten to bring home; she said that she kept running back and forth a million times. The parents tried to keep in close contact with Johan's teachers, but this was difficult as there were several teachers. The parents could only ensure that things were done if they knew about them and they were dependent on the teachers to keep them informed. On the bright side there were teachers in this school who had had experience with dyslexic children and were familiar with the condition.

The mother's opinion is that the school as an institution had some knowledge about dyslexia, but did not see the breadth of the problem. It was not only the classroom situation that needed to be handled, but other things as well, for instance remembering homework. Audio-recorded textbooks were not enough; now and then a teacher gave out a handout that was not possible to get in another format and Johan found himself in a troublesome situation. Incidents like this happened every day. Moreover, Johan was not as responsible as other children of his age. Eventually, this made the parents frustrated. They got into a negative spiral and conversations with Johan had a tendency to become arguments. This coincided with Johan entering puberty and trying to separate from his parents. He wanted to be independent but, at the same time, he could not cope without his mother. As he showed clearly that he wanted her to stay out of his business, she had to accept it even though it was very hard for her. She saw that he needed her support to manage his schoolwork and the situation got worse. To solve this, his parents were advised to seek help from a therapist. Johan's parents subsequently met with a counselor who helped them to break the negative spiral. Thanks to the counselor, they managed to see their daily life in another perspective and found new ways to communicate. His mother said that a child like Johan needs a lot of encouragement and support, not nagging or scolding. During this period, both parents worked full time and they felt exhausted dealing with Johan's needs as well as their other responsibilities.

It was very challenging to start secondary school and get settled in to the demands of this new level. In school, Johan found it hard to take notes even if he had a computer. Another way he took notes was to use his cell phone and take pictures of the blackboard or a text. Later on, in eighth grade, a special education teacher helped him take notes in natural science. The first time he received grades was in eighth grade. (The situation in Sweden has changed since then; now students receive grades starting from sixth grade.) At that time it was a four-grade scale: not passed, passed, passed with distinction and passed with extra distinction. Johan passed in all subjects and he passed with distinction in some subjects, such as music and sports.

Swedish schools have a tradition of holding one parent-teacher conference every semester. Johan's parents have asked for numerous meetings, but have also been summoned to more than usual. Sometimes the mother found it distressing that Johan sat in and listened to the discussion, as it is hard to be both encouraging and straightforward at the same time. As a consequence, she asked for two separate meetings. She also noted that when she and her husband had chosen an appointment time for the parent-teacher meeting, the teacher canceled the following session as it was understood that Johan's meetings took longer than the prescribed half an hour.

Johan sometimes was given extended time to do tests. The mother thinks this started in seventh grade, but she is not sure. She said that they had to fight for this. As Johan became older, he did not want to be singled out from his peers, and wanted to try to do the tests under the same conditions. Even though he always has been open about his dyslexia, it was something else to continuously be treated in a special way. Still, he said that he thinks one way to use his strengths to help with his weaknesses is that "I can do stuff orally instead of writing it."

In ninth grade, things started to look brighter for Johan. As he became older it felt easier for the mother. He not only passed exams, but in some subjects that he liked, such as social studies, he even improved. Of course, this boosted his self-esteem as well as comforted the parents. In fact, the mother said that Johan was very happy to have achieved better marks in ninth grade than in eighth grade. But, she added, there was much hard work behind that, both for him and for the teachers. His mother said that as the school has an obligation to support students in order to be successful in exams, the teachers clearly explained to Johan what he had to do to pass. Still, it was his responsibility to follow through and meet these requirements. Johan is proud of never having failed an exam or a test. For Johan, it is important to always try instead of giving up. This does not necessarily mean that he is always successful, but to have tried seems to be a motto for him. He said, "I think that you always should do your best." The worst thing about having dyslexia, he said, is "exactly that, that I can't read . . . everything takes such a long time." He is very satisfied with the support he has received in school and believes it was "excellent." When asked if there was any help with reading he did not receive, Johan explained he had a lot of reading help, but he referred only to scanned materials as opposed to actual reading instruction.

Teachers

During the period in middle school with numerous teacher changes, one special education teacher became a significant person for Johan. Although she was not a dyslexia specialist, she was very interested and keen to learn more about the condition. By the time Johan left middle school she had developed considerable knowledge of the impairment. She supported Johan with his reading, planning and organizing, and reminded him about homework and was in the mother's words, "Johan's salvation."

In secondary school Johan had help from another special teacher, which he really appreciated. This teacher did not have a special education certification although Johan referred to her as his special education teacher. She was a caring person who had a good way with teenagers; she was firm but compassionate and Johan liked her a lot. He saw her three times a week with a small group of students. It was also possible for Johan to go to her room even if he wasn't scheduled to be there. On those occasions, if she had time, she would help him with his assignment, or at least say "keep on working." Now and then, he took some tests in her room where she helped him to read the questions. She could also be present as a general support during ordinary lessons. The great thing about this teacher was, according to Johan, that she helped him to sort out the important content from texts. He said:

> I had a very good special education teacher from grade 7 to grade 9. She had a room you could go to. She could help and read stuff for you, and underline what she thought were the most important things in the text and so on . . . I thought she was really good. She could give me the help I

wanted and also hints about how things could be done. She could also, when asked, read through what I had written and say what she thought I should change.

In contrast, Johan mentioned a teacher he had in year three in primary school. This teacher "didn't know what dyslexia was." Johan felt that the teacher expected him to read as fast as the rest of the class, which was impossible for him. From Johan's point of view it is important that teachers give clear instructions, make sure all the material the students need is available on the school internet platform and understand that all individuals have different learning styles and instructional needs.

Learning Style

Johan is aware of his personal learning style as well as his strengths and weaknesses. The best way for him to learn is to listen, either when someone is talking or to get a text or a book read via a screen reader. One option is also to see an instructional video clip, but this does not occur often. Johan prefers to do a test or to write a paper to show what he has learnt if it doesn't involve too much writing. As it is easier for him to speak than to write, he has occasionally taken tests orally instead of writing them. He finds it acceptable to work in groups when the assignment is more of a discussion, but if the assignment is writing an essay, he prefers working by himself. Then he can decide how he wants to complete the assignment and he does not have to compare himself with others.

Johan has an extra spelling program on his computer and frequently uses screen reading. This is a tool he mainly uses for schoolwork, not for checking out music or chatting or such events. Most school material is published on a website (PowerPoints, documents, instructions etc.). School books, on the other hand, are sent to him from a service called Inläsningstjänst, which the school pays for. Inläsningstjänst is a company serving schools all over the country with learning materials in audio format. His favorite school subjects are history and social science. He dislikes English and Swedish, the latter due to his reading and spelling problem. His problem with English concerns translation of a part of a text or finding the right form of an irregular verb. His English comprehension derives from computer games, TV shows and audio books.

Homework

Johan spends an average of 3–5 hours a week on his homework. When Johan was asked if homework is a big or a small problem, he answered that without screen reading it would be impossible to manage. If he has a huge amount of homework, he feels stressed. He sometimes "reads" his homework going to or from school by listening to texts in his earphones from an app on his cell phone.

The mother's opinion is that homework has always been a big issue. It has been very problematic to get the right material from school to home on the right day and also to take it back on the right day. At secondary upper school, she has no control over his school assignments or homework. She sometimes tries to look in his bag to see if he has written down something for homework, a behavior that annoys Johan. She said, "Maybe he manages by himself now. Maybe it is I who shall learn to back away." If he told her what he wanted help with, she would take care of it or buy any technical equipment he might need. She finds one of Johan's challenges to be asking for help. He could get more help from school if he asked for it, but the whole issue of being different holds him back.

At home they have the rule of no computer games before homework is finished, so she asks him every day if he has any homework and if he has done it, which is the support she gives him nowadays. She estimates that he spends around one hour every day on his homework. At weekends he does not do any homework unless there is an upcoming test early on in the following week.

For now the mother does not know how he is coping in school and Johan sends clear signals that he wants to be independent. She is interested in finding out what his credentials will be after the first semester, but she is also a bit fearful. The most dreadful thing would be if she found out that he really was behind and had to spend his holiday doing homework, as happened one time in middle school. In upper secondary school, where Johan is now, parents are less involved in schoolwork. The mother has still not met any teacher or had any contact with the school, which for her is a completely new situation. Her first meeting with his class teacher is coming up next week, which conflicts with an important work matter for her. She feels that she has no other option than to choose the school meeting.

Social Development

Johan's mother is not completely sure that her picture of Johan is consistent with how he appears away from home. Not long ago, his mother worked with a group of adolescents in the church where she is employed as a deacon and she then saw another side of him, one that was more withdrawn than he is in the family. She says that he hangs out with two different groups of friends. One group is connected to church and the other group of friends she describes as more "cool." Johan has known one of the leading boys in that group since he was a child, which is why he hangs out with them his mother says. She estimates that three or four friends come to their home occasionally. One of his favorite activities is to hang out with friends. Johan also mentioned that being with friends is one way to cheer up. Even though Johan had a circle of friends, the start in upper secondary school was a bit troublesome and he changed groups after a short while. The mother explained "that there was no one in the first group he could be friends with." Friends are also mentioned by Johan as a reason why he quit the ji-jutsu club; "my friends stopped practicing, so I stopped too."

Johan is a big fan of computer games. He plays online with a group of friends against other groups. When they play, they use Skype so they can speak at the same time, and plan their playing. It is easy to spend a lot of time on computer games, as there is always a new level to reach and a new reward to achieve. Computer games are very efficient time consumers, particularly for adolescents, and Johan's mother describes his playing as almost an addictive behavior. The parents have had repeated conflicts in this area. In one way the mother can understand the urge to just vanish into a fantasy world, as the real world is hard and cruel. However, they have now come to the point where they have put time restrictions on the computer. Johan is not allowed to play before 18.00 and he has to have done all his homework before playing. He uses the computer for Facebook, too, mostly for arranging meetings with friends.

Self-Determination and Coping

Self-Efficacy and Motivation

Children with dyslexia often suffer from low academic self-esteem (Ingesson, 2007) and can have difficulties handling academic tasks. Johan has heard a few remarks about his dyslexia like "you are stupid and can't read." Johan's opinion is that it is the other person who is stupid, because if "you say such a thing you haven't understood what dyslexia is." He understands that there is no relationship between dyslexia and intelligence, and points out that many bright scientists, such as Leonardo da Vinci, had dyslexia. Still, as he explained, he would like to get rid of the dyslexia since it would make his life easier; things would go faster and he would be able to achieve more.

Two scales (Academic and Emotional) of the Self-Efficacy Questionnaire for Children (SEQ-C; Muris, 2001) were administered to Johan who explained how well he could do certain things on a scale of 1 to 5 (with 1 being low and 5 being high) on individual items pertaining to academic and emotional self-efficacy. Johan's answers show that he knows very well how to get help from teachers. He also seems to have good emotional control. The statements about being able to suppress unpleasant thoughts and not worry about things that might happen as well as statements about calming himself and controlling his feelings were all answered with "very well." There are only two items that are answered with 3; those concerned how well he can prevent himself from becoming nervous and how well he can pay attention during each class. The remaining items were answered with 4 and referred to statements such as satisfying his parents with his schoolwork, understanding subjects in school and finishing daily homework. Overall, Johan appears to be a boy who knows who he is, who has confidence in himself but does not go to extremes. He knows that he has limitations, but these shortcomings do not seem to bother him or make him depressed.

The Children's Hope Scale (Snyder et al., 1997) reveals children's perceptions of personal success. The results from this scale showed that Johan has a realistic view of himself with a modest hopeful attitude toward life. He can think of many ways to get things in life that matter to him and believes he is doing pretty well most of the time, which is an optimistic way to look upon life. He knows that he does not always do as well as others his age, but on the other hand he is convinced that things he has done in the past will help him in the future. He shows confidence when he says that even when others quit, he can often find ways to solve the problem. It should be noted that the Hope Scale is more of a global measure than the SEQ-C (Muris, 2001) and that it does not directly ask about school.

In order to gain more insight into Johan's motivation for studying, the Achievement Goal Disposition Survey (adapted from Hayamizu & Weiner, 1991) was administered. This survey examines a student's motivation for studying. Student responses are divided into three categories that identify motivation for studying: (1) learning mastery, (2) social approval, (3) goal achievement. This questionnaire reveals a picture of a young man who has good insight into who he is and who does not achieve for the approval of others. The reasons Johan gives for studying are that he is curious, enjoys getting to know new things and finds it is interesting to solve problems. He has a feeling of well-being when he overcomes obstacles and he likes to use his brain. To please others such as parents, teachers or peers is not a reason for Johan to study. His motivation neither arises from a wish to be praised nor a fear of being disliked. His motivation is connected to school success, securing a good job and reaching his goals. He would like to go to university and therefore needs good grades to achieve this goal.

Coping

Even if Johan has to struggle with homework and keeping up with school assignments, he seems to be fairly content with life. Both his mother and Johan describe his personality as "relaxed." Johan said that he deals with stress by winding down by listening to books or music, and then he is ready to "start again" with his work. When asked how he feels when he gets really stressed out, Johan hesitated and then said he doesn't really get stressed, that it is not a part of his nature. The only thing he can think of that would stress him is if he procrastinated.

He actually said that he was satisfied with the teaching he has received and generally happy with his grades. When asked how he coped with a bad grade he answered that he had not had a "bad rating yet," but admitted that once he was disappointed with the results of a test, but upon reflection, he took responsibility saying, "I felt that I could have done better, been more prepared." This last answer shows that he can see his role in the school work, and he also points out that "If the teacher has not given me the material I need then it is the teacher who has done wrong, but if it is I who did too little work, it's my fault." Johan's mother thinks he is mature, compared to his peers, and his ability to see things from more than one perspective confirms that impression. However, she also feels that he doesn't always access the assistance that is available to him for academic support.

When asked to identify a successful student in his class, Johan described a former classmate who he believed was successful in school because he studied a lot. He did not have many friends though, according to Johan. However, it is not Johan's objective to become one of the best in a class as he is satisfied with coping. His goal is not to become a doctor or such, just to be able to do the things he wants to do in life. He understands that if he wants to achieve more, he would need to increase his studying, but this is not his goal. When his mother was asked if Johan put forth effort in improving his reading performance, she replied, "No, I don't think he has. I don't think he thinks like that" because "he is satisfied" as "he has found a way that works for him."

Both Johan and the mother talk about the time the parents, and especially the mother, have dedicated to his school work. Johan acknowledged that his mother has made a difference in his progress; he points out that she has made him read books and helped him with homework. His mother talks about the endless hours of doing homework, nagging, pushing and encouraging him to do what was necessary. She has been there for him and she has been protective. It is hard for a child to go through school with dyslexia and she has fought many battles to ensure that he gets the support to which he is entitled. There is a rather marked contrast between the efforts and coping mechanisms of the mother and the son: Johan is content, relaxed and largely satisfied with his life, whilst the mother has been highly stressed from the ongoing battles with school trying to secure support for her son.

Impact on Mother

Johan's mother is torn between being proud of what she has accomplished with regard to Johan's school achievement and the fear that dyslexia and school problems have consumed their relationship. She hopes he thinks of her as a loving mother, even if there have been numerous conflicts between them over the years, nearly all of them related to school matters. The mother's reflections are closely aligned to results from studies about emotional stress for families with dyslexic children. Snowling, Muter and Carroll (2007) examined the impact of learning difficulties on families with children with dyslexia. That study showed that the majority of the parents (74%) reported an impact on family life from having a child with learning difficulties, especially the mothers of dyslexic children who had higher levels of stress and depression. A later study from an Italian context (Bonifacci, Montuschi, Lami & Snowling, 2014) revealed a somewhat different pattern. Even though this study indicated that parents of children with dyslexia had a higher level of parental stress than parents with normally developing children, the effect was found to be related to the experience of having a "difficult child," but also experiencing difficulties in the parent-child interaction pattern (Bonifacci et al., 2014). Johan's mother said that one aspect of having a child with special needs is that no one *really* understands what the parents have been through. No one sees all the hours they have spent with him and his schoolwork. Luckily, she has friends in whom she can confide and who can help her to see things more clearly, even though she has frequently prioritized her children over these friends.

In Johan's family everyone apart from the mother has dyslexia. From the beginning she had high expectations of her husband, as she thought he would understand from his own experience and be a good support. In fact, it worked the other way around. He felt frustrated by seeing his own school history being repeated and could be angry instead of supportive. He perceived that his children had many advantages that he had not been offered because there was very little understanding of dyslexia when he went to school and no technology for accommodations. So he did not always display the empathy his wife had expected. Moreover, with his own reading problems, it was hard for him to be of practical help with homework. In one way she has felt very lonely in her efforts to give her children the same opportunities as other children.

All the time she has spent helping Johan, talking to teachers and planning meetings has also affected her work. Her job has had very flexible hours and she chose for a period to work only when the children were in school so as to be at home to help with homework and then work again in the evenings. During other periods she has worked less than full time to accommodate the needs of her family. The family has been fortunate to have received some financial support from the Swedish government that is provided for parents of children with special needs. This monthly support is not something parents are given automatically. They have to apply for the stipend, which is a set sum; families can receive either the maximum sum, or 75%, 50% or 25%, depending on the severity of the disability and amount of time the child's disability is calculated to "steal" from the parents' working hours. Johan's parents have applied for this support three times and received it each time at the level of 25% (approximately 1,200 Swedish Krona or US$140). The support normally runs for two years, then a new application is needed. For now, the family is on the third round. Although the fianacial support is not significant, it has provided some assistance as well as the ackowledgment from the government that families with dyslexic children need help.

The mother feels frustrated with the school, as most initiatives for contact have come from her. She talked about how appreciative teachers have been toward her, telling her that she does a fantastic job as a mother. On such occasions she thinks "but this has almost killed me, I have hardly managed in my daily life, could you?!!" The mother also feels that some of Johan's teachers have been incredibly insensitive. She described a school meeting for all parents in the class in which the teacher had given a projected computer presentation to show daily activities at school. On one side of the screen were school pictures and on another side in smaller print was a teacher report specifying "written documentation about Johan, what Johan needs to do, and more things, all of them about Johan." The mother was shocked at the violation of confidentiality as she stated, "Everyone started to look at me and I didn't know what to do. Yes, this is what it is like and now everyone can see. And it wasn't a secret, but to be that odd person" was hurtful and embarrassing to the mother. When she emailed the teacher later and shared her feelings, the teacher defended herself with "thousands of excuses," but finally apologized. At this point, the mother expressed her sorrow and frustration with tears, explaining that people who have not experienced these challenges can never truly understand.

On the positive side, one thing she has learnt from being Johan's mother is that nothing is obvious, as she noted, "Many people struggle with different things, and life seldom turns out as you expected, but it can still be good." She also thinks that her children have learnt something in life from having dyslexia, including how to fight and to walk uphill. As she says, "A child with bad legs is not put in football-school, but these children with reading impairment, they have to struggle with their impairment every day."

Future Goals and Hopes

The mother's wish is that Johan will become "happy and a free spirit." She is proud of him as well as of her and her husband's part in his education. "Just think, we did this together!" she said. She looks forward to the day of his final graduation: "What speeches we shall hold then!" For now, she really wants him to learn to ask for help. If he does that and specifically lets others know what he needs, she thinks he will have better chances in life. She can see him working as a fireman. It is both a practical job and also a profession that is about helping other people. As Johan has a lot of compassion for other people, she can easily picture him in this profession. Earlier he wanted to be a policeman, according to his mother. It turns out that Johan still would like to be one. He thinks it could be fun to be a policeman and that "it feels like what policemen do is something I also would be able to do." As a policeman, Johan feels he could "help the community," which interests him. The only troublesome thing he can see with it is writing reports, which is a valid concern considering his dyslexia.

In the short run, Johan wants to get a driving license. He has started the process and gone to the first introduction class. He also wants to find a part-time job, to have some more pocket money. He seems confident that he will find one as he has had a job previously. In reference to school, his goal is to pass every subject. Johan's strategy to make this happen is to continue as he does; do his homework and ensure that he gets all school material in audio format. As he carefully points out, up to now he has "*at least* passed in everything" so he thinks this is a realistic goal. When Johan is given the opportunity to make three wishes, he asks for peace on earth, to get rid of his dyslexia and to have money. He is aware that the dyslexia will not disappear, and claims that he does not focus much on it, but still, sometimes, he thinks, "that it would be nice to not have it as things would go so much faster and smoother then."

Case Commentary

Johan's case is both a positive and a somewhat troublesome example of how effective compensatory tools can be. On the positive side there is Johan's satisfaction with himself and his progress. When previously interviewed, Johan was experiencing a lack of confidence in his abilities and school avoidant behaviors, which have been replaced by belief in his ability to succeed and a commitment to achievement. He has managed to enter the desired program at upper secondary school and is anticipating passing grades. The troublesome side is that his success is almost entirely built upon adjustments and adaption rather than reading improvement. Since he left primary school the main support he has received has been of two kinds: either technical support or personal resources that have helped him in school with organizing assignments. Both the technical support and personal resources are valuable, but Johan lacks reading remediation. One of the few things that have been validated as a path to improve reading is systematic intervention, preferably with an emphasis on phonological training (Wolff, 2014). In Johan's case, the emphasis has not been on improving reading skill, but to compensate the impaired reading with text in other formats, preferably audio format. Johan's mother claims that "reading is not performed with either eyes nor ears, it is the head that reads." In one way this is true; by reading audio books and using screen reading Johan will demonstrate intellectual achievement commensurate with peers, which may pave the way for his intended university studies. As McKendree and Snowling (2011) discovered in their medical school study, the condition of dyslexia does not necessarily predict lower performance in higher education. Still, when left without digital tools, by all accounts, there has been little improvement in Johan's reading since his diagnosis at the age of 9.

Recently, the Swedish Social Department ordered an in-depth investigation over the methods and tests used in Sweden for children with dyslexia. The investigation was performed by a group of researchers knowledgeable in the dyslexia field. They mapped the existing international research and found that very few tests or methods used in Sweden had been validated in a scientific way; that is, the studies did not include control groups and participants had not been selected in a random way (Statens beredning för medicinsk utvärdering, 2014). The literature search identified, for example, 644 abstracts about studies of alternative aids such as apps in cell phones. None of these passed the criteria (control group and randomized group of participants) for being scientifically valid. This does not mean that the tests and methods used are useless or worthless, but it means that there is no proof that they have any effect for increasing reading capacity (Statens beredning för medicinsk utvärdering, 2014). Thus, as a postscript, it may not be surprising that Johan did not have the literacy skills to pass in Swedish or Danish after the first semester in secondary upper school as was revealed when the researcher checked up on the family eight months after the interview.

Johan's case also shows clearly that Swedish schools lack clear guidelines for how to meet the needs of children with dyslexia. Several of Johan's teachers knew little or nothing about dyslexia; they misjudged his reading capacity and did not know how to support him. There seems to be a lack of consistency in dyslexia diagnosis as children with this condition demonstrate many different profiles (Fouganthine, 2012); thus, instruction that teachers have found successful for one child might not be suitable for another. Much focus needs to be directed toward how to instruct and remediate children with dyslexia (Vellutino, Fletcher, Snowling & Scanlon, 2004). In Johan's case, remediation seems to have been replaced with compensation. The mother is clear that "he has learnt to compensate" and in this way he has succeeded in school. Even so, the mother expresses a wish that he should be able to get through texts on his own. She sees how her husband suffers from not coping with that. She is not sure that Johan has the motivation to pursue the reading exercises as he seems content with the compensatory tools.

Johan has been fortunate to have been helped by a number of people; his mother and the special education teachers in primary school and secondary school served as an effective support system for him. Together they have formed a network around him to promote academic achievement and prevent the loss of self-confidence that dyslexic children often suffer (Carroll & Iles, 2006; Ingesson, 2007). Johan is an optimistic adolescent with an interest in learning and realistic goals for his future. While his life would be easier if his reading skills were improved and he had been able to meet his goal of passing all subjects, it does not seem likely that this obstacle will interfere with his successful life adjustment. As an adolescent, Johan's future seems brighter than it did during the primary school years and all indications suggest that he seems to be moving forward to the development of his potential.

References

Bonifacci, P., Montuschi, M., Lami, L., & Snowling, M. J. (2014). Parents of children with dyslexia: Cognitive, emotional and behavioural profile. *Dyslexia, 20,* 175–190.

Carroll, J. M., & Iles, J. E. (2006). An assessment of anxiety levels in dyslexic students in higher education. *British Journal of Educational Psychology, 76*(3), 651–662. doi:10.1348/000709905X66233

Fouganthine, A. (2012). *Dyslexi genom livet: Ett utvecklingsperspektiv på läs-och skrivsvårigheter* [Dyslexia through life: A developmental perspective on reading and writing difficulties]. Dissertation, University of Stockholm, Stockholm, Sweden.

Hayamizu, T., & Weiner, B. (1991). A test of Dweck's Model of achievement goals as related to perceptions of ability. *Journal of Experimental Education, 59,* 226–234.

Ingesson, G. (2007). *Growing up with dyslexia: Cognitive and psychosocial impact, and salutogenic factors*. Dissertation, University of Lund, Lund, Sweden. doi:10.1177/014303430708 5659

Ingesson, G. (2011). Johan, a case study of dyslexia in Sweden. In P. L. Anderson & R. Meier-Hedde (Eds.), *International Case Studies of Dyslexia* (pp. 82–98). London: Routledge.

McKendree, J., & Snowling, M. J. (2011). Examination results of medical students with dyslexia. *Medical education, 45*(2), 176–182. doi:10.1111/j.1365-2923.2010.03802.x

Muris, P. (2001). A brief questionnaire for measuring self-efficacy in youths. *Journal of Psychopathology and Behavioral Assessment, 23*, 145–149. doi:10.1300/J010v16n01_05

Regler för målstyrning. Gymnasieskolan: skollagen, gymnasieförordning, läroplan, ämnesplaner [Rules for governing. Upper secondary school: school law, statute, curriculum, learning objectives] (9th ed.). (2011). Upplands Väsby, Sweden: Svensk facklitteraturv.

Snowling, M. J., Muter, V., & Carroll, J. (2007). Children at family risk of dyslexia: A follow-up in early adolescence. *Journal of Child Psychology and Psychiatry, 48*, 609–618. doi:10.1111/j.1469-7610.2006.01725.x

Snyder, C. R., Hoza, B., Pelham, W. E., Rapoff, M., Ware, L., Danovsky, M., . . . Stahl, K. J. (1997). The development and validation of the Children's Hope Scale. *Journal of Pediatric Psychology, 22*, 399–421.

Statens beredning för medicinsk utvärdering [The Swedish Council on Health Technology Assessment]. (2014). *Dyslexi hos barn och ungdomar: tester och insatser; en systematisk litteraturöversikt* [Dyslexia in children and teenagers: Tests and interventions; a systematic literature review]. Stockholm: Statens beredning för medicinsk utvärdering (SBU).

Vellutino, F., Fletcher, J., Snowling, M., & Scanlon, D. (2004). Specific reading disability (dyslexia): What have we learned in the past four decades? *Journal of Child Psychology and Psychiatry, 45*, 2–40. doi:10.1046/j.0021-9630.2003.00305.x

Wechsler, D. (1999). Wechsler Intelligence Scale for Children (3rd ed.) (Svensk version, K. Sonnander, B. Ramund, & A.-Ch. Smedler, trans). Stockholm, Sweden: Psykologiförlaget.

Wolff, U. (2014). RAN as a predictor of reading skills, and vice versa: Results from a randomised reading intervention. *Annals of Dyslexia, 64*, 151–165. doi 10.1007/s11881-014-0091-6

4

GWYN, A CASE STUDY OF AN AUSTRALIAN ADOLESCENT WITH DYSLEXIA

Christina E. van Kraayenoord

At the time of the second interview Gwyn was 15 years old. He is a delightful and well-spoken adolescent who was diagnosed as dyslexic when he was 8 years old. Now he is a young man who is challenged by some aspects of his dyslexia, although he reads frequently and enjoys it very much.

Background

Diagnosis and Treatment

By Year 2, at the age of 6 years, it was clear that Gwyn's school achievement, especially in reading and writing, lagged behind that of his peers. However, it was not until Year 4 that a private educational psychologist diagnosed Gwyn with dyslexia. The psychologist then implemented his own reading intervention program, *Understanding Words* (Wright, n.d.) in the evenings for 40 minutes twice per week for 12 months, with Gwyn's mother undertaking the teaching of the program five times per week at home. Thereafter, the psychologist and mother used *Spelling Mastery* (Dixon, Engelmann, Meier, Steely & Wells, 1998) to develop Gwyn's writing skills for six months. At the end of this 18-month period, Gwyn's reading performance had vastly improved and he was much more confident about reading. In Years 4 and 5, Gwyn attended bi-weekly small-group-learning support sessions at his school. However, the mother mentioned in the previous interview that no systematic remedial instruction occurred during his learning support sessions. In Year 6, Gwyn left the state primary school and started at the same private school his brother attended. The school was made aware of Gwyn's learning preferences and the accommodations he would need prior to his arrival, and he was provided with learning support.

In Year 12, the psychologist who first diagnosed Gwyn assessed him again to determine eligibility for "special provisions" for the Queensland Core Skills examination, a test undertaken by all Year 12 students in Queensland. On behalf of Gwyn, the school applied for "special arrangements," which included practical adjustments to the test conditions, such as rest breaks, A3-size test materials and/or use of a computer. They do not entail the use of a scribe, reader, dictionaries or voice recognition technology because students taking the examination must do the required reading and writing themselves. Certain documentation (e.g., a psychologist's report) is required in order to support the application for special arrangements.

The psychologist's report detailed Gwyn's history of dyslexia and dysgraphia, which showed continued weakness in spelling and word-level reading skills, but also excellent comprehension skills when compared to grade level peers. In the spelling subtest of the Wechsler Individual Achievement Test (WIAT-II; Wechsler, 2005), he scored at the 14th percentile with word-level reading skills at the 14th to 19th percentile. His reading fluency was lower than 84% of his peers. In decoding non-words, his scores were even lower, at the 4th percentile. Despite the fact that reading is an effortful process for Gwyn, his comprehension still remains above average. The psychologist explained that Gwyn's above average intelligence and the use of other resources (e.g., his general knowledge and good vocabulary) supported his comprehension.

Family and Home Life

Gwyn lives with his parents in an upper middle class suburb of the Gold Coast, Queensland, Australia. His brother, Liam, moved out a year ago to begin his university studies. Gwyn always looks forward to his brother's visits home as he enjoys being with him. The family spends time at the beach, galleries and restaurants. They also enjoy bushwalking and family holidays in national parks and on islands off the coast of mainland Australia. The extended family gets together for barbeques and family events.

At home there is an expectation that Gwyn contributes to household tasks, such as emptying the dishwasher, cleaning his bathroom, helping with the laundry, working in the yard and mowing the lawn as well as cooking one meal for the family per week. He is not paid for these tasks, but instead is paid by his parents for "particular projects" around the home. Cooking and sharing food with family and friends has been an important interest since Gwyn's early years.

Medical and Psychological Aspects

Gwyn is tall and of slim build. According to his mother, he stoops and "has poor posture" because he is sensitive of his height, which makes him self-conscious. He is healthy and physically fit as he is involved in a range of family and individual activities such as gardening, swimming, snorkeling and tennis. He also takes part in sporting activities at school, especially swimming. Gwyn has no medical or psychological problems and does not take any medication. He is well-adjusted and engages in hobbies that are typical of adolescents including watching movies and listening to music.

Educational Perspectives

Reading Achievement and Progress

Gwyn has attended the same private school since middle school. In the first case study his mother reported that his reading was developing well. In the current interview, reflecting back on his reading four years earlier, she described it as "consolidated" because Gwyn read a lot. She stated that Gwyn had "continued along that path" and "still reads for leisure."

Four years ago, Gwyn rated his reading skills as 2.5 out of 5, while at the time of the current interview he rated them as 4, revealing a more positive assessment of his reading performance. When asked what made him a better reader now, Gwyn responded: "I like reading larger and better books . . . in Grade 7, I was reading 100-page novels, pretty silly plots. But now I am reading quite sophisticated plots and 400 to 500-page novels."

Gwyn reported that he did not enjoy reading aloud in class, although he enjoyed reading silently. When he had to read aloud he tried to read slowly in order to minimize mistakes. Gwyn added that he read a lot for enjoyment and when he read "in his head" he was able to read many books as he found silent reading much quicker. He stated that he read regularly, especially on the bus to and from school. He highlighted, "Most of my friends understand that I read heaps [and] I'm respected as a regular reader at school." When asked to name books he was currently reading, Gwyn enthusiastically reported some advanced titles including *Cloud Atlas* and *The Picture of Dorian Gray*.

In Year 8, at the start of high school, Gwyn chose not to take a foreign language or Religion in order to allow him to concentrate on core subjects. Throughout Year 8, Gwyn was involved in a structured learning support program in reading and writing, with one-to-one support and encouragement for six 40-minute class periods a week in a separate room. The school's Year 8 Literacy Support Program was organized by the secondary school learning support coordinator. Designed to develop spelling and reading comprehension, the program involved: (1) intensive drill exercises from *SuccessMaker: A Digital Learning Curriculum*, (2) weekly spelling activities, (3) *Comprehensive Assessment of Reading Strategies* (CARS), (4) weekly reading activities from *SRA Reading Labs*, (5) weekly grammar exercises, and (6) scaffolding and support for the mainstream English program. The students in the program were assessed at the start and at the end of the program. Gwyn's performance in spelling changed from Level 3.1 to Level 6.1, an improvement of 3.0 years. In *SRA Reading Labs* Gwyn's reading comprehension score translated to Year Level 4.1 and moved to Year Level 8.0, an improvement of 3.9 grade levels. For reading comprehension as assessed by the *Progressive Achievement Test— Reading* (PAT–R), Gwyn's score was in the 20th percentile at the start of the program while at the end of the program his score was at the 76th percentile. The learning support coordinator wrote in Gwyn's Year 8 report card that he had "worked very enthusiastically to gain far better knowledge of both spelling and comprehension" and it was a credit to him that he had made "such great progress." His mother reported that Gwyn appreciated both the physical and mental space offered by his participation in learning support. In addition, she believed that the documentation of his improvement in reading achievement "would have given him a lot of comfort too, that he was in the crowd and not lagging behind." Therefore, in this first year of high school there was considerable growth in his performance as assessed by the measures used in the learning support program. Gwyn's achievements were also documented in his report cards.

In the years that followed, Gwyn's achievement was reported according to a 5-point scale, with 5 being the highest level. In Year 8, Gwyn's teacher recorded a level of 5 for achievement in Language A—English, with a level of Outstanding for Effort in Semester 1 and a level of Good for Effort in Semester 2. His English teacher noted that he was "a diligent and attentive student who is always eager to deliver the very best."

In Year 9 Gwyn did not participate in any formal structured learning support program as there was no school funding for it, but he was still able to go to the learning support room in the available class periods. This was because Gwyn's parents paid additional fees to the school (AUS$1,998.00 (approx. US$1,789) in Year 9 and AUS$1,064 (approx. $US953) in Year 10—approximately AUS$54.00 (US$48) per session) so that he could receive assistance with his homework. Gwyn's report cards in Year 9 for English both showed a level of 4, with a level of Good for Effort in Semester 1 and a level of Outstanding for Effort in Semester 2. His English teacher wrote that he was "a highly intelligent and perceptive young man" with an "obvious zest for intellectual stimulation."

During Year 9, Gwyn sat for the mandatory, nationwide National Assessment Program – Literacy and Numeracy tests (NAPLAN) (Australian Curriculum Assessment and Reporting (ACARA)). These assessments are administered in May of each year to students in Year 3, 5, 7 and 9. Results for literacy and numeracy assessments across Years 3, 5, 7 and 9 are reported on a scale from Band 1 to Band 10. Results for Year 9 are reported across the range of Band 5 to Band 10, with Band 6 representing the national minimum standard for this year level. Gwyn's individual score in reading placed him in Band 7, within the range of achievement for the middle 60% of Australian Year 9 students, but below the national average score. Gwyn's individual score for persuasive writing placed him in Band 7, within the range of achievement for the middle 60% of Australian Year 9 students, but below the national average score. With respect to Language

Conventions—namely spelling, Gwyn's individual score placed him in Band 6, but outside the range of achievement for the middle 60% of Australian Year 9 students, and below the national average score. In the other area of Language Conventions tested, Gwyn's individual score in grammar and punctuation was in Band 8, which was within the range of achievement for the middle 60% of Australian Year 9 students, but above the national average score. With respect to Numeracy, Gwyn's individual score was in Band 8, which was within the range of achievement for the middle 60% of Australian Year 9 students, and in this case was above the national average score. Overall the results indicate that in reading, persuasive writing and spelling Gwyn's performance was at Band 6 or above (that is at or above the national minimum standard), even though within the particular Year 9 cohort across Australia, his scores in these areas were below the national average. In grammar and punctuation, as well as in numeracy he performed above the national average for that cohort of Year 9 students.

In Year 10 there were other periods during which Gwyn received learning support, mainly for the completion of assignments. As noted above, payment for this support was an additional fee that the parents paid to the school. The Year 10, Semester 2 Summary of Results on the report card for the subjects taken by Gwyn in Year 10 were as follows (the grade for Semester 1 appears in brackets): Language A: English 5 (5), Mathematics 4 (4), Sciences 4 (4), Humanities 5 (4), Physical Education 5 (6), Arts: Visual Arts 5 (5), Technology: Multimedia Studies 5 (5), Studies in Commerce 5 (4) and Personal Project 6. The Personal Project involves deciding on and implementing a project with an achievable and challenging goal that is self-selected. After implementing the project, students are required to reflect on their learning and evaluate the outcome against their own specifications for success, as well as to complete a project report. Gwyn's Personal Project involved planning, creating and sustaining a vegetable garden for his family and friends. The house tutor, who was the teacher for the Personal Project, also commented:

> The strength of your project lies in the fact that you chose something that is a source of interest to you. Your essay [Report] was of a good standard. Your enthusiasm enabled you to communicate a clear goal but your writing did at times lack depth in terms of the details and analysis surrounding your process. Gwyn, I am pleased that you did your best to meet the deadlines and that you have produced commendable work.

In the next section, descriptions are provided of all Gwyn's subject achievements. The descriptions provide an indication of his achievements across all curriculum areas at the time that Gwyn's data was collected for this case study. Gwyn's report cards provide information about effort, attitude, organization and time management for all subjects, which in Year 11 Term 1 were: English, Mathematics A, Biology, Business and Organization Management, Geography,

Physical Education and Metacognition. These competencies can be rated as "Unsatisfactory," "Satisfactory," "Good" and "Outstanding." In Term 1, Gwyn was rated as "Outstanding" in all four criteria in Physical Education and Biology, except for effort in Biology in which he was rated as "Good." He was rated as "Good" on all four criteria for all the other subjects. His house tutor commented that he had been impressed with Gwyn's leadership and "the positive ambitious and cooperative manner" in which he had approached Pastoral Care during that particular year.

In the last four years, Gwyn's overall reading performance has improved steadily and his mother mentioned that his tastes in reading have matured. However, his mother suspects that his recreational reading and reading in school might not always be accurate (that is, his decoding). Additionally, Gwyn still profits from his mother's support when it comes to content area books, for example, his mother stated that she sometimes pre-reads Biology chapters to him so that he is better prepared in class. He does well in his school subjects, and is considered to be someone who puts effort into his school work; he thoroughly enjoys reading a range of books and magazines for pleasure.

Teachers

As in the earlier years of his schooling, Gwyn's mother continued to advocate for him and was in regular contact with the school. She made herself known to Gwyn's teachers and consulted with them because often they did not know that he was dyslexic and would need support in his classroom activities as well as accommodations for his exams. His mother indicated that she had asked for someone to further assist him in reading and writing during class assessments so that Gwyn "didn't have to spend any energy on working out what the question meant and he could spend his energy on answering the question." Furthermore she was unsure if he even used the teachers' reading and writing support because he was reluctant to indicate during a lesson or examination that he was not able to read the questions.

Although he thinks he can read by himself, she encourages her son to ask for his school examinations to be read to him as she is afraid that he might not be getting the full meaning. She explained, "If I read him a question, he gets a far greater understanding than if he tries to read it himself, particularly under an exam pressure situation." Gwyn's mother thinks that he might miss the meaning of words particularly in multiple-choice questions and this makes it difficult for him to choose the correct answer. In order to individually remind each teacher of the accommodations that Gwyn required and after the distribution of report cards, Gwyn's mother attended parent-teacher meetings.

His mother felt that Gwyn got on well with his teachers and the comments on his report cards testify to this. As his mother indicated, "I think they all enjoy him very much." Nevertheless, Gwyn's mother suggested that most of her son's teachers had not really understood his reading problems because they did not "understand what it means to be dyslexic and he doesn't exhibit having problems, so they don't see it."

According to Gwyn, the best teacher he has had was his Year 9 English teacher. This teacher framed topics in current day contexts, encouraged the whole class to participate in learning and used humor in his teaching. Specifically, Gwyn thought that the best teachers were those who "vary the type of activities for the learning style," do not give much homework (i.e., homework should only consist of what had not been completed in class time) and who were not always strict. In contrast, a Technology teacher was one of his worst. Gwyn indicated that this teacher did not explain content well and he found it difficult to understand him. According to Gwyn, the teacher talked a great deal and not much work was done.

Learning Style

Gwyn indicated that he was "a visual learner" and that he needed "to see a teacher perform something or draw a diagram" to really understand it. He explained that he found his Year 11 Geography teacher to be "a really good teacher" because he does just that. He also commented that his current Year 11 English and Biology teachers understood that students have different learning needs. Commenting on the Biology teacher Gwyn said she understood that "different kids need different things" and that student learning style should be a consideration.

He reported that he demonstrated best what he had learned by discussing the topic. Relatedly, he indicated that he liked group discussions and preferred working in a group rather than alone in the classroom. He stated that when he and a friend participated in activities that they were required to do together, he found the activities "a lot easier." However, he also stated that he liked written assignments when he was at home and able to dictate the content to his mother who then typed it up. Gwyn thinks computers are useful for assignments, but he prefers not to take a laptop to school, but rather use a hard copy of the textbook. At his school, students did not often use individual laptops, as they could be a distraction. Gwyn's mother reported that there was a great deal of teacher talk and copying from the board or from an overhead transparency in all his classes. Gwyn reported he did not use a screen-reader or similar software, or make use of e-text-books. When asked to name things that he was not good at in school, he mentioned technology as he found working on paper easier to manage than working digitally. He also suggested that his difficulties with technology were related to the fact that he did not like the teacher.

Before Gwyn enrolled in Maths A, a more vocational, functional subject, there was considerable family discussion regarding subject selection in mathematics for Years 11 and 12. The main question was whether Gwyn should take Mathematics A or Mathematics B, a more theoretical subject. His Maths teacher later confirmed that his subject selection was indeed a good choice for him.

Homework

Gwyn suggested that homework should only involve completing work not finished in class. He completes it independently at home because he finds most of his homework "quite easy." His mother also reported that "he's extremely well organized" and has always had a very good understanding of the requirements of his homework. She noted that "He's got a mental plan about how he's going to get there." Indeed, his mother commented that Gwyn often planned ahead, letting her know when he needed her support typing his work. His mother emphasized that the family had enough capacity between her and her husband to assist Gwyn in all his subjects.

Even though the school asks students to use a school diary to record assignments and homework tasks, Gwyn keeps the requirements for the assignments in his head. His mother stated, "He's got where he is with each subject, what he needs to do, what's coming up, when it's coming up, when the draft is due, when the full thing [assignment] is due." Gwyn commented that he did get help from his mother with assignments, but he did not need assistance for homework completion. With respect to his assignments, typically, he dictated to his mother and she typed them, as well as correcting "a bit of grammatical errors involved and [she] changes up some words if there's a better word that can be used." His mother reported that Gwyn spent about 90 minutes completing homework and that if he was pushed, he could do more since the school had indicated that 180 minutes would probably be appropriate for students in Year 11.

Social Development

In his primary school years, Gwyn did not have a great number of friends, but those few that he did have were very good ones that he had maintained over the years. Now, in Year 11 and aged 15, Gwyn had a number of friends, whom his mother described as "quite nerdy." She reported that they liked to meet in groups and played *Real Life Minecraft*, spending hours in their character roles, "getting dirty," "building fires" and "hack[ing] down trees" in a friend's backyard. On other occasions, Gwyn went to LAN [local area network] parties, where they played non-stop computer games against each other for a 24-hour period.

In the first case study, Gwyn had experienced bullying on the school bus. However, in this current case study interview when Gwyn was asked if he had ever been bullied because of his dyslexia, he answered, "No, I don't think so. Most of my friends know. They mention it a couple of times, you know it's a joke. I find it a joke." Given this response it appears that the bullying on the bus was perceived by Gwyn not to be about his dyslexia or he had forgotten about it. His mother also reported that Gwyn had not been bullied in the last four years. It should be noted that all schools in Australia now have compulsory policies against bullying and a great deal of work is undertaken by teachers in relation to the prevention of bullying.

Gwyn gets along "extremely well" with other family members and with his peers, who according to his mother have "a great deal of affection for each other." His mother rated his social skills as 4 on a 5-point scale and commented that he was very comfortable talking with most people, adults and others. Gwyn regards himself as a "positive" person, who is "always involved." This involvement is manifested in assisting his friends with classroom work. She remarked that he was "a bit gormless around girls his age" and he did not initiate socializing with girls unless they happened to be in the group. His mother reported that he participated in volleyball and cross-country running as well as an out-of-school swimming squad.

He has had five or six good friends. In the eight months before the case study interview Gwyn started using Facebook, so he may well have had many "Facebook friends," but his mother thought "he's more of a sit and watch" Facebook user. Nevertheless, Gwyn did communicate regularly with his brother on the "private chat" part of Facebook. Gwyn's mother reported that she thought he had "pretty good" self-esteem although one of his teachers had mentioned that he might have low self-esteem because he "stooped" and was "quiet in class."

Self-Determination and Coping

Self-Efficacy and Motivation

The Academic as well as the Emotional Scale of the Self-Efficacy Questionnaire for Children (SEQ-C; Muris, 2001) was administered. The results from these scales provided information regarding Gwyn's perception of his abilities to handle academic tasks and to manage emotionally challenging events or contexts. Responses were made on a 1 to 5 scale, with 1 indicating that he could "not" do a certain task "at all" and 5 showing that he could do it "very well." All Gwyn's responses on the Academic Self-Efficacy Scale were either a 3 or 4. Thus with respect to having teachers to assist him with schoolwork, studying when there were other interesting things to do, studying a chapter for a test, succeeding in satisfying his parents with his school work and his success in passing a test, Gwyn believed that he could do all these moderately well (rating them at 3). He believed that he succeeded in finishing his homework, paid attention in every class and understood all subjects in school better than moderately well, but not very well (rating this at 4). With regard to the scores on the Emotional Self-Efficacy scale, Gwyn's ratings ranged between 2 and 5, although there were more highly-rated items than for the Academic Self-Efficacy scale. For example, Gwyn believed he was able to cheer himself up after an unpleasant event, could succeed in becoming calm when very scared, prevented himself from becoming nervous and succeeded in suppressing unpleasant thoughts (rating this at 4). In addition, he perceived that he could control his feelings very well (rating this at 5) and was able to give himself a pep talk when feeling low (rating this at 5). However, Gwyn believed that he would not be able to tell a friend that he did not feel well (rating of 2). Overall it appears that Gwyn has the capacity to deal with academic challenges while simultaneously mastering emotional challenges even better.

Additionally the Children's Hope Scale, which measures hopeful thinking in children (Snyder et al., 1997) was administered. The scale measures the capability to achieve desired goals and the ability to generate the means to achieve such goals, which are connected to hope. The findings showed that "most of the time" Gwyn thought that he was doing pretty well, was doing just as well as others his age and that "a lot of the time" he could think of ways to get the things in life that were important to him. He also indicated that he was able to solve his problems in many ways, and he thought that the things he had done in the past would help him in the future. Even when others gave up he thought he would be able to find ways to solve the problem "some of the time." The results of the scale revealed that Gwyn is hopeful with respect to what he is able to do and how to achieve his goals.

The third measure that was administered was the Achievement Goal Disposition Survey (adapted from Hayamizu & Weiner, 1991). This survey was used to examine Gwyn's motivation for studying. The responses are organized into three categories: (1) intellectual curiosity (learning mastery), (2) social approval, and (3) goal achievement. Gwyn was asked to respond to the survey items using "yes," "no" or "sometimes." For most of the items that dealt with intellectual curiosity, Gwyn responded positively ("yes") to items that referred to studying because he felt good when he overcame obstacles and failure and because he was curious. In addition, with respect to intellectual curiosity, he indicated "sometimes" to items relating to studying because he found it was interesting to solve a problem, because he liked to know new things and because he liked to use his brain. He showed that he was not interested in discovering how much he had improved. He did not derive his motivation for studying from the pleasure of tackling difficult problems.

Gwyn responded "no" to most of the social approval items. For example, he was neither interested in pleasing teachers and parents or getting praise from them nor in receiving recognition of his achievements from his peers. He indicated that "sometimes" he sought approval for studying because he wanted people to see how smart he was. With respect to goal achievement Gwyn was especially motivated because he had set goals for himself. He was "sometimes" motivated by prospects of success, such as getting grades as good as those of his peers, passing his exams, attending college or university, obtaining a good job in the future and having a good life. Thus, overall on the Achievement Goal Disposition Survey, Gwyn showed that he is motivated by more personal and internal reasons than external ones.

Coping

Gwyn reported that he was happy when he had time to relax and do the things he enjoyed such as playing games on PlayStation. He stated that he enjoyed being alone but also spending time with friends. He admitted that he is a big fan of fantasy games, historical-fiction, action-adventure and open world stealth video game series and also enjoys listening to music.

He only felt sad when he had a lot of school assignments to complete and on those occasions he said, "It took a lot of self-control to time-manage everything." To make himself feel better, typically Gwyn listened to music and then made a mental plan of what he needed to do and placed the activities "in order of priority." He reported that taking these steps calmed him down and let him "get on to the work straight away." Gwyn also reported that since Year 8 he no longer became frustrated with his reading difficulties.

Impact on Mother

The period of time that it took for Gwyn to be diagnosed and to receive intervention was a difficult and anxious time for his parents, however, the parents' relationship was impacted "only for the better" according to Gwyn's mother. She reported that her husband had begun to understand that his son's brain worked differently from his own and could "appreciate that difference." Gwyn's mother reported that the only matter the parents had questioned was whether the current school they had selected for Gwyn was and is the best school for him. She thought that his current school was too academic and she would rather he attended a more vocational-orientated school, although she also added, "But I'm probably coming to agree [with her husband] that where he is at the moment is certainly not doing him any harm and he seems to be enjoying it." The mother reported being a very involved parent and that parenting was a team effort with Gwyn's father.

The mother indicated that Gwyn's dyslexia did not bother her so much. However, she revealed that she wondered "how he's going to get on in the world and whether people are going to take advantage of him." She added, "But I think every mother has that concern about her child." She reported that she did not believe that his reading difficulties influenced her social or professional life. Gwyn's mother commented that she received "a lot of advice" from her sister who is dyslexic. She noted that since her sister did not have children, she provided "a bit of a fresh view" and that she took "advice from her more than anyone else."

The fact that Gwyn's parents ran a business from their home also meant that his mother was at home when he returned from school each day, which enabled him to recount the events of his day to her. Gwyn's mother revealed that over the years she had learned a great deal about parenting a child with dyslexia as well as understanding each of her children's needs. She did not appear to feel greatly stressed about parenting a child with dyslexia, rating her current level of stress as 2 on a scale of 1 to 5.

Future Goals and Hopes

Reflecting on his reading and writing Gwyn indicated that he did not have a reading disability anymore except for reading aloud, explaining he could comprehend well. However, he said that difficulties remained obvious in his spelling and punctuation whenever he wrote something. He also has fears for his future, especially if he chooses to go to university. Gwyn remarked, "I'm not sure how I will handle all that work." It appears Gwyn is afraid of not completing tasks in a timely manner especially without his mother's support in typing.

Gwyn mentioned that he wanted to go to the next level of swimming and athletic competitions before leaving school. Another goal was to "get an A– in at least half my subjects" so that by the end of the school year he would have an average of B+ or A–, hopefully A–. He intends to spend more time on his studies at home and to try his best in exams as well as in assignments where he gets most of his good marks in order to reach his academic goal. However, he acknowledges that time management would be the biggest obstacle to achieving both of these goals. When Gwyn was asked to prioritize these goals, he stated that the goal related to schoolwork was the most important.

When Gwyn's mother was asked about her son's plans after school, she highlighted the various options that might be available to him; he might travel, choose to go to university or get a job very readily. However, she hadn't actually talked to her son about that in detail. She reported that the school provided vocational counseling to all students, but she thought Gwyn assumed he would go to university because everyone else in the family did or still does. Nevertheless, she also stated that she did not make any assumptions that Gwyn would definitely attend university and that if Gwyn wanted "to go off for a year and work that would be fine."

When asked explicitly what kind of job he would like when he finished school, Gwyn said: "One that I'm interested in, one that provides new challenges, basically I reckon that would be fun. I also want to do something that lets me travel, mainly." When asked to elaborate on his response, he added:

> Maybe getting into something with geography or urban geography because I reckon that would be fun. I'd find that enjoyable, but also maybe health science because I'm doing PE [Physical Education] well sporting (sic) science, because I'm doing PE and Biology. Those are the two ideas that I've had.

When asked about three wishes, Gwyn replied that he would like to improve his logical sequencing of thoughts and ideas in order to do better on school tests. His second wish was to get better at swimming, and his third wish was to have more time to read books. He also added that he would like to be able to do things that he enjoys because he finds that he hardly has "enough time to read books."

It appears Gwyn's last wish is also in line with his mother's hopes for his future as she said: "Oh, I hope he wanders around the world and meets really interesting people and does really interesting things and has lots of really interesting experiences and finds people who really love him."

Case Commentary

In his early years at school Gwyn experienced severe difficulties in reading. A private educational psychologist diagnosed him with dyslexia when he was 8 years of age. The psychologist, in collaboration with Gwyn's mother, then began an 18-month intensive intervention program with him. The initial 12 months of the intervention focused on synthetic phonics instruction in which letter-sound correspondences, sight word reading and whole text reading were taught. The following six months involved the use of a commercial intervention program. Gwyn also received some learning support from his school in the first few school years, but this was not systematic and lacked intensity. Furthermore, his mother noticed that the school-based support did not address Gwyn's individual needs in a targeted way.

The results of the psychologist's intervention program indicate that his performance in reading noticeably improved, although he continued to have some difficulties. His new skills in decoding and comprehension resulted in increased confidence and self-esteem as well as an interest in recreational reading, although difficulties with writing, and especially spelling, remain. Thus, when Gwyn was interviewed four years ago he was an avid reader and enjoyed it very much.

Gwyn continued to receive intermittent support from his primary school until Year 6 when he enrolled in the same private school that his older brother attended. Gwyn's mother alerted the new school of his difficulties and accommodations were put in place so that classroom task requirements were adjusted. During Year 7 Gwyn participated in a dedicated learning support program in reading and writing where he made progress. Since then Gwyn has not participated in any specific learning support programs, but has continued to attend the learning support room where he has been assisted with his class work and assignments. Interestingly, the support has come about because his parents have paid additional fees to the school. According to his mother, Gwyn was grateful "for the opportunity to be able to go somewhere, talk to someone and have a bit of the load taken off." Thus, Gwyn is fully engaged in learning at school, and his teachers indicated that he participates in all classroom activities and especially enjoys contributing to classroom discussions. Research shows that classrooms in which instruction is adapted to students' developmental levels and individual needs, and where learning activities support students' autonomy, focus on students' interests, provide enjoyment and an appropriate level of challenge lead to student engagement (Shernoff, Csikszentmihalyi, Schneider & Shernoff, 2003). In addition, students with learning disabilities should receive on-going support including modification and adjustments to the curriculum; instruction and assessment are important because they allow these students to show what they know without being impeded by their learning disability. In addition, research shows that difficulties in word recognition, comprehension and written expression (especially in spelling) often continue during middle and secondary school level, despite intervention, and thus further intervention that targets specific knowledge and skills alongside additional support continues to be needed (Griffiths & Stuart, 2013; Snowling, 2013).

In primary school, Gwyn was bullied on the school bus, but this may not have been related to his dyslexia. Indeed when interviewed for the first case study Gwyn did not consider his reading difficulties to be a big concern and he had adopted the view, promoted by his parents, that individuals with dyslexia were unique. He was also aware that there were many influential and accomplished people with dyslexia in the world. His positive emotional state was also observed during the current case study. For example, the Self-Efficacy Questionnaire for Children (Muris, 2001) revealed that Gwyn had positive academic and emotional self-efficacy and the Children's Hope Scale (Snyder et al., 1997) showed that overall he had a hopeful outlook. His responses to the Achievement Goal Disposition Survey revealed that he had personal goals, he felt able to address challenges and he enjoyed discovering and finding out new things about the world.

Gwyn's emotional profile is different from other profiles described in much of the learning disability (LD) research. This type of research has provided profiles of helplessness, negative attributions, lower self-esteem, anxiety, depression and hopelessness in children with LD when compared to students without LD (e.g., Sideridis, 2007; Snowling, Muter & Carrol, 2007; Terras, Thompson & Minnus, 2009). As indicated in the first case study, the positive outcomes of his reading intervention program most likely have strongly contributed to Gwyn's positive emotional state. Indeed literature indicates that there are a number of factors that protect students with learning disabilities, such as dyslexia. These include social skills, self-esteem, family support and peer support (Hughes, Banks & Terras, 2013), and some writers have recommended that the teaching of skills in coping, assertiveness and resilience is effective for students with dyslexia (e.g., Firth, Frydenberg, Steeg & Bond, 2013).

In his leisure time Gwyn engages in individual sports like swimming and outdoor activities such as tending his vegetable garden or outings with his family. He likes computer games as well as reading books and magazines. Gwyn does not experience loneliness as is often reported in literature relating to students with learning disabilities (Al-Yagon, 2012). He has regular contact with his extended group of friends. During their get-togethers each person usually contributed to the social gatherings according to their different skills. For example, Gwyn's talent for cooking was appreciated by his friends as he usually shared something he baked. Recent research illustrates that patterns of online and offline communication are associated with both online friendships and relational closeness (Ledbetter & Kuznekoff, 2012). Such research may demonstrate how gaming contributed to the development of close bonds experienced by Gwyn and his friends.

Gwyn has continued to receive consistent assistance at home from his mother, particularly with typing and correcting assignments that he dictates. Gwyn signals when he requires his mother's assistance and indicates the type of assistance he needs. Both Gwyn and his mother noticed that he became stressed when he faced pressure due to time constraints regarding the completion of subject assignments. However, Gwyn was able to regulate this stress by being very well organized. Good organizational skills are not often observed in students with learning disabilities (Meltzer, 2007), but it appears that Gwyn is good at managing his time and his assignments. In this way Gwyn has developed coping strategies to mitigate stress and feelings of anxiety around work completion. His mother has also continued to advocate strongly for Gwyn at school and attended parent-teacher meetings to ensure that teachers are aware of his difficulties, especially as they are often not evident to the teachers. She attempted to make sure that he obtained the adjustments and support he needed, although it is not certain that they were consistently applied. It should be noted that although specific adjustments are not stated in legislation, both the Australian Government Disability Discrimination Act (1992) and the Australian Government Disability Standards for Education (2005) require "reasonable adjustments" to be made for students who require them at all levels of education.

Both Gwyn's parents have participated actively in his subject-selection for the senior years of schooling and his mother indicated that she and her husband have mostly common views related to Gwyn's learning and needs. Importantly, Gwyn's close relationship with his mother and father may be seen as another protective factor. Al-Yagon's (2012) research has pointed to the "possible protective role of adolescents' close relationships with significant adults (i.e., mothers, fathers, and teachers) in explaining adjustment in adolescents with and without LD" (p. 1308), with a close relationship with the mother being the most important for students with LD. In addition it is known that parents' educational expectations shape adolescents' own expectations (Dobbs & Arnold, 2009).

At the secondary school level, students interact with various subject area teachers in different classroom settings. Gwyn's secondary school report cards indicated that overall his teachers interacted positively with him. His mother also reported that the teachers mentioned that they liked teaching Gwyn. Surprisingly several of his teachers did not know that Gwyn had dyslexia, despite this information being available on his school records. This suggests that some of these teachers were not even aware that Gwyn occasionally encountered difficulties during their lessons. More importantly, if they had been aware, they would have been able to assist more efficaciously. When teachers are aware of students' difficulties they are able to convey empathy and concern, and develop a partnership with the students to involve them in assessing, planning and evaluating their learning needs and aspirations, which in turn empowers the students and allows them to be engaged in setting achievable targets (Long, MacBain & MacBain, 2007). In addition, teacher awareness and application of pedagogical practices known to facilitate struggling readers in high school might have been useful in Gwyn's situation. For example, pedagogical practices that simultaneously develop students' literacy skills and higher-order cognitive skills, in particular practices that enhance students' metacognitive and critical thinking skills, as well as practices that promote cooperative learning, have been found to be effective for high school students (Ivey & Fisher, 2006; Slavin, 2013).

In Gwyn's classes there was a preponderance of "chalk and talk" and little or no integration of assistive technologies. Such technologies have been found to support students with learning disabilities (Courtad & Bouck, 2013), and could have helped Gwyn in his classroom work. The non-use of assistive technologies meant that Gwyn's teachers had not tapped into Gwyn's "funds of knowledge" (Moll, Amanti, Neff & Gonzalez, 1992) or acknowledged his strengths related to computers as evidenced, for instance, by his gaming hobby. While it is clear that Gwyn did not enjoy and/or did not feel skilled in word processing, he was competent in a range of multiliteracies by using various modes for interaction such as image, sound, gesture, movement and text in computer games and LAN. These modes of interaction could have been used to enhance his learning. Thus, it is argued that teachers at secondary school level must enhance their knowledge relating to pedagogical content and effective practices that build on the skills and abilities that their students possess.

Currently, Gwyn is in his second-to-last year of high school where he is experiencing adolescence and preparing for future education and work. Although at first glance he is doing well at school, dyslexia has continued to affect his learning. The results from his recent evaluation by the psychologist who had worked with him in elementary school confirmed that his dyslexia and dysgraphia have persisted. She therefore recommended that he should get accommodations during his examinations. These provisions should include additional time, the use of a word processor and being allowed a 'reader' where appropriate in order for Gwyn to show what he knows. Due to the immense effort that Gwyn requires when writing by hand, the psychologist suggested the use of a computer as he can type considerably faster than he can write and his work would be legible.

Learning is not easy for Gwyn as he works effortfully to achieve good results. Nevertheless individuals diagnosed with dyslexia can compensate for their difficulties so that their word-reading accuracy and reading comprehension skills are similar to those of typical adults (Lefly & Pennington, 1991), and they are able to cope with the demands of tertiary education despite their remaining reading difficulties (Parrilla, Georgiou & Corkett, 2007). These research findings suggest that Gwyn, and students like him, have the potential to engage in higher education and this may then extend to a range of options for a productive work-life. In addition, Gwyn's own strengths and interests, his positive emotional status, his social skills and friendships, as well as the care of loving parents and his brother augur well for his future. It is anticipated that Gwyn's dreams and goals will lead to many opportunities and interesting and exciting prospects.

References

Al-Yagon, M. (2012). Adolescents with learning disabilities: Socio-emotional and behavioral functioning and attachment relationships with fathers, mothers, and teachers. *Journal of Youth Adolescence, 41*, 1294–1311.

Australian Curriculum Assessment and Reporting. (n.d.). *National Assessment Program – Literacy and Numeracy*. Retrieved from http://www.nap.edu.au/naplan

Australian Government. (1992). *Disability Discrimination Act, 1992*. Retrieved from http://www.comlaw.gov.au/Series/C2004A04426

Australian Government. (2005). *Disability Standards for Education, 2005*. Retrieved from http://education.gov.au/disability-standards-education

Comprehensive Assessment of Reading Strategies (CARS). Hawker Brownlow Education. Retrieved from http://www.hbe.com.au/series-cars-and-stars.html

Courtad, C. A., & Bouck, E. C. (2013). Assistive technology for students with learning disabilities. In J. P. Bakken, F. E. Obiakor, & A. F. Rotatori (Eds.), *Learning disabilities: Practice concerns and students with LD (Advances in Special Education*, pp. 153–173). Bingley, UK: Emerald.

Dixon, R., Engelmann, S., Meier, M., Steely, D., & Wells, T. (1998). *Spelling mastery: Teacher presentation book level A*. Columbus, OH: SRA/McGraw Hill.

Dobbs, J., & Arnold, D. H. (2009). The relationship between preschool teachers' reports of children's behavior and their behavior toward those children. *School Psychology Quarterly, 24*, 95–105.

Firth, N., Frydenberg, E., Steeg, C., & Bond, L. (2013). Coping successfully with dyslexia: An initial study of an inclusive school-based resilience programme. *Dyslexia, 19*, 113–130.

Griffiths, Y., & Stuart, M. (2013). Reviewing evidence-based practice for pupils with dyslexia and literacy difficulties. *Journal of Research in Reading, 36*, 96–116.

Hayamizu, T., & Weiner, B. (1991). A test of Dweck's model of achievement goals as related to perceptions of ability. *Journal of Experimental Education, 59*, 226–234.

Hughes, L. A., Banks, P., & Terras, M. M. (2013). Secondary school transition for children with special educational needs: A literature review. *Support for Learning, 28*(1), 24–34.

Ivey, G., & Fisher, D. (2006). *Creating literacy-rich schools for adolescents*. Alexandria, VA: ASCD.

Ledbetter, A. M., & Kuznekoff, J. H. (2012). More than a game: Friendship relational maintenance and attitudes toward Xbox LIVE communication. *Communication Research, 39*, 269–290.

Lefly, D. L., & Pennington, B. F. (1991). Spelling errors and reading fluency in compensated adult dyslexics. *Annals of Dyslexia, 41*, 143–162.

Long, L., MacBain, S., & MacBain, M. (2007). Supporting students with dyslexia at the secondary level: An emotional model of literacy. *Journal of Adolescent and Adult Literacy, 51*, 124–134.

Meltzer, L. (Ed.). (2007). *Executive function in education – From theory to practice.* New York: The Guilford Press.

Moll, L., Amanti, C., Neff, D., & Gonzalez, N. (1992). Funds of knowledge for teaching: Using a qualitative approach to connect homes and classrooms. *Theory Into Practice, 31*(2), 132–141.

Muris, P. (2001). A brief questionnaire for measuring self-efficacy in youths. *Journal of Psychopathology and Behavioral Assessment, 23,* 145–149.

Parrilla, R., Georgiou, G., & Corkett, J. (2007). University students with a significant history of reading difficulties: What is and is not compensated. *Exceptionality Education Canada, 17,* 195–220.

Progressive Achievement Tests in Reading—Fourth Edition (PAT Reading Fourth Edition). Australian Council for Educational Research. Retrieved from http://www.acer.edu.au/pat-reading

Shernoff, D. J., Csikszentmihalyi, M., Schneider, B., & Shernoff, E. S. (2003). Student engagement in high school classrooms from the perspective of Flow Theory. *School Psychology Quarterly, 18,* 158–176.

Sideridis, G. D. (2007). Why are students with LD depressed? A goal orientation model of depression vulnerability. *Journal of Learning Disabilities, 40,* 526–539.

Slavin, R. E. (2013). Effective programmes in reading and mathematics: Lessons from the Best Evidence Encyclopaedia. *School Effectiveness and School Improvement: An International Journal of Research, Policy and Practice, 24,* 383–391.

Snowling, M. J. (2013). Early identification and interventions for dyslexia: A contemporary view. *Journal of Research in Special Educational Needs, 13*(1), 7–14.

Snowling, M. J., Muter, V., & Carrol, J. (2007). Children at family risk of dyslexia: A follow-up in early adolescence. *Journal of Child Psychology and Psychiatry, 48,* 609–618.

Snyder, C. R., Hoza, B., Pelham, W. E., Rapoff, M., Ware, L., Danovsky, M., . . . Stahl, K. J. (1997). The development and validation of the Children's Hope Scale. *Journal of Pediatric Psychology, 22,* 399–421.

SRA Reading Labs. McGraw Hill Education. Retrieved from http://www.srareadinglabs.com/print/pages/home.php

SuccessMaker: A Digital Learning Curriculum. Pearson. Retrieved from www.pearsonschool.com/index.cfm?locator=PSZ4Z4&PMDbProgramId=55601

Terras, M. M., Thompson, L. C., & Minnus, H. (2009). Dyslexia and psycho-social functioning: An exploratory study of the role of self-esteem and understanding. *Dyslexia, 15,* 304–327.

Wechsler, D. (2005). *Wechsler Individual Achievement Test—Second Edition.* San Antonio, TX: Psychological Corporation.

Wright, C. (n.d.). *Understanding words.* Mermaid Beach, QLD, Australia: Author.

5
KA-HO, A CASE STUDY OF A CHINESE ADOLESCENT WITH DYSLEXIA

Steven S. W. Chu and Kevin K. H. Chung

Ka-ho is a 14-year-old Chinese adolescent, who was originally interviewed four years ago (see Chu, Chung & Ho, 2011). In the current interview he revealed problems coping with dyslexia and his feelings about not fitting into the Hong Kong educational system, which is well-known for its pressure to achieve good grades on standardized tests (Poon & Wong, 2008). Ka-ho was somewhat reluctant to discuss his frustrations with homework and reading as well as his relationships with teachers, peers and his father. This follow-up interview investigates Ka-ho's academic, social and emotional development during adolescence and highlights the challenges faced by Chinese students with dyslexia in high school and beyond.

Background

Diagnosis and Treatment

In second grade, Ka-ho took the Hong Kong Test of Specific Learning Difficulties in Reading and Writing for Primary School Students—Second Edition (HKT-P II; Ho et al., 2007), which revealed he was dyslexic. In the same year, he was administered a formal intelligence test (i.e., the Raven's Standard Progressive Matrices; Raven, Raven & Court, 2004) interpreted with reference to local norms (Hong Kong Education Department, 1986). The results showed that his nonverbal intelligence is within the normal range, with an intelligence quotient (IQ) of 98. Despite the fact that Ka-ho has normal intelligence and adequate learning opportunities, he consistently faces difficulties in orthographic knowledge and morphological awareness.

Chinese is best known for its visual complexity. Chinese characters have more visual information than English words. Each character is a perceptual unit that differs from thousands of others in its strokes and spatial configuration. Apart from visual complexity, Chinese characters are compounds, which can be segmented into sub-character components based on orthographic rules (see Chung & Ho, 2010 for more details). There are regularities in the positions and functions of the semantic and phonetic radicals of Chinese characters (Anderson et al., 2013; Chung & Leung, 2008). For example, the semantic radical 日 (jat6) often occurs on the left side of the character, indicating the meaning of the sun. The phonetic radical 青 (cing1) always appears on the right side, providing a cue to the pronunciation of the character. When the semantic and phonetic radicals are configured in their legal positions, a real or pseudo character can be formed. In the above example, a real character 晴 [sunny, (cing4)] is formed. However, Ka-ho finds it difficult to manipulate the regularities and functions of these semantic and phonetic radicals. In the interview, Ka-ho explained that he could not find a way to learn these regularities, which are rarely taught in class. He further complained that he was always required to correct his work multiple times (e.g. copying the correct characters ten times) once teachers identified his mistakes.

Another obstacle Ka-ho struggles with is perception and manipulation of the morphological structures of Chinese words. Because Chinese is a morphosyllabic writing system with a rich morphological structure, many words consist of multiple morphemes by combining different morphemes. Most words share the same morpheme such as 籃球 [basketball (laam4 kau4)], 足球 [football (zuk1 kau4)], 羽毛球 [badminton (jyu5 mou4 kau4)], all with a common morpheme 球 [ball (kau4)]. More than 70% of Chinese words are built and compounded from two or more morphemes (Institute of Language Teaching and Research [in China], 1986). An awareness and understanding of compounding or morphological structure is crucial for learning how to read and write in Chinese (Chung & Ho, 2010). Consequently, Ka-ho's deficit in understanding and manipulating morphological structures and word formation impedes his reading development. For example, Ka-ho would analyze 電腦 [computer (din6 nou5)] as "the electronic brain" instead of understanding that the compound words 電腦 [computer (din6 nou5)] must be perceived as a whole represented by only one morpheme. In short, Ka-ho overgeneralizes these implicit rules of word formation when he finds them confusing. He also faces difficulties in identifying and distinguishing Chinese homophones that share similar pronunciation such as 紫 [purple (zi2)], 紙 [paper (zi2)], and 子 [son (zi2)]. This reveals that Ka-ho is unable to map identical syllables onto new characters when he is required to do any reading and writing tasks in Chinese. In the interview, Ka-ho stated:

> It takes me lots of effort to identify words that sound similar. When I hear what my teachers read, I cannot locate the correct word in my mind. I think [the] Chinese language is so complicated. Reading is a huge problem for me.

Both Ka-ho and his mother mentioned that he made some progress in learning how to read and write Chinese in primary school (i.e., the first six years of schooling) where he attended after school tutoring sessions from grade three to grade six. He learned how to make use of phonetic radicals as a cue to the sound of the words and how to guess the meaning of some words such as 煎 [fry (zin1)], 煮 [cook (zyu2)] and 蒸 [steam (zing1)] that share the same semantic radical 灬 [fire (fo2)]. Unfortunately, Ka-ho could only read what his tutor taught him and was unable to generalize these skills to develop his reading achievement. He thinks that his reading might have improved if he had received similar teaching in mainstream Chinese lessons.

After finishing the sixth grade, Ka-ho was promoted to secondary school (i.e., grades seven through twelve). His secondary school has failed to provide any intervention or remedial programs despite the fact that his mother informed them of his reading and writing problems. At his current school, Ka-ho is provided only with homework allowances and extra examination time (i.e., half the amount of homework and an extra 15 minutes to complete exams), but no remedial support. The secondary school has never asked an educational psychologist to examine Ka-ho's reading and writing problems. At the interview the mother stated that "The school doesn't care too much about my son's reading problems. Without proper intervention and remediation, Ka-ho's academic performance has always been at the lowest end."

Ka-ho confirmed that no intervention program has been provided for him at the secondary school. Without much support from school, his Chinese literacy achievement has been disappointing. During the interview, he highlighted that he had always been the lowest performer in Chinese reading tests and examinations since grade seven. He reported that he could hardly score more than 30% on Chinese reading comprehension tests, which has caused him great frustration as reflected in his words, "School is no longer a suitable place for me. I'm a loser here. Reading is so difficult. My school is a hell for me!" Thus, Ka-ho's motivation has seriously deteriorated as his failures have multiplied.

Family and Home Life

Ka-ho lives with his parents in Sha Tin, a new town in Hong Kong. At the time of the interview, Ka-ho's younger brother, Ka-kit, was six years old and soon to be starting first grade. According to the mother, Ka-kit also shows some symptoms of dyslexia. Although Ka-kit's kindergarten teachers recommended a private educational psychologist for a formal assessment, the mother did not follow-up as she could not afford this evaluation. The family has been experiencing financial difficulties in the last year as the father was injured in an accident and the mother has become the sole bread winner. The mother stated, "My husband has become very depressed after the accident. He hits Ka-ho and Ka-kit when they score low marks in school. I've had some quarrels with him about this." Given that Ka-ho's father became very aggressive and emotional when he learned that the boys were not doing well in school, the mother will not allow her sons to report anything related to school to their father. She feels it is the best way to protect them from physical punishment. These recent changes have adversely affected the parents' relationship. The mother is particularly under stress as she must take care of an emotional and injured husband, protect her sons from physical punishment and earn a living for the family.

Ka-ho revealed he did not enjoy his family life. He admitted that his father's temper had become very bad since his injury. He confirmed his mother's perception of the family situation:

> My father can't work now. He hits us when we get low marks in school. My brother and I are so afraid of him. I wish I could leave school as soon as possible because I'm not good at that. I want to become a cook. When I've got a job I can help reduce my mother's financial burden.

His poor performance in school and the sudden change in the family situation have created a vicious cycle. His stress has further perpetuated failure, which is coupled with emotional and social strain. He feels the only solution is to quit school and get a job.

When Ka-ho was asked about his activities at home, he was quick to share that he enjoyed going online to play games and chat with new friends on Facebook. Every day he spends two hours surfing the internet. Ka-ho also sometimes helps his younger brother with his homework. Despite Ka-ho's deficits in reading and writing, Ka-ho can tutor his younger brother as the school work is simple. He reported:

> I like teaching my brother. I think he finds reading easier than I do. If I don't teach him, nobody can help him. My mother is too busy and my father will hit him if he doesn't know how to do homework.

However, when asked whether he liked reading at home, he quickly shook his head and said:

> I don't like reading. Reading is so difficult for me. I feel a headache when I read a long passage. I like reading comics, chatting with friends on Facebook, and playing online games.

Medical and Psychological Aspects

Ka-ho has not had any serious health problems in the past four years. However, both parents are concerned about his recent diagnosis of attention deficit disorder (ADD). Given that his teachers complained about his inattentiveness in class, the mother took Ka-ho to the government's psychiatric clinic for formal assessment in grade seven. After waiting for over a year, Ka-ho saw the psychiatric specialist at the end of eighth grade. The assessment results revealed that Ka-ho had ADD and he was prescribed Ritalin. Though the medication helped Ka-ho to be more attentive, he suffered from insomnia, a common side effect. Consequently, his mother stopped the medication without a psychiatrist's approval. Since then, Ka-ho has received no treatment for ADD and the mother has not taken him for any further appointments. The mother never told the school about his diagnosis of ADD, nor did the school ever inquire about Ka-ho's manifestations of ADD behavior. His ADD problem remains untreated.

Educational Perspectives

Reading Achievement and Progress

Given that Ka-ho is a slow, inaccurate reader, he has experienced tremendous difficulties in finishing reading tests and examinations. He told the interviewer that he could rarely finish half the questions on the reading tests and examinations that normally lasted for one and a half hours even though he receives an additional 15 minutes. When Ka-ho and his mother were asked to review the reading progress he had made in the last four years, they agreed that little achievement had been made. The mother indicated that Ka-ho's reading had declined, explaining:

> Ka-ho has made very limited progress in reading. He has never passed his reading tests and examinations in these four years. His reading scores were relatively low in secondary school when compared with what he scored in primary school. I don't see that he has made any achievement in reading. On the contrary, his reading performance has declined as he advanced to higher grades, especially when he was in grade eight. His teacher of Chinese [in the eighth grade] only blamed him for his inattentiveness and lack of effort. He [Ka-ho] was very upset about that.

In the current interview, Ka-ho and his mother were asked to rate his reading performance on a scale of 1 to 5 (1 being the lowest, 5 being the highest). Four years ago, the mother rated her son's reading as 2 and now rates it as a 1. Similarly Ka-ho rated his reading as 2 four years ago and 1 currently. It is evident that both Ka-ho and his mother are dissatisfied with his current reading achievement. His mother blames the school, noting "his secondary school hasn't provided him any reading remediation or tutorials. You can't imagine how a dyslexic student like my son could improve his reading without any support from school." Consistent with his mother's remarks, Ka-ho described the support he has received from his secondary school as being "close to zero." He feels that there are no teachers who really understand his reading difficulties. Both Ka-ho and his mother believe that some progress could have been made if the secondary school teachers had tried to understand and address his reading problems.

His mother believes that Ka-ho's limited reading achievement progress causes him substantial frustrations. However, she appreciates that Ka-ho never makes excuses to miss school and consistently tries his best to submit all homework. Ka-ho is aware of his parents' concerns:

> I know I'm not good at reading and my reading performance disappoints my parents, but I don't want to disappoint my mum and dad further. So I'll try my best to submit my homework and attend all school days.

Teachers

Ka-ho mentioned that he had a good teacher who was his remedial tutor when he was in primary school. He reported that this teacher "encouraged me a lot. I liked attending her remedial class because she was so patient and supportive. She never complained about my reading and writing problems." Ka-ho loved going to school when he was in the primary grades as he found most of his teachers caring and supportive. In contrast, Ka-ho would like to leave his secondary school as he noted:

> At my present school, my teachers just ignore me and they don't think I'm a good student because I'm not doing well in reading and writing. My teachers only ask me to do corrections many times when I write words wrongly. For every single word [miswritten], I have to copy ten times. I've tried my best to do better but my teachers don't understand my reading problems. I think they don't like me. To be honest, I don't like them either.

It is evident that Ka-ho does not get along well with his secondary school teachers. Perhaps, his teachers' ignorance of his reading and writing problems has significantly contributed to his poor adjustment, performance and desire to leave school early for work.

Echoing Ka-ho's views, the mother also feels that the secondary school teachers are not caring and supportive enough, particularly in comparison to primary school. She shared her disappointment with the way the secondary school teachers treat her son:

> My son has attention deficits and dyslexia. But they never approach me for understanding his problems. I feel that the teachers are ignoring his needs.

His homeroom teacher even persuaded us to send Ka-ho to another school which might have special programs for students with special educational needs.

Ka-ho's mother did not agree with the recommendation to transfer to another school as she believes that all teachers have the responsibility to support students with diverse learning needs. However, this expectation has not been met. Without understanding Ka-ho's special educational needs, one of his teachers even harassed him. The mother reported a very upsetting incident:

> When Ka-ho was in eighth grade, his teacher of Chinese openly discussed his reading problems in front of the class. My son told me that he just miswrote his name but his teacher made use of this opportunity to criticize my son for his illegible writing. I think this is a kind of humiliation and harassment.

Despite the fact that the mother believes this incident was humiliating, she never complained to the school principal as she was afraid that the teachers might label both Ka-ho and his parents as trouble makers. According to the mother's report, there is little communication between the teachers and the parents.

Learning Style

Ka-ho prefers learning by using his body, hands and sense of touch. However, he commented that his learning style has not been properly addressed in class as teaching was confined to the "chalk-and-talk" method. He further added, "I think I can learn better if my teachers design more activities which are hands-on in nature. I can't learn well if I have to read a lot." Also he doesn't like listening to lectures because he noted, "I can't follow my teachers' teaching when I only listen to them. They deliver their lessons so quickly. I think I'm a slow learner. I need more time to process my learning."

Ka-ho prefers to work in groups rather than working alone so he "can get some help" when he becomes "stuck." He believes that he would do better in school if he could demonstrate what he has learned through a presentation rather than written work. Ka-ho likes to use computers in school and finds them to be beneficial with his reading as he can look up vocabulary words he doesn't understand. He has never had any digital texts in school as his teachers use only printed books.

Ka-ho identified physical education and drama as his two academic strengths and reading and writing as his weaknesses. He is proud of his running and has won two medals for his school in competitions. Ka-ho is also good at cooking. He said, "I like cooking because I can learn how to cook by watching how people cook on YouTube and TV. Watching others' demonstration makes me grasp how to cook well." Ka-ho feels that since he is able to manage cooking and running, he could either become a cook or an athlete after leaving school.

Homework

Even though Ka-ho only has to complete half of his homework, it is still very troublesome for him. He described this as "a huge problem!" as he spends four hours daily on his homework. Because of his reading and writing problems, reading comprehension and writing Chinese characters are arduous demands. He finds it particularly difficult to remember and identify the stroke patterns of Chinese characters especially when some stroke patterns are similar in configurations. For example, he would confuse the Chinese characters 午 (afternoon) and 牛 (cow). He cited one example in the interview:

> When I write 午餐 (lunch), I might write it as 牛餐 (lunch for cow). I know that this is a silly mistake but I just make it sometimes. In grade eight, I made this silly mistake and my teacher of Chinese just discussed my problems publicly in class. I felt so embarrassed and I think the teacher was teasing me.

Unfortunately, his homework problems have not been properly addressed. Instead, he was teased. In order to help Ka-ho complete his homework, his mother has sent him to a fee-paying tutorial center since seventh grade, but Ka-ho does not think that the private tutorial center has helped. He stated:

> Sometimes, I approach some tutors asking for help but they reject me because they think I'm a slow learner. They feel that I'll waste their time . . . some tutors even just gave me the answers for copying. I don't like that because I'm not stupid.

Even though Ka-ho believes that going to the private tutorial center is useless, he cannot manage his homework on his own. The mother reported that she could not support his learning, as it is becoming more challenging and difficult as he advances to higher grades. The only solution Ka-ho can rely on is copying answers from the tutors at the tutorial center. Despite his reluctance to copy the answers, he feels he has no other alternative as he does not want to disappoint his mother or suffer harsh punishment from his father. This practice also helps him to avoid detention class for incomplete homework.

Social Development

Four years ago, Ka-ho reported that he did not have any problems getting along with teachers and peer students. He thought that his teachers and peers were helpful in spite of his reading and writing problems. However, when Ka-ho was asked whether he was getting along well with others in the current interview, he firmly answered:

> No. I think my classmates don't like me because I'm not doing as well as they do. Sometimes, my peers bully me by calling me nicknames. They either call me "idiot" or "dummy." I feel bad about these nicknames. I know I'm not good at reading and writing, but I'm not stupid. I've normal intelligence.

It seems that Ka-ho's dyslexia not only causes poor reading performance, but also affects how peers socialize with him. One prominent problem identified in the current interview is verbal bullying, which was initiated by his classmates when he was promoted to grade seven. Despite this bullying by his peers, Ka-ho has never reported these incidents to his teachers as he believes that they would not be able to stop it. He explained:

> It's useless to report any bullying incidents to my teachers. This kind of bullying is so common in my school, but my teachers never treat it seriously. They'll only handle a bullying case in a more serious way when someone was physically hurt by the bully.

Ka-ho's mother expressed her greatest concern over the issue of providing emotional support for her son's school frustrations. Ka-ho has faced increasing social challenges particularly since he started secondary school when the mother noticed that he began to have difficulty getting along with school teachers and his peers. She stated in the current interview:

> I've noticed that his classmates and teachers are not as nice as those in primary school. He [Ka-ho] can be very moody and frustrated when he is left alone by his teachers and classmates. I want to talk with him but he seldom talks with me about how he interacts with his classmates.

Undoubtedly, his mother would prefer to provide more emotional support, but her son's unwillingness to talk about his problems is an obstacle. The mother noted that Ka-ho has been getting along well with his younger brother, but she is gravely concerned about his interactions with his father since the accident. She believes the father's punitive behavior causes Ka-ho to be depressed and indicated that she would get the police involved if necessary as she is committed to protecting her children. She has not approached the school for counseling services because she does not want to disclose these family conflicts. This is unfortunate as the school could be a source of assistance in this situation.

Self-Determination and Coping

Self-Efficacy and Motivation

Ka-ho completed the Academic and Emotional Scales of the Self-Efficacy Questionnaire for Children (SEQ-C; Muris, 2001). The items of the academic self-efficacy questionnaire focused on how well he handles academic tasks; whereas the items of the emotional efficacy questionnaire address his ability to manage emotionally challenging situations.

Ka-ho's responses indicated that he has problems getting teachers to help him when he gets stuck on schoolwork, passing tests and understanding his subjects in school. In addition, he is challenged when studying for a test, paying attention to his studies when there are other interesting things to do, paying attention in every class and satisfying his parents with his schoolwork. The results indicated that Ka-ho has a low level of academic self-efficacy, and it seems likely that dyslexia and attention problems have adversely affected his academic performance and consequently his academic self-efficacy.

When it comes to the questions pertaining to emotional self-efficacy, Ka-ho exhibited similar low scoring. He believes that he is not good at controlling his feelings and is unsuccessful in suppressing unpleasant thoughts and cheering himself in the course of an unpleasant event. He noted that he gets furious when bullied by his classmates and teased by his teachers. The results of the emotional self-efficacy questionnaire showed that Ka-ho struggles with managing his emotions in challenging situations and is worried about the future. Without emotional support from significant figures such as peers, secondary school teachers and his father, Ka-ho's abilities in dealing with negative emotions have become very weak.

Ka-ho also completed the Children's Hope Scale (Snyder et al., 1997), which pertains to his confidence in abilities and problem solving. The results of the Hope Scale showed that most of the time Ka-ho does not think he is doing as well as other children of his age. He indicated that he could not come up with different ways to solve a problem most of the time. In addition, he was unable to understand how to achieve things that are important to him. Ka-ho has low confidence in his abilities and seems unable to explore or initiate different ways to solve the difficulties he faces. Perhaps, his accumulated failure in reading and disappointing school and home experiences have contributed to pessimistic perceptions.

The third measure that Ka-ho completed was the Achievement Goal Disposition Survey (adapted from Hayamizu & Weiner, 1991). This measure examined Ka-ho's motivation in learning as he rated himself on three categories of motivation: (1) intellectual curiosity (learning mastery), (2) social approval and (3) goal achievement. For most of the questions that dealt with goal achievement, Ka-ho agreed that he studies because he wants to get a good job in the future as he thinks a well-paying job could help him reduce his family's financial burden. In addition, Ka-ho feels that his motivation to learn is related to gaining social approval. He emphasized in the interview, "I study because I don't want to disappoint my mum and dad. I want to be praised by my parents, friends, and teachers." Ka-ho's intellectual curiosity is relatively low given that he shows little interest in learning new things, solving problems and overcoming obstacles. His responses on this measure show that he has a strong desire to obtain others' acceptance and approval and, most importantly, he perceives studying as a way to help him reduce his family's financial problems. Ka-ho's learning goals are seemingly rather extrinsic as his learning is not influenced by his intellectual curiosity, but rather is most strongly motivated by his desire to please others.

Coping

As Ka-ho advances to higher grades, he has encountered more problems in school. He feels that he is unable to cope with the increasing amount of homework and must rely on the support given by the fee-paying tutorial center, where he is not taught how to do the work but is instead given the answers. While this helps Ka-ho with his relationship with his father, specifically in avoiding physical punishment for failing to finish his homework, he is reluctant to discuss this matter with his mother. He admitted in the interview that he feels guilty about what he has been doing, but he has no other solution when neither his secondary school teachers nor his parents can or will offer homework assistance. In addition, Ka-ho feels particularly sad and stressed-out when his peers bully him and he is blamed and teased by his teachers. He strongly believes that his failure in reading has made him prone to bullying and his teachers' disapproval. He stated in the interview:

> Dyslexia has brought me lots of problems. My peers think I'm disabled so they bully me. My teachers don't like me because I've never attained what they expect me to do. My peers and teachers look down upon me because of my poor performance in reading and writing. I think I'm an abnormal student because I always fail.

When asked how he copes with the above-mentioned problems, his responses indicated that he has been using a cognitive-avoidance approach (e.g., Folkman & Lazarus, 1980) in facing challenges and difficulties. He stated: "There's not much I can do. I have no control over my problems associated with dyslexia. I want to forget how I'm doing in school and I wish I could leave this place [school] very soon."

Given that school is stressful for Ka-ho, he has turned to meeting new friends on Facebook and playing online video games. He was enthusiastic about these internet pastimes as he has found these to reduce stress because he does not have to disclose his reading problems. However, his mother disapproves and feels "he is spending too much time chatting with strangers."

Impact on Mother

Ka-ho's mother revealed that she had experienced tremendous stress in providing academic support to her son. She thinks that it is challenging to help with Ka-ho's homework as he advances to higher grades. In the absence of school support, she decided to send Ka-ho to a private tutorial center for homework assistance, which has caused the family extra financial burden and more stress. She believes that paying for outside tutoring is the only thing she can do for Ka-ho, because neither she nor her husband could help with his homework. Unfortunately, the father disagrees with her decision of a private tutorial center for homework support. He thinks that Ka-ho should finish his homework on his own. In the view of the father, Ka-ho's dyslexia would gradually disappear if he would work harder; he believes that his son's reading problems are associated with a lack of effort. Ka-ho's father fails to understand what dyslexia is and how it affects his child's school achievement. As the mother said, "My husband only thinks that our son is lazy. We have disputes over this issue from time to time."

As previously mentioned, the mother feels that Ka-ho's dyslexia has affected her relationship with her husband. She stated:

> My husband has not been involved too much in parenting Ka-ho because he's a very traditional Chinese father. He thinks it's a mother's duty to rear children. He always blames me for Ka-ho's poor academic performance. I think he should also help me support Ka-ho.

Having experienced disputes over the parenting of a dyslexic child, the mother feels helpless as she finds her husband only relies on punishment to "force" Ka-ho into performing better in reading. Disagreements over the practice of physical punishment have caused marital discord. She stated that she feels "very stressed and helpless" and sometimes she doesn't want to go home after work because the situation is so "heart-breaking" for her to face.

Not only has Ka-ho's dyslexia affected the mother's relationship with her husband, but it has also affected her social life. Because of the unavailability of support provided by family members, relatives and secondary school teachers, she spends most of her free time supervising Ka-ho with his reading at home. In light of this, she feels that she has less time available for friends and has been unable to share her difficulties and emotions with others outside family. Without much social support from friends, the mother thinks that parenting a child with dyslexia is very stressful.

In addition, the mother is anxious because of her concerns about Ka-ho's future which she attributes, in part, to the lack of teacher support. She stated in the interview:

> I don't think my son will have a good future because dyslexia has ruined his life. He won't be able to do well in the public examinations and can't go to university. I'm helpless because nobody can help him or advise me

what to do. The school teachers are not well trained in special education and it's apparent they don't know what to do with Ka-ho.

To sum up, the mother perceives that parenting a child with dyslexia is a difficult task for her. She feels that "Dyslexia is a curse. It doesn't only ruin Ka-ho's life, but it also affects the whole family. I feel tired, sometimes, but I can't give up. If not, his life could be much worse."

Future Goals and Hopes

When Ka-ho was asked to identify two goals that he would like to accomplish before leaving secondary school, he said that he wanted to submit all of his homework on time and to avoid punishment from his father. In order to complete his homework, he stated that he would rely on his private tutors, but if they could not help, he would "just copy some sentences from textbooks to fill in the blanks." Ka-ho's experiences have led him to believe that completing homework by any means is preferable to avoid punishment, but it is very unfortunate that there is no educational benefit to what appears to be an exercise in futility. In terms of his future goals after secondary school, Ka-ho, without much hesitation, admitted that he will not be able to attend university owing to his poor examination results. He pointed out:

> I won't dream of going to any university in Hong Kong. How can a dyslexic student like me do well in the Hong Kong Diploma of Secondary School Examination (HKDSE)? Only good grades guarantee university admission. I don't think I will succeed and I'm not daring enough to think about it [going to university].

Ka-ho wishes he could become an athlete when he leaves school as he stated:

> I like running so I want to become an athlete. But I know that being a full-time athlete could be a difficult task because I learned that not every athlete could make a good living. That's why I am also learning cooking. I can be a cook if I cook well, just in case I can't be an athlete.

Obviously, Ka-ho is aware of his difficulties in meeting the prescribed requirements of going to university. He also understands that few athletes can succeed in earning enough money to support the family so he has realistically included cooking in future career possibilities.

Consistent with Ka-ho's responses about his future goals and hopes, his mother explained that she has not demanded that her son do well on the secondary exams. She is more concerned that Ka-ho is able to find a good job to help the family. She made the following remarks in the interview:

I know he won't make it [going to university]. But I want him to be more focused. He wants to become an athlete, but I've never heard that an athlete could be able to make a living. I want him to become a cook because this career is more practical. His father has been unable able to work since the accident. I'm afraid he has to help share the family's financial burden.

Thus, both Ka-ho and his mother perceive cooking as a practical career that may earn a stable income for the family. Ka-ho still has a long way to go before taking the HKDSE in the twelfth grade and the mother wishes his teachers could provide more support to help him do better in this important exam, but it is probably unlikely. When Ka-ho was asked to name his three wishes, he promptly indicated that he wishes: (1) he would not be bullied by his peer classmates, (2) his teachers would provide him tutorials and (3) his dyslexia could be medically cured in the future.

Case Commentary

Ka-ho has gone through many troubling experiences at home and at school since the first interview four years ago. He went from a primary school that provided him with reading and tutorial support to a secondary school where he received no support at all and was bullied by his peers and ridiculed by his teachers. His mother is no longer able to help Ka-ho with his homework so she must pay private tutors to teach him skills to overcome his learning difficulties, which is a financial strain and doesn't help much as the tutors merely give him the answers with no instruction. Turning in his completed assignments on time allows Ka-ho to avoid physical punishment from his father, but does not help him to learn the content or improve his reading comprehension. School has become so difficult and frustrating for Ka-ho that he wants to leave and get a job to help support his family and feel successful. He feels powerless to deal with his dyslexia, as does his mother, who longs to help him. Since her husband lost his job, the mother's focus is on protecting her children's well-being from their increasingly physically abusive father and financially supporting the family. Ka-ho's school experience has gone downhill in the past four years. His negative experiences in secondary school demonstrate how Chinese students with dyslexia should be better supported in Hong Kong. This adolescent and his mother are doing everything possible, but they need the assistance of expert teachers who are committed to the needs of all students and they need knowledgeable school administrators who can provide the structure for necessary remediation and content support. The ineffectiveness of the secondary school, which focuses to the extreme on academic achievement in standardized tests, results in a meritocracy in which only the high achievers survive, and the rest are left to suffer many indignities (Riddick, 2010). It cannot be emphasized strongly enough that a major effort toward educating the public about dyslexia must be undertaken in Hong Kong.

Since 2007, dyslexia has been recognized as a form of disability in Hong Kong (Labour and Welfare Bureau, 2007). After its official recognition, mainstream schools in Hong Kong were mandated to adopt a Three-Tier Intervention Model to support students with specific learning difficulties (e.g., dyslexia, autism spectrum disorder, intellectual disability, physical disability, hearing impairments, attention deficit/hyperactivity disorder, and speech and language impairments) (Education Bureau, 2008). Based on the Three-Tier Intervention Model, students with mild learning difficulties are required to receive Tier 1 support (e.g., quality classroom teaching), whereas students who have persistent learning difficulties (e.g., dyslexia) should be provided with Tier 2 support (e.g., add-on interventions such as pull-out programs and group teaching). Finally, students who have persistent learning difficulties should be provided with intensive individualized support (e.g., Individualized Educational Plan) (Education Bureau, 2008). In addition, each primary and secondary school is mandated to set up Student Support Teams (SSTs) to monitor the progress made and to routinely meet with parents to provide them feedback on each student's performance (Education Bureau, 2012a, 2012b). Both the Three-Tier Intervention Model and the establishment of SSTs are important mechanisms that guide the operation of school-based support to students with dyslexia and various types of special educational needs in Hong Kong.

Despite the fact that every primary and secondary school is mandated to implement the Three-Tier Intervention Model and involve parent participation in supporting students with dyslexia, the implementation of such government policies has been inconsistent across schools, as indicated in the case of the secondary school Ka-ho attends. In Ka-ho's case, Tier 2 support in the form of regular after-school tutorials was provided to him through grades three to six, whereas it is clear that he received no support whatsoever in secondary school. It is critical to take note that every school is given HK$10,000 for the support of each and every eligible student on Tier 2. Even though Ka-ho was diagnosed as having dyslexia, he did not receive this support. It is not clear why he was ineligible, or whether the money was spent on other school-related activities rather than on dyslexic students. Given that parents of Chinese students with dyslexia are often ill-informed about the support and services that should be provided to their dyslexic children (Poon-McBrayer & McBrayer, 2013), it appears that there is no monitoring system that assesses how the Three-Tier Intervention Model as a framework has been implemented in Hong Kong schools. Thus, the effectiveness of the Three-Tier Intervention Model is unknown (Poon-McBrayer & McBrayer, 2013). This careless policy implementation results in a lack of support for students with special needs like Ka-ho.

The second significant issue in Ka-ho's case is the secondary school teachers' lack of readiness to support Chinese students with dyslexia and other developmental disorders. As implied throughout the current interview, Ka-ho's mother was aware of the importance of teacher training in special education because she had experienced the marked difference in the teacher support and attitude after Ka-ho's transition from primary to secondary school. She believed that her son could have been provided better assistance if the teachers were well trained in supporting Chinese students with dyslexia. Unfortunately, this is not likely to happen soon in the secondary school sector as the Office of the Ombudsman (2009), the watchdog of the government, found that only 11% of secondary school teachers had received basic training in catering for the diverse learning needs of students with dyslexia while 76% of the secondary schools did not have even one teacher trained in supporting students with dyslexia. To a certain extent, the secondary school teachers' attitudes toward students with dyslexia may also be related to their reluctance to integrate students with special needs in their classrooms. As suggested by recent studies (Horne & Timmons, 2009; Savolainen, Engelbrecht, Nel & Malinen, 2012), the successful implementation of inclusive education in mainstream settings for students with dyslexia is anchored by strong teacher training. Hence, the public has urged the government of Hong Kong to provide more training opportunities for teachers. In response, the Education Bureau has started to provide in-service teacher training in special education, beginning in 2007. However, another question pertains to teachers' initiative to take on more responsibilities when research has demonstrated that they are fully occupied by substantial teaching workloads and large class size (35–40 students per class) (Poon-McBrayer & McBrayer, 2013). Therefore, it appears that the government of Hong Kong needs to consider how the frontline teachers could be supported to take relevant training in special education, either by hiring more teachers and lowering current teacher workload and class size or by hiring special education teachers to provide services to students like Ka-ho.

The third issue highlighted in this case study is the ignorance on the part of Ka-ho's father about the condition of dyslexia. The father's use of corporal punishment to address inadequate school performance has had a devastating impact on Ka-ho's emotional development and family life. His aggression may be related to his injury and subsequent unemployment, marital discord and/or financial problems, all of which have been associated with parental use of physical punishment (Gershoff, 2002; Tang, 2006). Although the mother is able to prevent some of this punishment, the psychological effects of a history of harsh discipline will likely be long-lasting for this adolescent and may include depression and anxiety (Bender et al., 2007).

It is clear from the case study of Ka-ho that dyslexic children run the risk of failure not only academically, but also socially and emotionally. Like Ka-ho, the frustration of prolonged failure on a range of curriculum subjects resulting in feelings of insecurity and lack of confidence can have profound effects on social status, friendship patterns in class and acceptance and adjustment on the playground. The bullying incidents that Ka-ho has faced are, unfortunately, not unusual as research has suggested that this is a common occurrence for dyslexics (Anderson & Meier-Hedde, 2011; Singer, 2005). Ka-ho was not confident enough to seek support from teachers as he was afraid that he would be stigmatized and marginalized if he revealed the bullying incidents. It is troublesome that the school's policy on combating bullying shows its ignorance of the relationship of peer victimization and maladaptive adjustments such as depressive symptoms and suicidal thoughts (see Hawker & Boulton, 2000, for a review). As such, it appears imperative for the school administration to consider how bullying can be prevented to protect the well-being of Chinese dyslexic students. Furthermore, there is a pressing need for Ka-ho to be taught adaptive coping strategies to protect his self-esteem (Singer, 2007), which he describes as being very negative. Such descriptions are not surprising since dyslexic students often experience academic and social failure and receive negative feedback at school as well as at home. In the light of the evidence that students with dyslexia may experience behavioral, emotional and social deficits, it is important to identify those students at risk of experiencing such problems and to develop intervention programs to assist in these areas (Humphrey, 2002).

Despite all of the adversity Ka-ho has encountered, he perseveres by trying to do his best in school every day in the absence of encouragement or reinforcement. He demonstrates some sound strategies for reducing stress, such as online gaming and socializing, and is an obedient son and a loving, supportive brother who is committed to his family's well-being. Although he may not achieve the necessary public examination results to access a university education, Ka-ho has a clear vocational goal that he can realistically achieve in the future. In the face of enormous obstacles, he has demonstrated a measure of resilience to be a productive citizen and successfully adapt to the responsibilities of adulthood. Hopefully, when Ka-ho leaves school and the negativity associated with this time in his life, he will have positive work and social experiences that bolster his self-confidence and provide the personal fulfillment that has thus far eluded him.

References

Anderson, P. L., & Meier-Hedde, R. (2011). Cross-case analysis and reflections. In P. L. Anderson & R. Meier-Hedde (Eds.), *International case studies of dyslexia* (pp. 283–305). New York: Routledge.

Anderson, R. C., Ku, Y. M., Li, W., Chen, X., Wu, X., & Shu, H. (2013). Learning to see the patterns in Chinese characters. *Scientific Studies of Reading*, 17(1), 41–56. doi:10.1080/10888438.2012.689789

Bender, H. L., Allen, J. P., McElhaney, K. B., Antonishak, J., Moore, C. M., Kelly, H. O., & Davis, H. D. (2007). Use of harsh physical discipline and developmental outcomes in adolescence. *Development and Psychopathology*, 19, 227–242. doi:10.1017/S0954579407070125.

Chu, S. S. W., Chung, K. K. H., & Ho, F. C. (2011). Ka-ho, a case study of dyslexia in China. In P. L. Anderson & R. Meier-Hedde (Eds.), *International case studies of dyslexia* (pp. 46–64). New York: Routledge.

Chung, H. K., & Leung, M. T. (2008). Data analysis of Chinese characters in primary school corpora of Hong Kong and mainland China: Preliminary theoretical interpretations. *Clinical Linguistics & Phonetics, 22*, 379–389.

Chung, K. K. H., & Ho, C. S.-H. (2010). Dyslexia in Chinese language: An overview of research and practice. *Australian Journal of Learning Difficulties, 15*(2), 213–224.

Education Bureau. (2008). *Operation guide on the whole school approach to integrated education*. Retrieved from www.edb.gov.hk/attachment/en/edu-system/special/support/wsa/ie%20guide_en.pdf

Education Bureau. (2012a). *Education Bureau circular no. 12/2012: Learning support grant for primary schools*. Retrieved from www.edb.gov.hk/attachment/en/edu-system/special/support/wsa/primary/circular_LSGPS_e.pdf

Education Bureau. (2012b). *Education Bureau circular no. 13/2012: Learning support grant for secondary schools*. Retrieved from www.edb.gov.hk/attachment/en/edu-system/special/support/wsa/secondary/circular_LSGSS_e_6.8.2012.pdf

Folkman, S., & Lazarus, R. S. (1980). An analysis of coping in a middle-aged community sample. *Journal of Health and Social Behavior, 21*, 219–239.

Gershoff, E. T. (2002). Corporal punishment by parents and associated child behaviors and experiences: A meta-analytic and theoretical review. *Psychological Bulletin, 128*, 539–579. doi:10.1037//0033-2909.128.4.539

Hawker, D. S. J., & Boulton, M. J. (2000). Twenty years' research on peer victimization and psychosocial maladjustment: A meta-analytic review of cross-sectional studies. *Journal of Child Psychology and Psychiatry, 41*, 441–455.

Hayamizu, T., & Weiner, B. (1991). A test of Dweck's model of achievement goals as related to perceptions of ability. *Journal of Experimental Education, 59*, 226–234.

Ho, C. S. H., Chan, D. W., Chung, K. K. H., Tsang, S. M., Lee, S. H., & Cheng, R. W. Y. (2007). *The Hong Kong Test of Specific Learning Difficulties in Reading and Writing for Primary School Students—Second Edition*. Hong Kong: Hong Kong Specific Learning Difficulties Research Team.

Hong Kong Education Department. (1986). *Hong Kong supplement to guide to the Standard Progressive Matrices*. Hong Kong: Hong Kong Government.

Horne, P. E., & Timmons, V. (2009). Making it work: Teachers' perspectives on inclusion. *International Journal of Inclusive Education, 13*, 273–286.

Humphrey, N. (2002). Teacher and pupil ratings of self-esteem in developmental dyslexia. *British Journal of Special Education, 29*, 29–36.

Institute of Language Teaching and Research. (1986). *A frequency dictionary of modern Chinese*. Beijing: Beijing Language Institute Press.

Labour & Welfare Bureau. (2007). *Rehabilitation program plan 2007*. Retrieved from www.ability.org.hk/english/images/pr/rpp_report.pdf

Muris, P. (2001). A brief questionnaire for measuring self-efficacy in youths. *Journal of Psychopathology and Behavioral Assessment, 23*, 145–149.

Office of the Ombudsman. (2009). *Direct investigation on support services for students with specific learning difficulties*. Retrieved from www.ombudsman.hk/ombudsnews/ombe_3_0809.pdf

Poon, A. Y. K., & Wong, Y.-C. (2008). Education reform in Hong Kong: The "Through-Road" model and its societal consequences. *International Review of Education, 54*(1), 33–55. doi:10.1007/s11159-007-9073-9

Poon-McBrayer, K. F., & McBrayer, P. A. (2013). Parental account of support for specific learning difficulties in Hong Kong. *British Journal of Special Education, 40*(2), 65–71. doi:10.1111/1467-8578.12018

Raven, J., Raven, J. C., & Court, J. H. (2004). *Manual for Raven's Progressive Matrices and Vocabulary Scales*. San Antonio, TX: Harcourt Assessment.

Riddick, B. (2010). *Living with dyslexia* (2nd ed.). Abingdon, UK: Routledge.

Savolainen, H., Engelbrecht, P., Nel, M., & Malinen, O. P. (2012). Understanding teachers' attitudes and self-efficacy in inclusive education: Implications for pre-service and in-service teacher education. *European Journal of Special Needs Education, 27*(1), 51–68.

Singer, E. (2005). The strategies adopted by Dutch children with dyslexia to maintain their self-esteem when teased in school. *Journal of Learning Disabilities, 38*, 411–423. doi:10.1177/00222194050380050401

Singer, E. (2007). Coping with academic failure, a study of Dutch children with dyslexia. *Dyslexia, 14*, 314–333. doi:10.1002/dys.352

Snyder, C. R., Hoza, B., Pelham, W. E., Rapoff, M., Ware L., Danovsky M., . . . Stahl, K. J. (1997). The development and validation of the Children's Hope Scale. *Journal of Pediatric Psychology, 22*, 399–421.

Tang, C. S. (2006). Corporal punishment and physical maltreatment against children: A community study on Chinese parents in Hong Kong. *Child Abuse and Neglect, 30*, 893–907. doi:10.1016/j.chiabu.2006.02.012

6
XAVI, A CASE STUDY OF A SPANISH ADOLESCENT WITH DYSLEXIA

Rosa María González Seijas

At the time of the second interview, Xavi was 14 years and 11 months old. He was enthusiastic about this meeting and seemed willing and collaborative at all times. He was diagnosed with dyslexia at 9 years of age, when he was in fourth grade of elementary school. Until second grade of primary education, he was in a different school. Due to some unpleasant incidents with his teachers and the fact that he did not receive any help or support at school, his parents decided to switch schools. In the new school, he was diagnosed with dyslexia and received the necessary support so that, in addition to meeting the academic demands, various short- and long-term goals were established.

Background

Diagnosis and Treatment

Xavi was assessed in fourth grade with the Batería de Evaluación de los Procesos Lectores, Revisada [Reading Processes Assessment Battery, Revised] (PROLEC-R; Cuetos, Rodríguez, Ruano & Arribas, 2007). On the main indexes of this test, Xavi presented mild difficulty in naming letters, same-different word pairs, reading pseudowords and grammatical structures. He presented severe difficulties in reading words and punctuation marks, but his performance was normal in sentence comprehension, text comprehension and oral comprehension. The secondary indexes are included in the *precision indexes*, where Xavi was found to have some difficulties with naming letters, and reading words and pseudowords. Xavi had the greatest difficulties in the *speed indexes*. He had a low level of automation in naming letters, as his performance was slow. His score fell into the "very slow" category for the tasks of same-different, reading words and pseudowords and punctuation marks.

The Batería de Aptitudes Diferenciales y Generales [Differential and General Aptitudes Battery] (BADYG E2; Yuste, 2005) corresponding to third and fourth grade of elementary school was applied. This test includes primary factors such as verbal, numeric, spatial, memory and perceptive speed factors, which are considered to be reading skills (Rosselli, Matute & Ardilla, 2006) and are thought to be related to general intelligence. In the general intelligence index, he obtained a percentile rank of 71, which places him at a medium high profile.

The Evaluación de los Procesos de Escritura [Evaluation of Writing Process] (PROESC; Cuetos, Ramos & Ruano, 2004) with an internal consistency (alpha coefficient of 0.82) was used to assess writing, finding difficulties in the writing of dictated pseudowords and in the total test score. The aim of this test is to assess the main processes involved in writing, and it is administered from third grade of primary education to fourth grade of secondary education. The tasks are: syllable dictation, word dictation, pseudoword dictation, sentence dictation, writing a story, redacting a text. Difficulties were found in writing dictated pseudowords. He obtained a raw score of 95 in the total test, which is two standard deviations below the mean.

In fourth grade of elementary school, his mother decided to take him to special classes after school two days per week (one hour each day) so a tutor would help Xavi with his homework. In addition, he received intensive support in the school (outside of the classroom) from a support teacher trained to work with learning difficulties. Currently, Xavi still receives out-of-school support two days per week, for an hour and a half, in which he is provided with tutorial assistance to help him specifically with science, physics, chemistry and mathematics.

Xavi and his family also attended the program Mentes Unicas [Unique Minds] (Stern, 1999) for children with learning disabilities and their families, which involved eight weekly sessions of an hour and a half. Unique Minds was a program developed to address the socioemotional and cognitive-motivational difficulties of children with learning disabilities and the impact of these on the family. The Spanish version of Unique Minds (see Lopez-Larrosa, González-Seijas & Carpenter, 2016) drew from this program, adopting a novel proposal in which the group facilitators (one trained in family therapy and the other in learning difficulties and educational intervention) work concurrently with the children and their families. This program was adapted to Spanish at no cost either to the children or the families. It was carried out with small groups of parents and children. Xavi's family participated actively in the corresponding sessions. Unique Minds is based on the idea that families that share a common problem can help each other. The multi-family format means that several families with children with learning difficulties share positive and negative experiences. With regard to Xavi's case, he always attended promptly and was very motivated by the sessions. The mother, and sometimes the grandmother—considering that she was an important person in Xavi's education—attended the parents' sessions. Due to their participation in the Unique Minds program, Xavi's personal maladaptation and anxiety decreased although his negative attitude to school increased. With regard to family social climate, the mother believes that this program was a worthwhile experience that provided valuable assistance.

Family and Home Life

As Xavi's parents are divorced, he lives with his mother and stays with his father on alternate weekends. His mother is an assistant to a podiatrist and his father is a salesman who travels frequently. One day a week, Xavi stays with his grandmother with whom he has a close relationship. He is a very active youth and shares activities, such as going to the cinema, taking hikes, going to the beach and enjoying rural tourism, with his family. His home responsibilities, in addition to studying, are keeping his room neat and making his breakfast. Xavi is very responsible and usually does his tasks without having to be reminded. His mother noted that he has goals and hopes. He is just as affectionate as he was four years ago and continues to be, in his mother's description, a "good boy."

Medical and Psychological Aspects

Xavi is a healthy adolescent who is in good physical shape. He is over six feet tall and plays basketball four or five hours per week with his team. He currently has severe acne and is receiving treatment by a dermatologist. In the past four years, he has had braces placed on the top teeth and he wears glasses for nearsightedness. Since his last interview, he experienced one episode of missing school for several days because his legs hurt and he had a fever. The doctor described the condition as growing pains.

Educational Perspectives

Reading Achievement and Progress

Xavi is in the fourth grade of compulsory secondary education (CSE). He is a student who ultimately passes in all subjects, but must extend considerable effort to achieve this goal. He has obtained good grades and improved in reading and writing due to the support of his family and the tutorial assistance he received for all the courses. At school, he received specific academic assistance until the sixth grade of elementary school. His mother noted that his improvement has been achieved through the intensive support he has been given and the great effort he has made. She is not very worried about his reading and noted that he likes to read more than before. His mother thinks that Xavi is a slow, dysfluent reader, but has relatively good comprehension.

After the initial diagnosis of dyslexia, Xavi's reading was not reassessed until the week of this interview, at which time the PROLEC-SE (Ramos & Cuetos,

2009) was used to assess reading at the secondary level. This test takes lexical, syntactic and semantic processes into account. Xavi scored at a mean level in lexical and semantic processes, but he exhibited speed difficulties in single word reading and decoding pseudowords; Xavi's scores in these subtests fell respectively between the mean and one standard deviation below the mean. His performance ranged from normal to slightly lower in comparison with other students of his age and grade. When Xavi was asked to rate his reading four years ago on a scale of 1 to 5, he said it would have been "very low," at a 2, but today he believes that it would be a 4 as he has "improved greatly." Xavi attributes this improvement to spending more time and effort studying and never giving up in spite of the difficulty.

Xavi keeps up with all of his subjects, but becomes discouraged when he has studied a lot and does not obtain the expected grade. He sometimes reads magazines, newspapers and books about art and history; he particularly enjoys articles on Greco-Roman mythology. However, he admits he dedicates insufficient time to reading. If a teacher asks him to read in class, he gets nervous because he is afraid of doing badly or making mistakes. He makes more errors reading aloud than when reading silently. Xavi said that he had developed a reading strategy (or "trick" as he described it) to deal with this problem; by breathing properly, pausing and then reading mentally before reading out loud, he is able to increase his fluency. If he does not have enough time to read the text mentally, he tries to read it as calmly and as well as possible. Xavi says that even so, he sometimes makes mistakes, especially in the other official language of his autonomous community (i.e., Galician, which is also a transparent language) of the city where he lives. Looking back, Xavi says that he previously read much more haltingly with more errors and less confidence. Now he feels that his reading fluency has increased.

Xavi currently attends English classes three hours per week outside of school, at his own request because he believes he needs this language to be able to achieve his desired goals. Although English is not a transparent language, he shows no difficulties and his progress has been good, but he does need additional support.

Teachers

The interaction established between the teacher and the student at the precise time of teaching reading exerts considerable influence on reading performance. Since Xavi previously had some bad experiences with his teachers in his early years, some of this negativity remains today. Currently, Xavi's mother thinks that some teachers do not pay enough attention to him because they "cannot be bothered," but other teachers are not like this. She noted that it was not a problem to communicate with Xavi's teachers. Generally, the tutor-teacher (i.e., the teacher who is in charge of handling the problems a student from that class might encounter during that academic course; in this case, she was his math teacher) calls the mother every so often to report how things are going. This teacher often tells her that Xavi has to improve his reading and mathematics. (This tutor-teacher is not the one who helps him—as his extra classes are taught by a private teacher.) During the interview, Xavi commented that he recently had a problem with a teacher who chastised him for making a mistake when reading out loud; the teacher told him that he should know how to read at his age. Xavi felt bad, but he went to talk with the teacher and told her he was dyslexic and asked her to be patient with him. Since then, the teacher has accepted his reading difficulties and has not made further negative comments.

Xavi doesn't believe that most teachers are responsive to students who have different learning needs. He said:

> Some of them know it, but others just ignore it or avoid it for convenience. Teachers think that they do not have to teach you in a special way because you are different. I think that when someone is different, teachers should pay more attention and, above all, teachers should try not to pressure students so much because students will withdraw more and more.

Concerning his school, Xavi said he would like to change "the teachers who are not interested in their students, who just go to work to kill time, who do not explain well and make no effort to improve." He would change all the teachers who are "incompetent." He would not change the teachers who have just started, "only those who should have sought better training" and whose "skill level is insufficient to teach." Xavi believes that several teachers have no commitment to the profession of teaching and this is apparent. Their interests in teaching are merely self-serving (i.e., a job, a salary, a profession, etc.) and the students are not among their priorities. There are other teachers who obviously have a commitment to teaching and are dedicated to their students' learning, which makes it very motivating to be in their classes. Xavi believes that the best teachers he has had were those who explained concepts well and were very patient with him; these were mainly content teachers of natural sciences and history. Xavi described two of the teachers he had as "brilliant and friendly," extending, first and foremost, patience and applying effective teaching practices that increased his learning.

Learning Style

Xavi is very much aware of his personal learning style, as well as of his strengths and weaknesses. He knows he needs more time and effort than others and he does not give up when things become difficult. He especially likes history and knows that he also does well in art and music whereas mathematics and English are academic areas in which he is less strong. He noted that before he can master content, he must first understand it. Xavi does best when his teachers are good speakers and fully explain concepts in interesting ways. He does less well when he has teachers who "follow the book" instead of providing an explanation of the content. Therefore he needs teachers who clearly convey difficult content in a manner that increases comprehension and then he is able to memorize the information and apply it. Xavi believes that "the teacher is very important," but students also have a responsibility to follow up by reading and studying at home to reinforce concepts.

When asked how he can best demonstrate his knowledge of content, Xavi said that he prefers to orally explain it rather than write an exam or paper, etc. He sometimes likes to engage in group work, but "hates to depend on the work of others." He prefers to do schoolwork on his own, but if he has a group assignment, he "will try to do the best" that he can.

Xavi occasionally uses a computer to search for information at school, but he is more likely to use his books. None of his textbooks are digital, but his teachers use CDs that come with school books to demonstrate concepts on whiteboards. Xavi has little time to spend at the computer and he does not use it as a tool to help him learn. However, he strongly believes that "children should be taught from an early age to handle a computer because in the future if you are not able to handle a computer" it will be a disadvantage. He lamented that he was not taught these skills. He is aware of how technology could assist him in his learning efforts, but he has no Internet connection at home, which is why he says he uses his computer like a typewriter.

Homework

Xavi spends 1½ to 2 hours per day doing homework, depending upon the assignments he has. He generally does his homework independently, and, unless the homework is very complex, it is no problem for him. When in doubt, he asks his grandmother, especially about the areas of humanities, history, and art. If he has doubts about science, he asks his private tutor or an uncle who is a mathematician. Xavi thinks that homework is neither always easy nor always difficult. It has levels of difficulty and it also depends on whether he has sufficient time to complete it. He thinks that "you shouldn't try to do things; you should simply either do them or not do them." His mother thinks that Xavi needs to organize himself better because sometimes lack of organization results in wasted time.

Social Development

Xavi is a well-rounded adolescent who enjoys sports as well as the arts. He likes basketball very much as well as music, singing, and poetry. He plays the drums and the harmonica and has sung in plays in front of the whole school. As in the prior interview four years ago, Xavi identified the good health of his family and passing all of his subjects as things that make him happy. He feels very good and free when he does mountain climbing and reaches the top. He thinks he has about ten good friends (both male and female) as well as many school acquaintances with whom he socializes. His mother considers it very positive that Xavi relates well to older boys who are very studious. She has noticed a significant change with respect to increased maturity, particularly in the last year. When he finishes high school, Xavi wants to travel on the European Inter-Rail, which is why he attends English classes three hours per week. He thinks that by getting to know geographic places and their history, culture, and people, he will prepare himself practically for his career as a history teacher, which is his goal.

Self-Determination and Coping

Self-Efficacy and Motivation

Xavi has good self-esteem; he believes he is doing well and can achieve important things in life and reach his goals because of the effort he expends. With regard to academic self-efficacy and emotional self-efficacy as assessed by the Self-Efficacy Questionnaire for Children (SEQ-C; Muris, 2001), Xavi obtained high scores, reflecting his perception that he believes he has the necessary resources to deal with problems, both at school and in his daily life. He also scored high in academic requirements, such as finishing his homework every day, studying when there are other interesting things to do, paying attention in class every day and confirming his parents' satisfaction with his schoolwork. Xavi has proposed some goals and he knows that he will achieve them if he works diligently. With regard to emotional self-efficacy, Xavi thinks he can manage his thoughts and emotions successfully most of the time. He can cheer himself up when he feels low and avoid focusing on unpleasant thoughts. In the interview, Xavi stated that he thought it was necessary to make mistakes in order to learn from one's errors. He also said that he is grateful for the support he has received from his family and he acknowledges the effort they made to pay for the school, the academies and the private teachers to help him achieve his potential.

The results of the Children's Hope Scale (CHS; Snyder et al., 1997) revealed him to be an adolescent who perceives himself to be successful; Xavi is convinced that he is doing well, that he can achieve important things in life and that he can solve problems most of the time. He believes he is doing as well as other children in most areas. Xavi has confidence in his skills and understands the importance of perseverance for achieving goals.

In order to obtain a clearer view of his achievement goals, the Achievement Goal Disposition Survey (adapted from Hayamizu & Weiner, 1991) was administered. Xavi's responses indicated that his motivation for studying is intellectual curiosity (learning mastery) and goal achievement. He likes to discover new things and enjoys finding out how to improve. He likes the challenge of difficult problems and is gratified when he can overcome obstacles and failures. His profile on this measure indicated that he is usually intrinsically motivated for the sake of learning, but, occasionally, he is motivated to achieve for purposes of social approval (i.e., from his teachers, parents and friends) and competitiveness with peers. However, he also admitted that he does not want his classmates to make fun of him and he does not want to be rejected by his teachers.

Coping

Xavi is a youth who is at ease with himself; he is happy and relaxed when carrying out activities with his friends and family. If Xavi gets a poor grade, he is only discouraged for a short time, and interprets this as a signal that he must make a greater effort. He said, "I don't let myself be defeated," but admits that when he has studied very hard for an exam and fails it, he feels dejected. When he has some problem he cannot solve, he isolates it mentally and devotes himself to doing other things. If Xavi is feeling down or upset, he tries to "fix the problem, but when it is not possible," he compartmentalizes the problem and moves on to do other productive things. When he is stressed about something related to school, Xavi deals with the stress in a healthy way. He said:

> One activity that I like to do when I am angry or stressed is to release adrenaline with sports. Some people go to a gym in order to hit a punching bag, but I play basketball without stopping and then I feel calmed and relaxed as well.

Impact on Mother

Xavi's mother has made an extraordinary effort to give her son all the support he needs. She considers she is now gathering the fruit of her efforts because Xavi is a responsible, affectionate, sport-loving youth who enjoys studying and has passed every year, grade by grade, with a great effort. Presently, she is not concerned about Xavi's current reading problem or about his future because she sees he is a tenacious person who achieves what he proposes regardless of the effort. In the past few years, this has entailed significant economic resources from the mother as she does not receive much support from the father, which is a topic that usually generates conflict between the parents. Moreover, it is an aspect that affects Xavi because he says that one of the things that make him feel bad is when two people he loves fight. The grandmother's (a retired nurse) support is important, and both Xavi and his mother acknowledge this. Likewise, Xavi acknowledges the ongoing effort made by his parents to pay for his studies, the academies and private teachers.

The mother thinks that Xavi is a very good boy who is interested in everything, who always asks questions about all the things he does not understand and who needs some help because things are more difficult for him. The mother feels tranquil because as long as the child has people who help him, Xavi "will make progress."

Future Goals and Hopes

Xavi's mother believes that her son will go to university and will devote himself to teaching, which is what he likes. The mother only wants him to be happy, to be "good" and to achieve a job in whatever he likes. She hopes that, in the future, he will read more fluently and not be so "lazy" about reading. She considers that Xavi's reading problem is not an obstacle that will prevent him from going to university. She perceives him to be motivated, mature, spirited and goal-oriented, which she attributes to genes, maturity and the company he keeps (friends).

When Xavi is asked about the goals he would like to achieve before leaving school, he notes that he wants to achieve secondary school and his high school diploma, and maintain the relationships he has had, in addition to leaving good memories of himself in the school. He considers that the most important goal is to obtain his diploma because that is the most important thing for his future. Xavi articulated his specific goals for the future:

> I would like to go to the University of Santiago de Compostela, earn a history degree and then study for a Ph.D., and take the State exam to be able to work as a history professor at the University. I would very much like to teach my students everything that I learned when I was a student, and I would continue to learn in order to be able to teach them and make them feel as enthusiastic as I do about history.

When asked how he will achieve these goals, Xavi responded that he would do so by paying a lot of attention to the obstacles so that when they emerge, he can overcome them. It was rather disheartening to note that Xavi identified poor teaching as a possible obstacle to his goal. He also identified the skills that will help him to achieve his aspirations: his good memory, his great interest in ancient things and his special interest in history.

When asked about his three wishes, Xavi responded that the first one would be to travel in time and space from epoch to epoch and place to place. The second would be that all existing problems, whether his own or those of others, would be solved. Thus, there would be no more wars and the world would be a much better place; and the third wish would be to play with or meet his favorite music group, Guns and Roses.

Case Commentary

When Xavi was first interviewed four years ago, he had serious reading and writing problems. Xavi was not assessed and diagnosed until fourth grade, although his reading problems were identified in first grade of elementary education, and he only received support in fourth grade of primary education. This support was maintained during his primary education (fifth and sixth grade), but for less time than the three hours provided in fourth grade. At that time, he was an optimistic, very polite and sociable child, who was well integrated in his context, and these characteristics are still observed in the present interview. He had and still has the support of his family, teachers and friends. In the first interview, he already had future expectations that he has achieved and extended. At that time, he needed help with his reading and writing, but he only received this support for two more years, until sixth grade of elementary school. He has now developed reading strategies, but he still needs the help of a private tutor.

In transparent languages like Spanish, the grapheme-phoneme (reading) and phoneme-grapheme (writing) relationship is relatively simple and consistent (Carrillo & Alegría, 2009) so the dyslexic's difficulties are more apparent in reading speed than in reading precision (Cuetos, 2008; Jiménez, 2012). This explains why Xavi's mother thinks he lacks fluency whereas Xavi refers to a lack of agility when reading.

In Spanish, dyslexic children have problems with the automation of word recognition. These difficulties accessing the lexicon are explained by a deficient development of lexical and phonological processing (Jiménez, 2012). However, he still has reading difficulties in the other official language of the region where he lives, in spite of it also being a transparent language with similar grammatical and syntactical characteristics.

His specialist teacher thinks that one of the causes of this difficulty is the lack of specialist support in secondary education courses and the cutbacks of the time devoted to support in the last years of primary education. In Spain, the percentage of students who require additional support in the regular educational system is greater than the number of students who actually receive this support. This is true at all ages, but especially in secondary education. It could be said that the students who receive support at this educational stage are usually those with severe and/or permanent difficulties, or who display behavioral problems because there are fewer specialized personal resources than in the stage of primary education. Also, at this second stage, in general, the school community's organization and attitudes toward students with difficulties vary greatly, compared to the first stage. There is a lack of teachers' awareness about attention to these students, probably due to the scarce or non-existent pedagogical training they receive during their academic preparation. This is why the mother intensified the support with private teachers outside of the regular classes.

Many studies show that dyslexia persists in adolescence and adulthood; however, there are no studies on the prevalence of dyslexia in Spanish-speaking adolescents. In a study carried out with 945 randomly selected students to identify compulsory secondary education students with specific reading learning difficulties, from the teachers' curricular criterion and some specific diagnostic criteria based on psycholinguistic research, 291 students with specific learning difficulties were identified; that is, 30.8% of the total population. Within this population, 3.2% (n=30) were classified as dyslexic (Jiménez, 2012).

Xavi's family is not concerned about his future because they think he will achieve whatever he proposes. It is well known that the family setting is essential for emotional, social and psychological development and that many variables interact with and condition each other. For Xavi's mother, having a dyslexic child meant a great personal and economic effort, but she was committed to providing the necessary support so that Xavi could achieve his goals, and now she is sure that he will attend university.

Xavi has good friends in the different places where he carries out activities—the school, basketball training, private lessons; for him, "not having friends" would feel very strange. Socially, he has no problems because he is accepted and welcomed by his friends, so we can deduce that his reading difficulties have not interfered with or influenced his relations with his peer group. His mother thinks they are good friends who accompany him on his pathway and help him to achieve his dreams.

As for the contribution of the home literacy environment (i.e., the variety of resources and opportunities that are provided to children, as well as the parents' skills and willingness to provide these resources) (Burgess, Hetch & Lonigan, 2002), researchers in this field have focused especially on two essential aspects of the acquisition of reading skills and dyslexia: socioeconomic aspects (Noble, McCandliss & Farah, 2007) and shared reading activities (Sénéchal, LeFevre, Thomas & Daley, 1998). It has been shown that shared reading and writing activities in the family have a positive effect on the development of certain linguistic skills that are needed to acquire a solid level of reading (Mann & Foy 2003). It is important to remember that there are no activities of shared reading at home, except for the research Xavi shares with his grandmother. They are both interested in old cultures and sometimes they search for information in the books that the grandmother collects. If they are going to take a trip, then they read to find out more about the destination. Xavi does not devote much time to reading, and only uses the computer for some homework. This lack of time devoted to reading at home is not that unusual for dyslexic adolescents as Snowling, Muter and Carroll (2007) previously discovered. Their comparative study of the reading habits of dyslexic and nondyslexic adolescents found significant differences with regard to these children. The adolescents with reading difficulties in this study read magazines or newspapers less frequently in comparison to those without reading problems. Xavi reads to fulfill school requirements and he reads about the topics he enjoys, but he prefers sports to reading. Reading is a tiring activity for him and if he has other options, he prefers them to reading. In the case of Xavi, his parents tend to provide more opportunities for sports and leisure activities than for reading and writing. This is determined by the resources, the parents' available time and the relationship between the parents.

In Spain, it is necessary to establish definitions of special needs so that students like Xavi have specific diagnostic criteria, in addition to the curricular criteria that enable the identification of at-risk students as early as possible. In this way, the necessary support could be designed and adapted to the needs of each student in order to facilitate the development of full potential. The term "dyslexia" is no longer avoided in Spain. On the contrary, along with attention–deficit/hyperactivity disorder (ADHD), it is the most frequently used term to describe learning difficulties. Now educators must work to clarify dyslexia as currently it can be conceptualized as an umbrella term used to refer to a variety of learning difficulties. Recently there have been new publications devoted to this topic and in the schools there are work groups receiving dyslexia training. Hopefully, these efforts will result in more awareness of dyslexia as well as increased understanding of identification and treatment methods. Most secondary schools have Orientation Departments that are in charge of identifying dyslexic students and designing the necessary supports. The members of these departments participate in the meetings of the pedagogical coordination committee and the board of teachers. They are in charge of following up tutorial action plans for student learning needs and school adaptations. However, these Orientation Departments may not always be able to identify or assess students at risk because, in many cases, they must also share the work in different Child Education and Primary Education centers, which often involves an excessive number of students. Due to the Orientation Departments' demand for attention, priority is given to those with more severe educational needs, so the rest of the students are neglected to a great extent.

The results in reading and writing achievement obtained by Spanish students enrolled in compulsory education, both in national and international assessments, have shown scarce improvement, compared to the results of previous evaluations. Concerned by these results, various European countries have legislated the educational curricula. However, the methodological recommendations and the incorporation of key competencies in the prescriptive syllabus have failed to detect substantial changes in recent years either in the teachers' teaching and assessment habits or in the results of the students' learning process. In Spain in the last ten years, there have been continuous legislative changes concerning education, which have not helped to produce these changes in the teachers. As a result, the data of the international assessments point indirectly to teacher training as one of the causes of the poor literacy outcomes over the past decade (Guzmán-Simón, Navarro-Pablo & García-Jiménez, 2015).

While it is true that Xavi has faced a great deal of negativity at school and a lack of support for his reading problems, he has clearly demonstrated that he has the persistence to overcome any obstacles that dyslexia imposes. With the assistance of his supportive family and a few committed teachers, he has worked hard to substantially improve his reading and earn the grades that will move him closer to his goal of becoming a history scholar and professor, which is a reasonable aspiration for this adolescent considering his enthusiasm for learning and self-determination.

References

Burgess, S. R., Hecht, S. A., & Lonigan, C. J. (2002). Relations of the home literacy environment (HLE) to the development of reading-related abilities: A one-year longitudinal study. *Reading Research Quarterly, 37*, 408–426.

Carrillo, M., & Alegría, J. (2009). Mecanismos de identificación de palabras en niños disléxicos en español: ¿existen subtipos? [Mechanisms to identify words in dyslexic children in Spanish: Are there subtypes?] *Ciencias Psicológicas, III*(2), 135–152.

Cuetos F. (2008). *Psicología de la lectura*. Madrid: Wolters Kluwer.

Cuetos. F., Ramos, J. L., & Ruano, E. (2004). *PROESC Evaluación de los Procesos de escritura* [PROESC Assessment of Writing Processes]. Madrid: TEA Ediciones.

Cuetos. F., Rodríguez, B., Ruano, E., & Arribas, D. (2007). *Batería de Evaluación de los Procesos Lectores, Revisada* [Reading Processes Assessment Battery, revised]. Madrid: TEA Ediciones.

Guzmán-Simón, F, Navarro-Pablo, M, & García-Jiménez, E. (2015). *Escritura y lectura en educación infantil*. [Reading and writing in child education]. Madrid: Pirámide.

Jiménez, J. E. (Coord.) (2012). *Dislexia en español* [Dyslexia in Spanish]. Madrid: Pirámide.

Hayamizu, T., & Weiner, B. (1991). A test of Dweck's model of achievement goals as related to perceptions of ability. *Journal of Experimental Education, 59*, 226–234.

Lopez-Larrosa, S., González-Seijas, R. M., & Carpenter, J. S. W. (2016). Adapting the Unique Minds Program: Exploring the feasibility of a multiple family intervention for children with learning disabilities in the context of Spain. *Family Process* (Early View-online version). doi:10.1111/famp.12215

Mann, V. A., & Foy, J. G. (2003). Speech development, phonological awareness, and letter knowledge in preschool children. *Annals of Dyslexia, 53*, 149–173.

Muris, P. (2001). A brief questionnaire for measuring self-efficacy in youths. *Journal of Psychopathology and Behavioral Assessment, 23*, 145–149.

Noble, K. G., McCandliss, B. D., & Farah, M. J. (2007). Socioeconomic gradients predict individual differences in neurocognitive abilities. *Developmental Science, 10*, 464–480.

Ramos, J. L., & Cuetos, F. (2009). *Evaluación de los procesos lectores* [Assessment of Reading Processes]. Madrid: TEA Ediciones.

Rosselli, M., Matute, E., & Ardilla, A. (2006). Predictores neuropsicológicos de la lectura en español [Neuropsychological predictors of reading in Spanish]. *Revista de Neurología, 42*, 202–210.

Sénéchal, M., LeFevre, J. A., Thomas, E. M., & Daley, K. E. (1998). Differential effects of home literacy experiences on the development of oral and written language. *Reading Research Quarterly, 33*, 96–116.

Snowling, M., Muter, V., & Carroll, J. (2007). Children at family risk of dyslexia: A follow-up in early adolescence. *Journal of Child Psychology and Psychiatry, 48*, 609–618.

Snyder, C. R., Hoza, B., Pelham, W. E., Rapoff, M., Ware L., Danovsky, M., . . . & Stahl K. J. (1997). The development and validation of the Children's Hope Scale. *Journal of Pediatric Psychology, 22*, 399–421.

Stern, M. (1999). *Unique Minds program for children with learning disabilities and their families*. New York: Unique Minds Foundation.

Yuste, C. (2005). *Batería de Aptitudes Diferenciales y generales* [Differential and General Aptitudes Battery]. Madrid: CEPE.

7
PERCY, A CASE STUDY OF AN INDIAN ADOLESCENT WITH DYSLEXIA

Sunil Karande and Rukhshana F. Sholapurwala

At the time of the second interview Percy, a Parsi (Zoroastrian), was 14 years old and presented himself as a grounded, happy and well behaved adolescent, eager to talk about his experiences. He was diagnosed as having a specific learning disability in the areas of dyslexia, dysgraphia and dyscalculia when he was in fourth grade at the age of 8 years and 11 months.

Background

Diagnosis and Treatment

Percy's official diagnosis of dyslexia, dysgraphia and dyscalculia was based on a comprehensive assessment. His full scale quotient was 118 on the Indian adaptation of the Wechsler Intelligence Scale for Children-Revised Test (WISC-R; Bhatt, 1971). The results of the locally-devised Curriculum Based Test (CBT; Sholapurwala, 2010) revealed that he had severe problems in reading. The CBT evaluation described Percy as reading dysfluently with the help of his finger with numerous mispronunciations. He was very reluctant to write and preferred to answer orally. His spelling age was approximately a year below his age level. Percy could not compute simple sums without calculation errors. On the Wide Range Achievement Test 3 (WRAT 3; Wilkinson, 1993), Percy's reading performance was at the 23rd percentile with spelling at the 32nd percentile and arithmetic at the 39th percentile.

Although Percy's school offered remedial classes, his parents also hired a private special educator who worked with him on a one-to-one basis (one-hour sessions twice a week) mainly on reading and spelling. The remedial program included: phonics-based reading, language development (to improve comprehension) and completion of worksheets (as he was opposed to expository writing activities). Percy refused remedial sessions for his math problem. He continued this remedial program with the private special educator for a period of three years till he reached eighth grade when he became too busy with his private tuitions (tutoring) for his school subjects. During this period, Percy made limited progress although he also attended remedial sessions held in his school, which he continues to the present time. These 30-minute remedial sessions are held in the school library twice a week (one teacher working with three to four students). The teacher for these remedial sessions is actually a counselor as opposed to a qualified special educator. Percy's mother has no idea of the content of the remedial sessions as the school has not provided any reports of this program or discussed it during any of the biannual parent-teacher meetings. Fortunately, Percy's school has provided him with most of the prescribed accommodations (i.e., extra time for written examinations, no penalties for spelling errors and examinations being read to him). Also, since his handwriting was very poor and slow, he was allowed to photocopy his friend's notes and as he had problems in reading, he was exempted from oral reading in the classroom.

Although Percy never worked hard and was never really interested in his studies, he managed to pass every grade. Throughout the last four years he has shown little interest in reading and his school notes were always incomplete. Additionally, he had difficulty with math. When he was in seventh grade he would often fall asleep in class during history period for lack of interest in the subject. Consequently, the results of his exams were always at the lower end of the continuum and his teachers consistently remarked that he needed to work harder and that his handwriting needed improvement. The two accommodations that he was not allowed were dropping Hindi language as a subject (substituting it with a work experience subject) and receiving writing support during his written examinations in spite of these being permitted by law. Percy was unable to cope with the Hindi language subject and this created an enormous problem. Finally, just before his final ninth grade examinations he received the provision of dropping Hindi language and receiving the much needed writing support. To obtain these provisions, his mother had to repeatedly meet with the school principal and the remedial teacher to fight for this assistance.

Family and Home Life

Percy lives with his parents, paternal grandmother and elder brother (older by four years) in their Mumbai apartment. When they were younger, the two brothers did not get along too well, but now they are close. On weekends, Percy and his brother spend a lot of time playing video games.

During the work week, family members are busy in their own routines, but on weekends Percy's parents make it a point that the family spends time together going to movies, having dinners or just being at home. Every summer vacation, Percy's parents take their sons for a two week vacation to spend quality family time together. They have traveled to Switzerland and other European countries as well as exotic holiday resorts in Goa and Kerala in India.

At home Percy has the responsibility of putting the dishes in the kitchen sink after the family dinner. He does all the household errands willingly and his mother has no problems in dealing with him. But she always helps him in packing his school bag. She does this to save time and also to ensure that he does not forget anything.

Medical and Psychological Aspects

Percy is a healthy, physically fit and athletic adolescent. In the last three years his seasonal allergies and asthma have completely disappeared. He no longer takes any medications for these earlier complaints. Five years ago, Percy was diagnosed with attention-deficit/hyperactivity disorder-combined type (ADHD-C) as per DSM-IV-TR criteria (American Psychiatric Association, 2000) and has taken 40 mg. of Atomoxetine daily (except on weekends and during vacations) since that time. He has had no side effects and willingly swallows the tablet handed over to him by his mother, who was very pleased with the medication and had previously indicated that it had increased Percy's concentration and reduced his hyperactivity. However, since his original diagnosis, Percy has not met with his psychiatrist. During the interview his mother voiced her concern that the dosage may need to be increased as recently Percy's symptoms of inattentiveness and hyperactivity have resurfaced.

Percy's mother acknowledged that occasionally her son shows symptoms of stress related to homework completion and said that:

> He complains of headache when he wants to postpone doing homework. This occurs about once a month. I give him a paracetamol tablet and he will want to sleep. This used to happen even earlier, whenever he did not want to go for his private remedial sessions.

Percy too acknowledged that he does get stressed at times due to his homework:

> Then I don't go to school. This happens when lots of my homework is still incomplete. I tell my mother and I don't go to school for a day so that I can complete my homework. Sometimes I feel lazy or tired or just off-mood to go to school. This happens about once a month.

Educational Perspectives

Reading Achievement and Progress

When Percy was in eighth grade, his school principal instructed his mother to have Percy re-evaluated for his learning disability from a particular private clinic whose reports were accepted by the Indian Certificate of Secondary Education (ICSE) board (i.e., a private national educational board) based in New Delhi. This retesting was done solely for technical reasons, because a recent psycho-educational testing report was needed to be sent along with his Class 10 ICSE board examinations form to ICSE board head office. Without a recent psycho-educational testing report, Percy will not be able to receive the benefit of accommodations at his forthcoming Class 10 ICSE board examinations.

The testing included the Woodcock Johnson-III Tests of Achievement (WJ III; Woodcock, Schrank, Mather & McGrew, 2007) and the Wide Range Achievement Test 3 (WRAT 3; Wilkinson, 1993). The WJ III test revealed that Percy's reading fluency was comparable to that of the average individual in third grade, but compared to others at his grade level, his score was at the 3rd percentile. The report categorically stated that Percy would find it impossible to do grade-level tasks requiring reading of printed material and responding to questions in a timely manner. On the WRAT-III test, Percy's reading score placed him at the 14th percentile. The WRAT-III spelling score placed him at a percentile rank of 16 while the math score gave him a percentile rank of 44.

At school Percy was able to cope because he was getting extra time to finish his written examinations and the questions were being read, but his handwriting was very bad and teachers often commented on it. In the fifth grade, Percy experienced specific problems in Hindi and math. On her own volition, his mother started sending Percy for private tuition for all his regular school subjects, namely, English, Hindi, math, science, history and geography. The school provided him remedial classes twice a week and he attended private remedial classes twice weekly. In spite of this tutoring, till eighth grade, Percy's report card marks continued to be generally low (i.e., 45–50% with 35% being the pass mark).

Over the years, Percy's school teachers did not offer any specific advice to his mother for his academic problems. In Percy's school, parent-teacher conferences are mandatory every term. Over the last four and a half years, Percy's mother has attended every parent-teacher conference and his teachers have consistently reported that he has writing, attention and work completion problems. Percy continued to struggle with Hindi and just could not cope with it and was getting very poor marks. During one parent-teacher conference, when Percy was in eighth grade, his mother realized the severity of his Hindi problem and made up her mind that she would keep meeting the school principal until he received the Hindi exemption. During her interview Percy's mother remarked:

I would say that parent-teacher conferences were helpful. I came to know that his Hindi teacher understood his inability to cope up with the language and was helping him by being soft on him. Also through these meetings I could get acquainted with his school remedial teacher who then helped me in getting exemption from Hindi (as a second language) for my son.

In the ninth grade, Percy continued to show little interest in reading and consistently had incomplete notes and poor handwriting. His problems with Hindi also persisted along with math and physics difficulty. Although he is totally dependent on his mother to read everything to him while doing homework, he now realizes that he needs to get better marks and work harder with his studies. He refused to drop math and science, although that was permitted with his disability, as they are necessary to become an architect, which is his career goal. His mother expressed her concerns about his achievement:

School is surely becoming more difficult for him. The syllabus and subjects are getting tougher. Percy tends to forget what he has studied. Till now he had to remember the first term portion only for the first term examination. There was a separate portion for the second term (final) examination. Now when he goes to tenth grade, he will have to remember the entire first and second term portion for his final tenth grade board examinations. This is going to be a real challenge for him.

Percy's mother indicated that four years ago, she would have rated Percy's reading as a 1 (on a scale of 1 to 5 with 5 being the highest) whereas now she would rate it as 3. Percy himself rated his reading four years ago as 2 and today 2.5. Given this information, there would seem to be some progress. However, even though he has received regular private remedial sessions for a period of three years and has attended remedial classes at school for five years, his standardized test results indicate that Percy is still experiencing severe reading problems.

It is also significant to note that Percy rates the support he has received at school for his reading as "poor." During his interview Percy categorically stated that:

Most teachers did not understand my problems and did not pay any attention to me. But I don't think it was intentional. They were not bad to me. I would say that only one teacher understood my problems because that teacher would ask me again and again whether I have understood or not, whether I have written or not and whether something needs to be explained again.

His mother's observations were contrary to Percy's as she noted that:

> I think most of my son's teachers understood his reading problems. I say this because they were lenient with him. His reading problem has not affected his teachers' behavior towards him. Since the teachers knew that he has a learning disability, I guess they understood his problem.

So it would appear that mother and son interpreted this question differently: Percy believes that most of his teachers ignored his problem because they did not understand it while his mother believes that the leniency the teachers displayed indicated an understanding of dyslexia. Percy's interpretation may be closer to reality.

When Percy was asked what was missing in his school that he needed to help him with his reading, he was quite indifferent and said, "I don't know. I am not interested in reading." His mother's observations were not very different as she noted that his teachers have not commented on his reading progress. She does not believe that much reading is required at his school.

Percy detests reading and never reads on his own for enjoyment (e.g., even the informed consent form for his interview had to be read to him). He explained:

> I don't enjoy reading. I don't like to read on my own. Sometimes I look through magazines. I like to see pictures of clothes, perfumes and watches. Seeing these pictures is much better than reading a book.

Percy's mother offered an interesting insight into why her son doesn't want to read on his own when she said:

> He makes no effort to improve his reading performance. He is just not interested in reading. Firstly, he does not like to read. Also, he knows that it will take a longer time if he has to read. This will lessen the time that will be available for him to play. I think that is the main reason that he does not make any attempt to read. As regards his reading, he is not worried. He knows that I will read everything to him when he is doing his homework. He has stated that he doesn't want to read and that I should read out to him. I too have accepted this situation. This will continue till he joins college. After that I will not read out to him. I have made this very clear to him.

In spite of his difficulties, Percy appears to have a positive attitude and likes to go to school. His mother confirmed that she has no problems with school attendance. When Percy was asked whether he always tried to do his best in school, he answered "no," explaining that "till now I have never tried to do my best at school" as he wasn't interested in the curriculum. Now that he is going to tenth grade and will be facing board examinations, Percy has realized his responsibility toward his studies. He said, "This year I am going to work very hard and get good marks in school."

Teachers

Percy's mother has indicated that she is satisfied with the general support her son has been given by his school as she noted that communication has been good with his teachers and they have not required him to read out loud in the classroom. However, she explained that she could not comment on the reading support Percy had received as she had not received reports from the remedial teacher. Since the mother is such a strong advocate for her son, it is surprising that she has not investigated the reading instruction that Percy has received in his remedial classes. Thus, when she talks about her satisfaction with teacher support, she seems to be referring to leniency as opposed to remediation that would boost achievement.

Percy liked his ninth grade math teacher a lot and reported, "She is the best teacher I have ever had. She is strict, but she explains well and helps you to understand. She always pays attention to me and makes things interesting."

In Percy's opinion, a good teacher should have the following three attributes: "a good way of teaching" (i.e., "should check that student has understood"), "does not ignore students in the classroom" and "is not too serious" (i.e., "is approachable in the classroom").

Luckily, Percy has had only one bad teacher, his sixth grade English and Geography teacher, who was "the worst teacher that he ever had." Percy vividly remembered that:

> She would always be angry in class. She didn't like me and two other students. She would punish me. For example, because I had grown my hair long she was angry at me. As a punishment, she made me sit outside the staff room during the short and long recesses for one whole month. She would always ignore me in the classroom and didn't care for me.

However, Percy does not hold a grudge against any of his teachers. This was revealed when he expressed empathy even for his "worst teacher" when he said, "But I can understand her anger. She had recently lost her husband. Also her daughter had to get her leg amputated because a tree had fallen on it while she was returning home from work during the rainy season." Neither does he blame his teachers for all of his school problems. He said, "If I can't understand what the teacher is teaching or if I forget what has been taught then it's my fault. How can the teacher be blamed for this?"

Learning Style

Percy is very much aware of his personal learning style as well as his strengths and weaknesses. He knows that he learns best by listening and seeing:

> I remember things better by listening to a lecture, for example, when my mother reads out the subject to me. I can also remember well what I see

in a video and by watching a demonstration. For example, I learn very well in the laboratory when I see my teacher demonstrating an experiment.

Percy likes group projects because of the support he can receive from others. He admitted that he gets very nervous if asked to give an oral presentation. He could not identify any academic strength he had as he stated that he is not good in any particular subject because he has not taken his studies seriously until recently. He also noted that he is "not good at taking responsibility" as he views himself as "lazy" with regard to some school responsibilities. Percy believes that the best way for him to show that he has learned something would be to write an exam "because after a written examination, there are results and you are given marks, which is the best way to judge that the student has learned the subject."

Percy stated that he is good at quite a few things unrelated to school; in particular he excels in games (i.e., swimming, badminton, basketball and football), planning school picnics and B-boy (breakdance) dancing. During the interview he was very happy to state that: "I know B-boy dancing. I can rotate on my head while dancing. I have taken part in dance competitions and inter-school tournaments (swimming and badminton)."

Percy believes that most of his teachers are not aware that students have different needs and may require individual attention. He doesn't spend much time on the computer, usually only two hours on weekends playing computer games with his brother or social networking on Facebook. Also, he is unaware of technological assistive devices, such as screen readers and textbooks on CDs that could help him with his reading problems.

Homework

As Percy is a reluctant reader he has consistently experienced problems with his homework. His mother used to do most of his homework for him except his mathematics, which his mother could not do. She would also read his books for him. During his interview Percy categorically stated that "I am not good at doing homework. I barely manage to do it." Percy spends one hour on his homework per day and acknowledged that his mother takes a lot of personal interest in his homework. However, he claimed that he can do his homework independently. In reality, Percy is still totally dependent on his mother's support for doing his homework. His mother stated:

> He does not like to do homework. Given a chance he would like to play all the time outside his school hours. Over the years, I have had to do his homework with him. His teachers have been overlooking this and have been lenient. However, once when he was in fifth grade, the class teacher had made a remark that "Percy should be doing his homework himself!" Without me being around he will not do any homework at home. But he

has to do math and physics homework on his own. That's because I don't know math and physics too well to help him. Also for doing his math and physics homework he needs me to be near him for moral support.

Percy's main reason for being totally dependent on his mother is his refusal to read independently. When he was asked if homework is a big or a little problem he answered:

> It is a big problem. Some math sums are a big problem. I can't understand sums. I ask a friend to help me do the sum. I *WhatsApp* my friend and get the solved sum back from him. I even have another friend who lives in my building. I go to him and he explains the math sum to me.

Social Development

Percy has never had any problems getting along with others at school. His mother said:

> Everyone at school is fond of him. His school friends are very helpful. They lend him their notebooks for photocopying. That's because Percy is very responsible. He returns the notebooks properly and on time and never misplaces them. Percy also gets along with all his teachers. For example, if he does not understand something being taught in the class he will raise his hand and interact with the teacher to solve his problem. His teachers don't mind it at all. When I go for parent-teacher meetings I came to know that his teachers adore him.

Percy stated that he had never been bullied or teased about his reading. However, when he was in fifth grade, at times he was asked by his classmates why he went to the library twice weekly. Their curiosity about his attending his school remedial classes used to irritate him, but Percy has not faced any painful situations at school because of his disability.

Percy's mother stated: "My son is an extremely popular person both at school and outside. He has many friends in school. He is an extremely well behaved child and very mature for his age."

Self-Determination and Coping

Self-Efficacy and Motivation

In order to find out how Percy perceives his own ability to handle academic tasks and to manage emotionally challenging situations, two scales (Academic and Emotional) of the Self-Efficacy Questionnaire for Children (SEQ-C; Muris, 2001) were administered. Percy had to answer how well he can do certain things on a scale of 1 to 5 on individual items pertaining to academic and emotional self-efficacy.

When it comes to academic requirements, Percy indicated that he just could not "study when there are other interesting things to do." In his interview Percy stated that he would rate himself as being average at: "getting teachers to help him when he got stuck on schoolwork," "studying a chapter for a test," "finishing all his homework every day," "paying attention during every class," "succeeding in understanding all subjects in school" and "succeeding in passing a test." However, Percy stated that he was good at "succeeding in satisfying his parents with his schoolwork." With regard to emotional self-efficacy, Percy believes that he is not totally successful "in cheering himself up when an unpleasant event has happened," "becoming calm again when he is very scared" and "at giving himself a pep-talk when he feels low." Percy feels that he is successful in suppressing unpleasant thoughts most of the time and that he succeeds in not worrying about things that might happen. In his interview Percy stated that he would rate himself as being average at "preventing himself from becoming nervous," "controlling his feelings," "succeeding in suppressing unpleasant thoughts" and "succeeding in not worrying about things that might happen." Research has shown that there is a connection between low self-efficacy and depression (Muris, 2001). Looking at Percy's scores it is obvious that his levels of academic and emotional self-efficacy are both above average and that he is not at risk of developing depression. Percy's self-efficacy scores indicate that he does not lack confidence in his ability to meet the challenges of daily life stressors. Most probably, the reasons for having above average self-efficacy scores are: (1) being popular with most of his school teachers who have never treated him badly in school, (2) never having to repeat a grade as his school has allowed accommodations, (3) benefitting from the extensive and unconditional love, understanding and support of his mother and (4) having a group of close-knit friends. This view was supported by his mother who believes that he has high self-esteem and she is unaware of any reason for him to "feel low."

The results of the Children's Hope Scale (Snyder et al., 1997) revealed general feelings of confidence about life (i.e., optimism and ability to resolve problems and move forward in life in a positive manner). Percy perceives that "he is doing pretty well" most of the time. When he looks at his life right now, he feels he is doing fine because he enjoys going to school, he's popular with his teachers and has a wide circle of friends.

Percy perceives that "he is doing just as well as other kids of his age" most of the time. However, he lacks confidence and is ambivalent about his abilities to "think of many ways to get the things in life that are most important to him" and solve problems. When probed, he stated, "I have always preferred to work in groups because in a group I can take help from others if that's required." Percy has always been dependent on his mother to read to him and till recently has never been serious about his studies. Probably that's the reason that he is also unsure whether "the things that he has done in the past will help him in the future."

It should be noted that the Hope Scale is more of a global measure than the SEQ-C (Muris, 2001) and that it does not directly ask about school. Similar to Percy's above average scores pertaining to academic and emotional self-efficacy, the results of the Hope Scale also indicate that Percy does not lack confidence in his abilities to face life and that he believes he is doing as well as his peers. This is most probably due to the supportive home and school environment that he has experienced.

Another important reason that Percy does not lack confidence in his abilities to face life is most probably due to the success he has experienced in tasks which required the use of his talents. This became apparent when his mother stated that:

> Percy is very good with hand skills. He has very good imagination skills; he is very observant and creative. Currently, he is enjoying and doing well at technical drawing, a work experience subject chosen by him at school. He is good at scaling. He is learning skills for his future role as an architect.

In order to gain more insight into Percy's motivation for studying, the Achievement Goal Disposition Survey (adapted from Hayamizu & Weiner, 1991) was administered. This survey examines a student's motivation for studying. Student responses are analyzed in reference to three categories that identify motivation for studying: (1) intellectual curiosity (learning mastery), (2) social approval and (3) goal achievement. For three of the eight questions that dealt with studying for reasons of intellectual development, Percy indicated he does not like difficult problems, is not very curious and does not like to test his intellect, but he enjoys discovering how much he has improved, he likes to know new things and he feels good when he overcomes obstacles and failure. Also, Percy indicated that he "sometimes" studies because it's interesting to solve a problem and he is pleased when he can solve a difficult problem. Percy seems to be ambivalent about enjoying studying for reasons of intellectual stimulation. However, Percy commented to the researcher that:

> I am not interested in reading. I know that it's quite important to know how to read well because if one does not know to read properly it can create problems in the future, later on in life in your job, profession. But one should not feel bad or stupid if one cannot read properly.

Most of Percy's responses revealed that his motivation for studying is not dependent on wanting to be praised by his teachers or parents, demonstrating to others how smart or capable he is or avoiding teacher disapproval or teasing by classmates. However, Percy did indicate that he "sometimes" studies because he wants his friends to know that he is doing well in school and he does not want his parents to be disappointed with him. Percy indicated very clearly that he is motivated to study in order to achieve his future goals. His responses suggested that his motivation for studying is related to achieving grades similar to peers, feeling proud of good grades, admission to college, obtaining a good job, having a good life and achieving success in the future. Percy is aware that the achievement of his goals is dependent on the effort he puts in. In his interview Percy clearly stated:

> I know that till now I have not really bothered to study hard. I was just not interested. But now that I am going into tenth grade, I am determined to study very hard. I know that I should get good marks in my tenth grade board examinations so that I get admission to college. I have decided to become an architect. In ninth grade I have already chosen technical designing as a work experience subject. This will help me learn skills required for my future role as an architect. I like this subject and am doing well in it.

As Percy appears to be intrinsically motivated and has a pronounced technical interest, he will do well when he studies or works in a field that suits his talents.

Coping

Percy feels happy and relaxed when playing football or spending time with his friends and family. He is really sad if he has too much tuition (on weekends) and cannot play. Percy, however, hardly ever feels low and if he does "it goes out of my mind very soon." Physical activity appears to be the key to Percy's emotional well-being. His mother has understood his need to play games daily and has adjusted his and her own schedule accordingly. That Percy just cannot tolerate his play time being compromised also became apparent when he stated that:

> The only change that I want in my school is that I would like to see that the short recess is made longer. At present it is for only 15 minutes. I would like if it is much longer. The teacher keeps on teaching even after the short recess bell has rung. At times they make you wait outside the staff room for some work during recess time. This should change. Recess time should be recess time!

If Percy gets a bad grade he is only depressed for a very short while. He said, "I cope by studying more, by paying more attention and becoming more serious of my studies." His mother does not believe that he has any real frustrations as "he is a very happy child."

Percy is pretty much aware of what he should do to get better grades. He stated that he "would like to be smarter" and receive higher marks. He does not resent the tuition classes that he needs to attend or any of his private tuition teachers. In fact he praised his mother for starting these classes for him so that he could get better marks in school.

Percy is unapologetic of the fact that he is not interested in reading and his lack of ability to read fluently does not bother him. He wants to do better in his studies but not at the cost of giving up enjoyment. He doesn't want to become a bookworm. This became very apparent, when during the interview he described the best student in his class and mocked him by stating:

> He mugs (mugging is a slang term referring to rote learning) everything. He knows everything. He knows all the textbooks inside out. He knows what is written in which paragraph and in which line. He can open the book to any page where a particular line is written. He only studies, he doesn't play. He is pampered by his mother. His mother carries his school bag to school. When it rains, his mother is holding the umbrella over him even though she is getting wet.

Impact on Mother

Percy's mother has adjusted herself to his condition very well and has been a constant support to her son. When asked to rate the amount of stress that she feels in parenting Percy on a scale of 1 to 5, she said 2 (indicating a low level of stress). The main reason for this is that she compared parenting Percy with her experiences with parenting her elder son who had the same disability. She said:

> I would say 2 for Percy. But I would say it was 5 for his elder brother. When I compare Percy with his elder brother (when he was Percy's current age), I find Percy's behavior to be very mature. Percy is willing to study, unlike his elder brother. Percy understands that he has to study to achieve something worthwhile in life.

Percy is basically a very happy adolescent and shares a loving relationship with his mother who stated:

> I have not allowed Percy's dyslexia to influence my personal or social life. I am a homemaker. I have my husband's full support for all the decisions that I have taken related to Percy's dyslexia. Also, my mother and mother-in-law have always given me moral support.

However, on probing Percy's mother admitted that his dyslexia has affected her life. She said:

> I have no time for myself. I have to spend all my time coping up with Percy's dyslexia. I have to always sit with him when he is doing his homework. I have to read his books to him. He refuses to even make an attempt to read. I have to study his subjects so that I can help him with his homework. It's as if I have gone back to school again. But I don't mind doing all this. It's my duty as a mother. I have no choice and I have coped up well with the situation.

She also admitted that sometimes her husband disagrees with her parenting. She said:

> My husband at times says that I should stop reading to Percy while he is doing his homework. He feels that Percy should join a reading class. He has told me to stop helping him because very soon Percy will be going to college. My husband is worried that Percy will never learn to read well on his own.

Percy's mother never initiates discussions about her son's dyslexia with anyone, but sometimes other mothers with dyslexic children seek her advice. She believes her experiences may be helpful in providing guidance to others, but it doesn't personally help her to talk about them.

Notwithstanding all the adjustments that she has had to make in her own life in order to deal with Percy's learning disability, her unconditional love for her son and capacity for coping was revealed when she stated that:

> Actually it doesn't really matter if one's child has dyslexia. I think what matters to me as a parent is the behavior and temperament of my child. Percy is an ideal child. He is very loving and very understanding. I could not have asked for a better child. His condition has not affected my relationship with my husband or any family members. It's my duty as his mother to ensure that his dyslexia doesn't adversely affect him in any way. I have no choice and I have coped up well with the situation. I am not worried about his future. I am sure that things will work out well for him.

Future Goals and Hopes

Percy's mother's goals for him for the next four years are that "he learns to read on his own, especially by the time he is in college." She hopes that her wish materializes since she has resolved not to read his subjects to him once he is in college.

When Percy was asked about the goals he wants to achieve before he leaves school he pointed out that his first goal was to become the games captain of his school's football and basketball teams. The games captain is always chosen from a student who is in ninth or tenth grade. Percy wants to be the games captain so that he gets the privilege of choosing his team members and leading his team to victory in the school competition. His second goal was "to do better in math." When Percy was asked to prioritize these goals, he decided that doing better in math is much more important: "Once I do better in math I will get more marks and that will help me. Achieving this will make me very happy. Becoming a games captain is only for fun. It's not that important."

Asked how he would achieve his math goal, Percy had some strategies in mind and could identify some obstacles that would need to be overcome to make this plan a reality:

> To become better in math, I am taking private tuitions and I will now work hard and study a lot to do better. Till now I was not working hard but now I will try my best. I could have easily dropped math as a subject (an accommodation permitted to a student having a learning disability) but I have chosen not to drop math. I want to work hard and do well in math.

Percy is aware of the academic requirements to become an architect and believes that he has the talents that are required for his vocational aspirations. He is clear in his own mind that he wants to become an architect and help build big buildings:

> One should have good ideas, good knowledge. I am good at having new ideas and imagining new things. I am being taught technical designing in my school and I like this subject and am doing well in it. This training will also help me become a good architect. Also, an architect's job is not boring. In fact it is a nice job and it's quite relaxing. There is no rigorous work involved and I can also take help from others if needed. An architect can earn a good amount of money and this will motivate me a lot to be good at my job.

However, he may not be as realistic about the demands of the university education required to achieve this professional goal as he stated:

> I have found out from my brother and my friends (who are older than me and are in college) that it is not important to know to read properly in college. No teacher asks the student to read out loud in college. In college I will have more time to learn. I will take the help of my friends by asking them to read to me.

His mother says that, ever since he was in ninth grade, Percy has decided that he wants to go abroad to do his undergraduate and postgraduate studies in architecture. To accomplish this goal he has realized that he now needs to study very hard. Percy's mother agrees with her son that a profession as an architect would be a good match for his skills. She also feels that becoming an interior designer is another good option, but Percy only wants to become an architect. Additionally she hopes that: (1) he continues with his current resolve to take an interest in his studies and really work hard and (2) he makes genuine efforts to learn to read reasonably well on his own by the time he completes his schooling so that his current reading problem will not be too much of an obstacle for him in university education. Percy's mother is concerned that his reading problem *may* adversely affect her son's future to some extent and acknowledges that he will continue to have problems dealing with unfamiliar words. But she is very hopeful that things will fall in place provided he works hard. She perceives this to be a workable plan for the achievement of his goals. It is really important to her that Percy does well in life and can choose to be "whatever he wants."

Case Commentary

When Percy was first interviewed four years ago, he demonstrated severe reading, writing, spelling and math problems. However, his elementary school years were not marked by any feelings of inadequacy associated with reading failure. The main reason for this was that in his school it is not compulsory for students to read out loud in the classroom. Percy's learning disabilities were not diagnosed until the age of 8 years and 11 months. He was also soon diagnosed as having ADHD-C and has been on medication since then. For his learning disabilities Percy received remedial education from a private special educator, which focused on phonics based reading, language development (to improve comprehension) and writing worksheets. Percy refused to undergo any remediation for his writing and math problem. Simultaneously he has been receiving some sort of remediation in his school. In India, to date, there is no law to make remedial classes mandatory in schools or to monitor them (Karande, 2008). Percy received private remedial education regularly for three years till he reached eighth grade when his mother discontinued the remedial classes because of the demands of his school curriculum, homework and private tuition classes. Both Percy's mother and the private special educator believe that there has been improvement in his reading ability, albeit minimal. However, Percy thinks that there has been no real change in his reading ability. Percy's private special educator had documented the minimal improvement objectively by repeating the CBT even though standardized test results do not corroborate these results. The mother in all likelihood is interpreting Percy's willingness to try to read on his own and to do his math and physics homework as a slight improvement in his reading ability. In India there have been no published studies which have analyzed the effect of remedial education on the reading ability of children who have dyslexia.

In the past, Percy has been totally dependent on his mother to read his books to him for doing his homework and did not really care about his studies. Since he is now older and on the verge of entering tenth grade, wherein he will be facing a board examination, Percy has developed some responsibilty toward his studies. At present he is attending private tuition classes for his tenth grade, but he still wants his mother to read his books to him and help him study. Percy's mother, however, is unable to help him in math and physics. Even while doing his math and physics homework on his own, Percy wants his mother to be near him for moral support.

From a social/emotional perspective, Percy is doing very well. He has never been teased or bullied in school because of his learning disabilities. Percy is well behaved, friendly and makes friends easily. He is very popular with his teachers and classmates. He loves to play games in his school and will never miss playing games outside school daily for at least and hour and a half. The only thing that makes him sad is if a day passes when he does not get to play. Sometimes this does happen when his private tuition classes load increases. Percy's happy childhood and adolescence both at home, at school and even with his friends is an exception in India. Recently an Indian study has reported adolescents' recollections of their school years (Karande, Mahajan & Kulkarni, 2009). Adolescents have reported being teased by classmates, being insulted by their class teachers and even being ridiculed by their parents because of their disability. Another recent study (Karande & Venkataraman, 2012) has reported that the average age of detection of learning disabilities in Indian children is 12.5 years, by which time these children already feel "socially-excluded," have developed "emotional problems," are insecure about their future and perceive themselves as lacking in qualities for "social inclusiveness" (i.e., they feel that their peers and friends do not enjoy their company, do not understand their problems, do not care about their condition and find it difficult to develop social relationships).

Percy has had a happy childhood and early adolescence at school, home and in his social life. The credit for this is his own innate friendly nature and cooperative temperament and the unstinting support provided him by his mother. Percy's mother has, without any complaints, involved herself totally in ensuring that Percy gets the assistance he needs to lead a happy life and the accommodations necessary to do reasonably well at school. On school days Percy's daily schedule is hectic: school followed by tuitions. But his mother has allowed him to participate in inter-school games competitions and even play daily for two hours at the gymkhana. Being popular amongst his friends and teachers in school because of his success in sports is boosting his self-esteem. Other mothers of dyslexic children have reported doing well in sports can be very important for positive feelings of self-worth (Roll-Pettersson & Heimdahl Mattson, 2007).

Percy's mother has very good parenting skills and has ensured that there is no conflict in her relationship with her son. She has been accommodating as regards Percy's outright reluctance to read on his own. She has not made this an issue but instead taken upon herself the task of reading his subjects to him. She has, however, made it very clear to him that this will stop once he goes to college. Her good parenting skills has resulted in Percy growing up as an extremely well mannered adolescent. Percy too has never created a situation which has caused any trouble to her. A recent study (Karande & Kuril, 2011) has documented that positive parenting practices are crucial to ensure that good quality parent–child relationships develop in children with learning disabilities. This study has highlighted that these parents should be involved in parenting their children (i.e., they should ask their child about his day in school, help with homework and attend parent-teacher meetings). The study has also highlighted the benefits of practicing positive parenting (i.e., parents should praise or reward their child for obeying or behaving well and appreciate their child's help with housework). Lastly, this study has documented that negative parenting practices (i.e., poorly monitoring or supervising their child's activities, inconsistent discipline and indulging in corporal punishment) results in development of a poor quality parent-child relationship.

It is known that mothers of Indian children with learning disabilities have anxieties related to their children's poor future prospects in life (Karande, Kumbhare, Kulkarni & Shah, 2009). Both Percy and his mother have confidence in his skills and imagination that will help him become a good architect in the future. To achieve his aim Percy has chosen technical drawing as a subject in school and is doing well at it.

Percy's mother has been very fortunate to have the full support of her husband, mother and mother-in-law. Percy's learning disabilities have not affected her relationship with her husband or family members in any adverse way. Percy's mother has never felt left alone or stressed out because of her current situation. She has probably utilized her experience of parenting her older child who also had learning disabilities to learn coping strategies. However, she does not talk about Percy's problems with her friends as she doesn't feel the need to do so nor does it help her in any way.

For Percy's mother, having a son with dyslexia meant a great loss of personal time. But she has adjusted herself very well to the situation and not allowed her son's problems to affect her personal or social life. However, a recent Indian study (Karande & Kulkarni, 2009) has documented that mothers of children with learning disabilities have significantly poorer psychological health and social relationships, experience significantly fewer feelings of contentment and have a negative view of the future; and those having a male child with learning disabilities have less energy, enthusiasm and endurance to perform the necessary tasks of daily living.

With age, Percy is becoming mature enough to understand his responsibilities toward his studies. He is determined to become an architect and doesn't feel inadequate in any way as compared to his peers. For his ninth grade final examinations he has finally been allowed to drop Hindi language and also been given the services of a writer for his written examinations. This has resulted in an increase in his total marks of almost 15%. He is confident that he will be able to do well in his tenth grade board examinations next year and go on to college. Eventually he wants to go abroad to do his undergraduate and postgraduate studies in architecture. Percy is lucky to be born into a family that has sufficient financial resources to support his aspirations.

Percy's example cannot be extrapolated to all children with learning disabiities in India. The current educational situation in India does not provide the necessary support that dyslexic students need to achieve their potential (Karande, Sholapurwala & Kulkarni, 2011). Although over the last decade awareness about this invisible handicap has grown in India, much still needs to be done to ensure that each afflicted child gets an opportunity to achieve his/her full academic potential in regular mainstream schools. In order to achieve this ideal scenario, all 'regular' classroom teachers need to be sensitized to suspect this disability when the child is in primary school. School admnistrators need to become proactive to set up resource rooms and employ special educators to ensure that these children receive regular and affordable remedial education; and need to be diligent in ensuring that these children get the mandatory provisions both during school and board examinations. Lastly, the government of India needs to urgently recognize specific learning disability as a disability so that with the backing of the Right to Education Act 2010 these children benefit significantly (Karande, Sholapurwala & Kulkarni, 2011).

References

American Psychiatric Association. (2000). *Diagnostic and statistical manual of mental disorders* (4th ed., text rev.). Washington, DC: Author.

Bhatt, M. C. (1971). *Adaptation of the Wechsler Intelligence Scale for Children for Gujarati population* (Doctoral dissertation). University of Gujarat.

Hayamizu, T., & Weiner, B. (1991). A test of Dweck's model of achievement goals as related to perceptions of ability. *Journal of Experimental Education, 59*, 226–234.

Karande, S. (2008). Current challenges in managing specific learning disability in Indian children. *Journal of Postgraduate Medicine, 54*, 75–77.

Karande, S., & Kulkarni, S. (2009). Quality of life of parents of children with newly diagnosed specific learning disability. *Journal of Postgraduate Medicine, 55*, 97–103.

Karande, S., Kumbhare, N., Kulkarni, M., & Shah, N. (2009). Anxiety levels in mothers of children with specific learning disability. *Journal of Postgraduate Medicine, 55*, 165–170.

Karande, S., & Kuril, S. (2011). Impact of parenting practices on parent-child relationships in children with specific learning disability. *Journal of Postgraduate Medicine, 57*, 20–30.

Karande, S., Mahajan, V., & Kulkarni, M. (2009). Recollections of learning-disabled adolescents of their schooling experiences: A qualitative study. *Indian Journal of Medical Sciences, 63*, 382–391.

Karande, S., Sholapurwala, R., & Kulkarni, M. (2011). Managing specific learning disability in schools in India. *Indian Pediatrics, 48*, 515–520.

Karande, S., & Venkataraman, R. (2012). Self-perceived health-related quality of life of Indian children with specific learning disability. *Journal of Postgraduate Medicine, 58*, 246–254.

Muris, P. (2001). A brief questionnaire for measuring self-efficacy in youths. *Journal of Psychopathology and Behavioral Assessment, 23*, 145–149.

Roll-Pettersson, L., & Heimdahl Mattson, E. (2007). Perspectives of children with dyslexic difficulties concerning their encounters with school: A Swedish example. *European Journal of Special Needs Education, 22*, 409–423.

Sholapurwala, R.F. (2010). *Curriculum based test for educational evaluation of learning disability* (1st ed.). Mumbai, India: Jenaz Printers.

Snyder, C. R., Hoza, B., Pelham, W. E., Rapoff, M., Ware, L., Danovsky, M., Stahl, K. J. (1997). The development and validation of the Children's Hope Scale. *Journal of Pediatric Psychology, 22*, 399–421.

Wilkinson, G. S. (1993). *The Wide Range Achievement Test: Manual* (3rd ed.). Wilmington, DE: Wide Range.

Woodcock, R. W., Schrank, F. A., Mather, N., & McGrew, K. S. (2007). *Woodcock-Johnson III Tests of Achievement*. Rolling Meadows, IL: Riverside Publishing.

8

ALON, A CASE STUDY OF AN ISRAELI ADOLESCENT WITH DYSLEXIA

Talya Gur

Alon, 15 years old at the time of the second interview, collaborated with the interviewer. He was cooperative; however, his answers were short and brief and he did not volunteer information with ease. Alon was diagnosed as dyslexic at the age of 8.

Background

Diagnosis and Treatment

Alon was referred to the school psychologist for an evaluation during the summer holidays between the second and the third grades due to learning and emotional problems. His intelligence was found to be above normal (Hebrew version of the Wechsler Intelligence Scale for Children–R95 (WISC-R95, Cahan, 1998); Full scale IQ=120, Performance IQ=129, Verbal IQ=110). As no reading and spelling norms existed for Hebrew at that time, the evaluation of Alon's reading and spelling abilities were impressionistic. His reading of a passage was described as "partly accurate and extremely slow." While reading isolated words, he reread the words repeatedly until he managed to decode them accurately. His writing contained many homophonic spelling errors. On the basis of this evaluation, the psychologist diagnosed Alon as suffering from a reading disability and subsequently he started receiving one 45-minute weekly lesson from the school's reading specialist together with another pupil who had similar problems. In addition, he received assistance with his homework once a week from a private teacher after school.

Family and Home Life

Alon lives with his mother and younger sister in Haifa, a city in the north of Israel. His parents divorced when he was 11 years old and his father lives close by. Alon and his sister stay at the father's house twice a week and every second weekend, and their relationship is a close one. The father is an enthusiastic body builder and Alon has joined him in pursuing this hobby, working out at the gym five afternoons a week, usually with his father. When at home, Alon spends about three to four hours a day on his computer although none of this time is dedicated to schoolwork, and from time to time he plays board games with his mother and sister. On the weekends, they visit the mother's parents who live a half hour away. Alon also enjoys hanging out with friends and listening to music. According to the mother, he doesn't like traveling, but in the previous year the family went on a group tour to Europe. Although Alon did not want to go on the tour and it took him time to connect to other youngsters his age who were in the group, eventually he did manage to do so and really enjoyed it. When his mother has to go out in the evenings, Alon takes responsibility for his younger sister. In addition, he is in charge of making his bed every morning and keeping his room tidy, which he manages to do very well. If asked, he will wash the dishes and take out the garbage, too.

Medical and Psychological Aspects

Alon does not suffer from health problems and is in good physical shape. As he is an enthusiastic body builder, he is very concerned about his health and makes certain to eat nutritious food. In former years, on some mornings Alon reported he had abdominal pains, but his mother thinks that this was an attempt to avoid going to school and not a genuine problem. This year, he complained about these pains far less.

One of the recommendations of Alon's initial reading disability evaluation was a thorough investigation of his attention problems. Although this investigation indicated that there was a problem in maintaining attention, the neurologist could not determine if this problem was a primary one or a consequence of emotional difficulties. It was recommended that Alon start taking Ritalin, but his mother was ambivalent about this and gave it to him on an irregular basis. Alon reported that it helped him concentrate and read more accurately, but he complained about depression and headaches. As a result, during the fifth grade he decided that he didn't want to continue taking the treatment.

During the fourth grade, Alon started receiving help from a life coach who specialized in working with children with learning problems, which resulted in a significant improvement in his self-image and efficacy. He learned to see a more balanced picture of his abilities. For example, in the past, receiving the grade 60% would depress him, but now he can put this into perspective, understanding that he knows more than half of the things he should. As a consequence of this success, the mother would be very happy if Alon undertook psychological treatment that would continue to strengthen him emotionally, but he does not agree to do so.

Educational Perspectives

Reading Achievement and Progress

Alon's reading performance was not evaluated again by his teachers or a reading specialist during the fifth or sixth grades. The reason for this is that in Israel accommodations for test taking that will be valid till the end of high school and the matric exams must be based on evaluations that are given from the seventh grade (the first class of the middle school) onwards. In the fifth and sixth grades, Alon continued having difficulty with reading and copying from the blackboard, and generally meeting class requirements. These difficulties were emphasized in language-based subjects where his grades continued to be low. During these two school years, the school offered Alon remedial lessons. This plan was not implemented for two main reasons: his mother did not feel that these lessons helped him and Alon did not want to be removed from class and made to feel different from his classmates. In addition, he did not receive accommodations (e.g., answering fewer questions in tests, reducing homework load) that he had previously received. All this led to Alon being extremely unmotivated during his last two years of primary school. In order to help him cope with his difficulties Alon's parents arranged for him to have a one-hour private lesson, twice a week, at home after school. Although these lessons were meant to focus on learning strategies that would help him cope better and become a more independent student, Alon's mother says that they mainly completed homework during these sessions. During the sixth grade, Alon started taking two additional one-hour lessons a week, one in math and one in English.

In the summer before seventh grade when Alon was to start middle school (grades seven till nine), he underwent another psychological evaluation in order to obtain recommendations for test accommodations. Alon's mother does not recall the exact findings of this evaluation, but does remember the accommodations he received: an additional 25% time for exams, no penalty for spelling mistakes and having tests read to him. In addition, it was recommended that Alon should not learn a second foreign language (all Hebrew speaking Israeli pupils learn English as their first foreign language and Arabic or French as their second one). Furthermore, he was allowed to complete his exams orally if he chose. It is important to point out that the first three accommodations (additional time, ignoring spelling mistakes and reading of the test) are accommodations that are given in the matric examinations, too. The last accommodation (completing the test orally) is not specified as one that can be used in the matric examinations and is implemented in primary school or in the early years of middle school only. The summer before middle school, Alon started taking private lessons that focused on reading comprehension and organization skills. These lessons were held twice a week and as a consequence Alon started organizing his school bag independently when school began. The private teacher helped the mother understand that she must "let go" and enable Alon to take greater responsibility for his daily life. As a consequence, she decided she would stop reminding him to prepare his homework and that it would be his own responsibility. Alon's mother reported that this resulted in a drop in his grades. Although at the time it was hard, she said that she can now see the benefits as Alon takes much more responsibility for his schoolwork.

Alon did not receive any tutoring at school and although the private teacher continued working with him during the year, he finished the year with three failing grades in Hebrew, literature and history on his report card. In order to enter the eighth grade, Alon had to take two tests during the summer. At this stage the school wanted to move him into a special education class for learning disabled pupils, but the parents did not agree to this and they came to a school meeting during which they found out that none of the designated test accommodations were actually implemented during the school year. It was important for Alon and his parents that he stay in his original class and to achieve this he took extra private lessons during the summer and succeeded in getting passing grades in the tests. Consequently, the school agreed to leave him in his class and implement the test accommodations. Similar difficulties continued while Alon was in the eighth grade; he didn't always manage to copy everything from the blackboard and had problems with homework. The subject that Alon found hardest was Hebrew language, which includes reading comprehension, grammar and syntax. In fact, he failed this subject in the eighth grade, and got into an argument with the teacher regarding his behavior during class. This incident did not motivate him to work hard. Alon's mother says that "learning goes much more easily for Alon if the teacher manages to create a good relationship with him." Apart from the test accommodations, the school still did not suggest additional help and Alon continued getting three sessions of private tutoring at home after school hours in Hebrew, English and math. These lessons were usually designed to prepare some of the week's homework and catch up on the material that was learned in class. According to his mother, Alon's main problems are related to his difficulties associated with organization, copying from the blackboard, homework preparation and assumption of responsibility for his studies. Needless to say, these tasks are not getting any easier as the demands at school are increasing. For example, the teachers expect Alon to take more initiative and act in a responsible and mature way and come to them in order to find out when and where he should complete a test he didn't manage to finish in class. Because of his problems in organization and lack of responsibility for his conduct, Alon thinks that the teacher is the one who should notify him. This difference in expectations often creates crises. Alon defends himself by saying, "She didn't tell me so how should I know?"

In spite of these difficulties, the mother feels there is a trend toward improvement. Although she does not remember the percentiles associated with his reading scores, she rates his reading problem as a 3 (on a scale of 1 to 5 with 5 being the most significant). She believes that his reading has greatly improved in the last four years as she previously rated his problem as a 4. She explained this improvement by saying that Alon has started to read more for pleasure. This "transformation" happened in the sixth grade when she started reading Alon a book and he, on his own initiative and out of interest, continued reading it on his own. Currently, his mother says, he does no reading related to schoolwork, but spends about half an hour reading before he goes to bed. Alon rated his reading at the time of the previous interview as a 3 and his current reading ability as a 4. He stated, "I still don't read fluently, but there is a great improvement," and his explanation for this improvement is not related to the professional help he received as he explained, "I just started reading and slowly it improved." However, he also said:

> Although it's easier for me to read than it was in the past, when I read aloud it's harder for me (than reading silently) and the toughest thing is that many times I find it hard to understand what they are asking me, what they want me to do in the question.

In contrast to his mother's assertion that he reads every night before going to bed, Alon reported that this is not something he does on a regular basis, but rather from "time to time." He rated the help he received at school for his reading problems as "adequate" but could not remember specifics about any assistance he had received. This coincides with his mother's view of things as she stated that he rarely received help at school and all the assistance he received was given privately after school. His mother even stated that although the school saw that Alon had learning problems, they did not refer him to the "integrating" committee (*va'adat shiluv*) that pupils must be referred to in order to qualify for professional help at school.

In spite of this situation, Alon said that he is not frustrated by his reading problems, which are prominent mostly in Hebrew, and that his grades in the rest of the subjects are adequate. He said:

> There was a time when I used to get frustrated, but today if I see a passing grade I am happy . . . it's just a number. It doesn't indicate that I'm not good enough or that I'm not smart enough and it doesn't frustrate me. I just got a 70 the other day and I was very happy.

Teachers

Alon feels that the two most important things teachers should do for their pupils are to make sure they receive the test accommodations and care about their pupils. He said that in primary school there were fewer teachers of this kind compared to middle and high school. When asked to describe a good teacher he had had, he named his current home teacher and explained:

> She really cares. She helps and it's important for her that I get all that I deserve. It's very important for her that all the pupils succeed and she keeps on coming into class even if it's not her lesson and checking on us.

Alon's mother feels that most of her son's teachers do not understand the true nature of his problems and they focus on the average to strong pupils while disregarding the ones who have difficulties. She believes this is a consequence of the fact most of the teachers have no training in special education and she describes these teachers as "quite annoying." When asked about his worst teacher, Alon spoke about a gym teacher who accused him in front of the whole class of disrupting the lesson, which he claims he didn't do. The mother explained that Alon lost his temper, shouted at the teacher and was expelled from school for a few days.

According to the mother, no regular meetings with Alon's teachers have been held for the last four years, but she adds that communication has improved since middle school. Nevertheless, she feels that the teachers expect her to be the one to initiate the communication and make the calls. When she does this there is compliance, but she is so busy that she doesn't always manage to do this as much as she feels she should. She added that she would like the school to initiate communication on a more regular basis. When the home class teacher has initiated the communication, it has usually been when Alon has acted improperly and the call was made in order to complain about him rather than to give a full report on his academic achievements. His mother believes Alon gets along with most of his teachers and respects them, but he does have problems with specific teachers, such as the Hebrew language teacher. The mother feels that these problems occur because Alon takes their remarks too personally.

Learning Style

When asked what most helps him learn, Alon refers to several things: first, he takes responsibility for his own actions and says, "When I listen in class, it helps me the most," implying that he has not always concentrated in class and does not always listen during lessons. Alon says that he prefers listening to the teacher to reading material independently, and says that if the material is interesting he absorbs it better. When asked what interests him, he replies, "History that relates to wars and things connected to sport." It appears that Alon's insight regarding his personal learning style is quite developed. He adds that in order to remember something he has to really understand it. Mostly, evaluation is done by written exams and not by writing papers or other more creative ways of evaluation. Alon said he prefers exams as writing a paper is a long process. Technological assistive devices such as screen readers are not as available in Hebrew as they are in English. Nevertheless, all pupils have Bible lessons and a device that enables the reading aloud of the Old Testament does exist and due to the complexity of the biblical language could be very helpful to students with reading problems. As Alon has never been introduced to assistive technology for reading by his teachers, he stated that computers do not make learning easier for him.

Homework

Once a week a private teacher comes to Alon's house after school and helps him complete his homework. On the other days he spends about half an hour daily completing homework, which he usually does independently, although, if he asks for help, his mother will give it. On days he sees his father, he will also help if asked. If neither parent is available, Alon asks his friends to try to explain the material. If this doesn't work, he just gives up and doesn't complete the assignment. Alon says that usually he doesn't really feel like preparing his schoolwork and finds it hard to force himself to sit down and do it because "it's not the thing I really feel like doing when I'm tired." When asked if homework is a big problem for him, Alon said that it depends on the subject:

> In principle, we don't get too much homework . . . when I do sit down I find English and accounting homework easier, but find Hebrew grammar and language very complicated. I don't know why . . . I just don't understand the material.

Although Alon's mother believes homework is important, she tries not to get involved as she wants to avoid taking responsibility for his studying. She said that in the past her involvement in Alon's schoolwork took a toll on their relationship and that she understood that it wasn't worth it; she wants to be more of a mother and less of a teacher. On the days Alon doesn't have a private lesson he usually comes home tired after a workout in the gym, sits down for a meal, plays on the computer and reports that he doesn't know what the homework assignments are. His mother keeps to her resolution and doesn't remind him.

Social Development

In primary school Alon's social circle was quite limited. He had one or two good friends and apart from them had little connection with his classmates. To some extent, the pictures Alon and his mother paint regarding his current social development differ. Alon noted that in the past he had fewer friends, but says that since middle school he has a big circle of friends: "There is a big increase in the number of friends I have and I am continuing to make new friends all the time. The friends are not only from my class but also from higher classes, too." According to Alon's teacher, he has quite a few friends, but the mother has not met them. Although she knows he has two or three good friends, they don't visit him at home. She thinks that this may be a consequence of the divorce.

Alon said that he has not been ridiculed or bullied in the last few years, but his mother mentioned an incident that occurred two years ago. At school a few boys tried to remove his cap from his head. At first Alon warned them to stop and when they didn't, he got angry and threatened them.

The mother said that Alon's relationship with his sister varies from day to day. When he feels pressured with issues regarding school, he tends to be less patient with her: he is easily irritated and can shout at her. On other days, when Alon feels less stressed, he is calmer. His mother sees this as normal adolescent behavior. She described his maturity as average for his age. Alon will sometimes take the initiative and look for the teacher in order to find out what material he has to complete, a thing he would not do in the past. His immaturity, on the other hand, is still evident in the way he sometimes has temper tantrums and finds it hard to communicate when he feels that he is not treated with respect.

Self-Determination and Coping

Self-Efficacy and Motivation

Two scales (Academic and Emotional) of the Self-Efficacy Questionnaire for Children (SEQ-C; Muris, 2001), were administered to Alon with the aim of finding out what he feels regarding his capability to cope with academic tasks and emotionally challenging situations. He was asked to relate to specific items concerning academic and emotional self-efficacy and rank his ability in these areas. Alon's academic self-efficacy is slightly lower than his emotional self-efficacy. In the academic realm he ranked his ability to succeed in learning when there are things that distract him as very low. Nevertheless, he rated his ability to concentrate in class as medium but explained:

> If the class is quiet and if the material interests me, I can stay concentrated . . . if it doesn't interest me, I "log out" quite quickly, start messing with my cell phone and talking to friends. Today, no child just sits and learns the whole time. . . .

This explanation suggests that Alon is aware of the factors that influence his ability to stay focused during class and that he regards his behavior during lessons as similar to his fellow students. When relating to his ability to understand different subject matter in school, Alon makes a distinction that is compatible with the picture he described throughout the interview and said that his ability to understand Hebrew language is very low compared to his ability to comprehend other subjects.

Although Alon's emotional self-efficacy was to some degree higher than his academic efficacy, he found it harder to relate to these more personal questions and his tendency to be withdrawn was evident. When relating his ability to share feelings with friends he explained:

> Depends what happens. If it's something really personal, I don't trust anyone. I don't immediately "open up" and share . . . first of all, I'll approach my better friends, but there are things that I won't tell anyone.

The Children's Hope Scale (Snyder et al., 1997) relates to the way Alon perceives his ability in a broad sense and not directly to school. A comparison between his answers to this questionnaire and to the former one, the SEQ-C (Muris, 2001), revealed that he distinguishes between school related abilities, which he perceives as lower, and those that are not related to school, which are perceived as higher. Alon thinks that most of the time he succeeds if something is important to him. He also thinks that most of the time he can think of many different ways to achieve things that are important for him, solve problems and continue even when others lose faith in their ability. Alon's distinction between his school related abilities and general abilities is evident in his statement: "I am doing just as well as other kids my age." He said that although he may not always do as well as others in school, he does *better* than others in sports. Alon's developing maturity, that his mother described, is apparent in the way he perceives that things he has done in the past will help him in the future. Alon said, "Even if I did something bad, I will learn from it. This is what makes me what I am today."

The Achievement Goal Disposition Survey (adapted from Hayamizu & Weiner, 1991) sheds light on motivation for studying, which is classified into three types: intellectual curiosity (learning mastery), social approval and goal achievement. Alon's answers to this survey revealed that his main motivation for learning is meeting specific goals. But it is interesting to point out that the goals Alon wants to achieve are not related to the present (e.g., "I study because I want to be proud of getting good grades"), but to future goals (e.g., "I study because I want to get a good job in the future"). Nevertheless, Alon found it hard to relate to the statement regarding the connection between his current studying and being accepted for university because he says that he has never thought of studying at university. Alon's responses revealed that he is not motivated by intellectual curiosity or social approval.

Coping

As both Alon and his mother point out, working out in the gym plays an important role in his life. He described the workout as the thing that really makes him happy and relaxed. He adds that when he doesn't manage to engage in this activity he feels sad:

> I love it. I learn a lot about it. This isn't connected to learning in school. I sit at home and learn what makes the muscle grow . . . what are the things I should eat in order for it to grow.

Alon's mother agrees that going to the gym is the best way for him to reduce stress. Additional activities that he enjoys are playing basketball or football, hanging out with friends and playing card games. He adds that when he is sad these are also things that make him feel better.

Alon has experienced success with sports, but believes that one cannot succeed in every challenge. He explained, "One can't be successful in everything—even people that are good in many areas have things they are less good in," but added that he himself has never been faced with a challenge in which he did not succeed. When asked what brought him to this conclusion, he said that from a young age he was taught not to give up and keep on trying. Similar words were used by the mother when describing the ways she helps her son deal with his frustration. She said that she continuously tells him he must always keep trying and never give up.

It seems that his school difficulties are not perceived by Alon as a failure, but rather as a conscious decision on his behalf to engage in other activities and not devote his whole time to schoolwork. When asked about the success of a high achieving pupil in his class, Alon said, "That pupil sits at home all day long and learns. He doesn't do anything with his life, he just sits home and learns. He doesn't go out with his friends or go to the gym." He explained that "the fact that now I am not the best is probably because I don't work hard enough." Alon's balanced perception of success and failure is evident in the way he related his feelings when he gets low grades in school:

> It doesn't bother me that much. There were periods, towards the end of elementary school and the beginning of middle school in which I got many low grades and it stopped bothering me. And even today, it's only a number. It doesn't teach me that I am not good or not smart enough.

In spite of the various ways Alon tries to deal with his feelings, his mother said that sometimes he still finds it hard to deal with his frustration. In these instances, which can occur at home or at school, he gets very angry at his teachers and has tantrums. Three incidents in which he got very angry at his language teacher occurred in the current year. In all of these incidents Alon felt that a comment the teacher made was out of order and, as a consequence, he could not control an outburst of verbal criticism against the teacher.

Impact on Mother

Alon's mother rated the stress involved in being a mother of a child with a reading disability as very high and said that she feels the stress even more during school exam periods when conflicts increase. Problems relating to her son's reading difficulties have been part of her day to day life since he entered first grade. As the mother of a reading disabled son, stress has probably seeped into various parts of her life. The tension that was apparent at home had its effect on his sister too, who grew up in this situation. As the mother sees it, this stress has actually been reduced in the current year as Alon has matured and taken greater responsibility for his conduct and studies. In former years she was the one who had to urge him to wake up on time, organize himself and get to school on time, but currently things are somewhat easier. Alon still finds it very hard to wake up in the mornings and the organization problems still exist, but he manages to walk to school independently and actually get there on time.

Confiding in other people, especially professional figures who have worked with Alon, is the way the mother copes with stress. She says that the ability to share her difficulties, frustration and even fears enables her to feel less stressed and gives her the sense that she is not alone. Currently she feels less need to unburden herself by talking to others. Nevertheless, when specific situations arise she finds the people she can talk to. Alon's father is very involved with what happens at school and helps her to cope in stressful situations, too.

Motherhood is conceived by Alon's mother as a complicated mission. She describes it as a job that has many requirements and takes a lot of effort. When asked what advice she would give mothers who have sons with reading disabilities, she says that they have to remember to consider the perspective of time. They have to see the continuum and, especially in hard times, look back and see the way their children have already improved. She believes they have to strengthen the children and themselves continuously and find sources of support—friends, family, a teacher or a psychologist.

Future Goals and Hopes

Within the next four years, the mother would like to see Alon progressing in reading and doing well at school, but most of all becoming more independent and responsible. Alon's goals include finishing school with a full matric and succeeding in sports. In order to achieve the first goal, he understands he has to learn a lot and put more effort into his studies. He knows that he has to concentrate especially on the subject of Hebrew since he knows "that can bring me down . . ." In order to achieve his second goal, Alon explained that he has to learn more about sports, work hard, persist and eat and sleep well. While both goals are important, he stated, "Success in sports is first of all for myself. I don't see myself happy if I don't succeed in sports." He explained why this goal is important:

> It's something I am good at . . . I hear it all the time. Many people tell me that it's something I can succeed in. When my father just introduced me to the field, he told me that I have potential. There is nothing can stop me from achieving this goal.

Alon's mother is sure that his reading disability will continue to affect his life in the future, but she believes he will continue in higher education after he graduates from high school. When asked what occupation would be a good fit for Alon, she said that she sees him as working in technology or as a gym instructor. These two occupations seem right for him for different reasons. She would be happy seeing her son working in technology because of the good working conditions and salaries, but knows that his heart lies in the gym and that he would be good at it.

When asked what he could like to do in the future, Alon also talks about working in a gym and being a body builder. He explains that he would be good at this because:

> I have the genetics, I put in a lot of work, I like it. I had really good blood tests. I never miss a workout and if I continue this way there is no reason I won't be good at it.

Additional occupations that Alon sees as feasible for him would be business or accounting. While it is hard for him to explain what is expected from an accountant and why he would be a good one, he described his ability to be a businessman in the following way:

> I am just good at it. When I bought my first set of earphones I managed to buy them at a low price and when I sold them, I sold them at a high price. You also have to know many people and I do.

Alon's mother has quite a few concerns regarding her son's future life. Many of her fears focus on how he will manage during his army service, which is compulsory in Israel. Her main worry is how he will manage to overcome his anger and the occasional tantrum. She stated, "He is vulnerable and this vulnerability is connected to his reading disability." As regards her son's future, she said that she hopes he will be happy, choose a good occupation and have a family. Alon, on the other hand, wishes himself to be very smart, very strong and to succeed in all he does.

Case Commentary

Alon was diagnosed as reading disabled just before he entered third grade and since then has received help at school and private tutoring at home. While many times in Israel the assessment of a learning disability is not provided by the school, but by a private expert (Sharabi & Margalit, 2009), in Alon's case the educational system did take responsibility for his diagnosis. However, at the age of 10 (his age during the former interview), Alon still found it hard to cope in class. He especially found it difficult to read, comprehend written texts and copy from the blackboard, all skills which are related to language. His abilities in math were significantly higher.

A very similar picture regarding his weaknesses and strengths is found four years later. Alon and his mother both consider that his reading, although not up to the average of his fellow classmates, has improved. Nevertheless, they describe a significant difficulty in subjects related to the Hebrew language: syntax, grammar and reading comprehension. At the time of the current interview, Alon's major subject in school was accounting, which is consistent with his better mathematical abilities. The relationship between reading disability and language impairment, evident in the description of Alon's difficulties at both points in time, is recognized in the literature (McArthur & Castles, 2013). In fact, it has been determined that there is about a 50% overlap between reading and language disabilities (Eisenmajer, Ross & Pratt, 2005).

The mother feels that, although the law requires it, her son was not supported as he should have been in the last four years of school. During the last two years of primary school, Alon was offered extra lessons during school hours. As she felt that the help wasn't sufficient and since he did not want to leave the regular class to get extra tutoring as it made him feel different from his fellow classmates, Alon and his mother preferred that he have private lessons at home after school. After moving to middle school the only help Alon was offered was adjustments in tests; additional tutoring was not suggested by the school. This raises questions as Israel has a structured system designed to support learning disabled pupils, and this system is embedded in the special education law ("*hok ha'chinuch hameyuhad 1988*"). According to this law, pupils with special needs who learn in the regular educational system are entitled to additional teaching hours. Yet, the fact that Alon was not offered extra tutoring during his middle school years is consistent with data published by the Israeli Ministry of Education (2009), suggesting that the percentage of students requiring additional help in the regular educational system is higher than the number of pupils who actually receive this support. While there is no official prevalence of learning disability in Israel (Al-Yagon et al., 2013), approximately 15% of the children who participated in the Bagrut exams (the national matric examinations taken during the last three years of high school) were entitled to test accommodations because of some degree of learning disability (Sharabi & Margalit, 2009). However, the budget allocated for this purpose only covers treatment of about 5% of the students in the Israeli school system.

The mother emphasized that although Alon was entitled to test accommodations by law, she had to work very hard in order to make sure that they were put into effect. In fact, only when she intervened did the school apply the accommodations. This situation is not surprising when one looks at the findings of a survey conducted by Nitzan—the Israeli association for children and adults with learning disabilities (2009). This survey data revealed that only 35% of the parents of learning disabled pupils reported that the required test accommodations for their children were implemented in the schools. The situation is worse in middle school where only 22% of the schools provided all the accommodations for approved pupils. According to the report, after diagnosis and documentation of eligibility for test accommodations, parents in Israel have to battle with the school and the teachers to secure their children's rights.

In the former interview four years ago, Alon described himself as having only two good friends that he had been close to since kindergarten and said that if there were one thing he could change at school it would be to have more friends. The picture Alon painted concerning his social status in the current interview is altogether different. He described himself as having many friends, some of them from higher classes and said that he continues to make more friends every day. In fact, playing basketball with his friends or hanging out with them are two of the things that make Alon happy. His mother, on the other hand, is less enthusiastic and says that she has heard of two or three friends, but has actually not met any of them. In the survey conducted by Nitzan (2009) (see above), it was found that nearly a quarter of the parents whose children, aged 6 to 18, are diagnosed as learning disabled and/or having attention deficit disorder also reported social problems at school. This figure is high, especially when compared to the fact that only 6% of parents whose children were not referred for evaluation reported a similar problem. The different perceptions Alon and his mother have regarding his social situation is interesting and may stem from the different ways they conceive "friendship." While Alon considers guys he hangs out with as friends, his mother thinks of friendship as more binding and expects to meet these friends.

Throughout the interview, Alon referred to a few things that improve his motivation for learning. The first point he talks about, and which his mother also mentioned, is the relationship with his teacher; if this is a close relationship in which he feels that the teacher really cares about him, it's easier for him to learn. The literature, too, points to the relationship between the teacher and the pupil as an important characteristic that influences pupils' motivation for learning. Accordingly, improvement in teacher-student interactions has been found to result in gains in student achievement even a year after the completion of the intervention (Allen, Pianta, Gregory, Mikami & Lun, 2011). Furthermore, students themselves report that their success in school is largely due to their contact with their teachers (Pianta & Allen, 2008). The perspective that the teacher-pupil relationship is an important factor influencing achievement in class is increasingly accepted in the Israeli educational system. In fact, in recent years programs that emphasize this point are becoming a prominent part of teacher preparation.

Despite his relatively young age, Alon has quite a balanced perspective regarding his strengths and weaknesses. He distinguishes between his abilities in school, which he perceives as lower, and his abilities in other areas of life, such as sports, which he identifies as higher. Furthermore, he manages to distinguish between the different subjects and is able to pinpoint the exact subjects which he finds hard at school and those he feels more confident about. His lower self-efficacy in difficult subjects has not contaminated his sense of efficacy in other areas. Alon's mother explains his well-adjusted view of himself is a quality he learned from his life coach. This may be true. Nevertheless, the literature points to the fact that the family environment and parent-child interactions are related to high academic self-efficacy (Mihyeon, 2014). Thus, one can assume that the mother's involvement in her son's education played an important role in Alon's balanced perception of his abilities. The fact that Alon is so involved in sports, a field in which he excels, is very significant too as it balances the way he sees himself.

Learning disabilities are connected to a risk of undesirable life outcomes (Firth, Greaves & Frydenberg, 2010). At the same time it is becoming clear that the individual's coping patterns are significant in altering this path (Margalit, 2003). Firth et al. (2010) investigated the coping patterns of middle-school pupils with and without learning disabilities and found a larger use of nonproductive coping strategies such as ignoring one's difficulties or working less hard among the learning disabled sample. It seems that these findings can somewhat describe the way Alon copes with his academic difficulties. He mostly does not relate to his learning disability as a reason for his problems, but explains that if only he worked harder he would become a better student. He has made a conscious decision to invest less time in his schoolwork because he wants to leave time for additional activities he enjoys. Firth et al. also point to the fact that productive coping strategies such as involvement in sports, as in Alon's case, are actually thought to be used by some students as a way of compensating for their academic difficulties as it gives them an area in which their self-efficacy is higher. The way Alon describes his success in the gym supports this assumption.

According to achievement goal theory, students' motivation to achieve specific tasks is determined by the goals they want to accomplish (Ames, 1992; Dweck & Legget, 1988). It is clear from Alon's answers to the Achievement Goal Disposition Survey that his main aim for learning is not competence or performance goals, but rather meeting specific goals regarding success in the far future ("having a good life"). The scope of these goals is more in line with the ones that are mentioned in the expectancy-value theory (Wigfield & Eccles, 2000). According to this theory, students' self-efficacy and the way they perceive the task's value determine the goals they want to achieve while learning and, thus, their motivation for learning. Alon's motivation for learning is influenced by his mediocre self-efficacy. Yet, it seems, that the value, or the importance, that the school tasks hold for his life is not altogether clear to him. There seems to be a "missing link" between Alon's goals that are set in the far future ("having a better life") and the understanding that in order to achieve that "better life" he has to put in hard work in the present. Thus, it may be that determining proximal, "smaller" and closer goals for Alon is a way to access his more distal goals that could result in a stronger motivation for learning.

Parenting a learning disabled child is a complicated mission. Works investigating this subject suggest that parents, particularly those of low achieving children, perceive their children's education as an important goal (Barkauskiene, 2009). Pomerantz and Eaton (2001) suggested that parents of low-achieving children who are perceived as lacking competence have a tendency to be worried. In order to decrease their anxiety, parents tend to offer support such as assistance with or checking homework even when the child does not seek this kind of help. This kind of help is referred to as an example of parental control. One can expect that low achievers or learning disabled pupils receive this kind of parental support. Alon's mother described the support she offered her son in previous years in similar terms. Yet she also described a process in which she became aware of this pattern and resolved to loosen her control and encourage his independence.

An additional worry specific to Israeli parents of learning disabled adolescents, and which Alon's mother also mentioned, concerns their ability to cope during their army service, which is compulsory in Israel at the age of 18. The learning disabled find it more difficult to adjust to changing circumstances in comparison to the general population (Sellars, 2002). Thus, difficulty in dealing with authority that was observed during the school years can become even more challenging in a restricted military environment.

Research has shown that being a parent of a learning disabled child has a stressful impact on the family (Al-Yagon, 2009). These parents, compared to parents of children who do not suffer from a learning disability, describe higher levels of stress and parent-child problems (Al-Yagon, 2007). As a result, the challenges involved in parenting a learning disabled child may take a toll on the parents' time and energy, resulting in higher levels of parental pressure. In accordance with these findings Alon's mother rated the stress involved in being a mother of a learning disabled child as "very high." She described the stress as coming to a peak at exam times when she and Alon experienced increased conflict. She found that confiding in professionals who worked with her son helped lessen her anxiety and stress, enabling her to cope better with her son's needs. In fact, she stated that consultation with one of these professionals encouraged her to release control and transfer responsibility to her son, which resulted in a better relationship. In Israel today, the support for learning disabilities, defined by law, concentrates on the child himself with no mention of parental guidance or support. The significance of professional counseling for this family draws attention to the need to provide formal support for parents of children with learning disabilities in Israel.

At present, just as it was four years ago, Alon still finds it hard at school. Nevertheless, nowadays this ongoing, day to day struggle does not define him. He has found an area which is not connected to school and in which he excels, and pursuing this hobby strengthens him. His higher self-efficacy regarding his abilities in sports balances his lower academic self-efficacy and enables him to see himself in a relatively balanced way. This significantly increases the chances that Alon will live a fulfilling life as an adult, but the journey ahead holds quite a few challenges. At this point, Alon may be unable to define these challenges, but there is no doubt that they are clear to his mother. She in her clever and sensitive way is helping him deal with these challenges and is guiding him on this complex voyage, which increases the likelihood of his successful adjustment.

References

Al-Yagon, M. (2007). Socioemotional and behavioral adjustment among school-age children with learning disabilities: The moderating role of maternal personal resources. *Journal of Special Education, 40*, 205–17.

Al-Yagon, M. (2009). Comorbid LD and ADHD in childhood: Socioemotional and behavioural adjustment and parents' positive and negative affect. *European Journal of Special Needs Education, 24*, 371–391.

Al-Yagon, M., Cavensich, W., Cesare, C., Fawcett, A. J., Grunke, M., Hung, L., . . . Vio, C. (2013). The proposed changes for DSM-5 for SLD and ADHD: International perspectives—Australia, Germany, Greece, India, Israel, Italy, Spain, Taiwan, United Kingdom, and United States, *Journal of Learning Disabilities, 46*, 58–72.

Allen, J. P., Pianta, R. C., Gregory, A., Mikami, A, Y., & Lun, J. (2011). An interaction based approach to enhancing secondary school instruction and student motivation. *Science, 333*, 1034–1037.

Ames, C. (1992). Goals, structures, and student motivation. *Journal of Educational Psychology, 84*, 261–272.

Barkauskiene, R. (2009). The role of parenting for the adjustment of children with and without learning disabilities: A person-oriented approach. *Learning Disabilities: A Contemporary Journal, 7*(2), 1–7.

Cahan, S. (1998). *Manual for the WISC-R95 Intelligence Test*. Jerusalem: The Psychological Service, Israel Ministry of Education (in Hebrew).

Dweck, C. S., & Legget, E. (1988). A social-cognitive approach to motivation and personality. *Psychological Review, 95*, 256–273.

Eisenmajer, N., Ross, N., & Pratt, C. (2005). Specificity and characteristics of learning disabilities. *Journal of Child Psychology and Psychiatry, 46*, 1108–1115.

Firth, N., Greaves, D., & Frydenberg, E. (2010). Coping styles and strategies: A comparison of adolescent students with and without learning disabilities. *Journal of Learning Disabilities, 43*, 77–85.

Hayamizu, T., & Weiner, B. (1991). A test of Dweck's model of achievement goals as related to perceptions of ability. *Journal of Experimental Education, 59*, 226–234.

Margalit, M. (2003). Resilience model among individuals with learning disabilities: Proximal and distal influences. *Learning Disabilities: Research and Practice, 18*(2), 82–86.

McArthur, G., & Castles, A. (2013), Phonological processing deficits in specific reading disability and specific language impairment: Same or different? *Journal of Research in Reading, 36*, 280–302.

Mihyeon, K. (2014). Family background, students' academic self-efficacy, and students' career and life expectations. *International Journal for the Advancement of Counselling, 36*, 395–407.

Muris, P. (2001). A brief questionnaire for measuring self-efficacy in youths. *Journal of Psychopathology and Behavioral Assessment, 23*, 145–149.

Nitzan, The Israeli Association for Children and Adults with Learning Disabilities (2009). *2nd report of learning disabilities in Israel* (in Hebrew). Retrieved from http://www.nitzan-israel.org.il/home/תודוא-ניצ/רקחמ/דדמ-2.aspx

Pianta, R. C., & Allen, J. P. (2008). Transforming schools and community programs. In M. Shinn, & H. Yoshikawa (Eds.), *Towards positive youth development* (pp. 21–40). New York: Oxford University Press.

Pomerantz, E. M., & Eaton, M. M. (2001). Maternal intrusive support in the academic context: Transactional socialization processes. *Developmental Psychology, 37*, 174–186.

Sellars, C. (2002). *Risk assessment in people with learning disabilities*. Oxford: Blackwell.

Sharabi, A., & Margalit, M. (2009). Learning disabilities in Israel: From theory to research and intervention. In I. Levav (Ed.), *Psychiatric and behavioral disorders in Israel* (pp. 46–72). Jerusalem, Israel: Gefen.

Snyder, C. R., Hoza, B., Pelham, W. E., Rapoff, M., Ware, L., Danovsky, M., . . . Stahl, K. J. (1997). The development and validation of the Children's Hope Scale. *Journal of Pediatric Psychology, 22*, 399–421.

Wigfield, A., & Eccles, J. S. (2000). Expectancy-value theory of achievement motivation. *Contemporary Educational Psychology, 25*, 68–81.

9
JOÃO, A CASE STUDY OF A BRAZILIAN ADOLESCENT WITH DYSLEXIA

Giseli Donadon Germano and Simone Aparecida Capellini

At the time of the second interview, João was 14 years old and presented himself as an interested, but very shy and reserved adolescent. He was diagnosed as dyslexic at the beginning of second grade when he was 7 years old. During the interview he wasn't very comfortable sharing his experiences with dyslexia, but, after some conversation, he became less reticent and talked about his life in school and concerns for his future.

Background

Diagnosis and Treatment

When he received his official diagnosis of dyslexia, João was repeating first grade. It is common in Brazil for children who experience significant difficulties in learning to read to be retained in first grade (Conselho Estadual de Educação, 1997). Due to his difficulties, João was referred for assessment at the Centre of Study of Education and Health (CEES/UNESP-Marília-São Paulo, Brazil) and for an interdisciplinary evaluation at the Ambulatory of Child Neurology of the Clinical Hospital of the State University of São Paulo-FM/UNESP-Botucatu-São Paulo, Brazil. The results of the interdisciplinary assessment showed that João was dyslexic. In the neurological exam (Lefèvre, 1972), he exhibited difficulty in dynamic balance and motor persistence. The neuroimaging exam (Single Photon Emission Computed Tomography) revealed hypoperfusion (lower activity) in the left temporal lobe, indicating an under-activation of the auditory area of his brain that is commonly associated with poor auditory perception.

The neuropsychological examination showed a normal cognitive level with discrepant functioning between verbal intelligence (VIQ-83 points) and performance intelligence (PIQ-102 points) on the Wechsler Intelligence Scale III-Revised (WISC-R; Wechsler, 2002). In the phonological assessment, João demonstrated deficits in phonological awareness (i.e., phonemic, syllabic, rhyme and alliteration) demonstrating auditory perception difficulty. His fluency and comprehension in word and non-word reading tasks were found to be lower than expected for his age and grade level. Additionally he had problems in the writing of words and non-words.

After the dyslexia diagnosis, João's teachers were informed and he received one-to-one class reinforcement three times a week. Additionally, João attended sessions with a speech and language pathologist for three years. The therapist used the Play-On Software (Magnan & Ecalle, 2006), an audio visual computerized remediation program that has been proven effective (Germano & Capellini, 2008). This program fosters auditory perception of phonemes and the association between phonemes and graphemes necessary for learning the alphabetical writing system of the Portuguese language.

In the following year, the speech and language therapist implemented a reading program consisting of 18 different stories with various levels of difficulty, which facilitated the acquisition of reading skills (Germano, Pinheiro & Capellini, 2013). Activities involving manipulation of syllables and phonemes were used to enhance phonological awareness. In third grade, João continued with a meta-textual awareness program (Ferreira & Spinillo, 2003) administered by a university clinic speech therapist. The objective of this program was to teach the child to comprehend the elements of text structure.

After these three years, the results of João's therapy were positive as he showed progress in the acquisition of reading and writing skills. However, he still needed a continuation of therapy, but unfortunately the school started complaining about his absences as he was missing class to attend these therapy sessions and then his mother couldn't take him to the sessions anymore due to the demands of her job. In fourth grade João participated in school group sessions that supported him in Portuguese and math. After fourth grade, he did not even receive any accommodations for his special needs and no further interventions.

Family and Home Life

João is an only child who lives with his parents in Marília, São Paulo, Brazil. The family goes to church twice a week, watches TV together and during weekends they visit their relatives. At home João has different responsibilities such as making the beds, cleaning the backyard, doing the dishes and taking out the garbage. According to his mother, he is very disorganized and leaves his clothes and shoes scattered around the room. She has to remind him daily to maintain everything in order.

João doesn't have an extra job after school as his mother thinks he is too immature to handle that kind of responsibility. In addition, she is of the opinion that he has too much difficulty in school to take on extra work. She finds him shy and very lonely. He doesn't have many friends and enjoys spending time alone in his room. When he is at home, he plays video games and spends time playing with his dogs. He doesn't have any interest in computers. The family has a computer at home with no internet access, which he rarely uses. He doesn't have a Facebook account or other social media accounts. For his outdoor activities, he enjoys swimming and flying kites.

Medical and Psychological Aspects

João is a healthy and physically fit adolescent. His mother describes him as a teenager with a limited attention span. João has never been diagnosed with attention-deficit/hyperactivity disorder (ADHD), but recently he went to a child neurologist who prescribed Methylphenidate, a medication that is commonly used for children with ADHD. He hasn't taken the medication yet, but his mother has been very hopeful that it will help him improve his attention problems. João doesn't sleep well and when he is bored at home in his room he bites his fingernails.

Educational Perspectives

Reading Achievement and Progress

In fourth grade, João received support classes for 50 minutes per day to assist him in math, Portuguese and his homework. He attended this class with other children with learning difficulties. In order to assist him in the classroom, his teachers gave him more attention and seated him in the front row of the class. At that time his teachers reported that his performance was satisfactory. After fourth grade, João had to change schools. He had attended a municipal school from first to fourth grade, which was administered by the municipal government. Since fifth grade he has been in a state run school. In both schools, his teachers never re-evaluated his reading and spelling performance.

João has experienced increasing problems, especially in fifth grade, because he was slow in reading, writing and math. He explained that he used to be good at math but not anymore. He has difficulties with Portuguese grammar and all the other disciplines. The only class he said he was good at was gym. He noted that attending gym sometimes helped him to relieve the stress in other classes. Although his mother informed the teachers at the new school about his condition, they never gave him any special attention for his difficulties. Due to João's continued severe problems, his mother ended up requesting reinforcement classes. The only assistance that was offered him as a result of her complaint was specifically geared to providing support in mathematics.

At the new school, the students had a different teacher for each subject. According to his mother, João had difficulties with this constant change of teachers.

She stated, "He gets confused with the number of different disciplines and different teachers. The teachers come and go to the same classroom; I think it's confusing for him to associate the teacher with the discipline." The mother added that João was sometimes completely lost and he didn't even know which notebook to use for which subject. João's mother is very upset by this situation and has frequently complained to the school principal, but nothing ever changes. The school does not provide any support for him. The mother tries to think of further ways to help her son but as the family cannot afford a private tutor, she must rely on parent-teacher meetings where João's performance in assessments, homework and other activities are discussed. A further complaint from the mother is about other students' behavior and the noise they make in class. She argued that it keeps João from staying focused, something that has always been difficult for him.

Because João's reading has not been tested since fourth grade, it is not possible to determine the amount of progress that he has made. This is due to the fact that in Brazil it is not common to give standardized normative tests for basic skills. João's mother only remembers that his teachers said that he had "satisfactory performance," but she affirmed that he achieved better at school when he was having therapy sessions with a speech and language therapist. Four years ago, João rated his own reading as 3 (on a scale of 1 to 5, with 5 being the highest), but currently rates it as 1. His justification for this lower rating is that he stopped reading because he did not receive any support. However, his mother thought that he had improved a little due to his Bible group where he has to read aloud with less pressure.

It is also noteworthy that João rated the support he received for his reading problems in school as "poor." His mother's observations are consistent with João's as she noted that he "hardly got any support" and that only one teacher really understood his reading problems. After struggling for all these years, João has lost his motivation for reading, writing and going to school. In spite of his mother's constant requests for help, the school has failed to offer him even the slightest support. He rarely reads for enjoyment with the exception of the Bible or books with interesting stories. When asked to identify the hardest thing about having a reading problem, he responded, "I read too slow."

Because of his difficulties, João is not willing to do his best in school anymore. He stated, "No, I don't try to do my best. Because every time I try, I just can't do it." He believes that the school should give him more support, like extra classes and tutoring. His biggest fear is that he could be retained again as he was in first grade.

Teachers

João's mother feels that most of his teachers did not really pay any attention to his reading and spelling problems. Also, she says that at his current school, there are a lot of days when he has reduced hours of attendance. She says:

I think that the teachers stopped giving him attention. In fact, there were a lot of days when the teachers were absent from work and had no substitute. So he had no classes! . . . I used to complain a lot in the reunions [school conferences], like other parents. It has been the same from fifth till seventh grade. Nothing has changed.

The mother reported that it is easy to make appointments with João's educational coordinators, but it is pointless. As she noted:

When I go to the school, the education coordinator always talks to me. But if I complain about something, she says it's not true. For example, almost every Friday there are a lot of children missing school, so there is no class. My kid is sent back home. I ask them to offer some activities on those days, but they don't. I know that there are other parents that issue the same complaint, but the coordinator argues that it's not a problem of the school, but a government problem.

According to João's mother he used to have some support at his previous school, but his current school does not offer any. She pointed out that the reasons for insufficient help for the students are: the lack of teacher training focusing on reading disabilities, the lack of funding for special teachers and school programs and the lack of willingness of teachers to assume responsibility for reading problems.

João mentioned that there was one teacher who helped him with math in the seventh grade but that he also had two bad teachers:

One of my pre-school teachers always yelled at me. In fourth grade another teacher said if I didn't finish copying the activities from the board, I wouldn't be allowed to go to gym class. So I finished copying, but she didn't let me go anyway and yelled at me, too.

In João's opinion, a good teacher is one who always has patience with all students in the classroom and offers help. However, when he was asked whether his teachers understood his learning needs, João surprisingly answered "Yes," explaining that "they keep giving me some advice like 'attention' or 'do it faster, you know that you have difficulties.' "

Although João's mother said that the teachers did not pay attention to his problems, it is quite astonishing that she added, "I think they do understand." She, however, also stated, "They say that most of his difficulties are his fault. They think that he gives too many excuses, blaming the dyslexia." Looking at the teachers' comments and the way João is treated in class, it appears his teachers do not understand his learning needs as they are scolding him instead of supporting him.

Learning Style

João is not particularly aware of his personal learning style. He admitted that he learns better when someone reads to him. Even though he faces difficulties with all of his subjects, João said he prefers to work alone rather than in a group. This preference could be related to his problems with socialization or perhaps he is embarrassed by his low academic skills, but it would seem that group learning would have benefits for João as he would have some peer assistance instead of struggling through assignments by himself. He said that there aren't any learning support tools such as screen readers or textbooks and instructional materials in digital form at his school. He added that they don't use any PowerPoint presentations or videos in the classroom.

Homework

As João is slow in copying and is still facing reading problems, his homework is difficult for him, especially when it requires a lot of reading. His mother always tries to help him, but according to her:

> He doesn't understand what he has to do. So, we open the notebook together, and I see that he has a lot of incomplete activities. In the end, I think he can't explain to me what he has to do. Even he can't understand his own notes. Recently, he says that he doesn't have homework.

When questioned about homework, João answered that "If I would do all the homework, I would need at least 5 hours every day. But I don't do it all." According to his mother, he rarely spends more than an hour on his homework per day and he doesn't ask for assistance. He prefers reading alone. Sometimes he asks questions about things he doesn't understand. João's mother thinks that he could benefit from even more homework. She believes that João stopped making an effort to improve his reading because he did not receive support from his school.

Social Development

João's mother stated that her son has always been shy and reserved. He doesn't have many friends and he refuses to mix with other children. João rarely engages in conversation with others. He is good friends with his cousins, but has difficulty socializing with peers. João's mother does not think that his social development has been impacted by his reading problems. He exhibited behavioral problems in fifth grade, but this has changed for the better. His mother stated that she no longer receives any complaints. These were attributable to the new school as there were more students per class and the teachers seemed distant. João's mother said that after she received a notification of these behavioral problems from the school, she and his father had a serious conversation with him and since then she hasn't received any complaints.

In his free time, João does not participate in any group activities such as sports, clubs or dancing. The mother added that he does not use any social networking sites. Although João's mother thinks that his self-esteem is satisfactory, she rates his social skills as 1, on a scale of 1 to 5 with 5 being the most social.

When João was asked during the interview whether he had ever been bullied or teased because of his reading, he said he had not. His mother also confirms that she is not aware of any bullying incidents. However, four years ago when he was previously interviewed he indicated that he was teased by classmates for being so slow.

When asked about João's maturity, his mother stated: "He's not mature. He looks immature compared to other children of the same age. He looks like a 'big child.' He doesn't care about his looks, clothes, etc. He still plays games intended for 8 year-old children."

Self-Determination and Coping

Self-Efficacy and Motivation

In order to determine how João perceives his own ability to handle challenging situations, the Self-Efficacy Questionnaire for Children (SEQ-C; Muris, 2001) was administered. João was asked to evaluate his academic and emotional self-efficacy on a scale of 1 to 5. He indicated that he had great difficulty meeting academic requirements like finishing all his homework every day, studying when there are other interesting things to do, studying a chapter for a test, paying attention during every class and understanding all the subjects in school. With regard to emotional self-efficacy, João thinks he isn't capable of cheering himself up when an unpleasant event has happened and he also has difficulty in encouraging himself when he feels low. However, he believes that he is good at controlling his feelings and not worrying about things that might happen. He can also tell a friend when he doesn't feel well. Looking at João's scores it is obvious that his level of academic self-efficacy is very low and research has shown that there is a connection between self-efficacy and depression (Muris, 2001). João could be at risk of developing depression if he doesn't get help with his problems. It seems he also needs to learn that his success depends on his own effort. Studies have shown that children with dyslexia sometimes experience feelings of low self-esteem, depression and relationship problems. The feelings of frustration and failure may appear in various forms, from time to time, either due to their school work or interaction with colleagues and family. Children with dyslexia realize that they face obstacles that other children do not face. Many successfully maintain their self-esteem, despite the difficulties; but others end up being shy and isolated as a result of their problems (Frank, 2003; Selikowitz, 2001).

The Children's Hope Scale measures hopeful thinking in relation to achieving one's goals (Snyder et al., 1997). On this scale, João indicates that he is doing pretty well, although he responded that he never does as well as his peers. His response to a further statement shows that he finds solutions to problems most of the time. Some of João's answers show that he still possesses hopeful thinking and believes that he can generate ways to achieve his goals. This is probably due to the emotional support he receives from his family.

To determine if he derives his motivation for studying from intellectual curiosity, social approval or future goal achievement, the Achievement Goal Disposition Survey (adapted from Hayamizu & Weiner, 1991) was administered to João. He chose answers that showed his main motivation for studying is specific goal achievement. By studying, João hopes to have a good life, achieving success and finding a good job in the future. However, João's interview responses indicate that he does not attribute success to his own effort and interest, which makes it difficult for him to continue to pursue his goals in the face of difficulty or challenges. Similarly when things are not going well, he has no idea if it is his fault or someone else's. His answers reflect that João is motivated to a lesser extent by the desire to solve challenging problems and overcome obstacles and failure. Similarly, he is not strongly motivated to study for purposes of social approval. He does not study in order to be praised by his teachers; he just does not want to be disliked by them. Yet, he did indicate that he studies because he wants praise from his parents. It is important to him that he does not disappoint his parents.

Coping

João reported that there's nothing specific that makes him happy or sad. The researcher had to insist on some examples, but João's response was that he didn't have anything specific to share. When questioned about what he does to cheer himself up when he's feeling down, he answered, "I like to be alone." As mentioned by his mother, she always encourages him to make new friends, but he refuses to mix with other children except for his cousins. João can't describe his feelings about getting a bad grade or how he would tackle a challenge, but responded only by saying, "I'm afraid of being retained." Although this response did not address the interview question, it clearly reflected an ongoing fear that he has held since he had this devastating experience many years ago. The mother explained, "I really don't know if he is aware of his frustration. He has never mentioned it to me. The only time I remember that he felt frustrated was when he was retained in first grade."

Impact on Mother

It has been a struggle for João's mother to give her son the support he needs to deal with the challenges he faces due to his dyslexia. On a scale of 1 to 5, she rated the amount of stress she feels parenting a child with dyslexia as 5 (with 5 being the most stressful). She said, "It's very hard to see that he has a lot of difficulties every day, especially regarding his attention problem." She said that despite her son's problem, she and her husband always get along well and they make all decisions together. João's mother does not share her son's problems with friends or other mothers, but she talks to her own mother about it. She explained that in the beginning she didn't understand his problem and used to believe that he was lazy. But, after he received the diagnosis she better understood his needs. She said that if she had another child with the same problem, she would be able to quickly identify the signs of dyslexia. Regarding the impact of all this on her life, she reported, "It affected my professional life a lot of the time. I had to take him to school or to the speech therapist. He only had me to do this. I lost a lot of job opportunities."

Future Goals and Hopes

João's mother is concerned about his future and when asked what he will do after leaving school, she noted that "he will have to work. . . ." However, she believes that he is very immature and doesn't seriously think about his future as he mentioned that he wanted to work with video games. She added "I believe he would be a good veterinarian because he is good with animals." Her aspiration for him is that he'll be happy and will get a good job in the future.

When João was asked about his future goals, he indicated that he would like to get a job or to open a sports store. He prioritized obtaining a job because it would be more likely to happen. The job that he foresees for himself in the future is within the municipal government. However, he knows that he would have to put more effort into his studies in order to achieve his goals.

Case Commentary

During his first interview four years ago, João demonstrated severe reading and spelling problems. João's dyslexia was not diagnosed until the age of 7 after which he received remedial support from a speech and language therapist, which resulted in an improvement in performance. However, due to the school's complaints about his absences from class for therapy and the work conflicts his mother encountered taking him to therapy, the services were discontinued. After fifth grade he no longer received remediation. Unfortunately, in Brazil children with dyslexia still don't have legal support nor is there any public policy for them to get help in the classroom (Capellini & Germano, 2012; Conselho Nacional de Educação/Câmara de Ensino Básico, 2001). It is noteworthy that there is an increase in the enrollment of students with learning disabilities in regular schools. This was discovered through the census conducted by the National Institute for Educational Research and Study Anísio Teixeira (Instituto Nacional de Estudos e Pesquisas Educacionais Anísio Teixeira—INEP) (Instituto Brasileiro de Geografia e Estatística—IBGE, 2000). Despite this increase, it should be stressed that students with dyslexia and/or attention deficit hyperactivity disorder are not getting any special education intervention. The National Board of Education passed a resolution which contains operational guidelines in Article 4, identifying the following groups of students who qualify to receive special educational assistance (ESA) (Ministério da Educação. Conselho Nacional de Educação, 2009):

I – Students with disabilities: those who have long-term physical, mental, intellectual or sensory impairments.
II – Students with developmental disorders: Such as classic autism, Asperger's syndrome, Rett syndrome, childhood disintegrative disorder (psychoses) and pervasive developmental disorders not otherwise specified.
III – Students with high abilities/giftedness.

Some developments have been taking place in order to provide school children diagnosed as dyslexic and/or having attention deficit hyperactivity disorder with special educational assistance. A task force from the Ministry of Education has drawn up a document that provides guidance to support students with specific functional disorders. These guidelines have not yet been adopted at the national level of the educational system due to the fact that they still need to be clarified.

Studies have highlighted the difficulties faced by educators in improving dyslexic students' reading and writing. These problems mainly emanate from the fact that the educational policy still does not recognize dyslexia as a learning disability category and educators are not knowledgeable in written language disorders, which makes it difficult for them to detect the symptoms and complicates the diagnosis of dyslexia. Additionally, the pedagogical concepts in the Brazilian education system do not emphasize phonological instruction in the classroom, which causes problems for dyslexic children in acquiring reading and writing skills (Andrade, Prado & Capellini, 2011). In João's case, it is clear that the use of specific reading and writing strategies as well as supportive technological resources for dyslexic students are still far from being widely implemented. The lack of a public policy supporting dyslexic students has also resulted in João not being granted accommodations at school.

A study conducted by Oliveira and Leite (2011) showed that when it comes to the objectives, content and teaching strategies, the educational planning policy was the same for all children. When children are diagnosed with dyslexia, they still do not receive any special instruction that focuses on their unique demands. As pointed out by his mother, João's special needs were not met as the only assistance he received was in the form of group remedial lessons for math, Portuguese and homework problems. João would have benefitted more from a structured remedial reading program. In order to offer well targeted interventions, it is important for teachers who work with children with special educational needs in regular school settings to receive extra training to be able to use resources and educational methods that are designed specifically for this population (Omote, 2003).

From a social/emotional perspective, João is not doing that well. He is very reserved and his mother describes him as shy and lonely. Although he did not report this in the current interview, during the initial interview he indicated that he was teased by his classmates for being very slow. In this interview he pointed out that one of the elementary school teachers always yelled at him. Apparently this was so painful that he kept it in his memory.

João seems quite frustrated because frequently he cannot meet the requirements in school. Even though it is four years since the last interview, João still feels troubled by his slow reading and he would really like to have more support from his teachers and school, but unfortunately this is not likely to happen. It is sad to observe that João struggles a lot but lacks the means to change his situation.

For João's mother, having a son with dyslexia resulted in a great loss of personal time. She has had to adjust her lifestyle in order to try and support him. She is very concerned about the lack of classes and support. She has lodged complaints with the principal several times but to no avail. It seems that João's teachers and the principal do not even understand that with such a problem his academic career is in jeopardy. As a result João's mother worries about how his difficulties will affect his future. However, it is important to note that she always tries to do her best for him, just like all the other mothers of dyslexic children.

At the end of the first interview when he was finishing third grade, João's progress looked promising. It was very important to continue with the same quality and intensity of support that he received from the university clinic. He is currently not receiving any kind of help. This discontinuation of intensive remediation services seems to have been a turning point for this child. As we observed in this follow-up interview, it seems João and his mother are left to deal with his reading and spelling difficulties on their own. All too often families must bear the burden of dyslexia without the active support of the schools. It is crucial that João be provided with assistance from his school to help him attain an adequate education based on his particular needs. With specialized support, this adolescent would have the opportunity to successfully complete his education and become an independent adult.

References

Andrade, O. V. C. A., Prado, P. S. T., & Capellini, S. A. (2011). Developing pedagogical tools for early identification of students at risk for dyslexia. *Revista Psicopedagogia, 28*(85), 14–28.

Capellini, S. A., & Germano, G. D. (2012). Education for all: A review of literature about inclusive education in Brazil. *Civitas Educationis: Education, Politics and Culture, 1*(2), 105–115.

Conselho Estadual de Educação. (1997). *Indicação CEE no. 22/97*. Regime de Progressão Continuada. [State Board of Education. EEC No. Indication. 22/97. Continued Progression Scheme]. São Paulo. Retrieved from www.ceesp.sp.gov.br/indicacoes/in_22_97.htm

Conselho Nacional de Educação/Câmara de Ensino Básico. (2001). *Diretrizes nacionais para a Educação Especial na Educação Básica, Brasília*. [National Board of Education/Chamber of Formal Education. National Guidelines for Special Education in Basic Education]. Brazil.

Ferreira, A. L., & Spinillo, A. G. (2003). Desenvolvendo a habilidade de produção de textos em crianças a partir da consciência metatextual. In M. R. Maluf (Org.), *Metalinguagem e aquisição da escrita: contribuições da pesquisa para a prática da alfabetização* (pp. 119–148) [Developing the ability to produce texts in children from the metatextual awareness. In M. R. Maluf (Ed.), *Metalanguage and writing acquisition: research contributions to the practice of literacy*]. São Paulo: Casa do Psicólogo.

Frank, R. (2003). *A vida secreta da criança com dislexia* [The secret life of a child with dyslexia]. São Paulo: M. Books do Brazil.

Germano, G. D., Pinheiro, F. H., & Capellini, S. A. (2013). Performance of students with dyslexia in intervention programs: Metalinguistics and reading. *Psicologia Argumento, 31*(72), 11–22.

Germano, G. D., & Capellini, S. A. (2008). Efficacy of an audio-visual computerized remediation program in students with dyslexia. *Pró-Fono, 20*(4): 237–242.

Hayamizu, T., & Weiner, B. (1991). A test of Dweck's model of achievement goals as related to perceptions of ability. *Journal of Experimental Education, 59*, 226–234.

Instituto Brasileiro de Geografia e Estatística (2000). *Censo Demográfico*. [Brazilian Institute of Geography and Statistics. *Census Demographic*]. Brazil. Retrieved from http://portal.mec.gov.br/seesp/arquivos/pdf/Brazil.pdf

Lefèvre, A. B. (1972). *Exame neurológico evolutivo do pré-escolar normal* [*Evolutionary neurological examination normal preschool*]. São Paulo: Sarvier.

Magnan, A., & Ecalle, J. (2006). Audio-training in children with reading disabilities. *Computers & Education, 46*, 407–425.

Ministério da Educação. Conselho Nacional de Educação. (2009). Parecer CNE/CEB no. 13/2009, aprovado em 3 de junho de 2009. *Diretrizes Operacionais para o atendimento educacional especializado na Educação Básica, modalidade Educação Especial*. [Ministry of Education. National Board of Education. (2009). CNE/CEB No. 13/2009, approved on June 3, 2009. Operational Guidelines for specialized educational services in Elementary Education, Special Education model]. Brazil. Retrieved from http://portal.mec.gov.br/dmdocuments/pceb013_09_homolog.pdf

Muris, P. (2001). A brief questionnaire for measuring self-efficacy in youths. *Journal of Psychopathology and Behavioral Assessment, 23*, 145–149.

Oliveira, M. A. M., & Leite, L. P. (2011). Educação inclusiva: análise e intervenção em uma sala de recursos [Inclusive education: Analysis and intervention in a resource room]. *Paidéia, 21* (49), 197–205.

Omote, S. A. (2003). Formação do professor de educação especial na perspectiva da inclusão. In R. L. L. Barbosa (Org.). *Formação de educadores: desafios e perspectivas* (pp. 153–169). [Special education teacher's formation from the perspective of inclusion. In R. L. L. Barbosa (Ed.). *Teacher education: Challenges and perspectives*]. São Paulo: UNESP.

Selikowitz, M. (2001). *Dislexia e outras dificuldades de aprendizagem* [Dyslexia and other learning difficulties]. Rio de Janeiro: Revinter.

Snyder, C. R., Hoza, B., Pelham, W. E., Rapoff, M., Ware, L., Danovsky, M., . . . Stahl, K. J. (1997). The development and validation of the Children's Hope Scale. *Journal of Pediatric Psychology, 22*, 399–421.

Wechsler, D. (2002). *WISC-III: Escala de Inteligência Wechsler para Crianças: Manual* – 3ª ed. [Wechsler Intelligence Scale for Children – Manual Third Edition]. São Paulo, Brazil: Casa do Psicólogo.

10
VICENTE, A CASE STUDY OF A CHILEAN ADOLESCENT WITH DYSLEXIA

Arturo Pinto Guevara and María Pomés

Vicente was diagnosed as dyslexic when he was in first grade at the age of 6. Even though Vicente repeated second grade, his problems with reading and writing persisted. The diagnosis of dyslexia was confirmed when he was in fourth grade. At the time of the second interview Vicente was 15 years old and in his first year of high school. He has been at the same school since fourth grade and has not repeated any additional grades. Vicente was interested in participating in this interview and eager to share his new experiences.

Background

Diagnosis and Treatment

Vicente showed the first signs of reading difficulties during kindergarten when he was attending a private school. He had trouble recognizing colors, objects and letters. At that time, Vicente lost his enthusiasm for going to school as the teacher was giving him extra homework and repeating assignments in order to bring him up to the level of his peers. He did not show progress and was the last one in class to finish his schoolwork. Vicente's dyslexia diagnosis in first grade was made on the basis of the results of two standardized tests: Prueba de Dyslexia Específica (Condemarín & Blomquist, 1996) and Prueba de Comprensión Lectora de Complejidad Lingüística Progresiva (Alliende, Condemarín & Milicic, 1996). His scores on these tests placed him at the 5th and 6th percentiles respectively. The school was unable to offer specialized reading support or accommodations, and transferred the responsibility of providing assistance to the family. Vicente was referred to a private special education teacher (tutor) who reinforced the school curriculum two days per week, but unfortunately Vicente made little progress.

Vicente's diagnosis was confirmed in fourth grade. At that time, he attended a different school as his previous school recommended another grade retention, which his mother rejected. His new teacher noticed that Vicente had difficulty paying attention in addition to his reading problems. He was referred for another evaluation in a specialized center. The neurologist diagnosed him as having attention-deficit/hyperactivity disorder (ADHD) and prescribed medications. Reading assessment was repeated. Results in the same standardized tests placed him at the 3rd percentile. A mathematics test was also administered (i.e., Prueba de Evaluación Matemática; Benton & Luria, 2000), which placed Vicente's math performance at the 60th percentile. Considering these results, the school provided two hours per week of specialized assistance by a special education teacher who was able to adapt texts to meet Vicente's reading needs. Vicente's reading improved and he started to gain confidence. At the same time, the private tutor continued using a reading program based on phonetic and comprehension skills as well as strategies to support Vicente's writing. Self-monitoring strategies were also implemented. Positive results were observed since Vicente began fourth grade in this new school. A great improvement started to be evident when both the special education school teacher and the private tutor began to work together adapting reading materials, teaching strategic ways to monitor the learning process and reinforcing linguistic skills to improve reading comprehension.

Family and Home Life

Vicente lives with his parents and two siblings in an upper-middle-class neighborhood in Santiago. His hobbies include playing goalie for his soccer team and listening to pop music. Vicente also enjoys building cars and mechanical trucks. He perceives his talents to be playing soccer and making new friends.

Vicente's mother was formerly an early childhood teacher who is a homemaker. Since her children were born, she has worked at home taking care of her family. The father is an industrial engineer. Vicente's mother confirms her son's talents, saying that he is a friendly person who is very good at sports. She also noted that when Vicente pursues something, he usually accomplishes his goals successfully. When he is not at school, he plays and listens to music in his room. He has a computer and he uses it approximately three hours per day. Of that time, he spends about two hours engaging in social media and games, and one hour doing homework. Vicente also enjoys sharing time with his siblings practicing sports. In addition, he has other responsibilities, such as keeping his room clean, doing some shopping during weekends, watering the garden a couple of days during the week and helping his youngest sister. As a family, they like to spend time going out at weekends. They also enjoy going to their house on the beach near Santiago. The grandparents participate in these activities as do other relatives on occasion. The whole family shares holidays, sports and trips.

Medical and Psychological Aspects

Vicente is in good health and there have not been any changes since the last interview. As previously noted, he was diagnosed with ADHD in fourth grade, which has been controlled with medication (i.e., Concerta). He has no sensory problems or stress. However, Vicente's mother remembers one difficult incident in school. When her son was in sixth grade, he was admonished because of aggressive behavior; he pushed a classmate down the stairs. There has not been any repetition of similar aggression. Last year, school personnel asked Vicente to get an appointment with a psychologist in order to update relevant information, especially about his vocational aspirations.

Educational Perspectives

Reading Achievement and Progress

Since Vicente entered his current school in fourth grade, it has been possible to observe academic improvements, especially in tasks related to reading and writing. The mother indicated that her son has benefitted from the private special education assistance (one hour per week); he likes it and feels very supported. She recognizes that this type of help has been favorable as it has allowed Vicente to make progress and acquire a study system that brings him confidence and positive results.

Vicente explained that he sometimes feels frustrated because of his reading difficulties. However, he has developed some very beneficial strategies to deal with his problems and frustrations. When he experiences difficulty, he becomes angry at first, but then he is able to organize his mind and restart his work, acquiring positive outcomes. He indicated that the most difficult part of having reading problems is reading aloud in class and having insufficient time to complete assigned reading. Another difficulty mentioned by Vicente is not having enough time to finish homework because of problems reading or following written instructions. When asked about ways to overcome this problem, Vicente explained a strategy that helps him at home during homework or study time. The strategy includes reading out loud and then reading silently. He also turns the content into questions and replaces complex words with simple ones from his own vocabulary. After that, he finds important words or ideas within the text. Once he has identified those words, he tells a story about the content. He says that all of these steps take time, but the strategy is very helpful to him. He reads a few books and several magazines for enjoyment for approximately 10 minutes daily, which according to him is insufficient. In addition, he reads subtitles while he is watching movies and this can take a couple of hours. During the week, from Monday to Friday, he estimated that he spends approximately 90 minutes reading for homework, 20 minutes reading for fun and two hours reading on his computer. At the weekend, he spends approximately one hour doing homework, 15 minutes reading magazines for fun and 20 minutes reading on the computer. Four years ago, on a scale of 1 to 5 (5 being the highest), Vicente rated his reading skill with a 2. In contrast, he now rates it with a 4.

Vicente's reading improvement can be associated with several factors as mentioned before. The strategy that Vicente is using to improve his reading skills seems to transform the process into a reading system to achieve better results: "read aloud, then read silently, summarize the information, ask questions about the content, and make conceptual maps." Another factor that he recognizes as important is the usefulness of reading abilities to build knowledge and to establish social relationships. He mentioned that learning how to read is very important because all the information has to be found in texts and books. He also says, "If you do not read, you cannot interact with other people or technical media like computers."

Vicente stated that one thing that had been missing at school over the last four years was enough support for students with reading difficulties. He reported that nobody taught him to understand how to improve his reading or organize maps of content. In addition, he says that it would be very helpful if teachers would highlight the important content for each class so that students would know where to focus their study efforts. Vicente said that when he feels stressed with school activities, he tries to relax and asks for help; he only finds relief when he finishes homework and all the other school commitments.

The mother confirmed the improvements that Vicente has made in reading. On a scale of 1 to 5 with 5 being the highest, she identified 4 as the amount of improvement he had made in the last four years. She attributed this growth to more motivation and reading practice. She said that now he actually enjoys reading and reads homework and books that were impossible before. His mother's observations of her son's reading and homework load are similar to what Vicente reported except that she perceived his homework to be 60 minutes daily, as opposed to Vicente's estimate which was 90 minutes per day, and an additional hour on weekends. When Vicente has to read long books, the mother helps him by providing explanations and reading some chapters with him.

According to the mother, school challenges during the last years have decreased. Vicente's grades have improved. On a grading scale of 1 to 7, he has an average grade of 5.5. His mother explained that, "His grades could be better, but teachers do not provide enough help." Vicente has better grades in math (6.0). He stands out because of his motivation and interest in solving problems, even though he does not receive any help from school in math. He received a good final grade of 5.7 in science. Vicente spends time talking with his science teacher who provides clarification of content for him. In Spanish, his grade has gone up to 5.4, which is very good for him because in this subject students need to learn a lot of content and use a high level of reading comprehension. In history, Vicente received 5.2, which is important due to the fact that students have to process considerable information while they are reading text.

Teachers

Vicente complained that is the past few years, there has been an increased rotation of teachers in different classrooms that has caused some problems at school; this changing of staff has interfered with the learning process because of the lack of familiarity with his teachers. According to him, the type of support that teachers have provided in reading is "very poor." He remembers his best teacher as: "The one that worked with students outside the classroom and listened to his students respectfully. He explained my homework very carefully and, most importantly, the teacher was always assessing students." He also remembers his worst teacher. According to Vicente: "This was a math teacher, who asked me every time at the beginning of the class to go outside of the classroom, telling me that it would be better for me to play soccer than do math." Vicente interprets this as the teacher's lack of trust in his capabilities and failure to recognize his interest in learning mathematics. He described the most important qualities for teachers as: listening to their students, assessing the level of comprehension of the students and providing many opportunities to learn. In addition, he said that not all the teachers understand that there are students with special needs in the classroom. Vicente thinks "there are many students who have difficulties learning some subjects at school" and they need assistance from teachers to be successful in the classroom, which they do not always receive.

According to Vicente's mother, the school has not provided specific support during the last few years. According to her, "lack of support has been a limitation to Vicente's performance at school." She says that communication with school has been too superficial, and it has not had an impact on her son's needs. She does not attend parent conferences anymore as she has not found them to be beneficial. Neither does she believe that the teachers have been helpful, the only exception being the lead teacher who has shown interest in Vicente, but as she noted, "families carry everything else." The mother indicated that she would like to change the type of support given to all students at school. She would like to see "real help, which includes following up students' progress and effective communication with families." In her opinion, the problem with teachers is their unwillingness to help, their lack of preparation and their inadequate knowledge of how to address children's reading difficulties at school. The most important school support during the past few years has been meetings with Vicente's lead teacher who has helped him to organize his time and schoolwork. She also mentioned that in a certain way school is becoming easier for Vicente because instead of being presented with new content, teachers are reviewing previously taught content in preparation for the University Selection Assessment (PSU). This is a very important national test that is used for qualification and acceptance at universities in Chile.

Fortunately in spite of his challenges, Vicente likes school; he does not manifest school avoidance. His mother indicated that her son has good comprehension, which is the only way to do well in the PSU and enter university. The help that Vicente needs comes from a private special education teacher who continues to work with him for an hour a week. The program that the private special education teacher applies is based on phonemic awareness, phonics and reading comprehension in order to improve Vicente's reading as well as his processing and integration of information. In addition, this support program addresses independent study strategies and academic content. The lead teacher at school has indicated that this external support should be continued as it is highly valuable for Vicente's success.

Learning Style

According to Vicente's learning style, the most successful strategy for him is to combine different routes of information access. He is able to use visual and oral stimuli effectively and also to reinforce the meaning and relation of concepts by building graphs or maps. He established a study system, including oral and silent reading, elaboration of questions related to the specific content and implementation of graphic organizers, to synthesize the most relevant points. In addition, he indicated that the best way to demonstrate his learning is through the development of a computer presentation. The computer is a valuable tool that helps him with reading and solving tasks related to studying. He uses a desktop expansion with a larger auxiliary screen that helps him with reading. However, Vicente also indicated that school books are unfortunately not in digital format. Through presentations, he is able to orally express his knowledge in relation to content on a variety of topics to his classmates. Vicente mentioned that he enjoys working in groups and having the opportunity to lead the activity at some point. His interview answers on his academic strengths and weaknesses indicated that he is very good at working collaboratively on assigned topics.

When the mother was asked about her son's organization skills, she rated Vicente with a 4 on a scale of 1 to 5, which is quite strong considering his attentional difficulties. She says that her son is making a great effort that is supported by a system that Vicente has designed to improve his reading. She added that it is not easy, but Vicente does it very well. When he gets lower grades or feels frustrated with school activities, Vicente puts his study system in place, which usually improves his grades and helps him to present homework in front of his classmates.

Homework

Vicente indicated that now he is able to do his homework independently, spending approximately two hours per day; this involves 90 minutes of reading and 30 minutes of related preparation activities, such as writing. He considers that homework is currently not a problem because it is similar to the examples given during class; however, he indicated that "homework is very boring." Vicente also said that homework is almost always repeating examples from his school books, which means that he just needs to copy the content from the book. Thus, he perceives this repetition of homework to be tedious and useless for him. Other times, there are surprise assessments without previous notification, which make him nervous and anxious.

In Vicente's opinion, reading difficulties will not be a problem when he finishes high school. He recognizes that it will be necessary to spend more time reading in order to complete homework, especially when new information is involved. Vicente's mother mentioned that Vicente has trouble with long homework as he usually becomes bored. He does homework independently spending approximately one hour every day. According to her, homework does not contribute to Vicente's learning process or achievement. The biggest challenge today for her son is to perform well in assessments and homework to synthesize all the content that is taught.

Social Development

Vicente's reading difficulties have not influenced his positive interaction with classmates, friends and family members. According to his mother, sometimes he seems to be less mature than his classmates. For instance, he plays a lot on the computer, but at other times he seems to be mature enough when he has to interact with new people or make new friends. He has good interaction with peers, family members and friends, using social networks at least an hour per day. He is able to socialize with girls and since last year, he has had a girlfriend.

Vicente's self-esteem is considered normal by his mother. He maintains adequate interactions with teachers. In general, he does not have social or behavioral problems, does not drink alcohol and has never had problems with drugs or the police. He usually practices sports, and goes dancing at the "Club Español." When his mother rated her son's social skills on a scale of 1 to 5, she gave him a 4.

Self-Determination and Coping

Self-Efficacy and Motivation

Two scales (Academic and Emotional) of the Self-Efficacy Questionnaire for Children (SEQ-C; Muris, 2001) were administered. In general, Vicente's scores on the academic self-efficacy scale (29 points) were similar to those on the emotional self-efficacy (32 points). On this self-efficacy scale, children are asked to rate themselves on a series of questions related to academic and emotional competency; possible responses range from 1 to 5 with 5 indicating the greatest degree of self-efficacy. All of Vicente's responses were mostly 4s with a few 3s;

he did not respond to any items with 1, 2 or 5. There was some indication Vicente was slightly lower in his academic self-efficacy as he scored three of these items with a 3, lower than any of the emotional self-efficacy scores. The three academic questions that he scored lower were related to ability to obtain assistance from teachers when needed, studying when there were other interesting things to do and comprehension of school subjects. However, it should be noted that all other academic questions were rated with a 4, indicating strength in this area which addressed such factors as studying for exams, completion of homework, paying attention in class, satisfying parents with homework and passing exams. Vicente's responses of all 4s on the emotional self-efficacy questions also revealed strong self-efficacy in this area. Examples of these items included calming oneself, prevention of nervousness, sharing feelings with others and prevention of excessive worrying. In general, Vicente's responses indicated that he has positive academic and emotional self-perceptions that do not interfere with his achievement and sense of well-being.

Overcoming obstacles is not an easy task. Vicente mentioned that an effective way to overcome barriers is to be alert, prepared, attentive and to avoid making mistakes. On the Children's Hope Scale (Snyder et al., 1997), Vicente's responses again revealed that he is confident that he is "doing pretty well a lot of the time" and that "most of the time" he can think of many ways to attain things that are important to him. He also perceives himself to be a good problem solver "most of the time." Two areas in which he expressed some concern were comparing himself with peers (i.e., "doing as well as other kids my age") and benefitting from past experiences (i.e., "things I have done in the past will help me in the future"). Thus, his lowest scores were related to perceptions of his progress compared to his classmates and lack of confidence about the future.

In an effort to gain insight into Vicente's motivation for studying, the Achievement Goal Disposition Survey (adapted from Hayamizu & Weiner, 1991) was administered. This measure divides student responses into three categories that identify motivation for studying: (1) intellectual curiosity (learning mastery), (2) social approval and (3) goal achievement. Vicente's responses on this measure revealed that he shows a strong commitment toward studying for purposes of goal achievement (e.g., "I study because I want to get a good job in the future" and "I study because I have set goals for myself") and intellectual curiosity (e.g., "I study because I like to use my brain" and "I study because I like challenging difficult problems"). His responses suggested that he is not particularly interested in achievement for purposes of social approval, indicating that he does not study "to be praised by my teachers" or to avoid ridicule from peers; however, he sometimes studies for purposes of parental approval.

Self-awareness and coping are important aspects in Vicente's life. He indicates that sharing time with his friends and enjoying vacations make him very happy; on the other hand, relatives' illnesses make him sad. A coping strategy that Vicente uses when he feels down is "being with others, laughing and playing." When asked to provide an example of a situation in which he faced a challenge and succeeded, he explained that one day he did not have enough money to come back home so he decided to ask a lady in a drug store for money. The woman gave him two dollars and the next day, he returned the money to her, but this made him feel very embarrassed. Vicente says that he is successful as an adolescent. For a situation in which he faced a challenge and failed, he describes an opportunity when he had to design a presentation at school. Only 2 groups out of 12 would be randomly chosen to present in front of the class. Vicente's group decided not to study because there was a low probability they would be selected. However, unfortunately, his group was chosen to present. Even though they improvised, it was evident that they were not well prepared. He felt embarrassed and left a bad impression on the class. He lamented, "I did not know anything and it affected me for several days."

Vicente has strong opinions about learning difficulties and teaching opportunities. He said, "People can fail, machines cannot; we are people, not perfect machines." According to Vicente, the best student in his class is very quiet but "he's a show off who does not help anybody." Vicente definitely understands the relationship between effort and achievement as he said, "If I wanted to be the best student of my class, I would study all the time." When Vicente was asked what he would change about himself if he could, he mentioned that he would like to feel less awkward in certain situations. He indicated that he never has been bullied or teased because of his reading difficulties. He said, "I try to do my best at school because I do not want to fail." When asked whether it was his fault or the fault of teachers when things don't go well at school, he said, "It could be the responsibility of everybody," which is a mature interpretation. He also mentioned, "If the teacher explains topics clearly, that helps me to get better outcomes."

According to Vicente, the most important thing that his parents have done to support him with school is to provide a special education teacher at home. He recognizes that his parents are constantly talking with his teachers and always supporting him. When Vicente receives a good or bad grade, he tells his parents and asks for help to correct mistakes because, as he said, "I want to do better the next time." If Vicente could change something about school, he would like to change the way instruction is presented as his opinion is that "teachers talk too much and classes are boring," a thought that is most likely shared by many of his peers.

Impact on Mother

Vicente's reading difficulties have moderately stressed his mother. On a scale of 1 to 5 with 5 being the highest level of stress, she reported that she would rate her parenting stress at a 3. The time of highest tension was when Vicente had to repeat second grade and later the school recommended that he also repeat third grade. The mother did not accept this recommendation and moved him to a new school. She said that her son's reading difficulties have not affected her marital relationship or the relationship Vicente has with his siblings, although she admits that she spends more time with him than the other children. There are no specific situations that negatively affect her relationship with her son, but she mentioned that homework, guides and texts only repeat the work that Vicente does in class, and that upsets him.

Vicente's mother explained that at school parents with children with special needs are easily able to identify each other. They can talk and exchange knowledge and information. This is positive for mothers who have recently found out their children have learning disabilities. Vicente's difficulties do not affect her work as she is a homemaker and does not have responsibilities outside of the home. According to her, the best resource for Vicente has been the support provided by the private special education teacher. She said, "These classes make him happy" as Vicente and the teacher have a good relationship and share many conversations about sports. After these sessions, Vicente comes back home pleased and the mother believes that the instruction "really helps him." She indicated that having a child with special needs has helped her to see things differently, to have more patience, to see her children as diverse people and also to appreciate her son's friends as original and creative children. The advice she would give to the mothers of children with special needs is that they should have a broad positive view. They also have to trust in their children, support them and spend time with them. With regard to reading, the mother hopes that Vicente will read for fun, that he becomes interested in reading about his career and he will be able to grow culturally.

Future Goals and Hopes

Vicente wants to pursue important goals. First, he mentioned that he would like to "be one of the best at sports in his school." He understands that accomplishing that goal requires a lot of practice, playing for the team, and not making mistakes. The second goal is to travel to the United States again. In order to do that, Vicente's parents have asked him to get passing grades at school. When Vicente is asked to prioritize his goals, he indicates that traveling to the United States is the most important because he has great memories from his first visit there. He believes that he might understand things better now that he is older.

About the future, Vicente sees himself graduating from college as a mechanical engineer. In order to accomplish that, he believes he should "learn about engines and physics, have a car, be intelligent, know how to manage people, be very clean, and not waste time." Vicente also says that he would be good at this job because ever since he was a young child, he frequently visited his grandfather's workshop where he has watched him repair buses and trucks and now he understands everything that needs to be done. Finally, when he is asked what three wishes he would like to come true, he answered that he would like to be successful finishing high school, he would love to have a mechanic workshop for trucks and he would like to travel with his family.

Vicente's mother has high expectations for her son's future. She stated that Vicente will go to the university and he will be successful there. She said she believes he will attain his goal of becoming a mechanic because he really enjoys this as he has spent a lot of time in her father's shop. She believes he is highly motivated to achieve this vocational goal. She also wants him to be successful and happy. The mother indicated that she always will have concerns as a mother, but her wishes for Vicente are that "he is healthy, remains close to his family, becomes a hard worker and has good colleagues."

Case Commentary

Since his last interview, Vicente has continued his school life in an expected way; his academic performance has improved and he has not failed any subjects. He continues to enjoy building cars and playing soccer. He is able to develop this last activity with a high level of social acceptance. Vicente continues to make progress despite frequent changes in the school staff. It seems that these changes have not affected his positive interaction with school personnel. Although evidence suggests that the achievement gap appears even in first grade in children with reading difficulties and persists into adolescence, early intervention and teachers' specialized support may diminish the difference between typical and dyslexic readers. In order to narrow the achievement gap, reading interventions should be implemented during early years, when children are developing the basic skills to promote the reading process. Vicente had early private reading instruction, but no remedial support in school. Research findings suggest that when interventions are implemented later children may experience improvement and this instruction may prevent the reading gap from becoming wider, but it does not disappear (Compton & Steacy, 2015; Ferrer et al., 2015).

It is clear that school personnel should enhance their own willingness to support students who require additional intervention. The lack of specialized support and accommodations during Vicente's early years at school could be a risk factor for his academic performance. All teachers should be prepared to identify early signs of reading delays as they observe the learning process. Supporting and frequently assessing students according to their needs are important activities for teachers who must assume responsibility for monitoring their students' reading progress. In addition, they should provide diverse opportunities that allow students to demonstrate their learning achievements and use differentiated strategies to improve reading competencies, both of which could diminish reading delays (Bender, 2012; Lerner & Johns, 2015). Another aspect highlighted by Vicente's case is the importance of students working in teams and engaging in collaborative learning that will result in more positive outcomes and better academic development for all students. Moreover, the cooperative learning opportunities that Vicente has been provided at his school seem to have helped to overcome some of the academic barriers he has experienced.

In spite of the support Vicente has received, reading difficulties continue to be a source of difficulty that interferes with academic performance. Students with specific reading difficulties such as dyslexia have problems accurately recognizing words and reading fluently as well as difficulties with decoding and spelling (International Dyslexia Association [IDA], 2002; Jiménez, 2012). A natural consequence of these types of difficulties is comprehension problems and a slower, more arduous processing of printed language. Thus, it is not surprising that Vicente, like other struggling readers, rejects extensive homework that requires an unreasonable amount of time and effort, such as is the case when tasks involve reading long passages of text or involve following lengthy written instructions.

Currently, the amount of time Vicente spends meeting academic demands seems to be adequate as he is passing all academic subjects. Less attention is devoted to reading books and magazines; however, time for recreational reading associated with computer activities is a priority for Vicente. He has a positive self-perception of his ability to prioritize activities; he also has developed high expectations for his future. His family appears to be a crucial factor in his success as they support Vicente's needs and encourage his abilities. Even though evidence indicates that students with reading difficulties are more likely to display low self-esteem, family support appears to act as a protective factor that allows students to perceive themselves as capable of achieving academic goals. Family support is able to protect children's emotions and minimize the negative consequences experienced with dyslexia (Carawan, Blace, Nalavany & Jenkins, 2015; Nalavany, Carawan & Sauber, 2013). Adolescents and adults with reading difficulties are able to cope with emotional pressure when they are supported by family members. In general, Vicente attributes his academic success to his own effort and capabilities, showing a positive and healthy self-esteem. He also is able to acknowledge that his reading difficulties are an obstacle requiring great effort on his part, which is not always rewarded at school.

With his parents' support and commitment to him, Vicente is capable of facing and meeting academic difficulties and transforming these into manageable challenges. His parents were proactive in seeking a private special education teacher for Vicente who has helped him greatly with his reading and study skills, which has resulted in improved grades and achievement. A systematic and explicit intervention based on linguistic components has been successful for him. According to the literature, building phonological awareness, strengthening alphabetic principles, increasing vocabulary recognition and oral reading fluency along with self-efficacy and intrinsic motivation are basic principles that need to be considered as an integrated strategy to improve reading skills (Bravo, 2004; Carrillo & Alegría, 2009; Good & Kaminski, 2011; MacArthur, Philippakos & Ianetta, 2015; National Reading Panel, 2000; Pinto & Bermeosolo, 2007;

Vellutino & Scanlon, 1994). In addition, systematic phonics training and explicit instruction in executive functions may help students to focus, maintain attention, self-regulate, pursue goals, plan activities and continue working to complete a specific task. Executive function skills play an important role in working more efficiently to solve problems and interacting with other students in academic learning environments (MacArthur et al., 2015; Nielsen et al., 2016). Vicente has clear goals for his immediate future and some of them are related to achieving acceptable grades.

Vicente's mother agrees with her son's perception about the time that he spends studying, doing homework and reading on the computer. The mother believes that there is limited specialized school support for her son probably because teachers do not know how to assist students with special needs. Furthermore, most of the homework that he receives does not further enhance his learning skills. The mother noted that high school teachers put too much attention on the final school assessment that determines university selection (i.e., PSU). There is no systematic assistance for students with reading challenges at school. Although, Vincente's mother is aware of the lack of specific accommodations, she has always been willing to support her son with resources outside of school. She recognizes Vicente's development and the improvement in his grades in critical subjects such as math, science and history. She does not believe that Vicente's reading difficulties have significantly affected her life, except when Vicente had to repeat a grade and she had to find another school. This was a stressful time for her. Currently, she has positive expectations for her son's future. She believes he is going to be successful at meeting his personal and academic goals. Vicente's mother also highlighted the importance of having a parents' support group. She has found it very beneficial that she has been able to join other parents of children with special needs to develop a network for contacting one another and exchanging information and extending support.

Vicente's interview and assessment measures indicate a positive development in his academic skills, an ability to ask and receive assistance from teachers and his implementation of successful study strategies with consequent positive learning outcomes. Also, Vicente demonstrates the use of effective self-control strategies and an increased ability to express his feelings. Thus, it is not surprising that his parents are pleased with Vicente's motivation to overcome his reading and school achievement challenges. The social support system provided by his parents and others may play an important role in generating coping strategies and socio-emotional tools to overcome academic and social challenges (Classens & Lessing, 2015). Now, Vicente is at the point where he sometimes prefers academic tasks instead of recreational activities when he has the opportunity to choose. He demonstrates the ability to face and solve problems, and perceives himself as capable of successfully achieving his goals.

It has not always been easy for Vicente and his mother to face his school experiences with the challenge imposed by reading difficulties. From the beginning of his school experience, academic achievement has been based on the ability to design and implement a learning strategy of processing, integrating and repeating information to interpret printed text, which has not been easy for Vicente. It is clear that strategic learning is a powerful tool for students with learning difficulties, allowing them to select a strategy from a repertoire and use it appropriately in a specific context. Applying strategies correctly provides students with opportunities to develop self-confidence and independent learning (Reid, Ortiz & Hagaman, 2013). When Vicente, with the help of his private tutor, learned to develop his own personal learning strategy based on his strengths and weaknesses, he began to improve. Another crucial aspect also observed in this case is the fact that families of children with learning disabilities bear most of the responsibility for supporting achievement and emotional adjustment. Vicente has learned how to respond to teachers' instructions and to develop and implement study strategies; he has demonstrated a strong commitment to meet the academic standards in spite of his reading challenges, which, in turn, has shown a fortitude that has recently developed. The student is making a determined effort to succeed in his school environment without specialized support. The most important factors that have encouraged success include Vicente's self-determination, the consistent effort he extends, his ability to set clear goals and the assistance provided by his family. All of these factors have made an important difference, but have also made it possible for Vicente to successfully move forward in a challenging school environment.

References

Alliende, F., Condemarín, M., & Milicic, N. (1996). *Prueba de comprensión lectora de complejidad lingüística progresiva*. Santiago, Chile: Ediciones UC.

Bender, W. N. (2012). *Differentiating instruction for students with learning disabilities. New best practices for general and special educators*. Thousand Oaks, CA: Corwin.

Benton, A., & Luria, A. (2000). *Prueba de evaluación matemática*. Santiago, Chile: Ediciones UC.

Bravo, L. (2004). *Lectura inicial y psicología cognitiva*. Chile: Ediciones PUC.

Carawan, L. W., Blace, A., Nalavany, B. A., & Jenkins, C. (2015). Emotional experience with dyslexia and self-esteem: The protective role of perceived family support in late adulthood. *Aging and Mental Health, 20*(3), 284–294.

Carrillo, M., & Alegría, J. (2009). Mecanismos de identificación de palabras en niños disléxicos en español. *Ciencias Psicológicas, 3*, 135–152.

Classens, T., & Lessing, A. C. (2015). Young adult learners with dyslexia: Their socio-emotional support needs during adolescence. *Journal of Psychology in Africa, 25*(1), 32–36. doi:10.1080/14330237.2015.1007599

Compton, D. L., & Steacy, L. M. (2015). Reading intervention in perspective. In C. McDonald, & P. McCardle (Eds.), *Advances in reading intervention* (pp. 249–260). Baltimore, MD: Brookes.

Condemarín, M., & Blomquist, M. (1996). *Test exploratorio de dislexia específica*. Santiago, Chile: Biopsique.

Ferrer, E., Shaywitz, B. A., Holahan, J. M., Marchione, K. E., Michaels, R., & Shaywitz, S. E. (2015). Achievement gap in reading is present as early as first grade and persists through adolescence. *The Journal of Pediatrics*, *167*, 1121–1125. doi:10.1016/j.jpeds. 2015.07.045

Good, R., & Kaminski, R. (2011). *DIBELS Next(r) Assessment Manual*. Retrieved from www.d11.org/edss/assessment/DIBELS%20NextAmplify%20Resources/DIBELSNext_ AssessmentManual.pdf

Hayamizu, T., & Weiner, B. (1991). A test of Dweck's model of achievement goals as related to perceptions of ability. *Journal of Experimental Education*, *59*, 226–234. doi:10. 1080/00220973.1991.10806562

International Dyslexia Association. (2002). Retrieved from https://eida.org/definition-of-dyslexia

Jiménez, J. E. (2012). *Dislexia en español. Prevalencia e indicadores cognitivos, culturales, familiares y biológicos*. Madrid, Spain: Pirámide.

Lerner, J. W., & Johns, B. H. (2015). *Learning disabilities and related disabilities: Strategies for success*. Stamford, CT: Cengage Learning.

MacArthur, C. A., Philippakos, Z. A., & Ianetta, M. (2015). Self-regulated strategy instruction in college developmental writing. *Journal of Educational Psychology*, *107*(3), 855–867. doi:10.1037/edu0000011

Muris, P. (2001). A brief questionnaire for measuring self-efficacy in youths. *Journal of Psychopathology and Behavioral Assessment*, *23*, 145–149.

Nalavany, B. A., Carawan, L. W., & Sauber, S. (2013). Adults with dyslexia, an invisible disability: The mediational role of concealment on perceived family support and self-esteem. *British Journal of Social Work*, *45*, 568–586.

National Reading Panel. (2000). *Teaching children to read: An evidence based assessment of the scientific research literature on reading and its implications for reading instruction*. Retrieved from https://www.nichd.nih.gov/research/supported/Pages/nrp.aspx

Nielsen, K., Abbott, R., Griffin, W., Lott, J., Raskind, W., & Berninger, V. (2016). Evidence-based reading and writing assessment for dyslexia in adolescents and young adults. *Learning Disabilities 21*(1), 38–56. doi:10.18666/LDMJ-2016-V21-I1-6971

Pinto, A., & Bermeosolo, J. (2007). *Tratamiento e integración de niños con severas dificultades lectoras, utilizando estrategias con énfasis fonémico verbal*. Concepción, Chile: Paideia.

Reid, R., Ortiz, T., & Hagaman, J. (2013). *Strategy instruction for students with learning disabilities*. New York: Guilford.

Snyder, C. R., Hoza, B., Pelham, W. E., Rapoff, M., Ware, L., Danovsky, M., . . . Stahl, K. J. (1997). The development and validation of the Children's Hope Scale. *Journal of Pediatric Psychology*, *22*, 399–421. doi:10.1093/jpepsy/22.3.399

Vellutino, F., & Scanlon, D. (1994). *Componentes de la habilidad lectora su evaluación y tratamiento*. Lima, Peru: CEPAL.

11
JANKÓ, A CASE STUDY OF A HUNGARIAN ADOLESCENT WITH DYSLEXIA

Éva Gyarmathy

Jankó, a thin and sensitive boy, was almost 15 years old at the time of the second interview. He is not as talkative as he used to be and his attitude toward the world has changed radically compared with the first interview four years ago. He has become a reclusive guarded boy. He no longer calls himself "Jankó Strong" after a folk hero or conveys the impression of being able to achieve whatever he wants. During the last four years, he has struggled a lot with his learning endeavors, but more recently there have been some positive changes in his life, including a new school, which seems to be a good match for Jankó.

Background

Diagnosis and Treatment

In third grade, Jankó received his first professional diagnosis at the Educational Counselling Service. The results of the Ildkó Meixner Test (Meixner, 1993) and the Meeting Street School Screening Test (MSSST) (Denhoff, Siqueland, Komich & Hainsworth, 1968) revealed that Jankó's reading was slow and below developmental expectations. Additionally, he exhibited sequential visual perceptual and visual-motor problems as well as poor verbal memory. Jankó was diagnosed as dyslexic, but his mother insisted that the diagnosis be changed to "at risk" as she disagreed with the diagnosis. In fourth grade, the Gyarmathy-Smythe Cognitive Profile Test (Gyarmathy, 2009; Smythe, Gyarmathy & Everatt, 2002) was administered, the results of which reconfirmed that Jankó was dyslexic and additionally had math problems and difficulties in spatial-orientation. In fifth grade, Jankó went to another pedagogical counseling center where he received developmental and psychological therapy. As part of this therapy his reading abilities were reassessed, but no results were reported; however, for the first time a written certificate confirming Jankó's dyslexia was given to the mother.

Family and Home Life

Jankó lives with his father and younger brother in a large city in Hungary. A year and a half ago Jankó's mother decided to move out of their family home. The father agreed to this on condition that the boys stayed with him. Jankó's mother rented a flat, which she doesn't use anymore as she now sleeps in the family living-room. She does, however, spend more and more time at her new boyfriend's place. A sensitive issue for Jankó's mother is that she feels she has hardly any impact on her sons. Instead, it is the father who has a predominant influence. The mother feels that it is very hard for the boys when she and her husband cannot reach agreement on family issues. She cannot decide whether it would be better if she left or stayed.

There are no joint activities within the family. At times, the father engages in activities with Jankó, but unfortunately he is aggressive and brings his work problems home. Sometimes he takes the two boys to visit their great-grandfather. The father's side of the family gets together mainly on special days like holidays and birthdays. The mother's side of the family has harmonious relations and meets more frequently.

When Jankó is at home, he tends to take the easy road, sitting in front of the television and watching sports. Although he is already an adolescent, he still likes fairy tales and cartoons. He usually watches television for about one and a half to two hours daily, but there are days when he does not watch at all. When his father switches on the television, Jankó watches it with him.

Jankó is a highly sensitive boy who is deft and agile; his sense of balance is excellent. It is, however, not easy to communicate with him, as he has a rather peculiar way of thinking and expressing himself with very few words. His mother sent him to drama classes and it turns out he is very good at acting. Jankó currently plays soccer and previously played basketball for two years. He continues to enjoy weekly horseback riding, which has been a hobby of his for some time. Asked about his special talents or abilities, Jankó responded, "I don't know, let's not write anything here." Jankó can be highly motivated in competitions, but he cannot bear losing and his father does not alleviate the situation because he is very critical.

Medical and Psychological Aspects

Jankó's mother reported that her son did not have any serious illnesses; however, she stated that he usually has aches and pains all over his body, bad posture and is very sensitive. He does spine exercises and acroyoga for pain relief as well as to improve his posture. The mother explained that during the summer at an acroyoga session, Jankó consulted a seer who said that "his heart chakra was closing up." Jankó also has difficulty going to sleep and getting up, often complaining of being tired. He has quite serious allergies at times. During these episodes, his eyesight and hearing are severely affected. Alternative treatment methods have been tried, but nothing has worked. These allergy attacks finally abated when he changed schools. His mother believes that this switch to a better school might have a lot to do with the improvement of the allergies.

Jankó has significant difficulties paying attention. He took a hearing test, but no deficiencies were found. However, more recently he has been diagnosed with attention deficit hyperactivity disorder although he does not take any medication for this condition. His mother explained that during conversations he cannot focus for a long time. When the mother was young, she took medication for the same condition. The mother thinks Jankó lives in his own world and explains, "It is as if his soul was abused. As a child he used to be very open, and then he slowly shut the world out."

Educational Perspectives

Reading Achievement and Progress

Jankó has changed schools several times in the last four years. His mother has worked tirelessly to find a suitable educational placement for her son. He attended a Waldorf School, a public sports school and is currently at a polytechnic school.

In fifth grade, Jankó's problems were not acknowledged by his classroom teacher at the Waldorf School, therefore, he did not receive any support. The school claimed that the cause of his difficulties was family problems. Jankó would have benefitted from extra classes, but he did not get them. Thus, the family arranged for Jankó to change to another school. The only support he received at this stage was developmental and psychological therapy from the pedagogical counseling center.

Jankó was transferred to a sports school where he was placed in a class specializing in athletics. It was a fairly strong school, but his mother mentioned that they were not interested in his past records, which made her wonder how they would support his academic development. As the mother expected, Jankó's academic performance deteriorated. He did not receive any dyslexia-specific intervention in the classroom or in extra curricula settings. The school requirements forced him to catch up and he eventually reached the required level, but it was very hard for him.

In seventh grade, the mother enrolled him in a six-year polytechnic high school. At this school he failed computer science in the first year. Computer science and English are the subjects that Jankó particularly dislikes. He has little experience working with computers as there was a ban on them at his former school. This grade was basically the same experience for Jankó; there were no significant changes to improve his situation at school. Although his classroom teacher assisted him by teaching him learning strategies and he also received some computer science support, Jankó was at a disadvantage because the school did not offer support for his dyslexia. The only intervention that seemed helpful was provided by a special needs teacher who privately tutored him to develop his Hungarian. Jankó would be in the eighth grade now, but his mother requested that he be retained so he is repeating seventh grade.

Despite his lack of progress at school, Jankó's mother seems to think that his reading has undergone a significant development within the last four years. She rates the improvement as 4 on a scale of 1 to 5 with 1 being the least and 5 being the most. However, Jankó thinks his improvement is not as significant and places it at 3. The mother reported that changing to a more demanding school with his current Hungarian teacher has resulted in increased progress. The private tutoring also helped immensely, but unfortunately these sessions ended. At the polytechnic high school, his classroom teacher is now fulfilling the duties of his special needs teacher. She has been very helpful, but she does not really have time to provide this support.

Although Jankó regards reading as important, he still doesn't read a lot. He says he will read as much as he needs to, and he doesn't want to read any more than that. He seldom reads for his own pleasure, but infrequently he has read an entire book in one day. His current teachers think that Jankó has gone through a transformation. He is achieving more and puts more effort into school. He no longer plays the "I'm a dumb kid" card. The expectation to perform coupled with suitable developmental education were the driving forces behind Jankó's improvement. His mother is of the opinion that if Jankó had stayed at the Waldorf School, he would not have progressed so much and would not have been able to read and write.

Teachers

Jankó's mother believes there is a lack of teacher training focused on reading disabilities. Funding is lacking for special needs teachers and school programs for children with special educational needs; as a result, teachers fail to identify reading problems. Teachers are also not willing to assume responsibility for reading problems as they don't have the time and energy to deal with children individually in a differentiated way. The mother adds that Jankó's teachers don't make the children read enough. She did, however, admit that his current classroom teacher does everything he can as he agreed to give Jankó extra computer science sessions.

Jankó gets along well with most of his teachers but there are a few exceptions. His mother reported the following about his computer science teacher, "He would give him a one, the worst grade, simply if he deemed that Jankó wasn't paying attention." However, when Jankó was asked about the worst teacher he had ever had, he had nothing to say. When asked about the three most important things that a teacher should do for students, he said a good teacher should: (1) pay attention to students' questions, (2) enjoy teaching and (3) teach in a way that children like. Jankó believes that some of his teachers were aware of his learning needs as he reported that his math teacher as well as his arts teacher paid attention to him. This is quite surprising since he also reported that if he could change one thing about school it would be his math teacher.

According to his mother, Jankó's previous school failed to attend to his learning deficiencies; he did not get extra sessions and received inadequate support for his needs. His mother frequently visited the school, trying to ensure cooperation with the teachers. When Jankó changed to the polytechnic school, there was cooperation and joint teamwork in the students' interests. However, he still doesn't receive extra sessions to help him with his special learning needs. The mother adds that although the classroom teacher, a special needs teacher, is helping Jankó now, the kind of support he is receiving is not sufficient to make a significant difference. The mother admits that she has slipped into the background a little as she has grown tired of intervening and is now choosing to trust that the school will accomplish its task.

Learning Style

Jankó enjoys learning when things are fascinating. His ideal way of learning is reading something over and over again and he best displays what he has learnt through exams. He prefers working alone. His mother reported that he has no patience with electronic devices. He hardly uses the computer, only about 15 minutes a day at most, and even that tends to happen only when his young brother is playing and he joins in. Jankó also does not use the computer for schoolwork. He is even embarrassed in front of his classmates and friends for not being competent in using computers.

Homework

Jankó has to be forced to do his homework, which he is always trying to avoid. It is mainly the father who can get him to do his homework as opposed to his mother, who has little influence in this situation. His mother believes that Jankó plays his parents off against each other. Although he sometimes works independently, he dislikes spending time doing so, but is very happy when his work results in a good grade. However, his experiences of success do not influence him to be less resistant when it comes to studying. So far, Jankó's studying is restricted to reading material repeatedly, which is not particularly helpful because of his poor comprehension. English, math, chemistry, and Hungarian are difficult for him mainly because of spelling. He is unable to do his homework in math and English without assistance from his father. However, it is mainly the difficulties he faces in chemistry that cause frustration and tears.

Sometimes, Jankó crams his homework into a quarter of an hour so that he can watch TV. His mother thinks that homework is beneficial because during her childhood she experienced that going over what she had learned at school gave her a sense of security as it strengthened her knowledge. Unfortunately, Jankó does not feel the same way.

Social Development

Although Jankó does not really have responsibilities at home, he gets upset when he has to water the flowers or take out the garbage. He rarely ever does the shopping. His mother tries to allocate tasks to the children. She recently showed them how to start the washing machine. The younger brother, Matyi, is more independent. He gets up by himself, wakes Jankó and they eat breakfast together.

Jankó is physically less mature than his peers. His knowledge of what's going on in the world is also immature and naive. He does have some natural wisdom, however, which is uncharacteristic of his age group. As a result, he mostly gets along with adults. His sensitivity is exceptional. He sees and observes everything. His great-grandfather used to call him "a sharp-eyed kid." His mother reported that Jankó's reading problem has always influenced his social relationships. She stated, "Because of his fear of failure, he belittles himself and as such he's afraid to establish relationships. Even in existing relationships, he's always waiting for the other to make a move. He's afraid of rejection." Jankó has enormous inner strength, and will not simply go along with the majority view. However, due to his self-esteem problems, he is at times also highly vulnerable, which makes him a target for bullies. Although such occasions do not always come to light, one of the signs is that Jankó becomes withdrawn. For example, he accidentally mentioned an incident at home, and cried a lot about it. His father's reaction was, "If you don't stand up for yourself, everyone will stamp on you." This led to a major conflict within the family.

In the interview, Jankó's mother portrayed him as a child who is not easy to get along with. He used to fight with his brother Matyi all the time, but now there is less rivalry between them. Jankó's relationship with his father is also very complicated. His father's unresolved issues and work problems have a huge impact on his interaction with Jankó. The mother adds, "It bothers him to see his own weaknesses in the child." Jankó's mother also has a difficult relationship with her son, especially when he tries to manipulate her.

Although Jankó would like to connect with his peers, he is unable to do so and is quite shy. His mother stated, "His inner world is closed . . . he projects himself as though the external world did not exist." In addition, Jankó has a highly peculiar manner of expressing himself as he talks in riddles. These shortcomings are counter-productive in terms of forming friendships, which is why his mother is helping him by trying to build relations with peers. Until recently, Jankó didn't even have an email address or a Facebook account. While his peers would keep in contact with each other, he would close himself off from them. A few days before this interview, his coach pressed him on the subject. So now he is on Facebook and has already chatted with a female classmate. Jankó also had a good relationship with his soccer coach when he got into a better club in seventh grade. They got on so well that the good experience was the reason Jankó stayed at the school. Although Jankó's relationships are limited in terms of numbers, he has a few people with whom he gets along well.

His mother reported that friends never visit him. She clarifies that although he is on good terms with everyone, he's afraid to go into deeper relationships. The only friend he has is Kristóf, a boy from his former school. Kristóf is very fond of Jankó as Jankó supported him in first grade. In his present school there is one boy, Miha, with whom Jankó also gets along well. Jankó himself never takes the initiative regarding friendships. Miha helps Jankó with computer science, while Jankó helps him in turn with math. The fact that Jankó teaches something himself makes him feel really good.

Self-Determination and Coping

Self-Efficacy and Motivation

Jankó answered questions from the Self-Efficacy Questionnaire for Children (SEQ-C; Muris, 2001) in order to determine how well he can handle academic and emotional challenges. On a scale of 1 to 5 with 1 indicating that he can barely do something and 5 showing he does it very well, most of his self-efficacy answers ranged between 1 and 3. During the interview, Jankó's mother stated that he easily gets distracted in school when he tries to study. Jankó indicated that he had problems with some of the items that focused on academic self-efficacy (e.g., how well he passes tests, pays attention in class and finishes his homework), but was somewhat more confident on others (e.g., how well he succeeds in understanding subjects at school and how well he satisfies his parents with his schoolwork). However, during the interview, he indicated that he does not always try to do his best at school as he is not always in the mood to do so. With regard to emotional self-efficacy, on some of the items that focused on not worrying and preventing himself from getting nervous, Jankó scored a 3 whereas on other items (e.g., suppressing unpleasant thoughts and controlling his feelings), he scored himself lower. Looking at his overall scores, it appears Jankó has somewhat low academic and emotional self-efficacy.

Jankó also answered questions from the Children's Hope Scale (Snyder et al., 1997), which reveals the level of hopefulness in children. The results showed that Jankó sometimes thinks that he is doing pretty well although he is not so confident that he is doing as well as other kids his age. His lack of confidence in his progress was probably illustrated during the interview when he stated that being tense had become a natural state of mind for him. He reported, "I'm always tense. Not being tense at school, that's hard. I'm used to it. It's been like that for 7–8 years." On the other hand, the results of the Hope Scale indicated that on a few occasions he manages to think of ways to get the things in life that are most important to him as well as to come up with solutions when he has a problem. And on some occasions, when others want to quit, he believes he can find ways to solve the problem. With regard to his reading abilities, his mother stated during her interview that Jankó was quite accustomed to being passive as he used to have the "I'm a dumb kid" picture stuck in his head. This seems to have finally improved since he moved to the polytechnic school. The results of the Hope Scale indicate that although Jankó is hopeful some of the time, he also has doubts about his abilities.

The Achievement Goal Disposition Survey (adapted from Hayamizu & Weiner, 1991) was administered to Jankó in order to determine if he derives his motivation for studying from intellectual curiosity (learning mastery), social approval or achievement of goals. This survey revealed that Jankó is not usually motivated by intellectual curiosity. It is only "sometimes" that he studies because he likes learning new things and feels good when he overcomes obstacles and failure. Jankó indicated that he studies because he wants to be praised by his parents and that he did not want them to be disappointed in him, but he is not particularly interested in what his teachers and other people think. In general, his reasons for studying were quite mixed, but mostly indicate that he "sometimes" studies because he wants to get a good job in future, have a good life and achieve success. Although he studies because he does not want to fail exams, he has not yet set goals for himself for future educational endeavors. Both his interview and his mother's revealed that Jankó does not study much. However, his scores in the Achievement Goal Disposition Survey indicate that on the few occasions he does study, the main reasons behind it are related to parental approval and goal achievement rather than intellectual curiosity.

Coping

The mother reported that before Jankó transferred to the new school, he had become accustomed to passivity. Whenever he made an effort to be proactive, he never succeeded, which hurt his feelings. The self-image of a "dumb kid" worsened and passivity became his way of coping. As a result, he did not put his heart into his tasks, but merely skimmed the surface, not daring to be more deeply involved. Jankó himself revealed that he does not even make an effort, since "bad grades are the usual thing" for him.

When asked how her son copes with frustration, the mother explained that he removes himself from the situation. She added, "It's as if it wasn't happening, as if he wasn't there at all." Jankó's natural approach to life changed due to the many failures he encountered at school. He shut the world out because he was afraid of relationships and his fear of disappointments led him to declare that he won't even fall in love.

The mother now finally acknowledges that dyslexia is the cause of most of his difficulties. Jankó, however, does not. He rationalizes that he reads slowly so he can better understand the reading material. He doesn't want to face his weaknesses, just as he does not acknowledge his strengths. However, since he switched to the polytechnic high school, he enjoys going to school more. The current school is his favorite so far. His mother explained: "He is on good terms with everyone, and does not get involved in violence. He hates being so sensitive. It's not the physical pain that hurts, but the psychological." According to his mother, although he is not really motivated to do his schoolwork, she thinks that he mostly does it to fulfill the obligations expected of him. She is of the opinion that his organizational abilities are coming along well and that the new school might have played a role. The mother observes that Jankó is definitely changing. He likes sports and art lessons very much and is actually successful in them. He invests some effort in these areas in order to achieve better results.

Impact on Mother

When asked how she would rate the stress associated with parenting a child with dyslexia, on a scale of 1 to 5 with 5 being the highest amount of stress and 1 being the lowest amount of stress, Jankó's mother rated it at 5. She feels she has done everything she can. For instance, when Jankó was expected to read Nils Holgersson for school, she read it to him at home in order to reduce his agony because the reading level was much too difficult for him. In fact, she reads to him a lot. Yet she fears that her support is insufficient to help him improve.

Jankó's reading problem also put a great strain on her relationship with her husband and added to the parents' estrangement. The mother reported that when it comes to parenting questions, there is little agreement. Her husband considers Jankó's reading problem as a weakness and is impatient with him. He gets irritated by both Jankó and his wife, but not by the younger son Matyi. The mother's dyslexia as well as her inferiority complex did not help matters. All these factors including her husband humiliating her in front of the children eventually led to her deciding to separate from him.

Jankó's dyslexia also adversely affects his relationship with Matyi. Jankó is constantly trying to repress Matyi in order to prove himself. This usually leads to Jankó humiliating his young brother. The whole situation impacts on Matyi such that he still wets his bed and bites his nails.

When asked to advise other parents who suspect their children might have reading problems, the mother recommended having a sense of community. In fact, she helps out in a number of groups in the community. She eventually found a better school for Jankó and a special needs teacher to assist him based on recommendations from friends. Sharing the burden with people close to her helps her a lot. She believes in focusing on solutions rather than problems. She finds that such an attitude can improve the quality of one's life as well as the relationship one has with the child. For Jankó's mother, confidence in both herself and her child helps her to pull through. She also points out that believing her son is capable of achieving goals is also important, adding "If I don't, how can I expect him to?"

Jankó's mother reported that she has learnt a lot from raising a dyslexic child. She stated that setting an example is important in parenting. If she starts accepting herself including her own dyslexia, her feelings of inferiority and her vulnerability, then she may be able to set an example for her son. She believes parenting should begin with introspection because if parents can see themselves clearly, they will also come to see their children more clearly. She emphasized that she has put an end to self-defeating thoughts such as remorse and regret as she realized that it is detrimental both to herself and her son's progress.

Future Goals and Hopes

Jankó's mother is uncertain about his future, but stated that what will happen to him will depend on a lot of factors. She clarified that it depends mostly on the coming years and perhaps it even depends on the present case study interview as it might help her to reconsider options for him. She believes that acting would be the ideal career for him because it would enable him to slip into other people's perspectives and feelings. Although Jankó still does not have faith in himself, when he eventually does, he will have great inner strength. Jankó's mother hopes that he will learn from his experiences and someday stop fleeing from things. She wants him to be himself as well as to embrace his happiness and pain alike and to endorse himself before the world. What she really fears is Jankó becoming even more frustrated, shutting himself off from other people and living a lonely life.

Jankó's immediate future goal is to get into a better soccer team and he is aware that he has to train harder in order to improve. He considers this goal extremely important as he likes sport and participates in it competitively. His second goal is to improve in everything, but he does not seem to think that he has to make any effort in order to do so. When asked about his future job, he indicated that it should be related to soccer but that he was not yet sure what sort of job it would be. The interview also required him to identify three wishes, but he only expressed that he would like to possess a magic wand that he could use for "conjuring anything, including traits and abilities."

Case Commentary

The condition of dyslexia is not related to diminished intellectual capacity. Individuals with dyslexia may even be outstanding in other areas, such as is the case with Jankó who performs really well in sport and art. These strengths have long sustained his self-esteem and his internal resolve to cope, but his ongoing struggle with his reading disorder has slowly chipped away at his dwindling self-confidence in abilities. Over the years, Jankó has lost more faith in himself. His mother reported that he has little self-confidence and views himself as "no good," hence not valuing his other talents. He has bad posture, which reflects that he has a lot of problems. He seems to be carrying a heavy burden and always has his gaze fixed on the ground. Lack of self-esteem is a common consequence among dyslexic students because of their experience of learning failures (Alexander-Passe, 2004; Humphrey, 2003; MacKay, 2004). Self-perception is the sum of an individual's thoughts, feelings, attitude and beliefs in oneself and it evolves within a social environment. Unfortunately, the learning experience for dyslexic students is about them not being good enough as they frequently observe that learning seems to take less effort for their peers (Humphrey, 2002, 2003). It is particularly difficult for dyslexic students if the adults around them fail to identify dyslexia or if the teachers regard the condition as the individual's fault. Dyslexic children are unable to see themselves in a good light if their environment fails to do so. If dyslexic students' abilities are judged according to how well they read, they will tend to adopt the view that they are not good enough. This in turn makes it extremely hard for them to develop a positive self-image.

Jankó considers his slow reading to be something unchangeable because he thinks it is an integral part of his personality. He cannot imagine how his reading and his learning could significantly improve even with adequate intervention. He regards the situation as rooted in his own incapability. This self-image might spread from reading to his entire life and surroundings. This is to be expected, as anxiety experienced in relation to reading difficulties not only affects learning, but also one's perception of the world (Tsovili, 2004). Children with specific learning difficulties are, therefore, also at risk of developing socioemotional problems.

Although dyslexia is officially classified as a disability in Hungary (Gyarmathy & Vassné Kovács, 2004) and knowledge about it has reached increased levels, it is not yet acknowledged by everyone in the country. Therefore, it would not be uncommon for dyslexia or any other learning difficulty to elude identification until adolescence. A number of teachers are of the belief that dyslexic students fail due to their laziness and/or poor abilities. The majority of those teachers who do know and acknowledge the existence of dyslexia regard it as a disorder that needs to be cured. Even diagnosed dyslexic students presently do not receive suitable support. As illustrated by Jankó's case, at the late age of 10, he was diagnosed with dyslexia and yet no specific dyslexia targeted support was provided. This led to his sheer misery in terms of learning effort at school. Jankó's case is unique in that he attended a Waldorf School at the primary level. These types of schools don't pressure the students to acquire reading skills, but rather wait for the gradual development of their prerequisite abilities. Research shows that the reading performance of children without reading disabilities attending a Waldorf School will be the same as that of children learning at other schools, but they escape the anxiety caused by the early expectation of performance (Suggate, 2009). As Jankó's case shows, within this educational system children with specific needs do not receive sufficient assistance in order to adequately develop their reading abilities. Therapy and targeted dyslexia prevention strategies are necessary to ensure that neurologically-based differences do not lead to severe disorders.

Attendance at the Waldorf School resulted in Jankó having another disadvantage compared to his peers because of the ban on computers. He did not have sufficient experience of using computers for digital literacy and communication purposes. Additionally he could not benefit from the use of assistive technology, an aspect proven to provide significant support for dyslexic students in the area of reading and writing (Gregor, Dickinson, Macaffer & Andreasen, 2003). Despite this lack of sufficient support from the Waldorf School, Jankó's most beneficial and successful encounter was at the Waldorf Olympics. He wanted to stay at this school because he came third in the running competition, which was a wonderful event for him. His mother thinks that the Waldorf School saw his potential and gave him a chance.

Jankó is now in a non-state funded school where at the age of 14, he is receiving learning method training. It should be noted that such schools are actually quite rare in Hungary. At this polytechnic school, Jankó has new opportunities both academically and socially. He is beginning to build relationships with his peers. After the initial failures, the amiable side of Jankó's personality as well as his talent may provide the opportunity for him to feel strong once again and to cope with his difficulties. Hope for success has a paramount effect on abilities, which is why an appropriate environment and education are important for dyslexics (MacKay, 2004). Jankó appreciates that his mother increased his prospect of a positive future by constantly looking for better schools for him and supporting his needs.

References

Alexander-Passe, N. (2004, March). *A living nightmare: An investigation of how dyslexics cope in school*. Paper presented at the Sixth British Dyslexia Association International Conference, University of Warwick, Warwick, UK.

Denhoff, E., Siqueland, M. L., Komich, M. P., & Hainsworth, P. K. (1968). Developmental and predictive characteristics of items from the Meeting Street School Screening Test. *Developmental Medicine & Child Neurology, 10*, 220–232.

Gregor, P., Dickinson, A., Macaffer, A., & Andreasen, P. (2003). SeeWord—a personal word processing environment for dyslexic computer users. *British Journal of Educational Technology, 34*, 341–355.

Gyarmathy, É. (2009). Kognitív Profil Teszt. *Iskolakultúra*, 3–4, 60–73.

Gyarmathy, É., & Vassné Kovács, E. (2004). Dyslexia in Hungary. A guide to practice and resources. In I. Smythe, J. Everatt & R. Salter (Eds.), *International book of dyslexia* (pp. 116–121). Chichester, UK: Wiley.

Hayamizu, T., & Weiner, B. (1991). A test of Dweck's model of achievement goals as related to perceptions of ability. *Journal of Experimental Education, 59*, 226–234.

Humphrey, N. (2002). Teacher and pupil ratings of self-esteem in developmental dyslexia. *British Journal of Special Education, 29*(1), 29–36.
Humphrey, N. (2003). Facilitating a positive sense of self in pupils with dyslexia: The role of teachers and peers. *Support for Learning, 18*(3), 130–136.
MacKay, N. (2004, March). *Success comes in cans, not can'ts – accelerating learning for dyslexic learners in the mainstream classroom through metacognition and emotional intelligence.* Paper presented at the Sixth British Dyslexia Association International Conference, University of Warwick, Warwick, UK.
Meixner, I. (1993). *A dyslexia prevencio, reedukáció módszere* [Method of dyslexia prevention and re-education]. Budapest: BGGYTF.
Muris, P. (2001). A brief questionnaire for measuring self-efficacy in youths. *Journal of Psychopathology and Behavioral Assessment, 23*, 145–149.
Smythe, I., Gyarmathy, É., & Everatt, J. (2002). Olvasási zavarok különbözö nyelveken: egy nyelvközi kutatás elméleti és gyakorlati kérdései. [Reading difficulties in different languages: Theoretical and practical issues of a cross-linguistic study]. *Pszichológia, 22*, 387–406.
Snyder, C. R., Hoza, B., Pelham, W. E., Rapoff, M., Ware, L., Danovsky, M., . . . Stahl, K. J. (1997). The development and validation of the Children's Hope Scale. *Journal of Pediatric Psychology, 22*, 399–421.
Suggate, S. (2009). *Response to reading instruction and age related development.* Unpublished doctoral dissertation, University of Otago, New Zealand.
Tsovili, T. D. (2004). The relationship between language teachers' attitudes and the state-trait anxiety of adolescents with dyslexia. *Journal of Research in Reading, 27*(1), 69–86.

12
VALERIY, A CASE STUDY OF A RUSSIAN ADOLESCENT WITH DYSLEXIA

Olga Inshakova

Valeriy is a 15-year-old adolescent who was originally diagnosed as dyslexic when he was in the third grade at the age of 9. Valeriy is a very sensitive and compassionate boy and during the interview he was relaxed and gave answers willingly.

Background

Diagnosis and Treatment

When Valeriy was 3 years old, his mother felt he had developmental problems and needed special assistance. He was referred to a Medical Psychological Pedagogical Commission (MPPC), which included a speech therapist, a psychologist, a teacher and a physician, in order to examine his case thoroughly. Valeriy was diagnosed as language delayed and as a result he was placed in a kindergarten for children with speech problems where he was offered a specific remedial program in order to improve his phonological awareness, vocabulary and grammar. Valeriy also attended individual sessions three times per week with a private speech therapist. These interventions resulted in a significant improvement as this speech therapist coordinated her therapy with the kindergarten remedial program he was already receiving. Despite these improvements, Valeriy still had to repeat a year in kindergarten as he did not meet the required standards to proceed to first grade.

Due to the delay that was caused by his speech problems, he eventually started first grade when he was almost 8 years old. In first grade, Valeriy experienced difficulties in the acquisition of reading and writing. Although he was taught letters and their sounds by the speech therapist, it was hard for him to identify them at school. Consequently Valeriy was placed in a remedial class where he was taught by teachers who usually had received special education training. In second grade, Valeriy's problems at school became much worse. He couldn't understand math problems and had difficulty with Russian writing exercises and comprehension of texts. In third grade, Valeriy returned to the general education class. Because of his reading and spelling problems, the school sent Valeriy to the Institute of Pediatrics where he was thoroughly examined by different specialists. It was determined that his intellectual potential was within normal limits and he was diagnosed as dyslexic by a speech therapist. Therefore, tutoring by a dyslexia therapist was recommended. Valeriy attended these tutoring sessions for 45 minutes three times a week. As a result, his reading performance improved: he succeeded in comprehending text at school, his marks were better and his mother didn't have to help him do his homework all the time. In fourth grade, he made progress at school as he had nearly overcome his problems with math and made fewer mistakes in reading and writing.

Family and Home Life

Valeriy lives with his family in a large city in Russia. Since his last interview, his mother has remarried. Valeriy has two brothers and he gets on really well with them. They spend a lot of time together traveling around the country, going to theaters, concerts and museums and skiing in winter. In spite of his dyslexia, Valeriy takes an active part in reading aloud with his mother in the evenings. Valeriy has his own duties at home, which are feeding and taking care of the family's pets. In his free time the boy is fond of designing ship models. It is important to point out that though there is a computer in the family, the boys do not use it frequently. Valeriy has taken an interest in sports, especially basketball. He also enjoys classical music.

Medical and Psychological Aspects

Valeriy has a history of congenital problems with his mitral valve and has suffered from intracranial pressure from an early age. He often develops headaches. When the mother was asked if her son was taking any medication for his health problems, she explained that although medication was prescribed for him, the parents decided they would be able to cure Valeriy themselves and refused to give him the drugs. Valeriy does, however, have homeopathic treatment once a year. Valeriy has astigmatism and is also short-sighted, but no corrective measures have been taken for his vision problem. Additionally he had problems remembering things and was, therefore, examined by psychologists at the Institute of Pediatrics three years ago. The specialists came to the conclusion that the problem was due to Valeriy's dyslexia and dysgraphia, which, in their opinion, was the result of his delayed speech development during childhood. No special treatment was administered for this diagnosis. When Valeriy worries about something or gets excited, he makes involuntary movements with his fingers. This also happens when he tries to formulate his thoughts and ideas and while he is doing his homework.

Educational Perspectives

Reading Achievement and Progress

Valeriy attends a private Orthodox school. His mother reported that she noted a significant difference between the first four years and the last four years of his school experience. In primary school, he encountered many problems associated with dyslexia and dysgraphia and he had bad marks in most subjects. However, Valeriy's mother noted that he has greatly improved and currently receives marks ranging between good and excellent for all subjects with the exception of English, for which he receives a satisfactory mark. The mother attributes this improvement to the support her son received from his teachers as well as her decision to return him to the general education class. The school had organized a special class for children with the same problems as Valeriy but he attended only briefly as his mother believed that learning in this class did not give him enough motivation to improve his academic achievement. She perceives special classes for children with speech problems as being more detrimental than positive as she feels this instruction delays the children's mental development. The mother reported that being in the general education class really turned out to be more effective for Valeriy because he was motivated to try and catch up with his classmates, which increased his achievement.

When the mother was asked to estimate her son's progress in reading for the last four years on a scale of 1 to 5 with 5 being the highest, she rated it between 3 and 4. She attributed this improvement to his daily homework routine and to the rather high demands for written tasks at school. His mother actually rates his organization skills with regard to school at 5, which is the highest rating one could give. In similar questions, Valeriy was asked to rate his own reading skill at the time of the last interview on a scale of 1 to 5; he indicated that four years ago his reading would have been a 3 but today he was closer to a 4. He attributed his reading growth to increased practice. Valeriy said, "I came across a book which turned out to be interesting to me and after that I began to read much more." His mother reported that the last time Valeriy's reading performance was evaluated was in the fifth grade, and she described his problems associated with dyslexia at the time as quite serious. Over the last four years both Valeriy and his mother believe he has greatly improved. When Valeriy was asked to name areas in which he excelled, he mentioned sports, art, geography and biology. However, math and English are still quite difficult for him. Valeriy says one of the hardest things about having a reading problem is that he often lags behind in class. His mother continues to assist him, but mainly in writing essays. She thinks that "Although he can understand the books quite well, he is not good at formulating his ideas, especially in a written way."

Despite the challenges Valeriy faces with his schoolwork, he not only fulfills all his reading tasks for school, but also reads a lot for pleasure. He even mentions that reading is his hobby. He adds, "I try to read a lot for practice." When he was asked how long he read for school related purposes, he stated that he read 90 minutes per day on weekdays only. As for non-school related purposes he indicated that he read at least 30 minutes per day on weekdays but also that he spent much more time on recreational reading at weekends. Valeriy admitted that he always tries to do his best at school, but adds that "sometimes I am in low spirits . . . I don't like bad marks." He identifies extra classes as the most important thing his parents have done to support him.

Teachers

Valeriy's mother reported that his school teachers have always been helpful and attentive to his needs. They were considerate and usually explained tasks extra carefully for him and additionally stayed after classes if it was necessary in order to provide him with individual tutoring. She reported that Valeriy's teachers always tried to adjust their tasks and demands according to his capacity. She has consistently attended parental evenings at his school as she thinks it is essential to have a mutual understanding with Valeriy's teachers and to precisely explain her son's situation to them. Valeriy's mother remarked that in the beginning when the teachers first met him, they were rather puzzled by his problems, but after some time they began to sympathize with him and they got along well. The mother emphasized, "I have always been grateful to my son's teachers for their support and understanding."

With regard to his teachers, Valeriy thinks that one of the most important things that teachers can do for their students is to present lessons in simple but interesting ways. He is convinced that his teachers understood that students have individual learning needs since they certainly tried hard to find approaches that suited each student. However, when asked to reflect back and identify what else he would have needed in his educational program that he did not receive, he alluded to the fact that he could have benefitted from even more individual attention from his teachers as he says, "Sometimes, when I ask a question, a teacher doesn't answer because he is distracted by another pupil, and I still have questions without answers." Overall, Valeriy seems pretty content with his teachers since when he was asked what he would change about school he simply wished for "a bigger gym."

Learning Style

Valeriy's favorite style of learning is through lectures and reading. Valeriy added that he liked being the first to raise his hand in class and give answers to teachers' questions when he wanted to show his knowledge. He does not regard computers as a helpful tool for his studies and, therefore, does not use them for his schoolwork. No textbooks or other instructional materials in digital form are available to students at Valeriy's school.

Homework

It takes Valeriy about two hours to complete his homework per day. In primary school, he used to spend more time on tasks as he couldn't do them independently. His mother had to help him with his homework all the time. This was mostly due to his inability to express his thoughts, especially in writing. But as Valeriy has become motivated to succeed, he has learned to organize himself and can now do his homework independently. He has become more self-assured and knowledgeable. However, his mother clarified that this doesn't mean Valeriy enjoys going to school, but he understands that it is his responsibility. He is motivated to do his homework as he is eager to succeed in his schooling. Whenever he gets bad marks, he says he does his best to repeat the lesson in order to improve his result.

Social Development

During the interview, Valeriy claimed that he had never been bullied or teased by classmates because of his dyslexia, but his mother's perspective differed as she said: "There were a few incidents when he was bullied, especially, in the seventh grade. He was very depressed. Fortunately, his teacher kept the situation under control and fixed it eventually." Regarding Valeriy's social skills, his mother stated that he got along with his peers on a neutral basis, but sometimes avoids them. She added that he does not really socialize with girls except for his female cousins. Valeriy has three close friends, all of whom are younger than him. His mother thinks this is because her son is not as mature as his peers. She is of the opinion that his reading problems certainly influenced his relationship with his friends. Valeriy's mother explained that one of the greatest challenges Valeriy experienced in school was that "he is not confident enough in himself and even avoids long school trips with his classmates." She described his self-esteem as rather low. The mother later added that the most beneficial support her son has received from the school in the last four years is the fact that his teacher helped him improve his relationship with his classmates. However, Valeriy is not very enthusiastic about taking part in different extra-curricular activities as he does not consider them his top priority. Asked to rate his social skills, his mother placed them between 3 and 4 on a scale of 1 to 5, with 1 being the least social and 5 being the most sociable.

Self-Determination and Coping

Self-Efficacy and Motivation

The Academic and Emotional Scales of the Self-Efficacy Questionnaire for Children (SEQ-C; Muris, 2001) were administered to Valeriy in order to find out how he perceives his own ability to handle academic tasks and to manage emotionally challenging situations. Answers were rated on a scale of 1 to 5, with 1 showing that he could not do something while 5 indicated that he could do something very well. His responses to the questions reflected that he had a rather low emotional self-efficacy. He rated himself at 1 for his ability to avoid worrying about things that might happen. His ratings for his ability to suppress unpleasant thoughts, to give himself a pep talk when he is feeling low and calming himself when he is scared were nearly as low, at 2. Although he indicated that he is not very successful at cheering himself up after an unpleasant event occurs, when asked during the interview how he deals with school related stress he responded, "I pluck up my spirit and go ahead." His response indicates that he has the ability to motivate himself when faced with difficult situations. Despite his very low ratings for most of the emotional efficacy questions, Valeriy rated his ability to control his feelings at 4.

Valeriy rated himself quite highly when it came to the academic self-efficacy questions as he placed himself at 4 for almost all homework and other school related questions. The only exception was his rating of 2 for his ability to study when he had other more interesting things to do, showing that it was difficult for him. According to his ratings, he is pretty confident about his ability to concentrate during lessons at school and to satisfy his parents with his schoolwork as well as to study for exams. Valeriy doesn't consider doing homework to be a difficult task for him as he rated his success in concluding his daily homework as high. As a rule he can do it without help, but if he comes across a task that he can't manage on his own, he asks his mother to help him. Similarly at school, he indicated that he can easily ask teachers for assistance when he finds something particularly difficult.

In order to gain more insight into Valeriy's motivation for studying, the Achievement Goal Disposition Survey (adapted from Hayamizu & Weiner, 1991) was administered. According to the survey, the motivation for studying can be divided into three categories: intellectual curiosity (learning mastery), social approval and goal achievement. Judging by his answers to the questions which inquire about his motivation for success at school, Valeriy is mainly driven by the will to achieve certain goals. His answers in this survey portray him as a boy for whom it is important that everybody believes that he is smart; he is also afraid of lagging behind his peers at school and failing exams. He indicated that his motivation for studying is getting good marks, being admitted to university, finding a good job and being successful in the future.

Valeriy's studying efforts are not really influenced by intellectual curiosity as he is less interested in solving problems, knowing new things, challenging difficult problems and is not really curious. He is, however, quite pleased whenever he manages to solve a difficult problem and feels good when he can overcome obstacles and failure. Valeriy's studying habits are also partly motivated by social approval. Although he is not interested in getting praise from his parents or pleasing them, he does seem interested in what his peers and teachers think of him. He studies because he wants to perform just as well as his classmates and does not want others to make fun of him.

Valeriy's answers on the Children's Hope Scale (Snyder et al., 1997), which measures hopeful thinking in relation to achieving one's goals, indicated that sometimes he thinks he is doing as well as other children of his age. When he has a problem, he sometimes manages to come up with ways to solve it and he can often think of ways to get important things in life. But when others want to quit working on a problem because it is difficult, he usually feels the same. Yet, he is optimistic and most of the time he thinks the things he has done in the past will help him in the future.

Coping

Valeriy is a sensitive and sympathetic boy and his mother believes that this is in many ways a result of the hardships he has gone through in his life. He sometimes gets upset when his dyslexia affects his school results. After receiving a bad grade, he goes home and rereads the material, trying harder to understand it in order to remember it and then he takes the test again. In order to cope with the frustration caused by his reading problems, he pointed out that he first tries to overcome the problem and if he does not succeed, he asks for assistance from his parents and teachers. His mother also added that what helps him to cope is the fact that he confides in her and when he does she tries to take the situation lightly as she believes this is the only way to help her son overcome his difficulties.

When Valeriy was asked what situations he found most distressing, he mentioned the ones when he had made foolish mistakes and received bad marks for them. He even remarked that he would remember these moments for the rest of his life. On the other hand, books and sports make him really happy. He also identified jokes, funny stories and a cheerful atmosphere as things that can cheer him up after an unpleasant event. He thinks it is normal that people fail sometimes as he is aware that one cannot do everything. When asked whether he blames himself or his teachers when things do not go particularly well, he stated that it depended on the situation. On some occasions, he believes he is not attentive enough, but on other occasions, his teachers do not explain things to his satisfaction.

Impact on Mother

There is no doubt that Valeriy's problems have had an impact on his mother's life. She rates the amount of stress she feels from parenting a child with dyslexia at 5 on a scale of 1 to 5. She shared some of her stressful experiences:

> I consulted many different specialists, when my son was little and they diagnosed a variety of diseases like autism and oligophrenia (i.e., intellectual disability). It was kind of a shock to me and, in fact, I just couldn't believe them. Later it turned out, it was me who had been right. I think it is very important for mothers not only to find good specialists, but also to rely on their own intuition and instinct.

She was later confronted with an explanation of her son's reading problems, which were said to be the result of a mental disorder. (A likely explanation for this could be that in Russia difficulties in reading acquisition have been linked to mild mental retardation or delayed psychological development (Kornev, Rakhlin & Grigorenko, 2010).) Valeriy's mother's reaction to this predicament was to immediately make an appointment with a specialist from the Institute of Pediatrics. Fortunately, thorough examinations showed that these fears were groundless. It was then easier for Valeriy's mother to accept the diagnosis of dyslexia.

A child with this problem requires a lot of attention and selflessness on the mother's part. In order to fully devote her life to her son, she had to leave her job and stay at home so she could provide Valeriy with the necessary support. Additionally, she had to invest a lot of time helping him with his homework, to have constant contact with his teachers, making them understand her son's problems, and to consult with different specialists. The amount of time she devoted to her son also affected her relationship with her second husband. She explained, "He doesn't understand my being too careful with him." When the mother was asked if Valeriy's reading problems also affected his relationship with his siblings, she said, "His brothers can see that I'm more permissive with him and they don't understand it, but on the whole they are on good terms with each other."

In addition to all the challenges she faces, certain aspects of her son's behavior, which are related to his reading problem, are a constant source of stress for her. She confided that his problems with his classmates really upset her. When she was asked to advise other mothers whose children had similar problems, she emphasized the importance of finding good specialists to correctly diagnose a child and paying attention to personal intuition. She also recommended that children with dyslexia should not be separated from others as this may lead to a lack of motivation for making progress at school and life in general.

Future Goals and Hopes

According to both Valeriy and his mother, Valeriy's goal for the immediate future is to pass the exams at the end of ninth grade. Hence, his priority goal is to pass the graduation exams with good results because they can influence his opportunities in the future. He is aware that his reading problems are a huge obstacle to achieving this goal and that in order to become one of the best students at school, he will have to work hard. Valeriy was asked if he thought his reading difficulties might be problematic for him when he leaves school. He admitted that they might be as they cause misunderstandings or may even cause him to fail other subjects. Valeriy's mother also expressed her anxiety about how he will cope in his adult independent life. Her main wish is that her son will get a good education and realize his full potential.

Valeriy imagines himself pursuing a future career as either a veterinarian as he loves animals and would like to take care of them or, following in his mother's footsteps, as an art restorer. His mother agreed with him and explained:

> We still have not made up our minds what field he should deal with. On the one hand, he is interested in the arts, but, on the other hand, he is really fond of animals and a career as an animal doctor also seems like a good prospect.

Valeriy's mother wished to highlight the following characteristic of her son: "I would like to point out that my son is a very sensitive and compassionate boy, which in many ways is the result of his experiences. He can sympathize with other people and understand their problems."

This is not surprising as when Valeriy was asked what he would wish for if he could be granted three wishes, one of his wishes was for good health for his relatives. He also wished to get a good education and to find a good job.

Case Commentary

Valeriy's elementary school years were characterized by feelings of inadequacy due to his reading difficulties. Although in kindergarten Valeriy had sessions with a speech therapist three times a week to improve auditory discrimination and the acquisition of sound-letter correspondences, he could not identify letters and their corresponding sounds when he was in first grade. In Russia, children are expected to master basic reading skills during the first few years of school where they have to initially learn how to blend sounds into syllables and identify syllables before they are taught whole word reading (Kornev et al., 2010). As the syllable structure in the Russian language is very complex, it is an additional hurdle for children with reading difficulties to acquire the necessary decoding skills. This is probably why Valeriy's reading problems intensified and he exhibited additional spelling difficulties. Valeriy was subsequently diagnosed with dyslexia at the age of 9 after which he attended extra classes with a speech therapist.

Both Valeriy and his mother think that his reading skills greatly improved in fourth grade. By that time Valeriy had overcome his difficulties with math and he made fewer mistakes in reading and writing. He took up reading as a hobby after reading a book that turned out to be very interesting. Although he still has problems, he fulfills all his reading requirements for school and enjoys recreational reading. For a child with dyslexia, Valeriy reads a lot for pleasure as well as for school related purposes, which is the main reason for his improvement. This is quite a big difference from the common scenario in Russia as research has revealed a decreased interest in reading in all school-aged children (Kornev et al., 2010). Since his mother reported that the last time his reading was tested was in fifth grade, it is not possible to know the extent of Valeriy's improvement. The behavioral manifestations of dyslexia in Russia include difficulties with reading speed, accuracy and comprehension (Kornev et al., 2010). Therefore, despite Valeriy's reported improvements by his mother, he might still be facing challenges in these areas that are impeding him from reaching his highest reading potential. However, since he has not repeated a grade and there were no comments in the interview that revealed that he is in danger of failing, this might be a good indication that he is performing to an adequate standard.

In terms of potential areas for improvement, it is a pity that there are no screen readers, textbooks or instructional materials available to him in digital form at school. Electronic devices such as computers can potentially help to remediate reading difficulties in children with dyslexia (Elliot & Grigorenko, 2014). Unfortunately, the right to use a computer for written assignments or using a tape recorder instead of taking notes during oral presentations is not granted by any regulations or law and not even considered as an option for supporting dyslexic students. What is possible in Russia, even though it is not regulated by law, are the following accommodations which can be implemented when the teacher so chooses: not requiring the student to read aloud during lessons, not penalizing the student for spelling and handwriting problems, allowing the student to use a dictionary during lessons, granting a longer period for the execution of tasks and assignments and allowing the completion of written assignments through oral presentations (Grigorenko, 2010).

As for his social life and emotional balance, Valeriy has improved. He actively participates in a number of sporting activities, but he avoids class trips with more intensive social interaction. In the early days at school he had been bullied and teased because of his poor reading skills. It might be that he was quite distressed by the incidents as he denied being bullied in the current interview, and it was his mother who brought this to light. This is not unusual, for as they become older children with dyslexia tend to downplay their difficulties or even disguise them in order to fit in with their peers (Riddick, 2010). Valeriy still experiences problems in reading, but has succeeded in compensating for them through other activities and he makes sure that they don't interfere with other aspects of his life.

For Valeriy's mother, having a son with dyslexia has meant a great sacrifice of her professional and personal life. It has also deeply affected her emotionally as she has been committed to helping him with all of his challenges. When her son started school, she spent a lot of time helping him with his homework. As he is not very good at formulating his ideas, she still supports him with writing compositions. Mothers are usually the ones in charge of the family's health and therefore tend to be the ones that shoulder most of the responsibility that comes with raising a child with dyslexia, which includes practical as well as emotional support (Riddick, 2010). Without his mother's constant proactive dedication, Valeriy would not be at the level he is today. It is clear that she is indeed his pillar of strength in navigating his challenging journey. When asked if she shares her son's problems with dyslexia with others, she indicated that she confides in her close friends. She also invests a lot of time meeting with his teachers to discuss her son's problems and to reach a mutual understanding of his needs. A survey conducted among primary school teachers in Moscow revealed that only 30% of them were aware of the existence of dyslexia (Kornev et al., 2010). Valeriy was therefore fortunate enough that he always had helpful and sympathetic teachers who supported him. The support he has been receiving from his mother and his teachers has been a strong contributing factor toward his improvement in emotional and academic well-being.

In conclusion, one can foresee that Valeriy, as well as his mother, might face other challenges in future. He still has to take his final school exams and get accepted at university. Sadly, most children with dyslexia in Russia fail to pass the composition college entrance exam as they are not given sufficient and consistent assistance to achieve standard literacy requirements (Kornev et al., 2010). Despite all this, Valeriy has some clear goals and, obviously, will do his best to achieve them. His chances of success will be quite high if he continues working as hard as he has been doing.

References

Elliot, J. G., & Grigorenko, E. L. (2014). *The dyslexia debate*. New York: Cambridge University Press.

Grigorenko, E. L. (February, 2010). *Report on the Russian language for the World Dyslexia Forum 2010*. Paper presented at the World Dyslexia Forum at UNESCO, Paris.

Hayamizu, T., & Weiner, B. (1991). A test of Dweck's model of achievement goals as related to perceptions of ability. *Journal of Experimental Education*, *59*, 226–234.

Kornev, A. N., Rakhlin, N., & Grigorenko, E. L. (2010). Dyslexia from a cross-linguistic and crosscultural perspective: The case of Russian and Russia. *Learning Disabilities: A Contemporary Journal*, *8*, 41–69.

Muris, P. (2001). A brief questionnaire for measuring self-efficacy in youths. *Journal of Psychopathology and Behavioral Assessment, 23,* 145–149.

Riddick, B. (2010). *Living with dyslexia* (2nd ed.). London: NASEN Routledge.

Snyder, C. R., Hoza, B., Pelham, W. E., Rapoff, M., Ware, L., Danovsky, M., . . . Stahl, K. J. (1997). The development and validation of the Children's Hope Scale. *Journal of Pediatric Psychology, 22,* 399–421.

13

JACOB, A CASE STUDY OF A CANADIAN ADOLESCENT WITH DYSLEXIA

Brenda Linn, Barbara Bobrow and Ronald W. Stringer

Background

Diagnosis and Treatment

Jacob is the older of two children in a close-knit, middle-class family. His parents are both university educated: his father is a self-employed engineer and his mother is a chartered accountant. Although Jacob had some minor medical difficulties in his infancy, he began first grade as a robust, healthy boy who related well to his peers, loved physical activity and showed promise as an athlete. His mother recalls him as having been "very verbal," although he had some articulation difficulties in his pre-school years. As is quite common in the large multicultural city in which the family lives, Jacob attended a tri-lingual parochial school (English, French and Hebrew). His kindergarten year seems to have gone very well. However, Jacob began to develop difficulties with attention and behavior during the first and second grades of elementary school. Concerned that her son might acquire a reputation as a troublemaker, his mother arranged for him to be assessed at a learning disabilities clinic that had a good working relationship with Jacob's school. The clinician who assessed Jacob found his overall IQ score to be in the high to superior range, but she noted that his phonological awareness and spelling skills were very weak for his age, and that his reading comprehension was far below the level that would have been predicted from his scores on oral verbal measures. The clinician who tested him noted some "anxious defensiveness" in his interactions. If he could not answer a question, for example, he commented, "This must be a university question!" Jacob's difficulties with attention appeared to be confined to the school setting, and were therefore seen as a probable consequence of his learning difficulties.

When Jacob's diagnosis of dyslexia was shared with the teachers at his school, the staff immediately arranged for him to have intensive remedial reading instruction in English, as well as curriculum adaptations in his other two languages (French and Hebrew). Specifically, Jacob's evaluation in French and Hebrew was to be based primarily on oral rather than written work. In addition, Jacob's parents enrolled him in a summer reading camp run by the clinic where his assessment was done. Both the school resource teacher and the remedial specialist at the clinic and camp used a modified version of *Words in Colour* (Gattegno, 1962), a synthetic phonics program. Jacob's mother was very impressed by her son's interest in, and mastery of, the *Words in Colour* sound chart. Jacob's father also found a computer-based phonics program that helped him greatly.

During fifth grade, Jacob would not accept pullout support for reading. At his own request, he received in-class support only. This support tended to focus specifically on tests, for which, because of his dyslexia diagnosis, he also was permitted to have a reader. At the end of year his report card was generally good, although his teacher commented that he talked too much. In sixth grade, Jacob accepted some 15-minute pullout sessions focused on tests, and he continued to have a reader. He also began to see a French tutor for one hour per week. This was not unusual, as the class expectations were very high, and many children were receiving tutoring. His report in sixth grade was very positive, and included the comment that he had a good attitude. In fifth and sixth grades, Jacob seems to have done some reading for pleasure outside of school. In the summer after sixth grade, he read six books for pleasure, all from the *Percy Jackson* series.

Seventh grade, which in Quebec is the first year of high school, was a challenging year for Jacob. He continued in the private school system, but transferred to a highly prestigious secular school where he had only two, rather than three, languages to cope with. The transition to the new school, and perhaps the transition to puberty caused him considerable anxiety. The new school provided an hour of remediation each week, which once again focused on preparing for tests rather than reading instruction. The whole class was given instruction in organizational skills (e.g., the use of an agenda, etc.). He did not have a private tutor that year, but completed seventh grade as an honors student. In eighth grade, Jacob found that memorizing facts was not one of his strengths. His teacher provided him with cues, and helped him review his notes in order to prepare for exams. His accommodations on exams, including the right to a reader and to extra time, have continued. At the end of the year, Jacob was once again on the honor roll. His only mark below 80% was history, in which he received a very respectable 79%.

Family and Home Life

Jacob lives at home with his parents and his younger sister. In the early grades, Jacob's school difficulties worried his parents, but the high level of cooperation and support that they received from the school and the learning disabilities clinic appears to have enabled the family to cope without undue stress or conflict. Jacob is passionate about sport, an interest that he shares with the rest of his family. Jacob's success as an athlete has provided him with the greatest sense of achievement and satisfaction. When not engaged in athletics, Jacob relaxes mostly by watching TV or spending time at the computer.

Medical and Psychological Aspects

Throughout his school life, Jacob has been a healthy and active child. Once he began receiving help for his reading and writing difficulties, and some extra coaching for examinations, Jacob's behavior difficulties quickly resolved. He gave up the role as class clown that he had briefly adopted in second grade and no longer came into conflict with his peers. On an emotional level, Jacob's mother finds that he is sometimes quite anxious, and Jacob certainly does not deny having been stressed out, anxious or scared. However, neither his parents nor the school have considered that his anxiety was serious enough to warrant any professional help.

Educational Perspectives

Reading Achievement and Progress

Jacob's reading and spelling skills were retested when he was in the middle of sixth grade, his final year of elementary school. At that time, all of his reading and spelling scores were in the average range for his age. The only remaining signs of dyslexia were his tendency to tire easily when reading and writing, and the fact that his listening comprehension remained superior to his reading comprehension. The clinician who originally diagnosed Jacob with dyslexia also did the follow-up testing for the present study. She commented she would have questioned both the earlier diagnosis and the need for accommodations if she had not done the earlier testing herself.

Jacob and his mother agreed that Jacob's reading problem no longer has much of an impact on his school performance. His mother rated the impact of her son's reading problem as "somewhat significant:" a 2 on a scale of 1 to 5. She reported that, every day of the week, Jacob spends half an hour working on the computer and/or reading for pleasure. Jacob clarified that the time he spends on the computer for pleasure is rarely spent reading—he does not look at Facebook or Twitter or anything of that kind. He said that he continues to read books (fiction) for enjoyment, and does so for about an hour at a time, but at most once a week. Like his mother, Jacob remembered clearly how much difficulty he previously had in reading. He rated his reading skill at the present time as 4 on a scale of 1 to 5, compared to a 2 in his early elementary school years. He attributed his improvement partly to tutoring, and partly to his own hard work. He credited his parents, too, with ensuring that he received the help needed.

Teachers

According to his mother, Jacob "loves his school," but she admits that he would much rather sleep in than get up and go off to class. Jacob's mother also highly regards the school. She commented, "I would not say I was satisfied with the school: rather, I *love* the school." She explained that constant communication between the teachers and the parents has ensured that Jacob "may slide at times, but he doesn't fall." She has found most teachers quite understanding of dyslexia, at least in the sense that they understand Jacob's need for accommodations and extra support. In fact, one of the teachers, who herself has dyslexia, has taught Jacob studying "tricks" using cue cards. Another teacher has invited Jacob to work on the school yearbook next year. Jacob's mother said that she has attended all the parent-teacher conferences during the past four years. At these meetings, the teachers have expressed satisfaction with Jacob's progress.

Jacob himself rates the help he has received at school as "satisfactory." He said that most of his teachers "realize that different students learn in different ways," and that they "can see that a student needs extra help and make accommodations." He particularly appreciated a teacher who treated him as a person, and would talk to him outside of class in a friendly way. He resented a teacher who was rigid in insisting that work be done independently, and who responded to requests for clarification by saying, simply, "Read the textbook." Since Jacob prefers to work in groups, rather than alone, it is not difficult to see why this approach would alienate him. Jacob's sociable nature is clearly one of his strengths—a strength that he uses to compensate for his relative difficulty in working alone and directly from the text. Interestingly, he did not mention this when he was asked how he drew on his strengths to compensate for his areas of weakness. Instead, he spoke about the way he used his strength in math to boost his performance in science.

Learning Style

Jacob's strongest subjects are English and mathematics, subjects in which his good reasoning skills are more important than his capacity for what he sees as rote verbal memory. His difficulty recalling facts is exacerbated when the facts are presented in French, as is the case in his history course. He considers the course boring; whether this is because he does not understand it very well is unclear. What is clear is that French remains Jacob's greatest academic challenge. He has moved into a higher-level French program, which requires him to take one of his core subjects in that language. His mother thinks that a large part of his difficulty with French is simply a lack of confidence that causes stress and anxiety. Jacob also has difficulty remembering facts and theory in science. This difficulty may also be directly related to language, and specifically, to phonological memory; he finds it particularly hard to remember the terminology.

Jacob does not appear to have any explicit metacognitive strategies for dealing with this difficulty, apart from a frequently reiterated belief in the value of hard work. He attributes the success of the best student in his class to a combination of being "smart" and working hard. But he commented, rather bitterly, that in order to become one of the best students in his school, he would have to quit sports and work all day, a prospect that does not appeal to him at all. He does not appear to have considered the possibility that working more strategically, rather than simply spending more time studying, might be an alternative more compatible with his love of athletics. The impression that Jacob does not strategize is drawn from the fact that when he does not do well, he simply blames himself for not working hard enough. He does not mention his tendency to leave things to the last minute, although, of course, he may see this as being just a part of not working hard enough rather than as a problem in its own right. However, Jacob does recognize that, in drawing on his strong math skills to boost his science marks, he is using a strength to help an area of weakness. He also finds that he remembers things better when he writes them down—apparently he does not particularly care whether they are presented visually or in some other modality. In math and science, he finds working through examples is the most helpful way of making sure that he understands the material.

Jacob is aware that there are resources (texts, study guides, etc.) available to him in digital form, but he did not comment on the value of these. He has never used a screen reader. However, he strongly prefers to write on the computer as he finds it easier than writing by hand, and in addition, he appreciates the spell check and the grammar check. (His mother wonders if perhaps he is too dependent on the spell-check feature.)

When asked how he could best demonstrate his knowledge, Jacob seemed not to understand the question. It did not appear that he has ever been offered any other way of showing what he has learned, apart from writing exams (for which he is given extra time). On the other hand, his mother reported that Jacob is beginning to see the results of mastering the material and not leaving studying to the last minute. He apparently commented recently, "Tests go well (or are fun) when you know the work!"

Homework

Jacob and his mother agree that he prefers to finish his work at school, but that he does an average of half an hour at home in the evening. His mother offers help willingly; she believes that homework is useful in reinforcing new concepts. However, Jacob works mostly independently, and on the whole resists and perhaps resents his mother's interference. His mother feels that he needs more study skills, not necessarily skills specific to dyslexia, but skills that will allow him to organize, plan and break his work into steps that would facilitate mastery of content. When Jacob himself was asked if homework was a little problem or a big problem, he was not willing to commit himself. His mother observed that she felt it might become a problem when the time demands increase in the higher grades. When asked how he coped when faced with an assignment he thought he could not do, he had no answer. Jacob's mother explained that her son only accepted her help "at the eleventh hour." Neither she nor Jacob clarified how frequently last minute crises arose.

Social Development

Jacob is a sociable person. On a scale of 1 to 5, with 5 being the most social, Jacob's mother believes he would be at 4. According to his mother, he has about six close friends, relates well to his peers and is a popular student. So far Jacob only socializes with boys—perhaps because he attends a boys' school, and none of his athletic activities is co-educational. Jacob's mother perceived his social development as being more mature than that of his peers and explained that he is not the type of adolescent who would "go with the crowd if he thinks it is not the right thing to do." She finds that, in general, Jacob shows good judgment, and is able to anticipate the consequences of his actions. She feels that his peers respect him for his leadership qualities. Jacob's mother indicated that she did not believe that his reading problem has influenced his relationship with friends, but Jacob commented that he personally finds that the most difficult thing about having a reading problem is that other kids do not understand.

Jacob's mother feels that her son has become a responsible person, who is in some ways very mature for his age. She did not mention any specific responsibilities that Jacob has around the house, but at school, he has volunteered to coach younger students in several sports.

Self Determination and Coping

Self-Efficacy and Motivation

Jacob reported without hesitation that daily sports make him happy, and that school makes him sad. However, at this point in the interview, his responses became rather laconic and he became withdrawn, almost to the point of being sullen. This style of responding, or not responding, is sometimes indicative of depression, and indeed, Jacob's mother recalled that in ninth grade, Jacob did seem quite depressed at times, a fact she attributed to difficulties in his relationship with an athletic coach at his school.

When asked to complete the Self-Efficacy Scale for Children (Muris, 2001), Jacob reported that he was very good at giving himself a pep talk and preventing himself from being nervous. He felt he was "quite good" at suppressing unpleasant thoughts. He gave himself a middle score for related skills such as calming down after being scared, or telling a friend he was not feeling well. His overall score for Emotional Self-Efficacy was 29 out of 40, which placed him above the mean of 26.5 (Muris, 2001). On the academically focused items from the same scale, Jacob gave himself middle ratings on almost all the items, although he reported being very good at passing tests, and rather poor at studying a chapter for a test. This contradiction may be resolved if we assume that he finds studying from a chapter in a book quite difficult, but has found ways to overcome or compensate for this difficulty. His overall score for Academic Self-Efficacy was 27 out of 40, which is again above the mean of 23.9 (Muris, 2001).

On the Children's Hope Scale (Snyder et al., 1997), Jacob's modal response was "some of the time." This represents a 3 on a six-point scale, which is slightly leaning toward the lower end, with an overall score at the 38th percentile (Bickman et al., 2007). He responded with "some of the time" to statements including, "I think I am doing pretty well" and "I think what I have learned will help me in the future," and also to statements about his ability to solve problems. This questionnaire was the only context in which Jacob allowed himself to sound just a little bit discouraged. But even here, in response to the statement, "I am doing just as well as other kids my age," he chose, "Most of the time."

In an effort to gain insight into Jacob's motivation for studying, the Achievement Goal Disposition Survey (adapted from Hayamizu & Weiner, 1991) was administered. This measure analyzes student responses in reference to three categories that identify motivation for studying: (1) intellectual curiosity (learning mastery), (2) social approval or (3) goal achievement. Jacob's responses to this measure overwhelmingly indicated that the first and foremost reason he studies is to achieve specific goals. He responded with an unequivocal "yes" to all of the goal-related items, including wanting to get as good grades as his peers, wanting to be admitted to university, wanting not to fail his exams and wanting to achieve success and have a good life. Jacob's responses indicate very clearly that he regards schoolwork primarily as a means to an end, and that the end is eventual success, including a university education and a good job. There does not seem to be any obvious reason that this goal-oriented approach to school would be more common in a student with reading difficulties than with any other student, unless, of course, the combination of struggle and focus on extrinsic rewards such as marks and the prospect of a good job have combined to dampen the student's love of learning for its own sake (Lepper & Greene, 1978, 2015). In Jacob's case, it may be unnecessary to invoke this rather sad possibility, since the goal-orientated motivation seems to reflect the values of his family and his school culture.

Jacob gave an unequivocal "no" to five of the eight items intended to probe intellectual curiosity, suggesting that he is generally not motivated to study for this purpose. It should be noted, however, that several of these items on the face of it appear to relate more directly to the student's sense of his own competence as a learner than to any intrinsic interest in the subject matter. Jacob indicated that he *sometimes* studied because it felt good to overcome a difficult problem or challenge, and that he *sometimes* studied because he was "very curious." When asked if he studied because he was pleased when he was able to solve a difficult problem, he responded "yes," although moments earlier he had indicated that he did *not* study because he found it interesting to solve a difficult problem. His responses, taken as a whole, suggest some ambivalence toward intellectual pursuits—as if he sometimes gets interested in spite of himself. Social comparisons, and social approval, appear to motivate Jacob's studying more than any intrinsic interest in learning. Jacob indicated that he did *not* study to avoid being made fun of, being disliked by his teachers or disappointing his parents, but he did sometimes study to obtain praise or respect from his teachers, parents or friends. His mother corroborated this, noting that Jacob is very competitive and wants to be one of the smartest kids in his class.

Coping

When he was asked about how he dealt with challenges, Jacob replied that he did not have any major challenges. When asked how he dealt with failure, he could not think of an instance of having failed. Perhaps he was thinking of failure in the literal sense of failing an exam or a grade, because he went on to agree that in life it was normal for everyone to fail at times. He explained, "I am fine with it, I just accept it." Never in the course of the interview did Jacob draw any connection or parallel between academics and sports. He never, for instance, used a sports-related example to explain how he dealt with a challenge, or a failure, or a disappointment.

In spite of the reticence he showed during this part of the interview, Jacob said that when he was feeling down, the thing that helped most was talking about it. This perhaps explains why his favorite teacher was the one who would talk to him, outside of class, as a friend. His mother confirmed the fact that, when Jacob is upset, he will "talk it out," either with her or with his father. Jacob also reiterated that when he was feeling stressed about school he watched television to take his mind off the problem. In addition to some episodes of mild depression, Jacob's mother says that he continues to suffer from mild anxiety. For example, he will still sometimes freeze during an exam. The strategies his mother suggests for dealing with this include taking a deep breath, moving around and "managing the anxiety." Jacob's other strategy for coping was simply to "try harder." This seemed, in fact, to be the only strategy he could think of to improve his performance either in school or on the playing field.

Impact on Mother

When Jacob's mother was asked whether she could identify specific times in Jacob's schooling and/or personal life when his reading disability was particularly hard for her as a mother, she said she could not. Yet later, she recounted her dismay and anger at discovering, when Jacob began second grade, that he was obviously struggling with reading and spelling, and that his first grade teacher had not communicated with her about this in any way. When confronted, the first grade teacher apparently explained that she thought Jacob would acquire reading skills in his own time, and should be allowed to do so. Although this was indeed the prevailing view in education when this particular teacher was trained (Goodman, 1986), Jacob's mother, and apparently the other teachers at his school, regarded this *laissez-faire* approach as evidence of laziness and a lack of concern. Jacob's mother recalls that, until her son was assessed and diagnosed with dyslexia, she also associated his poor schoolwork and his avoidance of reading with the child's laziness and lack of effort. Once she understood the nature of Jacob's difficulties, she felt "terrible" for having been hard on him in this way.

Jacob's mother says that she does not recall a time when her son's reading difficulties had a negative impact on her marriage. She explained that her husband is a person of infinite patience, and has always been understanding and kind to their son. Jacob seems to have a good relationship with his younger sister, but his mother wonders if he is perhaps a little envious of the ease with which she acquired basic academic skills. She recalls an incident when Jacob's sister, at the age of four, responded like lightening to a question about fractions (of the pizza they were sharing), and Jacob stomped off in frustration. Such incidents have been few, however, and have not been a major factor in their relationship.

Jacob's mother feels that her son does experience some daily stress related to his reading, that he tends to avoid subjects that involve a lot of reading and that he becomes quite anxious at times. However, she does not see this as causing stress in her own life. When she was asked to rate the amount of stress associated with parenting a child with dyslexia on a scale of 1 to 5, she chose 2. She explained, in general terms, that she tends not to become stressed—instead she focuses on finding a solution. Thus, when she first learned that her son was dyslexic, she responded by informing herself about dyslexia and by becoming very active in an organization that helps dyslexic children. She also has maintained close contact with Jacob's schools to ensure that his needs are met and that he is keeping up with the demands of his program. She is very open about sharing her experiences related to dyslexia with others. She shares her experiences in the hope of raising awareness of the problem, and creating greater understanding of her son, rather than as a means of relieving her own stress or anxiety. She clearly appreciates the fact that her son is accepted, understood and valued. Speaking in retrospect of his elementary school, she recalls, "They loved him." This statement was independently confirmed by teachers at the school.

Jacob's mother is proud of the way her son has coped with the challenge of his reading difficulties, but she does worry about his ability and/or willingness to deal with the increasing time demands of the higher grades and university. She also is concerned about the fact that, according to the rules of the Ministry of Education in the province of Quebec, Jacob will need to be retested in order to continue to qualify for accommodations. She fears that he may become a victim of his own success, and that the progress he has made may result in him losing the right to accommodations on which he depends. However, she regards this as a problem to be solved when the time comes. In general, neither she nor her son dwells on the emotional impact of Jacob's dyslexia, and they are reluctant to talk about how it affects them on an emotional level. When they do become upset, Jacob's mother prefers to express her emotions at the time, while Jacob has a tendency to withdraw, seek distractions and talk about it later when he has calmed down.

Future Goals and Hopes

Jacob's goals for the rest of his time in high school include doing well in history and doing even better in sports. He feels that the second of these goals matters more because he likes sports better. When asked what obstacles he might have to overcome to achieve these goals, he replied that the main obstacle would be other people—people who are better than he is. Once again, he identified hard work as the means of achieving both goals. He defined hard work, as it relates to sports, as "developing physical skills and techniques." He did not have a comparable explanation of what hard work in history would entail.

Jacob's mother said that her son is hoping to pursue a career in engineering, following in the footsteps of his father. She said that he is on his own now, that she cannot set goals for him and what is most important is simply that he be happy in what he does. She worries that his anxiety may get in the way of him achieving his goals. Jacob explained that he felt studying was important in order to attend a good university and get a good job to be successful in life. He had already explained he would like to play professional sports, but he did not reiterate this when asked directly about his future plans. Instead he became somewhat taciturn, and replied, "I don't know," with a shrug, to questions about what would be required to qualify for his chosen career. When asked what he would wish for if he could have three wishes, he replied without hesitation (or perhaps much thought), "money, a car, and physical skills."

Case Commentary

Jacob was diagnosed with dyslexia when he was 7 years old at the beginning of second grade. At that time he was a highly verbal, active, athletic little boy who was beginning to find ways of masking his reading difficulty by clowning and was showing signs of anxiety and hostility. He was in fact very like the boy with dyslexia described in the excellent children's book, *The Alphabet War* (Robb, 2004). Despite his high to superior verbal intelligence, Jacob's phonological awareness, word identification and spelling scores were all a standard deviation below the mean. A significant discrepancy between oral comprehension and reading comprehension has been proposed as the most meaningful way of identifying specific reading disability/dyslexia (Siegel, 1989; Stanovich, 2000). However, in Jacob's case, the older practice of focusing on an IQ-achievement discrepancy would also have supported this diagnosis.

Jacob's reading was reassessed when he was in the sixth grade. At that time, his reading and spelling scores had improved greatly, and were all within the average range for his age. He continued to find reading and writing effortful, and appreciated the accommodation (extra time) that he continued to receive. Jacob is now an honors student in the ninth grade at a prestigious private school. He is still given extra time for tests and examinations, and is able to use a computer with a spelling and grammar check for his assignments. With these measures in place, he feels that his reading difficulties no longer have a significant impact on his life.

The fact that Jacob was diagnosed with dyslexia when he was only 7 years old meant that the support he received in school fell somewhere in between prevention and intervention. Its effectiveness is consistent with findings on both. Early intervention greatly enhances children's chances of overcoming their reading difficulties (Vellutino, Scanlon, Small & Fanuele, 2006). Moreover, a systematic, synthetic phonics approach to reading instruction was identified by the National Reading Panel as the most effective means of preventing reading difficulties in at-risk children (National Institute of Child Health and Human Development, 2000). Certainly the use of such a program, both in school and in the summer reading camp, seems to have prevented Jacob from falling victim to "Matthew Effects," that is, to the exponential widening of the gap between good and poor readers that takes place over the course of elementary school (Nagy & Anderson, 1984; Stanovich, 1986).

Unfortunately, Jacob's situation must be seen as optimal rather than typical. He was fortunate in having vigilant parents and an attentive teacher, and also in having access to a private clinic where he received a formal psycho-educational assessment at an early stage of his schooling. Moats, Foorman and Taylor (2006) sharply criticized the practice of reserving early intensive intervention and/or accommodations for those students who have received a formal diagnosis based on a comprehensive psycho-educational assessment, since these are often beyond the means of many parents and/or school districts. Without the advocacy of his family, and without access to private resources, Jacob would not have received a full assessment and formal diagnosis until much later in his schooling, if indeed at all.

Jacob was also fortunate in attending a school that was able and willing to implement the recommendations of his assessment as soon as they received them. Specifically, he was fortunate that the school was able to provide him with an intensive, systematic course in synthetic phonics. This situation, at least in Canada, is relatively rare. Unlike England and Wales, provincial ministries of education in Canada do not tend to endorse synthetic phonics programs, or indeed, systematic phonics programs of any kind. The English program, *Jolly Phonics*, has been used to good effect in Canadian schools, but it has no official sanction.

Jacob's situation was also optimal in that his resource teachers were not only willing to implement the recommended instructional approach, they were able to do so effectively. Even in jurisdictions where code-based teaching has official support and sanction, there is no guarantee that students will receive what Rose (2006) described as "high quality phonics instruction." A large proportion of teachers lack the necessary knowledge and training to teach a code-based reading program effectively (Coltheart & Prior, 2007; Cunningham, Zibulsky & Callahan 2009; McCombes-Tolis & Spear-Swerling, 2011; Moats & Foorman, 2003). Moreover, these teachers tend to be unaware that their knowledge of the reading process is inadequate (Cunningham, Perry, Stanovich & Stanovich, 2004). This is a serious problem since, as Piasta and colleagues (2009) discovered, poor quality phonics instruction can be worse than no phonics instruction at all. Unfortunately, teachers' preparation to teach phonics effectively is unlikely to improve any time soon, since instructors in faculties of education tend also to lack the specialized knowledge that such instruction requires (Binks-Cantrell, Washburn, Joshi & Hougen, 2012; Joshi, Binks, Hougen, Dahlgren, Ocker–Dean & Smith, 2009) and are unfamiliar with the basic research that explains why code-based instruction is so important (Linn, 2013). Information that might improve this situation is not typically to be found in the textbooks used in most university education courses (Joshi, Binks, Graham, Ocker–Dean, Smith & Boulware–Gooden, 2009).

In Quebec, as in most parts of Canada, students are technically eligible for extra resource help and an Individualized Education Plan (IEP) even if they have not had a complete psycho-educational assessment and a formal diagnosis. This policy is intended to give students an opportunity to "respond to intervention" before receiving any formal diagnosis (McIntosh et al., 2011). The implementation of a "response to intervention" model in Canada (as well as the United States and the United Kingdom) is commended by Bond and colleagues (2010) as a means of discriminating between "casualties of instruction" and persons with true dyslexia. Clearly, the usefulness of this model depends upon the nature and quality of the intervention received, and therefore all of the difficulties discussed in the previous paragraph are pertinent here.

An additional complicating factor is that in Canada the ministries of education tend to avoid the terms *dyslexia* and *reading disability* altogether, even in describing children who do not respond to intervention. They prefer the more neutral term "learning difficulty in the area of reading." This may reflect the kind of confusion around the terminology that recently led Elliott and Grigorenko (2014) to propose getting rid of the term dyslexia entirely. However, the avoidance of the term dyslexia in ministry guidelines may, in turn, explain why many teachers, even resource teachers, are unclear about what dyslexia may entail. In one Quebec school, when the resource teacher was told that one of her students had dyslexia, she asked the clinician with great concern, "You don't think he might have a learning disability, do you?"

Jacob's situation is complicated by the fact that, although the term dyslexia is not commonly used by the ministries of education, it must appear in a student's psychological assessment in order for the student to receive certain accommodations, such as the right to take examinations orally, or to dictate answers to a "scribe." Moreover, the student must be reassessed at intervals in order to confirm that the diagnosis still applies. In Jacob's case, this may be a problem, since Jacob did, indeed, respond to early intervention. As noted earlier, the clinician who diagnosed him, and then retested him four years later, reported that she would have questioned the diagnosis if she had not made it herself.

The policy of requiring students to be retested to determine whether they are "still dyslexic" is problematic. It draws a sharp dichotomy between children who learn to read quite well if, and only if, they receive an early intensive prevention or intervention program that most children do not require, and those who continue to struggle in spite of these programs. Bond and colleagues (2010) suggested drawing this distinction in the context of their proposal that dyslexia be legally classified as a disability. On the other hand, it is difficult to justify excluding the former group from ongoing extra support in school as long as their success requires extra effort and causes stress beyond that experienced by those students who have never experienced any particular difficulty with reading. Unfortunately under the current Quebec regulations, this may be exactly Jacob's situation when the time comes for him to be reassessed to see if his dyslexia has "gone away."

For the time being, however, Jacob is one of the lucky ones, at least as far as his English reading is concerned. However, he continues to struggle with French, which is not only a challenging subject in its own right, but also the language of instruction for one of his other academic courses. Jacob's dyslexia does not appear to have come with more generalized language impairments that interfere with second language learning (Nash, Hulme, Gooch & Snowling, 2013). On the other hand, phonological processing difficulties affect reading in any alphabetic language (Gottardo, Chiappe & Siegel, 2002). Jacob does not appear to have received the systematic, explicit teaching of phonological awareness and phonics in French that he received in English, and his decoding in French may still be weak for his grade. Unfortunately, Jacob's mastery of French was not assessed during his recent evaluation, so this explanation must remain a conjecture.

Although he struggles with French, Jacob does not consider that his reading problem has much impact on schoolwork or his life any more. He does find, though, that he still needs extra time for examinations and access to a spell-check. The fact that his fellow students do not understand his need for accommodations is what distresses him most about his dyslexia at this point. This is understandable, since he is a very sociable boy, who values the good opinion of his peers. Jacob's social success is very much in keeping with Bruck and Melnyk's (2004) finding that the majority of dyslexic children have better than average social skills. These skills, and his athletic ability, will probably prove to be a source of resilience, as well as a way of compensating for his residual academic difficulties. Sports are what make him happiest, and they also provide an outlet for his competitive nature since in school he has to be content with being an honors student rather than being one of the very "smartest" in his class.

Jacob's motivation for doing well in school seems to be primarily extrinsic: he cares about winning the respect of his teachers and peers, and more importantly, he sees success in school as essential to having a good life, going to university and earning a good living. Although he sometimes gets interested in a subject or a problem for its own sake, it appears that focusing on the external rewards of doing well in school, together with the fact that school has been a struggle for him at times, may have undermined his innate interest in learning, at least to some degree (Lepper & Greene, 1978). This is particularly unfortunate as it relates to reading for pleasure. Unless Jacob becomes an avid, as well as a competent reader, he will miss out on the benefits of exposure to print that have been so clearly documented by Cipielewski and Stanovich (1992). These include vocabulary growth, verbal reasoning and general knowledge, all of which become increasingly important for students who, like Jacob, wish to excel in school and hope to pursue a professional career. On the positive side, Lepper and Greene (1978, 2015) have found that intrinsic motivation can be protected and reinforced by genuine praise and encouragement. The fact that Jacob has been invited to work on the school yearbook, for example, should reinforce his pleasure in working with words and ideas for their own sake, rather as a means to some future material goal.

Jacob's choice of goals for the present and for the future was interesting. He was clear about his short-term goals—he would like to do better in sports and in history. In making this choice, Jacob seemed quite consciously to balance sports against school, using the pleasure he derives from the one to counter-balance the aversive demands of the other. Jacob was able to break his sports goal down into sub-goals—acquiring physical strength and specific physical skills. He did not do this with his goal of improving in history, but simply spoke in general terms of working harder. This seems rather typical of dyslexic students, and probably of ordinary high school students as well. Jacob would benefit from some explicit instruction in analyzing an academic task, and in identifying the specific skills and steps that success in that task demands. In fact, explicit instruction in study skills is probably what would make the greatest difference to Jacob's prospects at this point in his school career. This would help him shift his focus from working "harder" to working more strategically and efficiently.

When he was asked about his long-terms goals, Jacob hesitated. One suspects that he fears he may have to make a choice between what he loves most, and what he sees as the only path to what he calls "a good life." Jacob may also have some doubts about his ability to achieve academically at university level. His mother says he wants to attend university and to become an engineer like his father. But Jacob himself said he didn't know what he wanted to do, and his responses on the Children's Hope Scale leaned just slightly toward the pessimistic end of the scale. Especially when he leaves home, Jacob may need help managing his occasional negative thoughts and his moments of panic. That said, Jacob's overall assessment of his abilities appears to be realistic and reasonably positive, very much in keeping with Burden's (2008) contention that dyslexic students are by no means doomed to have a low sense of self-efficacy and self-esteem.

Jacob has benefitted from explicit instruction in reading, and from a proactive, supportive home environment. He would now benefit from explicit instruction in stress management that would wean him somewhat from his dependence on his parents to help him work through his moments of anxiety. It would be good for Jacob to realize that even students with no specific learning problems often need support in this area. It appears, in fact, that the majority of adolescents have no specific strategies, beyond distraction, for coping with stress (Shapiro, Heath & Carsley, 2016) and that this, in turn, increases the risk of anxiety disorders, depression, immune disorders and conditions that directly affect students' ability to learn (Washington, 2009). There is a new, research-based stress management program recently developed at McGill University and being piloted in the schools in Jacob's community that might meet his needs very well (Shapiro et al., 2016).

Although it is desirable that Jacob become somewhat more independent in managing the stresses and demands of his schoolwork, Jacob's family is likely to remain one of the great sources of resilience in his life. His mother continues to be very proactive in assuring that Jacob has the help he needs in order to cope with the demands of his academic program. She has also shared what she has learned from Jacob's reading difficulties in the hope of improving the lives of other families with dyslexia. She feels that this is how she avoids becoming stressed herself—she focuses on finding solutions. She readily acknowledges that her ability to do this successfully has depended to a considerable degree on the fact that her husband has been entirely supportive, both of her and of Jacob, and also on the fact that she has had the resources to arrange a private assessment, to choose excellent schools and to provide Jacob with a tutor when he needed one. She is clearly proud of her son, and appreciates his maturity and his sense of responsibility. Jacob, in turn, is appreciative of his parents' support, and credits them with ensuring that he received the support he needed to deal with his reading difficulties. The family has worked together to overcome the various hurdles that they have encountered, and one feels that in the future, they will continue to do so.

References

Bickman, L., Riemer, M., Lambert, E. W., Kelley, S. D., Breda, C., Dew, S. E., . . . Vides de Andrade, A. R. (Eds.). (2007). *Manual of the Peabody treatment progress battery*

[Electronic version]. Nashville, TN: Vanderbilt University. Retrieved from http://peabody.vanderbilt.edu/ptpb

Binks-Cantrell, E., Washburn, E. K., Joshi, R. M., & Hougen, M. (2012). Peter effect in the preparation of reading teachers. *Scientific Studies of Reading, 16*, 526–536.

Bond, J., Coltheart, M., Connell, T., Firth, N., Hardy, M., Nayton, M., ... Weeks, A. (2010). *Helping people with dyslexia: A national action agenda. Report to the Hon Bill Shorten, Parliamentary Secretary for disabilities and children's services.* Retrieved from https://www.researchgate.net/publication/242485434

Bruck, M., & Melnyk, L. (2004). Individual differences in children's suggestibility: A review and synthesis. *Applied Cognitive Psychology, 8*, 947–996.

Burden, R. (2008). Is dyslexia necessarily associated with negative feelings of self-worth? A review and implications for future research. *Dyslexia, 14*, 188–196.

Cipielewski, J., & Stanovich, K. E. (1992). Predicting growth in reading ability from children's exposure to print. *Journal of Experimental Child Psychology, 54*, 74–89.

Coltheart, M., & Prior, M. (2007). Learning to read in Australia [occasional paper]. *The Academy of the Social Sciences in Australia, 1*, 1–11.

Cunningham, A. E., Perry, K. E., Stanovich, K. E., & Stanovich, P. J. (2004). Disciplinary knowledge of K-3 teachers and their knowledge calibration in the domain of early literacy. *Annals of Dyslexia, 54*, 139–167.

Cunningham, A. E., Zibulsky, J., & Callahan, M. D. (2009). Starting small: Building preschool teacher knowledge that supports early literacy development. *Reading and Writing, 22*(4), 487–510.

Elliott, J. G., & Grigorenko, E. L. (2014). *The dyslexia debate* (No. 14). New York: Cambridge University Press.

Gattegno, C. (1962). *Words in color: Background and principles.* Chicago: Encyclopedia Britannica Press.

Goodman, K. S. (1986). *What's whole in whole language? A parent/teacher guide to children's learning.* Portsmouth, NH: Heinemann Educational Books.

Gottardo, A., Chiappe, P., & Siegel, L. S. (2002). Reading-related skills of kindergarteners from diverse linguistic backgrounds. *Psychology Faculty Publications*, Paper 1. Retrieved from http://scholars.wlu.ca/psyc_faculty/1

Hayamizu, T., & Weiner, B. (1991). A test of Dweck's model of achievement goals as related to perceptions of ability. *The Journal of Experimental Education, 59*(3), 226–234.

Joshi, R. M., Binks, E., Graham, L., Ocker-Dean, E., Smith, D. L., & Boulware-Gooden, R. (2009). Do textbooks used in university reading education courses conform to the instructional recommendations of the National Reading Panel? *Journal of Learning Disabilities, 42*(5), 458–463.

Joshi, R. M., Binks, E., Hougen, M., Dahlgren, M. E., Ocker-Dean, E., & Smith, D. L. (2009). Why elementary teachers might be inadequately prepared to teach reading. *Journal of Learning Disabilities, 42*, 392–402.

Lepper, M. R., & Greene, D. (1978). *The hidden costs of reward: New perspectives on the psychology of human behavior.* Hillsdale, NY: Erlbaum.

Lepper, M. R., & Greene, D. (Eds.). (2015). *The hidden costs of reward: New perspectives on the psychology of human motivation.* Hillsdale, NJ: Psychology Press.

Linn, B. M. (2013). *In the wake of the reading wars: Cognitive psychologists' and teacher educators' familiarity with and evaluation of cognitive reading research.* Doctoral dissertation in the Department of Educational and Counselling Psychology and the Department of Integrated Studies, McGill University.

McCombes-Tolis, J., & Spear-Swerling, L. (2011). The preparation of preservice elementary educators in understanding and applying the terms, concepts, and practices associated with response to intervention in early reading contexts. *Journal of School Leadership, 21*, 360–389.

McIntosh, K., MacKay, L. D., Andreou, T., Brown, J. A., Mathews, S., Gietz, C., & Bennett, J. L. (2011). Response to intervention in Canada: Definitions, the evidence base, and future directions. *Canadian Journal of School Psychology, 26*(1), 18–43.

Moats, L. (2015, October 21). Defending the "D" word ... dyslexia [Web log post]. Retrieved from http://blog.voyagersopris.com/defending-the-d-word-dyslexia

Moats, L., & Foorman, B. R. (2003). Measuring teachers' content knowledge of language and reading. *Annals of Dyslexia, 53*, 23–45.

Moats, L., Foorman, B., & Taylor, P. (2006). How quality of writing instruction impacts high-risk fourth graders' writing. *Reading and Writing, 19*, 363–391.

Moats, L. C. (1994). The missing foundation in teacher education: Knowledge of the structure of spoken and written language. *Annals of Dyslexia, 44*, 81–102.

Muris, P. (2001). A brief questionnaire for measuring self-efficacy in youths. *Journal of Psychopathology and Behavioral Assessment, 23*, 145–149.

Nagy, W. E., & Anderson, R. C. (1984). How many words are there in printed school English? *Reading Research Quarterly, 14*, 304–330.

Nash, H. N., Hulme, C., Gooch, D., & Snowling, M. J. (2013). Preschool language profiles of children at family risk of dyslexia: Continuities with specific language impairment. *Journal of Child Psychology and Psychiatry, 54*, 958–968.

National Institute of Child Health and Human Development. (2000). *Report of the National Reading Panel. Teaching children to read: An evidence-based assessment of the scientific research literature on reading and its implications for reading instruction* (NIH Publication No. 00–4769). Washington, DC: U.S. Government Printing Office.

Piasta, C. A., Connor, C. M., Fishman, B. J., & Morrison, F. J. (2009). Teachers' knowledge of literacy concepts, classroom practices, and student reading growth. *Scientific Studies of Reading, 13*, 224–248.

Robb, D. B. (2004). *The alphabet war*. Park Ridge, IL: Albert Whitman.

Rose, J. (2006). *Independent review of the teaching of early reading*. Nottingham, UK: Department for Education & Skills Publication.

Shapiro, A. J., Heath, N. L., & Carsley, D. (2016). Pilot evaluation of the feasibility and acceptability of StressOFF Strategies: A single-session school-based stress management program for adolescents. *Advances in School Mental Health Promotion, 9*(1), 12–28.

Siegel, L. S. (1989). IQ is irrelevant to the definition of learning disabilities. *Journal of Learning Disabilities, 22*, 469–478.

Snyder, C. R., Hoza, B., Pelham, W. E., Rapoff, M., Ware, L., Danovsky, M., ... Stahl, K. J. (1997). The development and validation of the Children's Hope Scale. *Journal of Pediatric Psychology, 22*, 399–421.

Stanovich, K. E. (1986). Matthew effects in reading: Some consequences of individual differences in the acquisition of literacy. *Reading Research Quarterly, 22*, 360–407.

Stanovich, K. E. (2000). The future of a mistake: Will discrepancy measurement continue to make the learning disabilities field a pseudoscience? *Learning Disability Quarterly, 28*, 103–106.

Vellutino, F. R., Scanlon, D. M., Small, S., & Fanuele, D. P. (2006). Response to intervention as a vehicle for distinguishing between children with and without reading disabilities: Evidence for the role of kindergarten and first-grade interventions. *Journal of Learning Disabilities, 39*, 157–169.

Washington, T. D. (2009). Psychological stress and anxiety in middle to late childhood and early adolescence: Manifestations and management. *Journal of Pediatric Nursing, 24*(4), 302–313.

14
CHRISTIAN, A CASE STUDY OF A GERMAN ADOLESCENT WITH DYSLEXIA

Regine Meier-Hedde

Four years after the first interview, Christian was 16 years old and eager to share his story. He was diagnosed with dyslexia in second grade at the age of 9. Christian is a communicative young man with a wide variety of interests.

Background

Diagnosis and Treatment

During his second year of elementary school when Christian's reading achievement did not improve in comparison to his peers, he was evaluated and diagnosed with dyslexia. To evaluate his reading ability, the school administered the Züricher Lesetest (ZLT; Linder & Grissemann, 2000), which yields information about letter and word identification skills and oral passage reading competence. As Christian did not complete the entire oral passage reading task because it was too strenuous for him, the test results only displayed letter identification and word reading problems. Christian's word reading speed (1st percentile) was more affected than his accuracy (26–50th percentile). Additionally, Christian demonstrated severe spelling problems. In the two spelling tests, the Lory Rechtschreibtest and Sätze nach Bauer (see Kultursministerium, 1996), he scored at the 5th percentile with errors in phonetic and orthographic spelling. To assess his overall intellectual ability, the Hamburg-Wechsler-Intelligenztest für Kinder (Hawik-III; Tewes, Rossmann & Schallberger, 1999) was administered. The test results revealed that his intellectual potential was in the superior range (FSIQ=121, VIQ=123, PIQ=114).

After the diagnostic procedure had been completed, he was transferred to a different school with special classes for dyslexic children where he had to repeat second grade. By the end of third grade, he still could not read despite being in a special class that catered for children with reading and spelling problems. At the teacher's recommendation, he was admitted to a special clinic for children and adolescents with psychological, psychiatric, neurological and psychosomatic problems. The clinical diagnosis he received there included three disabilities: maladaptive social functioning, dyslexia and both fine and gross motor deficits. As a result, he was attended to by a reading specialist and received reading and spelling remediation as well as behavioral and perceptual therapy. The clinical therapist, was very well trained and had developed her own teaching programs for dyslexic children, hence, for the first time in years, Christian began to show significant improvement in reading. Christian's reading was tested again in fifth grade before the remedial program at the new school started, but the results were never communicated to the mother. He has since then not been assessed as his school does not offer such evaluation.

Family and Home Life

Christian lives with his parents in a small rural town in the eastern part of Germany. He maintains close contact with his older sister who lives in a different city with her husband and two young children. Since his grandmother, with whom he had an intimate relationship, recently passed away, Christian is often alone after school and is responsible for himself during this time as his parents both have demanding jobs. His friends don't live in the same village as he does, which is why he spends a lot of his free time with his cousin and their grandfather. Together they engage in wine making as a hobby. He also visits his other grandmother who lives across the street and, according to his mother, "spoils him a lot." At home he has household responsibilities, which mainly entail helping his father in the garden. Christian enjoys spending time with his immediate family and they like traveling together to different European cities and visiting museums. Their last vacation was a bike tour in Lithuania, which was his confirmation gift from his parents.

In summer, Christian uses his bike as a means of transportation. One of his favorite activities is cycling to the lake to meet his friends. During winter, he is quite secluded from his friends and spends a lot of time at home on his computer in order to communicate with them. This is because he is dependent on one bus, which takes him to his village, but runs only in the afternoons. Christian has just started working on getting his driver's license in order to improve his mobility and attain his independence. He also spends time listening to music online especially rock and heavy metal suggested by his friends. Christian engages in other social group activities; for instance, he traveled to France with his church group and to Auschwitz with the Anne Frank Society.

His mother reported that he is open minded and interested in a variety of topics like history, science and politics. Christian stated in his interview that he was very good at remembering history facts. He was quite passionate about his last project where he had to interview people from a different generation about his country's history. His mother added that she read newspaper articles to him so that he could be well informed of important issues. When asked what special talents or abilities her son had, she said, "He has an emotional talent, he easily makes friends, has a lot of empathy, he has a special social competence."

Medical and Psychological Aspects

Christian is a physically healthy young man for the most part. However, his mother reported that at times he suffers from back pain, dizziness and mood swings. He was earlier diagnosed with a corneal irregularity, but his eye sight has since greatly improved. During the interview, Christian was not taking medication of any kind but his mother said that at times he gets restless, withdrawn and rather anxious at night.

Educational Perspectives

Reading Achievement and Progress

In the last interview four years ago, Christian was in fifth grade. After fourth grade, he changed schools to his current school. It appears this change was for the better as his mother reported a significant difference between the elementary years of her son's schooling and the past four years. She stated that after the last change of school, Christian had a more stable environment with more continuity, which was important for his progress. He is still attending the same public school and is now in ninth grade.

In the sixth grade, the clinical therapist from the special education clinic that he attended in third grade trained some of Christian's school teachers by using a well-established program for dyslexic children that she and her colleagues had re-designed and updated (Koschay, 2014), which was then used to remediate the students. He received the dyslexia therapy in a group with other students, but unfortunately Christian did not get along with the remedial teacher who was in charge of the program and made limited progress.

In Christian's sixth grade end of year report, his class teacher commended him for his good general knowledge, which always enriched the class discussions. His report card also showed that Christian employs complex thinking strategies; however, compared to his cognitive skills his reading skills were lagging behind. He still needed to put much effort into reading texts, which slowed him down immensely. Regarding written tasks, the report card also indicated that he needed a lot of time to complete tasks, but managed to compensate for this shortfall with good oral participation. Christian's grade in German was a 3 on a scale of 1 to 6 with 1 being the best grade. This grade was quite satisfactory considering his reading and spelling difficulties. Looking at his report card, it is noteworthy that his performance in technical and science related subjects is particularly good as he received a grade of 2.

In order to receive further assistance for his problems in seventh grade, Christian's mother had to apply for social-emotional support, which could be provided to students according to school regulations. As Christian sometimes seemed emotionally distant, he was granted such help. Social-emotional support was provided by a teacher who assisted him during lessons by showing him how to work on certain tasks as well as by helping him with learning strategies. His mother commented that since Christian usually began a task, but rarely ever completed it due to poor time management, the program helped him in this regard. Additionally the new remedial teacher prepared interesting worksheets and a variety of games to meet his individual needs. In order to combine both reading and writing, they used a computer program that was more interesting than writing by hand. Regarding the nature of Christian's reading problems, the mother added: "He can read a word like 'Krokodil,' but words that are similar like 'schlief, viel, kriecht' cause problems for him. He has problems with endings of words, which change the tense of a word." Additionally, she reported that Christian struggles with reading comprehension. Because he takes a very long time to read, he ends up not comprehending the text.

Unfortunately, the new remedial teacher who had been helping Christian only stayed for a year. Christian's mother commented that this teacher was of the opinion that the program should have been continued for a few more years in order to adjust it to his needs and to allow real progress to take effect. His seventh grade report card indicated that he had difficulties in English as he was graded with a 4. He, however, showed an improvement in math from the previous year and for his new subjects such as geography and history he achieved a 2 which is quite a high grade. His teachers additionally mentioned that Christian structured his workload in a much better way. They also noted that his self-esteem had greatly improved and hence he was able to work on much more challenging tasks.

Christian had four new subjects in eighth grade. It is noteworthy that his overall performance deteriorated mainly due to the low marks in these new subjects where he was graded with a 4 in three of the subjects including English. In his report card, his teachers pointed out Christian was aware that he had to invest more time and effort into his schoolwork in order to have better results. His teachers acknowledged that his deteriorated performance was partly due to the disturbances from other students in class. During this period he was only actively involved in the subjects that were of interest to him. The report card also noted that the way he executed his mandate as class speaker boosted his self-confidence and was also very helpful for the rest of the class. In ninth grade, Christian's grades greatly improved; he was graded with eleven 2s and four 3s. For his project in history he achieved the best grade possible.

His mother pointed out that he has good grades in subjects like astronomy, maths and social studies as he is given the chance to display his abilities through class participation during lessons. She highlighted that he still had problems with his reading performance and that he needed the extended time that he was given to perform tasks. Christian's mother expressed concern and did not understand why, although her son can communicate quite well, he still had such a low reading performance level. She stated that she felt that most of Christian's teachers also did not understand the nature of the problem. An exception was his German teacher who conducted the social-emotional support that Christian received in eighth grade. For the first time after three years, she understood the complexity of the problems that a dyslexic child had to deal with as she worked on a one-to-one basis with him.

When asked to rate his own reading skill four years ago, on a scale of 1 to 5 with 1 being the lowest level and 5 being the highest, Christian indicated 4. When asked again to rate his reading during the follow-up interview, he placed himself at 3. Four years ago when Christian rated himself, he had just experienced a significant improvement from not being able to read at all to reading small text passages. His current progress is not as pronounced as it was earlier, hence his lower rating. Christian's mother rated her son's reading improvement level in the last four years at 2 on a scale of 1 to 5. She rated him so low because she had expected greater progress. Although her son reads newspapers and history books for pleasure, his mother thinks that this is insufficient and that he could put more effort into practicing on his own. However, he does not do so to avoid emotional distress. His mother reported that she sometimes reads him articles to make the task easier for him. When asked to rate the significance of his reading problem on a scale of 1 to 5, with 5 being the most serious, she rated it at 2. According to her, Christian spends about an hour reading on weekdays and this time is split between homework tasks, leisure reading and the use of a computer for reading purposes. Both Christian and his mother agree that he spends much more time reading during weekends.

Teachers

According to Christian's mother, there are some teachers with whom her son gets along quite well and some he does not get along with at all. Christian identifies his best teacher as his classroom teacher who is also his music teacher. He explained that she engages with the whole class and is very fair. Christian also credited his classroom teacher for understanding that students have different learning needs. He stated, "If you have a problem, you can talk to her. . . . And when she asks questions in class she doesn't address me." To clarify his statement, he added, "If we read a text in class and the text is difficult, I will never be asked to read it out loud." However, he explained that he has no problem reading text he has written himself out loud to the whole class.

Another teacher who was also quite helpful to him was his remedial reading teacher. In addition, his elementary school teacher from fourth grade also seems to have made a lasting impression on him, as he reported, "She always told me not to let things get me down and keep going. She really supported me." On the other hand, he said his worst teachers were his German teacher and his math teacher with whom he had disagreements regarding his working materials. Sometimes he felt personally attacked by these teachers. Although he doesn't want to say he has "lazy" teachers, it annoys him when they rely on worksheets instead of teaching students. And he doesn't like it when a teacher has an extended leave of absence for which the school fails to provide a substitute, which was the case for his German teacher who was out for five weeks. He also reported some negative memories about a first grade teacher who always told him that he was "dumb" and could not accomplish anything. His mother reported, "It's very important how he gets along with teachers. If they have different moods, he has a lot of problems with it."

When asked for his opinion on three of the most important things that a teacher should do for students, Christian stated that they should understand when one has certain weaknesses, explain to other students when someone is going through a tough time at home and lastly intervene and deal with students who interrupt a lesson as they can interfere with other students' learning. His teachers also confirmed that Christian thrives best in a quiet atmosphere.

Christian's mother now has to engage with more teachers compared to elementary school where students had only one teacher as opposed to the new school where he has a different teacher for every subject. Although she is grateful that her son gets support from his teachers, she wishes they would take a greater initiative in contacting her. Christian's mother reported that she is not really given any updates regarding his reading progress. For instance, when she asked the German teacher for feedback, the teacher avoided talking about Christian's performance. On the other hand, the mother appreciates that this particular teacher is considerate enough not to make Christian read difficult text aloud in class.

Overall, Christian's mother is not satisfied with the reading support that her son has received over the years from his teachers. Reasons for this insufficient support included the fact that teachers are not adequately trained on how to deal with children with reading and spelling disabilities, and insufficient funding for children with learning problems. The mother is of the opinion that the teachers in their state are also not motivated because they are not very well paid. She added, "Most teachers start with a lot of motivation, but after ten years they don't want to do things against the mainstream and they are exhausted."

Learning Style

Christian reported that he learns best by seeing and listening at the same time, as long as he does not have to do much reading. The ideal situation for him is when someone makes a presentation with visual elements. Similarly, the best way for him to demonstrate what he has learned is through oral presentations which he eagerly reported that he is very good at: "I had to give a presentation and I didn't use any visual aids. I just presented it orally and I'm really good at that. And I received an 'A' for that."

Christian's mother admitted, "I am always very happy when he finds something where he feels acknowledged so that other people can witness his abilities." Christian also prefers working in groups so that someone else can perform the writing task that he is not too fond of because he thinks that other students write better than he does. He would rather be the one that stands in front of the class to explain the visual aid that someone else has prepared. If he could change one thing about his learning environment, Christian would prefer that the lessons took place in smaller groups of 15 or fewer students. Another factor that he thinks could be improved is the font size on worksheets, which should be enlarged.

As is the case with most students, Christian would also like his education to be relevant and connected to his world. He would like to apply what he has learned in the classroom to the real world. He is most highly motivated to learn when his teachers connect the instruction to his environment as he noted, "I ask myself what it's good for that I know the Theorem of Pythagoras, if I don't know in which context it could be applied." Although none of his textbooks or instructional materials are available in digital form, computers still play a rather influential role in assisting him with his school tasks. He mentioned that when he has problems, he simply uses Skype to talk to his classmates and ask for help. Further, he identified his use of a computer as the main factor which influences his reading. He also uses it as his main means of communication with his friends. In summer he spends between two and three hours on the computer and in winter between four and five hours on a daily basis. Although very little of this time is related to schoolwork, Christian believes his recreational activities on the computer actually contribute to his reading development. He explained that:

> When you read on Facebook, you just try to get the main information, because if somebody writes to you, you cannot take ten minutes to respond . . . You have to write immediately and then you get your response. I also use it to ask my friend what he will be doing during the weekend and if he has time for me . . .

Homework

Christian's mother used to help him with his homework before but since seventh grade, she felt that it was his responsibility. Although she thinks that repeating the content of the lessons could be beneficial, she does not really believe in the value of homework and she thinks that the eight hours of school per day are sufficient. Christian spends about 10 to 30 minutes on his homework every school day. He also executes it pretty independently as his parents are both always at work and also lack the knowledge to assist him with difficult math problems as well as English. Christian does, however, experience difficulties in doing his homework as he is usually very tired after school. His mother describes his attitude, "He doesn't really take it too seriously and doing his homework annoys him as he thinks it is not necessary." Christian defended his actions:

> I'm too lazy to do it. I'm not a person who comes home after eight hours of school and wants do half an hour of homework. When I leave our house at 6:30 in the morning and come home at 4 o'clock, I'm not in the mood to do my homework.

When he cannot complete a certain assignment he simply copies it from his classmate in order to avoid punishment by his teacher. His mother admits that it is important for Christian to have time for himself to do nothing and just relax.

Social Development

When asked to describe Christian's self-esteem, his mother pointed out that he has two different sides, one that is afraid, shy and introverted and another side which is self-assured and confident. She explained that the side that comes out depends on how secure he feels in particular surroundings, adding, "If his environment scares him, it takes a little to make him feel insecure. He pretends like he is absent." His mother also describes him as someone who sometimes is sincere, more mature than his peers, has a clever outlook on issues and knows exactly what he wants. To illustrate these qualities, his mother recalled a situation whereby Christian had to end a relationship with his girlfriend as he felt that he always got caught up in the middle of the problems she experienced with her mother. She stated:

> And that emotionally drained him a lot. Then I told him that he can't take over responsibility for his girlfriend and that he doesn't have to endure situations which he can't stand. We supported him and Christian thought about it for a long time and he decided to end the relationship. His decision showed emotional maturity.

Christian's reading difficulties have not affected his relationship with his real friends, but his mother reported that he was once bullied simply because he was allowed more time during exams, hence, some students had the perception that he received special attention at school. Christian acknowledged and recalled some of the bullying incidents. His mother shed more light on another case that Christian did not mention: "The others excluded him from their group and, his classmates discriminated him, bullied him. He suffered a lot from that."

Despite the emotional turmoil these bullying incidents inflicted on Christian, he still displayed a great sense of resolve. When he was asked how he handled everything, he responded, "I did my own thing and knew that he [the bully] wouldn't be in the same class with me in fifth grade." It was of more importance to him that he got along well with other students in fourth grade. His mother reported that he also gets along very well with family members as well as his friends but tries to avoid the dominant students in his class. She explained:

> He complains about his classmates. He's more careful, because there are only a few in his class who are very dominant, which is the problem for him. They interrupt the lessons in school then Christian loses focus on the entire lesson. He is somebody who wants to study. He cannot concentrate when there is such a distraction in the classroom.

Christian has three good friends who include his cousin and two other classmates with whom he identifies as they are both reserved individuals. Christian participates in group activities such as his railroad club, although he would much rather meet his friends for a beer or two by the lake. His mother proudly reported that her son took part in a dragon boat competition and that their team did quite well. She also added that Christian's team, which is comprised of both girls and boys, interacts very harmoniously and that he has no problems socializing with the opposite sex. When asked to rate her son's social skills on a scale of 1 to 5 with 5 being the most social, she placed him at 4. His report cards also rate his social competence as excellent and show that he is very well mannered.

Self-Determination and Coping

Self-Efficacy and Motivation

The Academic and Emotional scales of the Self-Efficacy Questionnaire for Children (SEQ-C; Muris, 2001) were administered in order to find out how Christian perceives his own ability to handle academic tasks and to manage emotionally challenging situations. The scales ranged from 1 to 5, with 1 indicating that he cannot do something at all and 5 indicating that he does it very well. In relation to his academic efficacy, he indicated that he was good at paying attention during class and satisfying his parents with his schoolwork, both of which he rated at 4. He appeared to be quite moderate at other academic efficacy related aspects as he rated them at 3. This rating reveals that Christian believes he is moderately good at the following: getting help from his teachers when he gets stuck on a subject, studying for a test, completing his homework daily, understanding all subjects in school and passing tests. The only academic self-efficacy aspect which he rated at 2 was studying when there are other more interesting things to do.

In terms of emotional self-efficacy, Christian's answers displayed that he thinks he has the ability to calm himself down when he is scared, prevent himself from being nervous and remotivate himself again when he is feeling low as he indicated that he succeeds in doing these things quite well with a rating of 4. Christian rated the following aspects of emotional self-efficacy at 3: suppressing unpleasant thoughts, not worrying about things that might happen, conveying to a friend that he is unwell, controlling his feelings and picking himself up again after an unpleasant event. His answers to the self-efficacy questionnaire reflect a moderate to quite good general self-efficacy.

Christian also responded to questions from the Children's Hope Scale (Snyder et al., 1997), which measures hopeful thinking in relation to children's goals. According to this scale, Christian thinks that most of the time he is doing very well; he can think of numerous ways to acquire the important things in his life and he is doing just as well as his peers. A lot of the time Christian comes up with ways to solve his own problems and he believes the things he has done in the past will help him in the future. Sometimes he can find a solution to a problem even when others want to quit. The results from the Hope Scale illustrate Christian's positivity and hopeful thinking. Such a positive outlook is probably a contributing factor to his improvement in his school performance after his deterioration in eighth grade.

To determine if he derives his motivation for studying from intellectual curiosity, social approval or future goal orientation, the Achievement Goal Disposition Survey (adapted from Hayamizu & Weiner, 1991) was administered to Christian. In order to have an insight into his motivation for studying, Christian had to indicate "yes," "no" or "sometimes" to various possible statements that fall under three categories: intellectual curiosity (learning mastery), social approval and personal goal setting. Overall, it appears he mainly studies out of intellectual curiosity and in order to achieve future goals since he answered "yes" to most of the reasons in these segments. For the motivations classified under intellectual curiosity, he only "sometimes" studies because it is interesting to solve a problem, but he does not derive his motivation for studying from the mere pleasure of tackling difficult tasks nor from seeing how much he has improved. Social approval plays very little to no part in Christian's motivation for studying as he indicated "no" to most of the reasons under this section. It is only "sometimes" that he studies because he wants to be praised by his parents and does not want them to be disappointed in him. He did indicate though that he does not want others to think that he's incapable. Although his answers show that he also derives his motivation for studying from the goals he has set for himself (e.g., to be successful, to have a good life and a good job in the future), he is not interested in being admitted to university.

Coping

Christian's mother explained that when her son is frustrated due to school pressure or reading difficulties, he withdraws from his environment and uses avoidance strategies in order to cope with the situation. Both parents try to assist him as much as they can by letting him travel to different countries so that he can diversify his experiences beyond his academic life. His mother also added, "My husband also supports him by working with him in the garden so that he can do things that are totally different from school work." She further explained that although he is very motivated, he is not so confident. She added that, "He is very afraid of new things and he doesn't want that someone sees that he can't do certain things."

Christian nonetheless values his family's support and the acceptance he gets from his friends. He elaborated that what makes him really happy is that he has nice friends with whom he can spend his free time. He is glad that they listen to him, accept his dyslexia and include him as a member of their group. When asked what he does when he feels down, he described that he distracts himself by taking a walk through the neighborhood with good friends. He added that it is a nice feeling to know that there are people who are there for him when he is feeling low.

Christian identified his need for much more time to finish a task than his peers as the hardest thing about having a reading problem. In order to keep up, he says he tries to read as fast as possible and also gets help from his classmate who sits next to him. Christian has no wish to be the best in his class as it would mean that he would have to work harder and consequently sacrifice his social life, a price he is not willing to pay.

Impact on Mother

Christian's mother rated the amount of stress associated with parenting a child with dyslexia at 4 on a scale of 1 to 5 with 5 being the highest amount of stress. The most difficult time for the mother was when Christian was in first grade. She felt very helpless as she had no idea what was causing his problems with regard to reading acquisition. When Christian was diagnosed in second grade, she endured health and diet related problems due to the constant stress. Christian made little progress at the time and the family barely had a normal life for the next five years, but are now taking things step by step as they believe it is beneficial for all of them. His mother pointed out, "My husband and I needed time to live with it, but now that's in the past." She also emphasized, "You have to accept your child the way he is. Who else should give him this acceptance?" Thankfully, Christian's dyslexia has not affected her relationship with her husband in any way. However, even though her husband does not take an active part in their son's school life, he and Christian still engage in a number of activities together such as shooting and working in the garden. The highest amount of stress they experience as a family is usually at the end of the school year before Christian receives his report card when he already knows that the results are not very satisfactory or if he had problems with one of his teachers.

Regarding Christian's severe reading problems, his mother observed that "teachers always think that if [the child] practiced more [he] wouldn't have the problem." It is quite difficult for mothers to cope with their dyslexic children alone especially when teachers do not understand the extent of the problem. This is why she thinks it is crucial that she actively takes part in teacher-parent conferences twice a year and that she always takes Christian along with her in order to enable him to also express his views as well as hear first-hand what his teachers have to say about his performance.

Although Christian's mother is very supportive of her son and is always prepared to go to his school when he requests it, she also expects him to directly approach his subject teachers or his class teacher if he is experiencing problems with any of them. During the elementary school years when she had to help him with his schoolwork, she had less time for herself and other things, but now she seems grateful that she mainly just provides him with moral support. In addition to being her son's pillar of strength, she also gives him a lot of advice:

> I tell him that it will be easier after he has left school and started working in a job. He has to find something that really suits him, but people have different careers and sometimes they only find out later what they really want. So it doesn't really matter which profession he chooses first. He will find out if it's the right choice for him and I think we will have to support him for a longer time.

Understandably, Christian's mother also needs some form of support herself, which is why when it comes to her son's dyslexia related problems, she usually confides in her sister, her parents or one of her own employees whose daughter has dyscalculia. She reasons:

> I can speak to people who have an understanding with these problems. But I don't talk to everybody. It's his problem and I don't want to make it public because it only belongs to him.

She is specifically grateful to her son's pediatrician, the clinical therapist and his seventh grade remedial teacher all of whom understood his problems quite well and managed to adequately help him. Christian's mother noted the continued support of her husband who also calmly supported her son's every effort. Through her experience with raising her son, Christian's mother admits that she has become a good advisor to other people who face similar challenges. She cautions parents with dyslexic children to be patient and not be too hasty in expecting results. Regarding the lessons she has learnt from parenting a child with dyslexia, she declared:

> I have learnt to be patient and it was more than I expected from myself. And that everybody has to be accepted as he is. I learnt not to expect too

much and just to be content when my son is happy and to let him take his own steps. If I let go a little bit, it brings us closer together. I tell him what I expect from him, but the decision is his. That's what tolerance is about.

When asked what advice she would give to other mothers who suspect that their children might have reading problems, she recommended that they should concentrate on the needs of the child and seek expert help instead of concealing the problem. Her additional advice for parents and teachers alike, who have direct contact with children with special needs like Christian, is:

That teachers or assistants should read the instructions to the student so that he knows what he has to do. That parents should realize what wonderful children they have. It's always hard for parents to see what their children can do. You always see first what they can't do.

Future Goals and Hopes

Christian's most important short-term goals are to improve his grade point average and to pass his tenth grade exam. He acknowledges that he has to pay more attention in class and not get too worried before an exam in order to achieve these goals. He remarked, "I have to read a lot in German and in English and these are the biggest obstacles I have to overcome." His mother reported that she reminded him that he would have to use his last report card to apply for an apprenticeship, therefore, he needs to ensure that he gets good grades during his last year in school. She wishes that he could stop using avoidance strategies and practice his reading on a more regular basis in order to improve his reading ability.

Christian does seem quite aware of the importance of learning how to read and illustrates this with the following comment, "You have to know where you put your signatures later on. Somebody sells something to you, 10 vacuum cleaners ... you should read that before." Christian understands that reading will play an essential role in order to properly execute one's job in the future, but he also indicated that this was highly dependent on the type of job one chooses to pursue. When asked what kind of a job he would like to have when he finished school, Christian stated that he wanted to be a carpenter or metal constructor. He added, "A job where I don't have to read too much." He explained that he previously did an internship at a blacksmith's and enjoyed the experience as he understood everything that he was expected to do. His mother has always thought that since he is very good at communicating he would use this skill to decide on a career path. She acknowledges that although he wants to work with his hands she does not believe that he will do that for the rest of his life. The main thing is that she simply wants him to be happy regardless of which field he pursues. She witnessed him happy for the first time during his internship at the blacksmith's shop as she had not expected him to like that line of work. Due to this experience, she stated: "I think if he starts with an apprenticeship, it will be better for him. Maybe later on he might say that this is not enough. Then he will have the strength to try something else." Christian also mentioned that if he could change something in his life, it would be to pursue the academic school track instead of the vocational track as he believes that "With a high school degree, you can be more successful," even though he does not want to pursue a career with significant literacy demands.

At the present moment, the mother thinks that it is important for him to move to his own apartment soon so as to improve his organizational skills. She justified herself by explaining that she always has to remind him of how much time is left before the bus leaves in the morning, or else he would lose track of time. If she could change any aspect of her son's schooling system, Christian's mother would recommend that the subject matter of what they are taught be reduced. She thinks that:

> They don't learn important things they need in life, like how to communicate properly or how to manage time. I always see that when I have interns in my book store. They are not able to listen to an instruction and cannot execute it correctly.

Like any mother, she wishes her son well, but when asked in what way she thought her son's reading problems might affect him in future, she openly expressed her fears:

> He will become afraid in certain situations, he cannot perform in a way he would like to and he will come to his limits. . . . he will get very ambitious, but then he very quickly reaches his limits. He wants more, but I think his environment won't give him the opportunity . . .

Christian's mother thinks that her fears might be the result of everything that her son had to go through because of his reading problems. She constantly pointed out during the interview that he has to put so much extra effort to meet the demands at school and is thus always exhausted. This pushes him to his limits as it tires him out and prevents him from displaying his full potential. With Christian's above average IQ, his good grades and successful oral presentations, he has probably much more potential than his mother believes. As evidenced by the teachers' comments in his report cards, his teachers do not share his mother's fears. She nonetheless hopes that her son will receive enough support to build a solid foundation on which he can fall back in the future so as to be able to live a happy, healthy and normal life. When asked what he would wish for if he were to be granted any three wishes, Christian simply wished for a driver's license, enough money to maintain his car, to live for the moment and not have to do things.

Case Commentary

When Christian was interviewed four years ago, he was quite a vibrant and socially engaged child. He was diagnosed with dyslexia at the age of 9 when he was in second grade. Unfortunately his elementary school years were characterized by demoralizing experiences as he received no support from his teacher who scolded him in front of his classmates for his reading difficulties. In comparison with the first six years of his school life, he has gradually adapted to living with his reading disability over the last four years. The older he got, the more his academic performance improved but he still encountered severe problems in reading and spelling. Although the reasons are unknown, most dyslexic children who receive adequate support experience only minor improvement in reading and spelling (Schulte-Koerne, 2010). Christian received a highly professional intervention that unfortunately only lasted for a limited time. While there is still no concrete research regarding the duration of support for dyslexic children, it is clear that such support should be sustained since the child's needs change according to the growing reading demands at school (Elliott & Grigorenko, 2014). Christian's case demonstrates the importance of individualized programs administered by specially trained educators or therapists in supporting dyslexic children. There is, however, no nationally recognized training for dyslexia therapists in Germany, but the German association for dyslexia and dyscalculia (Bundesverband Legasthenie und Dyskalkulie e.V.) has recently established an initiative that certifies training programs where the graduates receive extensive theoretical and practical training (Schulte-Koerne 2010).

At the end of sixth grade, at a students' evaluation meeting held by Christian's teachers, it was recommended that he pursue the track that ends with an exam at the end of tenth grade leading to an apprenticeship or employment. The German school system provides three different kinds of tracks, two of which are more vocational oriented and the third track is more academic based. When attending the first two tracks, students are more likely to go straight into an apprenticeship or employment and upon graduating from the third track they have the necessary prerequisites (high school diploma) to pursue an academic career at a college or university. Based on Christian's current grades, it is possible for him to transfer to a school that leads to a high school diploma. The mother, however, felt that Christian might be over-burdened by this option due to the higher standards in high school. She acknowledged that after completing an apprenticeship, Christian might still choose this career path as he had acknowledged in his interview that he would like to get his high school diploma. On the other hand, he could face further difficulties after school since in this evolving world where there are constantly changing academic and professional expectations, dyslexia can continue to cause problems during one's career (Mugnaini, Lassi, La Malfa & Albertini, 2009).

The growing academic demands faced by students as they get older exert extra pressure on a dyslexic student since reading is a pivotal part of most tasks. Christian has thus experienced various challenges and has undergone a lot of emotional distress. Being misunderstood by teachers, having to deal with reading and spelling problems, with associated bullying and having to put a tremendous amount of effort in his school work made his life stressful. An additional factor that his mother pointed out is that Christian always wants to have everything under control and uses a lot of energy to do so. Sometimes Christian's mother notices a side of him that is shy, frustrated, afraid and withdrawn from his environment. A review of various studies shows that dyslexia is a contributing factor to depression and anxiety in children of school age (Mugnaini et al., 2009). Fortunately, the supportive atmosphere Christian has at home as well as the good relationships he has with his friends and extended family, combined with the experienced assistance from his clinical therapist, give him the stability he needs to handle the challenges. A study conducted with dyslexic adults regarding the long-term emotional effects of living with learning difficulties since their childhood revealed that professional and parental support plays an important role in reducing the recurrence and magnitude of negative experiences (McNulty, 2003). Christian's strong bond with his friends and cousin provide a pleasant social buffer for him to compensate for his experiences with his persistent learning difficulties. His mother agrees and pointed out that he enjoyed socializing with his friends and rated his social skills at 4 on a scale from 1 to 5 with 5 indicating the most sociable. Research has established that good relationships with family and peers promote a positive self-esteem by encouraging healthy psycho-social adjustment (Terras, Thompson & Minnus, 2009). This is true for Christian, but greatly depends on how secure he feels. His confident side is more likely to dominate his personality if he experiences a secure environment most of the time. This might happen when Christian finds a job he enjoys and in which he succeeds.

Despite the hardships Christian has had to endure, he is very fortunate to have different positive aspects that give him the conducive environment he needs to cope and develop himself. His teachers, parents, therapist and a great social circle have played an important role in ensuring his success. It is very important to have such a supportive and cooperative atmosphere for a dyslexic child to reach his potential. If he continues on such a positive path, he is likely to achieve a great deal more in the future.

The interviewer and Christian's clinical therapist stayed in contact with Christian and his mother after the completion of the interview and he happily communicated that he had successfully passed his tenth grade exam with good to very good grades in all subjects except for German, which he passed with a lower grade. Christian could have continued to obtain his high school diploma, but decided to first enter an apprenticeship program in a technical field. As is common in Germany, in this program he works in an office and also goes to school. His new German teacher praises him for his reasoning abilities and his valuable contributions to the classroom discussions. For the first time, Christian is receiving good grades in German. Christian and his mother are both very relieved and feel that they have chosen a path with many opportunities for future job success and life happiness.

References

Elliott, J. G., & Grigorenko, E. L. (2014). *The dyslexia debate*. New York: Cambridge University Press.

Hayamizu, T., & Weiner, B. (1991). A test of Dweck's model of achievement goals as related to perceptions of ability. *Journal of Experimental Education, 59*, 226–234. doi:10.1080/00220973.1991.10806562

Koschay, E. (2014). Silben-Stämme-Stolperstellen [Syllables-roots-stumbling blocks]. In S. M. Behrndt, H. Hoffmann, & E. Koschay (Eds.), *Kompedium. Zum Abbau von Schwierigkeiten beim Lesen und beim Rechtschreiben* [Compedium for the reduction of difficulties in reading and spelling]. Rostock, Germany: Eigenverlag Greifswald.

Kultursministerium (Hrsg). (1996). *Erlass zur Förderung von Schülern mit Lese-Rechtschreibschwierigkeiten und einer förmlich festgestellten Legasthenie* [Regulations for the remediation of students with reading and spelling difficulties and for officially recognized dyslexia]. Schwerin, Germany: Mittlbl. Des Kulturministeriums Mecklenburg-Vorpommern.

Linder, M., & Grissemann, H. (2000). *Züricher Lesetest (6. Auflage)* [Zurich Reading Test (6th ed.)]. Bern, Switzerland: Huber.

McNulty, M. A. (2003). Dyslexia and the life course. *Journal of Learning Disabilities, 36*, 363–381. doi:10.1177/00222194030360040701

Mugnaini, D., Lassi, S., La Malfa, G., & Albertini, G. (2009). Internalizing correlates of dyslexia. *World Journal of Paediatrics 5*, 255–264. doi:10.1007/s12519-009-0049-7

Muris, P. (2001). A brief questionnaire for measuring self-efficacy in youths. *Journal of Psychopathology and Behavioral Assessment, 23*, 145–149. doi:10.1023/A:1010961119608

Schulte-Koerne, G. (2010). The prevention, diagnosis and treatment of dyslexia. *Deutsches Ärzteblatt International 107*, 718–727.

Snyder, C. R., Hoza, B., Pelham, W. E., Rapoff, M., Ware, L., Danovsky, M., . . . & Stahl, K. J. (1997). The development and validation of the Children's Hope Scale. *Journal of Pediatric Psychology, 22*, 399–421. doi:10.2466/pr0.1999.84.1.206

Terras, M. M., Thompson, L. C., & Minnus, H. (2009). Dyslexia and psycho-social functioning: An exploratory study of the role of self-esteem and understanding. *Dyslexia, 15*, 304–327. doi: 10.1002/dys.386

Tewes, U., Rossmann, P., & Schallberger, U. (1999) *Hamburg.Wechsler-Intelligenztest für Kinder dritte Auflage (Hawik-III)* [Hamburg Wechsler Intelligence Scale for Children]. Bern, Switzerland: Huber.

15

JIM, A CASE STUDY OF AN AMERICAN ADOLESCENT WITH DYSLEXIA

Peggy L. Anderson

At the time of the follow-up interview, Jim was 14 years old and presented as an interested adolescent with a very pleasant personality. As Jim attends boarding school on the East Coast, this interview took place when he was home for spring break. Even though he was giving up break time from school for the lengthy interview, he did not seem to mind. At the time of the previous interview four years ago, he had some difficulty staying seated as he preferred to walk around the room during the questioning. During the current interview, he did not appear to have any difficulty staying in his chair. He was slightly fidgety, but very attentive. Although he was quite engaged in the interview, his gaze was often averted. Jim was originally diagnosed with a reading disability at the age of 7.

Background

Diagnosis and Treatment

When Jim began preschool at the age of 3, he experienced problems learning the names of letters and sounds and writing his name, skills he was unable to accomplish during the three years he spent at that school. He started kindergarten at the age of 6 and four months later was placed on an Individual Literacy Plan (ILP), which involved the provision of pull-out services (i.e., the child is taken out of the classroom and provided with supplementary reading instruction) for purposes of learning letters and associated sounds. In midyear, school personnel determined that Jim had made insufficient progress and referred him for a full evaluation. Referral reasons included: "unusual behaviors in class, including little or no eye contact, self-stimulation, high anxiety, overt need for a large amount of personal space, slight aggression when angry, difficulty with associating letter names, sounds and form, spatial awareness and perception, weak fine motor skills" as well as achievement scores well below expectations. Although Jim was originally given the Wechsler Preschool and Primary Scales of Intelligence-Third Edition (WPPSI-III; Wechsler, 2002) at the age of 5 when he was evaluated for anxiety by a psychiatrist, his comprehensive evaluation for the school referral included a second IQ test (i.e., the WISC-IV; Wechsler, 2003) that measured Jim's intelligence to be within the average range. The results of this IQ testing were consistent with the previous results: average intellectual functioning with strengths in verbal comprehension and weaknesses in processing speed. The speech and language evaluation revealed strong expressive and receptive language skills with weakness noted in pragmatic and social skills, particularly in terms of need to increase eye contact. The Woodcock Johnson Tests of Achievement III (W-J III; Woodcock, Shrank, Mather & McGrew, 2007) placed his oral language skills at the 70th percentile while performance on the Test of Early Reading Ability—Third Edition (TERA-III; Reid, Hresko & Hammill, 2002) placed his reading at the 1st percentile. The discrepancy model of evaluation was implemented and Jim was identified with a specific learning disability in the area of reading. Subsequently, an Individualized Educational Plan (IEP) was developed to address his instructional needs in the areas of reading and writing. This IEP stipulated that Jim would receive two hours per week of resource support (small group instruction in a special education class) in addition to one hour of supplementary support in the general education classroom. Thirty minutes of weekly consultation was also to be provided to his classroom teacher in an effort to assist her in providing appropriate instruction for Jim. In spite of this support, Jim did not show much, if any, improvement in reading and his self-esteem worsened. The homework demands were overwhelming for Jim and his family; he worked an hour and a half most evenings to try to keep up. After three years in the public school, the parents became disillusioned and decided to investigate other schools that might be better able to provide Jim with the reading support he needed.

After much consideration, the parents decided to send Jim to a private school that provided specialized instruction for students with average to above average potential and learning differences, such as dyslexia and attention-deficit/hyperactivity disorder (ADHD). This school was located in Denver, 95 miles from their home in a small mountain community in Colorado, and necessitated a move that separated the family as the mother took an apartment in the city for herself and Jim while the father and younger son stayed in the family home. At the beginning of third grade, Jim was given another evaluation as part of the application process for his new school. This evaluation included another administration of the WISC-IV (Wechsler, 2003), which provided confirmation of previous results (i.e., IQ within the average range with the same pattern of strengths in verbal comprehension and weaknesses in processing speed). The W-J III Tests of Achievement (Woodcock et al., 2007) were also repeated and revealed continued weakness in reading (Broad Reading Cluster Score at the 4th percentile) and average functioning in math (Broad Math Cluster at the 48th percentile).

In general the move to the new school was a positive one and Jim immediately seemed to do better. His mother said at that time, "It seemed like the greatest thing in the world." He got along with both teachers and peers and seemed to really enjoy school for the first time. His reading program, the F.A.S.T. Reading System (Tattum, 1998), used a multisensory approach that focused on auditory processing, phonics and literature-based instruction that was aligned with the National Reading Panel's (NICHD, 2000) five essential components of reading instruction (i.e., phonemic awareness, phonics, vocabulary, comprehension and fluency). The homework policy was vastly different from the public school; Jim was only required to spend approximately 30–45 minutes on homework per evening, 15 of which were devoted to reading. This school appeared to be an excellent match for Jim's needs and he continued there from third grade through the beginning of eighth grade. He seemed to be making progress in reading, but as he moved into adolescence, things started falling apart at home as Jim began making less effort and exhibiting more behavior problems. Although his teachers reported few problems at school, Jim's defiance and poor anger control at home were causing major problems and his parents decided to investigate residential schools.

Two months into the eighth grade, at the age of 14, Jim was sent to a short-term outdoor education program for students with learning and behavioral difficulties. At this time, Jim's parents sought a comprehensive evaluation to obtain recommendations regarding alternative educational placements. This evaluation included Jim's fourth intelligence test (i.e., WISC-IV; Wechsler, 2003), which confirmed previous results (i.e., average intelligence with strength in verbal comprehension and weaknesses in processing speed). This evaluation also included academic testing with the Wechsler Individual Achievement Test—Third Edition (WIAT-III; Wechsler, 2009) as well as an emotional and behavioral assessment. The psychologist's report included the following diagnoses: reading disorder, mathematics disorder, disorder of written expression, ADHD (combined type), depressive disorder, oppositional defiant disorder and generalized anxiety. The psychologist recommended a boarding school on the Eastern Seaboard of the United States that specialized in working with adolescents with learning and behavioral problems where Jim was placed after his two months with the outdoor education program. After six months in this program, his parents are fairly pleased with the progress he has made. At this point it has not been determined if he will return home to resume attendance at his private school or will continue in his boarding school in the East for the remainder of high school.

Family and Home Life

Jim has a younger brother, a dog and a pet mouse. According to the mother, Jim does a good job with his chores at home, which include taking care of the pets, setting and clearing the table, making his lunch and cleaning his room. This is a close-knit family that enjoys hiking, riding bikes, taking walks and attending sporting events together. The family is also close to their extended families whom they travel to visit every year. Jim's parents made the decision that the mother would not work outside of the home so that she could give all of her energy and effort to Jim and his brother. This decision was made, in part, because of the additional support Jim needed. She and her husband believe that it is important "to have one person who can be solely dedicated to the job" of parenting as the mother described it. After it became clear that the private school was a good match for Jim, the father and younger brother moved to Denver and the father now commutes 95 miles to the mountain community for his work.

Prior to placement in boarding school, home life had become increasingly stressful due to Jim's behavioral problems. There were reports of lying, stealing and experimenting with alcohol and marijuana. He had always been very close to his mother, but their relationship has deteriorated in the last couple of years as Jim moved into adolescence. In the past, she was consistently the parent he would listen to—the one who could calm him. Since her "relationship with Jim started crumbling," she has noticed that he has become increasingly manipulative and on occasion has even threatened her. The mother told Jim's psychologist, "He used to listen to me more, but lately that has not been true." There has always been an increased level of stress between Jim and his father as Jim told the psychologist, "We are both really stubborn and we don't walk away from fights." In recent years, there have been physical altercations between the father and the son. Jim has also been physically aggressive toward his brother and has damaged things in the home during times when he could not control his anger. In one situation, the family was experiencing a stressful incident that included missing a plane to go on vacation and returning home to find a dangerous gas leak. Jim's anxiety and frustration levels became so high that he picked up a hammer and used it in a threatening manner; the family resorted to calling the police because of the volatility of the incident. The officers who responded were well versed in this type of episode and calmly helped Jim to reduce his anger and give up the hammer. He did not have to go to the police station and the mother was pleased by the way the officers defused the tension and handled the situation without exaggerating the offense.

Jim's relationship with individual family members has been complicated by his learning and behavior problems. His mother said that, "It has been bad for all three of us;" however, it has probably influenced Jim's younger brother less than the parents. This is because the younger brother has become more involved with sports and other activities outside of the home and is less focused on Jim's problems.

Medical and Psychological Aspects

Jim's early development was typical until the age of 3 when he developed self-restricted eating patterns; at one point he had stopped eating all foods except for peanut butter and bread. He also experienced excessive crying problems and challenges associated with tolerating boisterous preschool and social activities that seemed to overwhelm him. In spite of the pediatrician's advice not to worry, the parents sought a psychiatric evaluation at a university-affiliated medical center, which resulted in a diagnosis of generalized anxiety disorder at age 5. Jim received play therapy for three years; however, this did not seem to help so the parents eventually agreed to have him medicated with Zoloft. He continued with Zoloft for several years and then was switched to Wellbutrin, which he currently takes along with Abilify to increase the effects. The mother believes this has been beneficial to some extent. He also has taken different medications to control the symptoms of ADHD and currently takes Intuitiv. From ages 4 to 9, Jim benefitted from sensory integration therapy to address his discomfort with tactility, eating and anxiety issues as well as fine motor problems. During the fourth grade at the age of 10, Jim began seeing a psychologist for support for his behavior and academic problems. Jim likes this therapist and the mother feels this has been a valuable therapeutic relationship. She has indicated that Jim will probably continue with the therapist when he returns home.

As noted in the previous section, Jim has recently been diagnosed as having oppositional defiant disorder and depression in addition to his reading problems. Although he denies the depression, the psychologist believes that he is "vulnerable to experiencing mild depressive symptoms . . . sadness, guilt, self-criticalness, tearfulness, agitation, and loss of interest."

Jim's history of medical problems includes eye tracking difficulties that were addressed with orthoptic exercises. The mother and his current ophthalmologist do not believe that these exercises were effective and he continues to have difficulty with visual tracking. Recently Jim broke his arm in the outdoor education program when he fell off a pile of logs. He had to undergo surgery for the compound break that required the insertion of metal plates for support and consequently has a lengthy scar on the inside of his arm, but he has had full recovery of functionality.

Educational Perspectives

Reading Achievement and Progress

It is difficult to discern how much reading progress Jim has made since he was diagnosed with a reading disability in kindergarten. Over the course of his school career, he was given many different achievement tests often with inconsistent results. For example, at the end of Jim's sixth grade year, he was given the Kaufman Test of Educational Achievement—Second Edition (KETA-2; Kaufman & Kaufman, 2004), which was the test that the private school used to assess progress. The results of the KETA-2 measured his Letter and Word Recognition at a standard score of 92 and his Comprehension with a standard score of 90. However, the most recent Wechsler Individual Achievement Test—Third Edition

(WIAT-III; Wechsler, 2009) given midyear of eighth grade, measured his Word Reading at the 4th percentile, Decoding at the 7th percentile and his Reading Comprehension at the 53rd percentile. To further complicate Jim's test performance, he has widely discrepant performances on the two Iowa Tests of Basic Skills (Hoover, Dunbar & Frisbie, 2005) that he took in sixth and seventh grade. In the sixth grade, his Vocabulary Reading score was at the 36th percentile and Comprehension at the 75th percentile with Spelling at the 3rd percentile and in seventh grade, his Vocabulary Reading score was at the 74th percentile and his Comprehension was at the 19th percentile with Spelling at the 2nd percentile. This discrepant performance (i.e., reversal of strengths and weaknesses in comprehension and word recognition) may have been the result of level of effort, which is one of Jim's challenges. He may not be motivated to do his best on tasks that are stressful for him. And it is virtually impossible to compare group and individual tests with any degree of confidence or individual tests with varying subtests. However, an examination of most of Jim's testing over the course of his school history seems to indicate that he is making very slow improvement in decoding and fluency, but substantial gains in reading comprehension. One would have hoped that given the multisensory linguistic instruction he experienced at his private school he would have showed more progress in decoding, but such has not been the case. Perhaps the small group instruction that he received over the course of the five years was insufficiently intense to move him closer to grade level achievement. Or perhaps Jim did not have the commitment or attention to push forward to improve his decoding skills. Although this is disappointing, Jim's comprehension is improving in spite of his poor decoding. His mother has noted that sometimes she can't believe that he is able to read technical instruction manuals and recognize so few words, yet be able to understand the directions sufficiently to build fairly complicated electrical models. She has noticed improvement in comprehension, but this improvement has not been to the extent that she would have anticipated. When asked how much Jim has improved his reading in the last four years on a scale of 1 to 5 with 5 being the most improvement, she identified 3 as the closest match. When asked to describe the severity of Jim's reading problem on a scale of 1 to 5 with 5 being the most significant reading problem, she indicated that it would be a 4. In similar questions, Jim was asked to rate his own reading skill at the time of the last interview on a scale of 1 to 5 with 5 being the highest; he indicated that four years ago his reading would have been a 2 but today he was "about a 3 right now—I'm pretty much average."

The fact that Jim believes his reading is average is likely related to his report cards that generally show a history of solid academic performance. From the third through sixth grade, his private school used a report card evaluation system of 1–4, with 4 = Exceeds Expectations, 3 = Meets Expectations, 2 = Below Expectations and 1 = Well Below Expectations. These numerical designations were accompanied by a narrative in which the teachers would provide fairly detailed descriptions of Jim's performance across skill and subskill areas. For the most part, Jim earned 3s; however, there were some consistent patterns of 2s in reading (spelling, word attack skills and fluency) and math fact fluency (difficulty memorizing math facts) as well as cooperation, class participation, homework completion and responsible behavior. And yet in spite of these 2s indicting below expected performance, the teachers wrote mostly positive narratives about solid progress and improvement. In the seventh grade, which was the beginning of middle school, grades replaced the numerical rating system and teachers continued to provide explanatory narratives. Jim's grades were divided fairly evenly between As, B+s and Bs with a few B-s. In almost all of these narratives, the teachers were overwhelmingly positive about Jim's progress. The exception was a narrative written by a physical education teacher who noted some problems with Jim "often times laughing or remarking negatively about the mistakes or failures of other students in the class." Otherwise Jim's seventh and eighth grade reports indicated high marks, which have continued at his current boarding school. Thus, it is not surprising that Jim stated his reading achievement was average, as he was likely comparing himself to his peers, most of whom also have reading problems.

Teachers

When asked to rate the level of support (i.e., excellent, satisfactory or poor) Jim had received for his reading problem since he started school, he identified satisfactory as the best description. His mother, though, has appreciated the solid support of the teachers at the private school and feels that that they have been a big help. It has been easy for her to communicate with all of his teachers. They are all responsive and she feels that these teachers are excellent as they are highly trained. She noted that the public school teachers were not as responsive, nor did they have the same level of skills to address Jim's problems. She was under the impression that those teachers were waiting for Jim's reading skills to naturally develop, as opposed to working on remediation to boost skill development. She noted that she did not think they were using a multisensory approach to reading, so she and her husband "saw the writing on the wall and said, 'we're out of here.'" They "weren't going to wait around" for improvements that might not be forthcoming. They knew that the private school provided multisensory remedial instruction and they decided this could make a difference for Jim. He doesn't believe that the teachers in his public school understood that some students need individual attention. Rather, he said, "The teachers were all the same; they did not want to do anything else for different students—just give everyone the same thing." The best teacher Jim has ever had was a social studies teacher at his private school. This teacher was dynamic and used "a lot of hands-on stuff—usually it was highly interactive." In contrast, the worst teacher that Jim has ever had was during his primary years at his public schools. He described this teacher as follows: "Her classes were really boring. They didn't have that great of focus . . . she was always yelling at students. It just wasn't a good fit."

Jim believes that the three most important things that a teacher should do for students would be: (1) help with work when needed; (2) challenge their students with "the right amount of difficulty . . . not push too much or too little, but exactly the right amount;" and (3) make their classes engaging.

Learning Style

Jim is aware of his optimal learning style. He explained that the best way for him to learn is through "hands-on . . . and building things." He also believes that watching videos helps greatly. The best way for him to demonstrate that he has learned content is to show this knowledge through "a computer presentation or making a model." He likes to work independently sometimes, and other times he appreciates the assistance of a peer group, as he noted:

> It sort of depends on what the activity is and what the group is like. If the group is functioning well then that's fine, but if the activity is something that can be done quickly, I would rather do it myself because it would take longer in a group . . . it wouldn't be as efficient.

Jim likes to use computers for his schoolwork, particularly research (as the search tools are all available in one place), but does not find them helpful for reading. When asked about various screen readers and reading software, he did not seem to be familiar with these. In spite of his problems with math facts, Jim identified math as one of his school strengths as well as social studies and chemistry. Two areas that he identified as weaknesses for him were literature class and textbook work because he did not find them engaging and he said he is "not good at reading." Jim thinks that the most difficult thing about having a reading problem is that it causes him to skip over lines when the content doesn't make sense (most likely because of weak decoding). He feels that he spends a lot of time doing the work, but he often doesn't understand it, which is very frustrating for him. He has developed some special strategies that have helped him with reading. He tries to find reading material with pictures, showing a preference for reading magazines, and he places a sheet of paper under lines to keep his place. He reads magazines for enjoyment, but doesn't spend much time on books as he finds them too arduous.

Homework

Although homework was a problem for Jim and his family in first and second grades of his public school, it was not a problem at the private school. The terrible clashes that occurred over homework disappeared when Jim changed schools. The mother feels grateful that the private school took much of the pressure off families and students as she has always been the parent who dealt with the responsibilities of homework. She said that the private school takes the position that "parents are not responsible for homework" and that the "the student must advocate for himself and go to the teachers if he can't do his homework." The only homework problems he typically had were those related to his 15 minutes of required fiction reading. He was very resistant to this, but his mother is aware of the value of this practice and the potential benefits to increase his reading achievement. Jim sometimes spends a lot of energy trying to avoid this responsibility, which is upsetting to the mother because she knows he cannot move ahead without the practice and persistence.

Social Development

In the preschool and primary years, Jim had some problems getting along with others at school and in social situations. His generalized anxiety caused him to become uncomfortable in certain situations where there was a lot of commotion. He was also teased because of his poor reading, which undermined his social confidence. (It should be noted that during the current interview he denied the teasing that he had originally described in his first interview four years ago.) The mother feels that Jim has a difficult time picking up social cues his peers are giving and, therefore, has trouble reading some social situations. For example, she indicated that if the family is at a party or gathering and there is one child who is behaving inappropriately, most of the other kids, including Jim's brother, would ignore the behavior and stay away from the child. However, Jim would continue to interact with the child and then complain or "tell on" the child to draw attention to the situation and create tension. He appears to demonstrate a certain degree of social immaturity. Yet, Jim enjoyed the socialization of the private school and made friends there. Perhaps these socialization experiences were less stressful because his peers had similar learning challenges. He participated in soccer in eighth grade before he left for boarding school, which his mother sees as a substantial step in socialization as "he put himself out there and was comfortable with his coach, which was a big thing." In other words, he took a chance and had a positive experience that likely assisted in his social development. On a scale of 1 to 5 with 5 being the most social, the mother judged his social development to be at 3.5 and noted that he usually does better with adults than other kids, but at the current boarding school he seems to have a small group of friends. He is not really interested in social networking, but occasionally will spend some time on Facebook.

Self-Determination and Coping

Self-Efficacy and Motivation

Jim's motivation to achieve is an area of concern for his family. His mother believes that his slow reading progress is due to that fact that he does only what is required of him, "just enough and no more." The mother perceives his greatest school challenge is whether he will decide to "push through when something is really hard and say 'I'm still going to go for it' instead of saying 'I just can't.'" She is concerned that he doesn't seem to care when he misreads things; instead of trying to learn the words, he seems to easily accept that these words are not in his reading vocabulary. She attributes his limited growth in reading to his lack of interest and effort in working on these skills. She believes he is resistant because:

> It's really hard and it's hard to have the inner strength to do something that is really hard and in knowing that in the end you are still not going to be as good as others even after putting forth all that effort.

Jim believes that he tries to do his best most of the time, but sometimes he admits that his moods and distractibility interfere with these intentions. When things aren't going well in school, he accepts personal responsibility instead of blaming his teachers. It is interesting that Jim seems to understand the path to being a better student ("get my work done" and "do a small amount above average"), but he is not inclined to follow through. It is also interesting, but not surprising, that Jim shows strong motivation for reading technical manuals that are well above his reading level when he is engaged in activities such as building circuitry for an electronics project. He doesn't really find grades to be a source of stress. This is probably related to the fact that his private school had a liberal policy of grading to relieve this stress for students with learning problems. He is rather philosophical about occasionally receiving a bad grade as he said, "Well, I guess, I don't think it really matters much. I just look at it like it's not the end of the world. Grades go up and down."

Two scales (Academic and Emotional) of the Self-Efficacy Questionnaire for Children (SEQ-C; Muris, 2001) were administered to Jim to investigate his interpretation of his abilities in these areas. According to Jim's responses on the Academic Scale, he admits to struggling with attention when he is trying to study if there are other interesting things to do and when he is in class. He also disclosed some homework completion problems and difficulties satisfying his parents with his schoolwork. For the most part, Jim expressed confidence in fulfilling academic challenges. On the Emotional Scale, he shared some problems with mood (feeling down), controlling his feelings and worrying, but, on the whole, he expressed good emotional stability without extreme variability across items.

On the Children's Hope Scale (Snyder et al., 1997), Jim's responses again revealed that he is confident that he is "doing pretty well," and that most of the time he "can think of many ways to get the things in life that are most important" to him and he is a good problem solver (i.e., "I know that I can find ways to solve problems"). Two areas in which he expressed some concern were comparing himself with peers (i.e., "doing as well as other kids my age") and benefitting from past experiences (i.e., "things I have done in the past will help me in the future"). These concerns were also voiced in the interview. Jim had indicated that at the time of the previous interview four years ago he was reading below average, but in the current interview he expressed ambivalence. At one point, he said he feels he is "pretty much average." Yet, on several different occasions in the interview, Jim referred specifically to his "reading problem" and when asked if he could change one thing about himself, he replied, "I would probably say that I would like to change the fact that I do have challenged reading. That is a small issue, but I would like to have easier reading."

In an effort to gain insight into Jim's motivation for studying, the Achievement Goal Disposition Survey (adapted from Hayamizu & Weiner, 1991) was administered. This measure divides student responses into three categories that identify motivation for studying: (1) intellectual curiosity (learning mastery), (2) social approval or (3) goal achievement. Jim's responses on this measure revealed that he shows a strong commitment toward studying for purposes of goal achievement (e.g., "I study because I want to get a good job in the future" and "I study because I have set goals for myself"). His responses also suggested that he is not particularly interested in achievement for purposes of social approval (e.g., answering negatively to "I study because I want to be praised by my teachers" and "I study because I want my friends to know that I do well in school"). He was equivocal about the questions that addressed intellectual curiosity, suggesting that he has mixed feelings about challenging himself.

Coping

Jim's greatest challenge may well be in the area of coping with stress and frustration. He has a repertoire of strategies to help him deal with difficult situations such as frustration associated with reading problems. For example, Jim said that when he becomes frustrated with reading, "I try to put the book down and calm down and then go at it again later." He finds this strategy usually helps. He uses a similar strategy when he becomes overwhelmed by a difficult homework assignment and thinks he can't do it. He said "I guess I put it aside and I try to find some solution, either through the Internet or my parents and then I go back to it and try to get it done." Jim believes that his parents provide an effective support system for him as he says that he often relieves school stress by talking to his parents about an incident that might be bothering him. In Jim's opinion, the most important thing that his parents have done to support his school achievement is "Giving me help when I need it and not giving me help when I don't need it." When listening to Jim, one is struck by the sincerity of his perceptions. However, it appears that he may be describing his aspirations for coping rather than reality. There is no question about the sincerity of his desire to effectively use these strategies, but the reality may be different. His mother specifically noted, "My major concerns are his poor coping skills. Strategies that he has used are not working well."

In general, Jim wishes that school could be a more positive experience. In spite of all the support that he has received, he believes that school is generally a negative environment. Looking back over his school years, Jim regrets that he wasn't given sufficient help for his reading problem early on. He clearly remembers the emotional pain of being told "go read this" and not having the skills to comply. He wanted the teacher to help him because as he said, "I couldn't read" and he didn't know what to do.

When Jim is feeling down, being with one of his pets can help him feel better. And he counts on his parents for major assistance when he is at home. While it is a positive move on his part to use his parents as an effective support system, this reliance is also the source of stress at home. Jim's inclination to do the minimum for academics and his tendency to argue and make excuses can lead to bickering and full blown arguments. Jim is the first to admit that his failure to control his anger at home has caused major problems. Now that he is in boarding school, he will need to rely more on his teachers as his parents will not be there to support him. This change in environment may give him the opportunity to develop more successful coping skills, which he will need to become a well-adjusted adult.

Impact on Mother

Jim's mother is totally committed to her son's development and well-being, but it has been a real struggle for her to determine how best to support him. When asked to rate the amount of stress associated with parenting a child with dyslexia on a scale of 1 to 5 with 5 being the greatest amount of stress, she doesn't hesitate before saying, "That would be a 5." Jim's early problems in preschool and kindergarten, the teasing for poor reading, diminishing feelings of self-worth and relinquishing him to boarding school were particularly difficult times for the mother. On a daily basis she feels stress associated with the possibility that he may "not achieve a basic level of reading to exist in life," and the long-term repercussions of this conceivable outcome.

Jim's reading difficulties have influenced both her personal and family life. She does not work outside of the home, in large part because of Jim's needs as well as her commitment to the family. She and her husband have not had major disagreements about Jim's education since he started the private school in third grade. They are "usually together" about the course that should be pursued and if there is some disagreement, they often defer to the recommendations of the school. They feel comfortable sharing home problems with the school staff because they are so supportive and helpful in generating solutions. Jim's relationship with his brother has been influenced by Jim's learning and behavior problems. The mother feels that Jim used to try to hide it from the brother, but now he seems to be less inclined to do so. She is hoping that Jim is "trying to let that go" and accept himself with all of his strengths and weaknesses. The mother has felt some resentment at times because she was the designated parent to address Jim's challenges, which meant that sometimes she felt that she always had to be home, foregoing some outside interests and causing her to feel frustrated. She has found great support in the teachers at the private school and other mothers of Jim's classmates. She does not speak freely to friends about Jim's problems as she does not feel that they would understand because many of her friends are parents of high achieving children. She could easily confide in other private school mothers as they share her concerns, which makes her feel less alone in her parenting situation.

When Jim's mother reflects about what she has learned about parenting and life in general in relation to having a child with a reading problem, she is quick to answer, "We're all stronger than we think. I'm strong enough to make the tough decisions if I think they are the right decisions and Jim is stronger than he thinks and he is capable of change." She would advise other mothers of children with dyslexia to "keep searching, always keep trying" to find solutions and not to give up hope even when some decisions "don't turn out to be the answer." The mother feels that Jim is on a long and difficult journey of trying to accept himself and come to terms with his problems to fulfill his potential. Her son's journey has also changed the course of her life.

Future Goals and Hopes

The mother's reading goals for Jim for the next four years are focused on increasing his fluency to the point that he will be at a functional level of reading. Specifically she would like him to successfully pass his driver's license test. She knows that this will be a challenge for him. She was very pleased that he recently passed the written test for scuba diver certification, but this test was given to him orally and she does not know if that is a possibility for the driver's test. She knows his reading problem will affect his future, but she does not want him to think that he must limit himself as there are reasonable accommodations that can support his success. At this point, Jim does not aspire to college, but he does want to continue his education. Previously, the mother felt that Jim would go to university, but now she believes that he could be very successful in a technical career that requires less formal education. He shows a lot of talent in electronics; he is very adept at building LED circuit boards and fixing anything mechanical. Her dreams for his future are for "him to be happy and functioning well . . . and that's the way I would define success for him."

Jim showed good evidence of realistic goal planning. The primary goal he would like to accomplish before leaving school is to "graduate on a good note," which to him means having "decent grades" so he can obtain a successful job. When he was asked to break down this goal into steps, he indicated that he "would need to find out what my job will be in advance, take classes that would help in that job and do well in these classes." In addition to being able to articulate his long-term goals and the steps to accomplish these, Jim could also identify potential obstacles that might interfere with his achievement of the goals (i.e., "trying not to give up and not letting my mood get in the way") and a strategy for addressing these that includes taking each day at a time and trying "to remind myself that this day could make a difference in my future." Jim has already explored vocational opportunities as his private school provided a few classes on welding. He did well in these classes and looks forward to the possibility of pursuing that career because "it's a good interactive job and I think it fits my style." Jim showed solid knowledge of the requirements of welding; he noted that a welder had to have a high tolerance for heat, excellent coordination, good eye sight and a working knowledge of the chemistry of welding. He understands himself well enough to know that he wants a job "in the field" and he doesn't want to be "cooped up in an office." The chances seem good that Jim will be successful in pursuing employment in a technical career that he enjoys.

Case Commentary

Four years ago Jim was a 10 year-old with severe reading and spelling problems who was finishing his second year at a private school for students with learning differences. His evaluations at that time revealed that he had the classic characteristics of dyslexia (i.e., decoding, fluency and spelling problems typically related to a phonological deficit that is unexpected in relation to cognitive abilities and instructional opportunities) as described by Lyon, Shaywitz and Shaywitz (2003). In addition to his reading disability, Jim struggled with generalized anxiety and ADHD. He did not display significant behavior problems at the age of 10, but he was somewhat resistant to fulfilling the school's reading requirements.

Today at 14 years of age, Jim continues to demonstrate significant decoding and spelling problems similar to those that he displayed four years ago. Given the fact that he has had the benefit of a structured multisensory linguistic reading program in a small group for an hour per day for almost four years, one would have anticipated some additional growth. It is difficult to speculate why this has not come about, but it is important to note that many children with dyslexia continue to have decoding and fluency problems in spite of exposure to systematic phonics-based remedial programs. In a review of intensive reading interventions, Vaughn, Denton and Fletcher (2010) identified factors such as remedial group size as well as frequency, length and duration of intervention to be influential variables affecting growth rate of learners with reading difficulties. For example, these researchers found that remedial groups of 1 to 3 students per instructor yielded more significant outcomes than larger groups of 10 or more students. Likewise, intervention for extended periods every day (approximately two hours) resulted in dramatic gains for those with severe reading problems. Thus, it could be that Jim's remedial group size exceeded the optimal number of students to maximize reading achievement or that the one hour of instruction he received daily was less than what he needed to make significant strides. Perhaps Jim's lack of progress could also be related to the fact that from kindergarten through the second grade, he did not have instruction at the intensity necessary to achieve gains. By the time he started private school at the age of 9, he was already past the optimal time for achieving maximum benefits of early intervention (Lyon & Fletcher, 2001). Or conceivably inadequate growth in decoding could be related to his lack of concentrated effort, which is his mother's concern. And finally, it is also possible that Jim's ADHD and slow processing speed has interfered with his reading growth because of executive function deficits (Mahone, 2011).

On the positive side, Jim's comprehension has improved. Inconsistent test scores make it difficult to describe the magnitude of these gains, but all indications suggest that there has been considerable growth. In fact, in sixth grade his scores indicated that he was above average in comprehension. Even though the following year these gains had disappeared, his reading comprehension testing during eighth grade placed him at the 53rd percentile. It may seem unlikely for a child with word level reading at the 4th percentile to achieve a comprehension score that high, but research has previously demonstrated that decoding and comprehension may be dissociated for dyslexics (Bruck, 1990, 1993) as well as skilled readers (Landi, 2010) as age level advances. The close relationship between decoding and spelling and comprehension that is observed in beginning readers may be supplanted in adolescence and young adulthood by vocabulary, which becomes a strong predictor of reading comprehension (Braze, Tabor, Shankweiler & Mencl, 2007). Jim's strength in oral language will hopefully continue to increase his reading comprehension, bringing him closer to the functional level of reading that will insure he can pass his driver's license test and any technical tests associated with a career he pursues.

In addition to Jim's improvement in reading comprehension, there is also noticeable growth in his maturity with regard to realistic goal setting for the future. He was easily able to identify goals for the next four years of schooling (i.e., earn required grades for graduation to obtain a successful job upon completion) and specific steps that would move him toward the achievement of this goal (i.e., investigate job qualifications, take classes to prepare for a specific job and do well in these classes). At this point, he already has his sights set on a realistic career that he believes is a good match for his skills and is of considerable interest to him. While it is true that he does not want to exert himself to improve his reading, this may be an endeavor that is simply too hard or results in too few rewards to be worth the effort for him. Jim is probably not alone in his lack of motivation for increasing reading achievement through intensive personal efforts. Many dyslexic students cannot continue to sustain this type of effort over a long period of time because it becomes too grueling. Adults can avoid careers that require sitting in cubicles for eight hours a day, or arguing complicated cases in a courtroom or selling designer fragrances in malls, etc., according to individual preferences, but children cannot avoid reading, not even for one day, during their school careers. This kind of day-to-day experience can be unbelievably arduous and personally devastating.

Jim's behavior problems have escalated over the past four years and are of concern, but may not be completely unexpected. Many adolescents with dyslexia have comorbid problems such as anxiety, depression, and/or aggression that interfere with progress or complicate the condition (Dahle & Knivsberg, 2014; Eissa, 2010). In fact, even early in development, reading problems are reliable predictors of behavior problems (Morgan, Farkas, Tufis & Sperling, 2008) and vice versa (Sanson, Prior & Smart, 1996), suggesting a link albeit one that is unclear as it is not known if dyslexia and behavior difficulties are causally related. It could well be that for Jim these increased behavioral difficulties are related to the stress associated with his reading problems. However, it is also possible that his problems with anger control and defiance have been triggered or exacerbated by adolescent development. The conflict he created in the home environment is not that unusual for adolescents who are striving to separate from their parents. Regardless of the cause, these behaviors needed to be addressed so that they do not interfere with this adolescent's development and progress. Jim's parents took steps to control these unacceptable behaviors that interfered with family life as well as his social and emotional development. Their responsiveness and willingness to take action may well have averted more serious behavioral difficulties. The outdoor education program and his current boarding school that focuses on behavioral development will hopefully provide Jim with the guidance he needs to learn new coping strategies for his frustrations and stress. In spite of the challenges that he has had at home, there was very little mention of behavioral difficulty at his private school, which is a positive indicator for an optimistic prognosis. When behavioral problems are persistent across numerous environments, they are likely more resistant to treatment.

It is significant to note that families and particularly mothers of children with dyslexia have more than a full time job taking care of the needs of these children. As revealed by Jim's story, this is not usually an easy job even under the best of circumstances and it is a full time job with lots of overtime. In some countries, such as Sweden, the government recognizes the magnitude of this contribution and makes financial allowances by providing quarter or half salaries for the primary caretaker of a child with dyslexia (Ingesson, 2011). Of course, there is no financial support of this kind in the United States and very little emotional support other than from one's family. When teachers, such as those at Jim's private school, are responsive and sensitive to the child and the family, the stress of parenting a child or adolescent with dyslexia can be greatly minimized as Jim's mother attests. The ability to work successfully with families may be as important as the ability to successfully teach the child.

Finally, it is important to remember that the likelihood of successful adjustment for Jim is greatly enhanced by the support his parents have consistently provided, and the fact that they continue to present a united front. This is a family that is so committed to their child's optimal development that they moved 95 miles for a school that provided better instructional opportunities and then four years later made the difficult boarding school decision to address problem behaviors. The mother believes that these challenges come with the territory of parenting and that her role is to keep searching for the best treatments and solutions for Jim. As the presence of a strong support system for children and adolescents with reading disabilities is one of the factors predictive of a positive outcome, there is a good likelihood that Jim will overcome his current behavioral challenges and capitalize on his unique strengths to achieve fulfillment and personal success in adulthood. Although his journey will not be easy, he will not be alone.

References

Braze, D., Tabor, W., Shankweiler, D. P., & Mencl, W. E. (2007). Speaking up for vocabulary: Reading skill differences in young adults. *Journal of Learning Disabilities, 40*, 226–243. doi:10.1177/00222194070400030401

Bruck, M. (1990). Word recognition skills of adults with childhood diagnoses of dyslexia. *Developmental Psychology, 26*, 439–454. doi:10.1037/0012-1649.26.3.439

Bruck, M. (1993). Component spelling skills of college students with childhood diagnoses of dyslexia. *Learning Disabilities Quarterly, 16*, 171–184. doi:10.2307/1511325

Dahle, A. E., & Knivsberg, A. M. (2014). Internalizing, externalizing and attention problems in dyslexia. *Scandinavian Journal of Disability Research, 16*, 179–193. doi:10.1080/15017419.2013.781953

Eissa, M. (2010). Behavioral and emotional problems associated with dyslexia. *Current Psychiatry, 17*(1), 39–47.

Hayamizu, T., & Weiner, B. (1991). A test of Dweck's model of achievement goals as related to perceptions of ability. *Journal of Experimental Education, 59*, 226–234. doi:10.1080/00220973.1991.10806562

Hoover, H. D., Dunbar, S. B., & Frisbie, D. A. (2005). *Iowa Tests of Basic Skills*. Rolling Meadows, IL: Riverside Publishing.

Ingesson, G. (2011). Johan, a case study of dyslexia in Sweden. In Peggy L. Anderson & R. Meier-Hedde (Eds.), *International case studies of dyslexia* (pp. 82–98). New York: Routledge Publishing.

Kaufman, A. S., & Kaufman, N. L. (2004). *Kaufman Test of Educational Achievement* (2nd ed.). Circle Pines, MN: AGS Publishing.

Landi, N. (2010). An examination of the relationship between reading comprehension, higher-level and lower-level subskills in adults. *Reading and Writing, 23*, 701–717. doi:10.1007/s11145-009-9180-z

Lyon, G. R., & Fletcher, J. M. (2001). Early warning system. *Education Next*, 23–29. Retrieved from www.educationnext.org/20012/22.html

Lyon, G. R., Shaywitz, S. E., & Shaywitz, B. A. (2003). Defining dyslexia, comorbidity, teachers' knowledge of language and reading: A definition of dyslexia. *Annals of Dyslexia, 53*, 1–14. doi:10.1007/s11881-003-0001-9

Mahone, E. M. (2011). The effects of ADHD (beyond decoding accuracy) on fluency and comprehension. *New Horizons for Learning, IV*(1). Retrieved from http://education.jhu.edu/PD/newhorizons/Journals/Winter2011/Mahone

Morgan, P. L., Farkas, G., Tufis, P. A., & Sperling, R. A. (2008). Are reading and behavior problems risk factors for each other? *Journal of Learning Disabilities, 41*, 417–436. doi:10.1177/0022219408321123

Muris, P. (2001). A brief questionnaire for measuring self-efficacy in youths. *Journal of Psychopathology and Behavioral Assessment, 23*, 145–149.

National Institute of Child Health and Human Development. (2000). Report of the National Reading Panel. *Teaching children to read: An evidence-based assessment of the scientific research literature on reading and its implications for reading instruction* (NIH Publication No. 00–4769). Washington, DC: U.S. Government Printing Office.

Reid, D., Hresko, W., & Hammill, D. (2002). *Test of Early Reading Ability* (3rd ed.). Austin, TX: PROED.

Sanson, A., Prior, M., & Smart, D. (1996). Reading disabilities with and without behavior problems at 7–8 years: Prediction from longitudinal data from infancy to 6 years. *Child Psychology and Psychiatry, 37*, 529–41.

Snyder, C. R., Hoza, B., Pelham, W. E., Rapoff, M., Ware, L., Danovsky, M., . . . Stahl K. J. (1997). The development and validation of the Children's Hope Scale. *Journal of Pediatric Psychology, 22*, 399–421. doi:10.1093/jpepsy/22.3.399

Tattum, S. (1998). *F.A.S.T. Reading System*. Denver, CO: F.A.S.T. Learning.

Vaughn, S., Denton, C. A., & Fletcher, J. M. (2010). Why intensive interventions are necessary for students with severe reading difficulties. *Psychology in the Schools, 47*, 432–444. doi:10.1002/pits.20481

Wechsler, D. (2002). *Wechsler Preschool and Primary Scale of Intelligence—Third Edition*. San Antonio, TX: Psychological Corporation.

Wechsler, D. (2003). *Wechsler Intelligence Scale for Children—Fourth Edition*. San Antonio, TX: Psychological Corporation.

Wechsler, D. (2009). *Wechsler Individual Achievement Test—Third Edition*. San Antonio, TX: Psychological Corporation.

Woodcock, R. W., Schrank, F. A., Mather, N., & McGrew, K. S. (2007). *Woodcock-Johnson III Tests of Achievement*. Rolling Meadows, IL: Riverside Publishing.

16
CROSS-CASE ANALYSIS AND REFLECTIONS

Peggy L. Anderson and Regine Meier-Hedde

The voices of these adolescents and their mothers clearly articulated their challenges, accomplishments and concerns. The developmental period of adolescence is marked by increasingly complex challenges that can be exacerbated by dyslexia and give way to failure, recriminations and maladjustment. Overall, we did not find this to be the case for most of the participants in this study as the predominant theme that emerged from our conversations with these adolescents and their mothers was one of healthy adjustment and resilience. While it is true that some of the participants in this study were experiencing more difficulty than others including frustration, disappointment and despair related to their dyslexia, they were not representative of the group as a whole. More often than not, the adolescents expressed positive feelings about their lives and a genuine desire to move ahead to meet specific goals and become successful. Yet, as this is a *story of the stories*, all voices are equally important and relevant as the major objective of the study is to understand and appreciate the experience of each adolescent. Some of the results in this chapter are reported by case numbers that do not correspond to the order of case study chapters and initials that are not consistent with the names of the adolescents to preclude positive and negative associations with particular countries. As we are unaware of any countries with reputations for provision of excellent or poor services to children with dyslexia, we wanted to avoid summary results that would erroneously corroborate either perception. The aggregated findings are shared to examine possible trends, but the individual case studies always assume primacy. The cross-case synthesis is included to provide additional insight and recommendations that will hopefully be of value for families, teachers and future researchers.

Success Attributes

As described in Chapter 2, the Frostig Center studies (Goldberg, Higgins, Raskind & Herman, 2003; Raskind, Goldberg, Higgins & Herman, 1999; Spekman, Goldberg & Herman, 1992) identified six attributes that discriminated between the more and less successful individuals who were former students. The data from these studies revealed the predictive value of the following success attributes: self-awareness, proactivity, perseverance, emotional stability, use of effective support systems and appropriate goal setting. The current study used this theoretical construct, in part, to qualitatively analyze participant interviews in consideration of the operationalized success attributes (Raskind et al., 1999). Discrete analysis of interview responses and holistic analysis of the case studies were both included. Table 16.1 provides a summary of the success attribute strength for the group as well as a measure of the variable strength for each adolescent. On this table, a score of 1 is interpreted as a marker of insufficiency indicating the least successful adjustment whereas 2 would be a satisfactory level and 3 would be considered highly desirable and predictive of the most successful adjustment.

Self-Awareness

Raskind and his colleagues (1999) divided self-awareness into two parts: acceptance of the learning disability and general self-awareness. Acceptance of the learning disability was operationalized by criteria requiring that the individual

TABLE 16.1 Evaluation of Success Attributes for Adolescents with Dyslexia

	Self-Awareness	Proactivity	Perseverance	Emotional Stability	Use of Support	Goal-Setting
Case 1	3	3	2	3	3	3
Case 2	2	1	1	1	2	2
Case 3	3	1	1	2	3	2
Case 4	3	3	3	3	3	3
Case 5	3	1	1	1	2	3
Case 6	3	2	2	2	2	3
Case 7	2	2	2	1	2	2
Case 8	3	3	2	3	2	2
Case 9	2	3	2	2	3	3
Case 10	3	2	2	2	3	3
Case 11	3	3	3	3	3	3
Case 12	3	2	2	3	3	3
Case 13	3	3	2	1	3	3
Totals	**36**	**29**	**25**	**27**	**34**	**35**

Note: 1= low strength, 2 = medium strength, 3 = high strength.

refers to self as learning disabled, describes events in reference to his/her disability and compartmentalizes the disability as one aspect of personality rather than the predominant characteristic of self. For the current study, we addressed the criteria of learning difference (as opposed to disability) and general self-awareness with interview questions that focused on the adolescents' understanding of school-related strengths and weaknesses, optimal ways to learn and demonstrate knowledge, personal talents (outside of school) and ability to use strengths to compensate for weaknesses as well as other areas of self-understanding.

This analysis revealed that these dyslexic adolescents as a group demonstrated strong self-awareness with numerical values exceeding that of all other success attribute areas. The majority of adolescents had no difficulty identifying school-related strengths, which were predominantly in the area of sports. They perceived these to be "school things" because most of these activities occurred during recess or after school. Physical activity has been identified as a stress reliever for adolescents by reducing depression and anxiety while improving self-esteem (Biddle & Asare, 2011; Liu, Wu & Ming, 2015) so it is not unexpected that many adolescents with dyslexia pursue athletics (Edwards, 1994; McNulty, 2003). Some mothers of children with dyslexia have specifically noted that sports have been helpful in improving self-esteem (Anderson & Meier-Hedde, 2011; Roll-Pettersson & Heimdahl Mattson, 2007). There was only one adolescent who could not identify two strengths: he named gym as his first strength, but try as he might, he could not name another, saying, "I used to be good in math, but not anymore." All of the adolescents, except for that boy, could readily identify their talents outside of school, covering a wide range from cooking, video game-playing, music, running, dancing, swimming, basketball, etc. with most of these, again, being sports related. As would be anticipated, most adolescents acknowledged that their greatest challenges were reading-related and/or learning English as a second language. Second language learning associated with the high school curriculum is particularly challenging for students with dyslexia (Chung & Ho, 2010; Helland & Kaasa, 2005; Palladino, Bellagamba, Ferrari & Cornoldi, 2013) and this group of adolescents was no different.

It is important for students to understand that although people are not born with innate learning styles, they often find that they learn more efficiently through certain methods and this self-awareness has the potential to be an enormous benefit (Reiff & Ofiesh, 2016). The adolescents were asked to explain their preferred ways to learn to discern if they possessed this awareness. In a related question, they were asked to identify the optimal way to demonstrate what they had learned. From a universal design for learning (UDL) perspective, both teachers and students need to have knowledge of optimal ways for individual students to receive information for comprehension/retention and to express what they have learned (Meyer, Rose & Gordon, 2014). One of the prominent themes that emerged from this analysis was that these adolescents as a group reported that listening in class was a preferred method of learning academic content.

Obviously this makes sense as these students all had literacy problems that interfered with the acquisition of content through reading. Thus, it was essential that their teachers delivered oral explanations in a very clear fashion as they perceived their mastery of content to be closely tied to these. If they didn't understand something in class, it was improbable they would acquire the content from the textbook because of their reading difficulties. Some adolescents also preferred that oral class content be supported with videos so that they could have the dual experience of listening and viewing to reinforce instruction. All of the adolescents gave responses indicating they were highly aware of their learning needs except for one student with a very low reading level who responded that he learned best by rereading the material many times, which is generally considered to be one of the least preferable ways for students to learn (Karpicke, Butler & Roediger, 2009; Roediger, 2013) and may be particularly ineffective for students with dyslexia who have decreased decoding and vocabulary skills. These students identified oral and computer presentations as preferred methods of demonstrating learned content. Additionally, having exams read to them and dictating written assignments were also mentioned as preferences for showing what they had learned. All of the adolescents except for one could readily identify productive ways of demonstrating knowledge of academic material that would accommodate their reading difficulties and allow them to have comparable content progress with classmates.

When these adolescents were asked whether they preferred to work alone or in groups, over half indicated that group work was preferable. As one student said, "I like to work in groups rather than working alone because I can get some help when I get stuck" while another echoed the same sentiment saying, "I prefer to work in groups because in a group I can take help from others." The value of cooperative learning for students with learning disabilities has been well documented (Jenkins, Antil, Wayne & Vadasy, 2003) even though associated achievement gains have been questioned (McMaster & Fuchs, 2002). However, Sencibaugh and Sencibaugh (2016) recently conducted an efficacy study from which they concluded that cooperative learning has the potential to "positively impact the achievement of students with learning problems" (p. 362) if teachers carefully instruct students about the protocol for the specific cooperative learning activity and provide sufficient attention to individual accountability to maximize the effects of this learning strategy. Although there are many other group strategies, cooperative learning may be one of the most effective.

It is highly valuable for students with learning problems to come to understand their strengths and weaknesses in such a way that they learn compensatory strategies (Reiff & Ofiesh, 2016; Reis, McGuire & Neu, 2000). When we asked these adolescents if they ever used their strengths to compensate for their weaknesses, approximately half of the 13 adolescents did not seem to understand the question regardless of prompts, but the other half gave excellent examples of using such a strategy. Several of these responses referred to using strong oral skills to compensate for weak writing as one boy explained:

> I like to work in groups because there is always someone who writes better than I do. I can make my point of view clear by presenting it orally. But if I had to write something, everybody would ask, "What is that?" which wouldn't be good for me. So it's better when I only speak about the issues. If someone else makes the visual aid, I can stand in front of the class and explain it.

Another boy explained how he participated in student versus teacher sports competitions, allowing him to forge relationships with his teachers as he is talented in sports and weak in communicating with instructors. The result, as he explained it, was that "all the teachers know me well and they like me and talk to me." Such relationships help teachers to perceive dyslexic students holistically, encouraging emphasis on the positive aspects of the child and motivating teachers to provide supportive guidance (Nielsen, 2011). Another adolescent discussed how he used a complicated mnemonic system that involved the association of number combinations with specific language rules as he possessed an excellent memory for number associations and a marked weakness in languages.

Proactivity

This success attribute referred to the premise that successful students are those who are socially engaged with their families, schools and communities, proactively make decisions and believe that they have the power to make changes in their lives (Raskind et al., 1999). We asked the mothers to assess socialization with reference to family, peers and teacher relationships as well as engagement in organized community activities. The mothers also rated their sons' social skills on a scale of 1 to 5, with 5 indicating the most well developed social skills. As a measure of proactive decision making, the adolescents described a challenge they had faced and succeeded in accomplishing as well as a challenge they had faced and failed. These questions focused on the students' initiative in solving the challenges and demonstrating control over their lives. Additionally, two questions on the Children's Hope Scale (Snyder et al., 1997) were analyzed in this section as they addressed the ability to make positive changes in one's life ("I can think of many ways to get the things in life that are most important to me" and "When I have a problem, I come up with many ways to solve it").

As indicated in Table 16.1, proactivity for the group was evident, but less so than what was observed for self-awareness. With regard to family relationships, the majority of mothers indicated that their sons got along very well with family members, but 4 of the 13 shared problems related to behavioral reactions to school pressure and difficulties at home. One mother explained that her husband "blames our son for being lazy" and punished him for his lack of achievement, causing the son to be fearful. The majority of these adolescents had excellent peer relationships; however, two of the boys who experienced significant problems with peers also had family problems. For both of these boys, the peer problems were related to dyslexia and underachievement in the classroom. Only one adolescent had significant problems with most of his teachers; his mother attributed these to the teachers losing their temper and ridiculing him in the classroom. There was evidence that another four adolescents had problems with specific teachers, but reasonably good relationships with others. These poor relationships adversely affected their school performance, which is not unexpected as the connection between adolescents and their teachers is a powerful predictor of academic success (Milsom & Glanville, 2010; Wang & Eccles, 2012). The majority of the adolescents were active participants in organized activities in their schools and/or communities with only four boys not participating (three of these had other relationship problems), expressing a preference to be alone in their free time. On the social scale, seven of the mothers evaluated their sons' social skills as high, at 4 to 5 with three of the mothers indicating social skills at 3 to 3.5 and three indicating that social skills were 1 to 2.5. Slightly more than half of the group appeared to have very strong social skills while 23% had some problems in this area and another 23% had significant social problems. Socialization is a critical skill for successful school adjustment and it may well be a predictor of future well-being (Holopainen, Lappalainen, Junttila & Savolainen, 2012). There is considerable evidence suggesting that students with reading difficulties and learning disabilities have less social competence (Bryan, 2005; Kavale, & Forness, 1996; Milligan, Phillips & Morgan, 2016; Smidt, Prah & Ĉagran, 2014). However, the current study found that slightly over half actually had social skill strengths and only a few had pronounced social difficulties. Multidimensional studies of social engagement have revealed that good parent and peer relationships are very important for successful adjustment, but the student-teacher relationship is particularly influential for school success and has far-reaching implications for typical adolescents (Wang & Eccles, 2012) as well as those with learning disabilities (Pham & Murray, 2016).

Nine of the 13 boys had no difficulty explaining a specific challenge they had faced and how they had succeeded by effective problem solving. For example, one boy described a time when he found himself in a situation where he had no bus fare to get home and decided to ask a shopkeeper for a loan that he repaid the following day. Another boy talked about a sports challenge: "My challenge was to win a football match. I was very angry with the opposing team. I got serious and with my team planned a strategy, played the match, and we won." The nine boys who were able to answer this question came up with specific instances in which they effectively resolved a dilemma, the other four adolescents could not answer this question. With regard to facing a challenge and failing (learning from one's mistakes and showing capacity for change), five of the boys indicated that they did not remember or know of a situation when they had been unable to successfully meet a challenge. One of these boys said, "No, from a young age I was taught not to give up" while another said, "I do not remember any situation because I am a hard working person and I almost always get it." Those who identified specific situations recounted such problems as not being able to overcome challenges learning English, losing soccer matches by playing poorly and being unable to stop teasing by teachers and bullying by peers. The boy who was teased said, "I can't fight back. Nobody is interested in knowing my experiences," meaning that he could not count on his teachers to help as they also ridiculed him and he could not think of any solutions. Some of these responses indicated a pattern of helplessness, while others showed strong reflective thinking on the part of the boys who understood why they had been unsuccessful and how to change this in future situations. For the most part these adolescents revealed capability in resolving problems and achieving the goals they desired.

In reference to the ratings of the two questions dealing with the ability to make positive changes in one's life, ten of the adolescents indicated that they could "think of ways to get things in life that are most important to me" "a lot of the time" to "most of the time" and eight of the adolescents believed that they could come up with ways to solve problems "a lot of the time" to "all of the time." These responses collectively suggested some confidence in exerting control over life and problem-solving circumstances. Historically, there has been quite a bit of research indicating that locus of control was a problem for those with reading difficulties and learning disabilities, although most of this research was conducted 30 years ago (Lewis & Lawrence-Patterson, 1989; Rogers & Saklofske, 1985). This locus of control research suggested that students with learning disabilities did not feel that they were in control of their lives, giving way to feelings of learned helplessness that further incapacitated them. More recent research has questioned this finding. Mamlin, Harris and Case (2001) reviewed 22 studies that had identified locus of control problems for students with learning disabilities and concluded that these studies were methodologically flawed, advising against perpetuating the assumption that these students have external locus of control that interferes with their capacity to demonstrate initiative in problem solving. The results of the current study would support this cautionary note as only a few of the adolescents could have been described as such.

Perseverance

Raskind et al. (1999) addressed three factors in the operational definition of perseverance: ability to move forward in spite of adversity, understanding that difficulties are necessary for learning and refusal to quit in difficult circumstances. Perseverance is related to proactivity with the distinction being that the former refers more to the ability to keep going when things become very difficult while the latter refers more to taking control of events and situations to achieve a desired outcome. We asked the adolescents four questions about how they handled challenging school-related situations: (1) reading frustration ("What do you do when you become frustrated by your reading problem?"), (2) homework challenges ("When you have an assignment that you think you can't do, what do you do?"), (3) doing one's best at school ("Do you always do your best at school? Why or why not?"), (4) coping with a bad grade ("How do you cope when you receive a bad grade?") and (5) quitting in the face of difficult problem solving ("Even when others want to quit, I know that I can find ways to solve the problem"), an item on the Children's Hope Scale (Snyder et al., 1997).

Evidence of perseverance for this group was not as strong as self-awareness, being similar to proactivity with only two boys scoring at the highest level. In spite of their significant literacy difficulties, five of the adolescents said that they do not experience reading frustration. These boys were somewhat vague in their responses, mostly simply stating that this did not happen to them. One boy said, "Most people know that I need more time to read and so they adjust their expectations and just accept it" while another said, "I find I don't really get that anymore. I used to get it a lot." In reviewing the case studies, it would appear that this frustration may have been mitigated by the decrease in their actual reading of print. These particular adolescents were relying on audio materials or their parents' reading and actually did very little reading themselves. Of the eight adolescents who admitted to reading frustration, six showed sound strategies for dealing with this stress. These adolescents gave responses that revealed a pattern of perseverance; none of these adolescents said that they gave up and discontinued reading. Responses such as, "I calm down, take a deep breath" and continue to read, "I feel angry, but then I organize my ideas and start over again," "I try to overcome them, if I fail I ask for teachers or parents to help" and "I just try to put the book down and calm down and then go at it again later" suggested that these boys had a reasonable plan for dealing with the stress as opposed to one of the adolescents who admitted to being greatly distressed by reading frustration, but indicated that he had no idea what to do when he experienced this problem.

With regard to homework challenges, the majority of the adolescents said that they would pursue help from their parents, tutors or friends, but some of this help was less constructive ("I copy it from my classmate because I don't want to get punished by my teacher") and other assistance was more beneficial ("I guess I put it aside and I try to find some solution for it, either through the Internet or my parents and then I go back and try to get it done"). Two of the adolescents simply said that they did not know what they would do and another two said they would try, but if they couldn't resolve it, they would just "leave it." And finally, one very determined boy whose response represented the essence of perseverance said:

I usually think that I am able to do it. I think that everybody is able to do all subjects, but they have to try. There is an idiomatic expression that I like a lot: "Do not *try*, do it or don't do it."

The question about coping with a bad grade probed the issue of whether a bad mark would be an impetus for improvement or a disillusioning event that would give way to quitting. We know that grades are very influential as high grades encourage students to move forward in their academic careers while low grades are associated with dropping out of school (Kemp, 2006). This is particularly true for students with reading difficulties who drop out of high school at a much higher rate than those without these problems (Cortiella & Horowitz, 2014). Only three of the adolescents responded that a bad grade could actually be the precipitant for learning improvement. One boy said, "I talk with my parents and ask for help to see where I made mistakes. I want to do better next time," while another said, "I cope by studying more, by paying attention and becoming more serious of my studies." The other 10 adolescents did not seem too concerned about bad grades and considered this to be a typical occurrence. Responses such as "Just accept it. Doesn't bother me. Forget about it," "I don't talk about it. A month later I think it is like it is," "With me, bad grades are usual" and "Well, I guess I don't think it really matters much. I just look at it like it's not the end of the world. Grades go up and down." One boy was quite philosophical about the school grading system in relation to his abilities, saying:

> It doesn't bother me that much. There were periods, toward the end of elementary school and the beginning of middle school when I got low grades and it stopped bothering me. And even today it's only a number. It doesn't teach me that I am not good or not smart enough.

On one hand, it would be defeatist to encourage rumination about poor grades, yet it seems escapist to ignore them. Dyslexic children who try to ignore bad grades, pretending they don't matter and saying they don't care may well be trying desperately to protect self-esteem (Singer, 2007). It would be preferable for the students to go to their teachers and discuss the grade in relation to the content and studying guidance. This would help on two counts: the student would likely benefit from the advocacy process and possibly increase communication to establish an improved working relationship with the teacher, both of which could be highly valuable for increased achievement (Milsom & Glanville, 2010).

A little over half of these adolescents indicated that they always tried their best at school although the responses suggested that sometimes this was difficult. One adolescent said, "Yes, always, but sometimes I am in low spirits because I don't like bad marks," while another said "Yes, I do not want them to think I am lazy or someone who is not worried about anything." Those who revealed that they did not always do their best complained of boring subject material, feeling personally attacked by certain teachers and dealing with bad moods. For the question about quitting from the Children's Hope Scale (Snyder, et al., 1997), three boys responded that it would be unlikely they could persevere if a problem was so difficult that others quit while five thought there would be some chance of solving the problem and another five thought there would be a good chance. None of the adolescents indicated that their chances would be very good ("most of the time") or excellent ("all of the time"). This question focused on abilities in relation to peers, apparently causing feelings of insecurity. Dyslexics may well perceive themselves as less competent than peers and have trouble envisioning scenarios where they would demonstrate skills equal to or exceeding that of their peers (Alexander-Passe, 2006, 2015).

Emotional Stability

This success attribute referred to ability to manage stress, cope with frustrations, be socially active, demonstrate good peer relationships and express a hopeful outlook (Raskind et al., 1999). The results from the current study regarding social relationships and coping with frustration will not be repeated in this section, and hopeful thinking will be subsequently addressed in an analysis of the Children's Hope Scale (Snyder et al., 1997). In this part of the interview, the adolescents were asked questions about feelings ("Tell me what makes you happy," "Tell me what makes you sad" and "When you are sometimes feeling down, what is the single most important thing that can make you feel better?"), as well as a question dealing with stress ("If you become stressed at school, what do you do to deal with the stress?"). Both the adolescents and their mothers were also asked about teasing or bullying and coping mechanisms. Additionally, the mothers rated their sons' self-esteem. It should be noted that this success attribute was assessed more holistically than any other as the adolescents' emotionality permeated all aspects of the interview.

Emotional stability emerged as a strength for five of the boys and a weakness for four, with the group showing less resilience compared to most of the other areas. Twelve of the 13 adolescents easily identified things that made them happy (e.g., "when I don't need to read," "nice friends who understand dyslexia," "working out in the gym," "going out with friends and playing sports") as well as things that made them sad (e.g., "low marks and punishments from my father," "when I make stupid mistakes on a test and get bad marks" and "when two people I love fight each other"). There was only one boy who could not identify what made him happy and sad. When this boy was asked what made him feel better when he was feeling down, he said, "I like to be on my own." This child had some emotional difficulties, evident in several different sections of the interview as his responses seemed to indicate that he was socially isolated, verified by his mother who reported, "He refuses to be with other children" apart from his cousins. The other 12 boys identified a range of strategies for making themselves feel better including "go online and chat with friends," "to be with friends and know they are with you when you don't feel good" and "do something that makes me feel happy like be with friends, watch TV shows."

Dealing with school stress revealed a wide variation of responses. Three of the boys indicated that they do not experience much stress associated with school. One of these boys said, "I'm not as stressed as other people, but I just try and get the work done if I do feel stressed. I think, 'If I need to do this why am I sitting here feeling stressed.'" At the other end of the continuum, one adolescent said he did not have a strategy for dealing with stress as he had always been tense for the past seven or eight years, which would have coincided with the start of school. Other adolescents had excellent strategies, such as playing basketball until they felt calm and relaxed, listening to music or sharing feelings with parents or friends. Some strategies for dealing with stress were less productive. For example, one adolescent indicated that about once a month when he felt stressed about school, he just stayed home. While avoiding the source of acute stress seems reasonable for events that do not occur often, it is not optimal for dealing with pressure related to school. With regard to self-esteem, a little over half of the mothers reported that their sons had normal to high self-esteem while four of the mothers indicated their children had low self-esteem that was cause for concern. The other two mothers were equivocal, reporting that their sons' self-esteem varied depending on the situation. One of these mothers said:

> There are two D—s [name of child]. There is the D— who is afraid, shy introverted. And there is another D— who knows about his abilities, who makes his position clear. It depends on how secure he feels. If his environment scares him, and it takes little to make him feel insecure, he pretends like he is not there.

It seemed clear from the responses of both the mothers and the adolescents that the history of school struggle had a negative impact on approximately half of these boys, and vestiges of this troubling experience had adversely impacted self-worth. Such an equivocal finding is fairly consistent with the literature on self-esteem, with many studies showing problems (Edwards, 1994; McNulty, 2003; Terras, Thompson & Minnis, 2009) and others reporting few (Burden & Burdett, 2005; Lindeblad, Svensson & Gustafson, 2016).

When these boys were interviewed four years ago, almost all of them complained of persistent teasing by peers and these problems rose to the level of bullying for two of the children (Anderson & Meier-Hedde, 2011). In addition, four of the children had been either physically or verbally abused by their teachers. The connection between teasing and dyslexia has been established by a number of studies (Edwards, 1994; Riddick, 2010; Singer, 2005) so this link was not unforeseen; however, it was unexpected to find that this pattern had changed in adolescence. Only four adolescents in the current study admitted to ever having been teased or bullied in spite of what the group previously shared in the first study. One of these adolescents complained of teasing by both peers and teachers, saying that his peers called him "idiot" or "dummy" and he had no idea how to stop it, as he said, "I can't fight back. I will get into more trouble." This adolescent did not feel he could go to his teachers for help as they had also teased and ridiculed him. His mother confirmed that he had been severely castigated by his teachers for "his poor handwriting and the mistakes he makes in homework." Another adolescent complained of being ridiculed by a teacher when he was asked to read out loud in class. This teacher said, "I think you should be able to read by now," causing him to become very nervous and make increasingly more errors as he read. After class this boy went to talk to his teacher and explained that he had dyslexia and asked her to be patient with him. This proactive strategy was very successful and nothing like that ever happened again. A third adolescent described a situation where a student who was the leader of a certain social group ostracized him, causing him to "suffer a lot," but the boy indicated that he handled the situation by keeping to himself and socializing with classmates that were not under the control of this bully. And a fourth adolescent's mother explained that her son had been bullied for one full year in a terrible situation; however, the adolescent denied this, saying that he had never been teased or bullied. Several observations could be drawn from this area of inquiry: (1) there was a marked decrease in teasing and bullying, (2) many of the children who complained about the abusive teasing in the early elementary years did not recall (or professed not to recall) these episodes and (3) some of those who were teased or bullied implemented proactive strategies for dealing with the problem and associated emotional pain. There is scant research that would help to explain this decrease in teasing/bullying, but as Ingesson (2007) suggested, it appears that the early school years may be more difficult for children with dyslexia as their self-esteem is very vulnerable at the time when they first face the significance of their reading difficulties and then later their self-worth is less threatened by the stigma as they learn to compartmentalize the condition.

Use of Effective Support Systems

In the Frostig study, use of effective support systems referred to individual's active use of the support of others, such as parents, teachers and significant others (Raskind et al., 1999). For the current study, we evaluated the adolescents' and mothers' interviews in terms of three categories of responses: understanding the need for support, valuing of support and initiating use of available support. As indicated in Table 16.1, this group showed a high level of support system use.

Every single adolescent in this study gave responses indicating a valuing of the support that had been provided for their reading and an explanation of its importance in relation to needs. This support varied in terms of the structure of the assistance as some of these adolescents had tutoring sessions while others had small group remedial sessions, homework assistance or direct assistance from the parents and/or peers. When the adolescents were asked "What is the single most important thing that your parents have done to support your school achievement?" 12 of the boys were very specific in their responses, indicating type of support and appreciation of assistance. Typical responses included the following: "My mother sent me to a private tutor center for homework support," "to give me a special teacher, to talk with teachers and always support me" and "made sure I got help." One boy said: "My parents have paid for my studies since childhood. They always try to pay my private schools and private teachers to get the best for me." Another adolescent said: "They invest a lot of time and money in private teachers and to drive me to them. They speak to the teachers to make sure I get what I deserve." This question seemed to elicit a genuine outpouring of gratitude from the adolescents for the assistance the parents had provided. The one adolescent who did not identify specific academic support for the parent question said, "They are always with me," probably meaning that he feels that they always supported him. Previously he had indicated that he had made the most improvement when he had been provided with remedial help from a university clinic and he lamented that he no longer had access to these services as his mother's job prevented her from taking him. (It was not clear why he could not take public transportation to the clinic.)

The question "How well can you get teachers to help you when you are stuck on school work?" from the Self-Efficacy Questionnaire for Children (Muris, 2001) was examined as an indicator of student's ability to seek and obtain support. The adolescents responded on a scale of 1 to 5, with 1 designated as "not very well" and 5 indicating "very well." Only four of the adolescents responded with 4s and 5s while over half responded with 3s, suggesting that most did not feel confident they could easily engage teacher support. The other two adolescents gave this question a 1 and a 2, conveying that help would not be forthcoming from their classroom teachers or they would be hesitant or fearful of requesting such support. These adolescents valued remedial support, but were not as positive when they had to rely on their classroom teachers whom they viewed as being less supportive. Perhaps this lack of confidence in securing support from classroom teachers was related to their teachers' lack of confidence in meeting their needs. In general, teachers have expressed feelings of insecurity about meeting the needs of students with dyslexia because of their insufficient knowledge (Bell, 2013), which appears to be related to their lack of training (Gwernan-Jones & Burden, 2009; Sicherer, 2014). Although this may be a pervasive problem across all levels, secondary teachers seem to be particularly uninformed about dyslexia and may not understand that challenging content cannot be easily acquired without attention to the presenting reading problem (Wadlington & Wadlington, 2005).

Appropriate Goal Setting

The ability to develop goals and demonstrate self-direction is a substantial asset for successful adaptation. Raskind et al. (1999) operationalized appropriate goal setting as the ability to set attainable goals and explain how these can be accomplished in a step-by-step manner. For our study, we asked the adolescents to identify goals to be accomplished by the end of secondary school and the steps by which these could be achieved. We also asked the adolescents to prioritize their goals with a rationale. In terms of postsecondary options, we extended this area to include vocational aspirations, associated requirements and the suitability of the job for individual skills and interests.

As indicated in Table 16.1, goal setting was definitely an area of strength for these adolescents. All of them identified two goals to accomplish before the end of secondary school. Twelve of these adolescents identified a school-related goal as one of these. These goals included "try to get an A– in half of my subjects," "do good in history," "submitting all of my homework on time" and "pass graduation exams successfully." In terms of prioritizing their goals, the overwhelming majority identified the academic goal as the most important mainly because of how it would influence their future (e.g., "because it lays the foundation to be able to go to college or get a job" and "it will be the most important in the future"). One boy summed up the importance of prioritizing academics over sports by saying, "Once I do better in math, I will get more marks and that will help me. Achieving this will make me very happy. Becoming games captain is only for fun. It's not that important."

For those who did not prioritize the academic goal, sports was identified as having primacy. One of the boys explained:

> Success in sports is first. I don't see myself happy if I don't succeed in sports. It's something I am good at. I hear it all the time. Many people tell me that it's something I can succeed in. When my father introduced me to the field he told me that I have potential. There is nothing can stop me from achieving this goal.

As this adolescent's career goal was to be a body builder, it would seem to be quite logical to prioritize this goal as it most likely does not have an academic requirement.

Five of the 13 adolescents identified professional jobs requiring higher education as vocational aspirations (i.e., university professor, veterinarian, architect and two engineers). The majority reported that they would not go on to university, which was somewhat inconsistent with previous research (Cortiella & Horowitz, 2014; McNulty, 2003). They identified office jobs and manual labor positions as their vocational choices, some of which required trade school or apprenticeships. Although most of these adolescents could articulate why their chosen jobs were a good match for them (e.g., they had previous experience or great interest in the area), very few could explain the associated requirements of the vocation they had chosen. It certainly should not be considered unusual for children between 14 and 16 years of age to have set their sights on jobs for which they have only vague familiarity. It is laudable that they have demonstrated evidence of planning for the future and that many of these goals seemed eminently attainable. There is some concern that only five were, at this point, seeking higher prestige jobs as all of the adolescents have average to above average intellect. Some of the manual labor jobs may be unnecessarily restrictive and based on the adolescents' perceptions of limitations or weak self-efficacy unless the individuals selected these based on a realistic assessment of interests, skills and values (Rojewski, Lee, Gregg & Gemici, 2012). Some of the boys in this study who chose manual labor vocations were actually interested in jobs requiring more education, but seemed fearful of the challenges associated with university matriculation and lacked confidence in their chances of success. Ingesson (2007) discovered that most of the adolescents with dyslexia she interviewed chose not to pursue further study after high school because the academic demands were too arduous. It wasn't that they could not be successful with the increased educational requirements of these professions, but rather they did not choose to continue down this road. We do not know the extent to which teachers or school counselors may have influenced the adolescents' expectations in our study, but we do know that some research has determined that school personnel unwittingly impose restrictions on the career aspirations of those with learning disabilities because of their lack of understanding of this condition whereas parents have more positive perceptions of potential (Diakogiori & Tsiligirian, 2016). Indeed, Richard Rogers, a gifted architect with dyslexia, explained his determination to follow his desired career trajectory as follows:

> Because I was very close to my parents, especially my mother, who never gave up, I learned that when people said "it's impossible," it's not impossible. That was probably the most important lesson I learned. So when people said, "go join the police force and don't go to university," I didn't believe it.
> (Yale Center for Dyslexia & Creativity, 2016)

Achievement Goal Dispositions

Motivation for studying was examined with an adapted version of the Achievement Goal Dispositions Survey (Hayamizu & Weiner, 1991) that separated sources of incentive into three categories: social approval, learning mastery (intellectual curiosity) and attainment of specific goals. The adolescents in this investigation showed a marked preference for studying to achieve specific goals, such as university admission, securing a good job and attaining self-selected goals.

Of the thirteen boys, nine indicated goal achievement as the primary reason for studying while another three boys scored this area the same or a close second to the other areas. Only one boy selected social approval as his primary motivation for studying with learning mastery being a very distant third choice. Studying for purposes of social approval has often been interpreted as avoidance of rejection (Hayamizu & Weiner, 1991), which may be the case for this boy as his father frequently punished him for school underachievement and teachers routinely ridiculed him for reading and writing errors he made in class. Learning mastery was the second most frequently identified reason for studying, but it was well below goal attainment. Only one boy consistently rated learning mastery as a primary reason for studying. Social approval was in last place as a motivation for studying, well below both goal attainment and intellectual curiosity. Previous research with students with learning disabilities compared to those without has determined that the former were less interested in learning for purposes of intellectual stimulation (learning mastery), less motivated for securing social approval and equally motivated to achieve attainment of specific goals (performance goals) (González-Pienda et al., 2000). The current results are consistent with these findings. The adolescents in this study seemed to be focused on setting their own personal goals and striving to meet these, a finding that was further verified in the previous section on goal setting as a success attribute. However, it is helpful to keep in mind that students are rarely motivated to adopt a single goal exclusively, but rather show preferences for different goals depending upon the circumstances (Núñez, et al., 2011) and that the highest levels of motivation may be associated with a combination of high learning mastery and high goal achievement (Bouffard, Boisvert, Vezeau & Larouche, 1995), which was the profile for only one adolescent in the current study.

Self-Efficacy

According to Bandura (1997), self-efficacy refers to an individual's belief in his/her ability to execute behaviors necessary to produce specific performance attainments. In other words, self-efficacy reflects an individual's confidence in achieving important goals. In this study, self-efficacy was measured, in part, by responses to two scales (Academic and Emotional) on the Self-Efficacy Questionnaire for Children (SEQ; Muris 2001). Table 16.2 shows that nine of the adolescents in the current study scored at or above the mean on the Academic Scale; four of these boys had scores that were a standard deviation or more above the mean. The four boys who were below the mean had very significant reading problems and had made limited, if any, reading progress in the past four years. The results of the Emotional Scale revealed that there were five adolescents whose scores fell below the mean; four of these boys were the same who had scored below the mean on the Academic Scale. This is not surprising since Muris reported the subscales as being intercorrelated (.40, $p < .001$).

TABLE 16.2 Total Scores for Self-Efficacy Questionnaire for Children

Adolescents	Academic Self-Efficacy	Emotional Self-Efficacy
Case 1	27	31
Case 2	20	24
Case 3	27	29
Case 4	29	32
Case 5	14	16
Case 6	25	27
Case 7	20	21
Case 8	23	23
Case 9	24	27
Case 10	30	21
Case 11	32	33
Case 12	33	35
Case 13	27	27

Note: Mean scores for normative sample (Muris, 2001) are 23.9 (SD = 5.7) for the Academic Scale and 26.5 (SD = 4.5) for the Emotional Scale.

The other adolescent whose score was a full standard deviation below the mean on the Emotional Scale had scored a full standard deviation above the mean on the Academic Scale. This adolescent's scores revealed a pattern of consistency within each scale, showing a marked difference between academic and emotional competency. The results of the self-efficacy measure were important as they suggested that the majority of these adolescents with dyslexia were confident about their academic and emotional competence, a finding supported by previous research (Burden & Burdett, 2005; Lindeblad et al., 2016). However, there is some concern about the four adolescents with low scores on both scales as Muris (2001) has identified a significant correlation between scores on the SEQ with measures of depression; the lower the SEQ scores, the higher the level of depression in the adolescent. The possibility of depression can be observed in the words of one adolescent with low academic and emotional self-efficacy scores:

> I find that most of my secondary teachers ignore me and they don't pay attention to the problems that I encounter. It seems that they can't accept that I'm different and I have dyslexia . . . Many people can succeed, except me . . . I want to be normal. I don't want dyslexia.

Another adolescent with low scores in both areas showed his lack of confidence throughout his interview responses. He was the same adolescent who was unable to name two school strengths. This adolescent also expressed a fear of being retained and said that he did not always try to do his best at school because "every time I try, I just can't do it." He had described the level of support he had received for his reading as "poor" and indicated that if he could change one thing about school, it would be to receive tutoring for his reading. This boy's plight as well as that of the other boys with low scores on this self-efficacy measure is concerning for a number of reasons including the co-morbidity of depression associated with dyslexia (Burden, 2005; Koulopoulou, 2010; Nelson & Harwood, 2011).

Three of the four adolescents who scored the lowest on both the Academic and Emotional Scales seemed withdrawn and somewhat isolated. These boys also seemed to feel helpless in the face of school demands, not knowing how to make things better. They felt trapped by their reading problems, fearful of consequences and saw few options to experience success at school, a finding consistent with that of other self-efficacy researchers (Lackaye, Margalit, Ziv & Ziman, 2006). These adolescents in particular seemed to be at risk for depression. The fourth adolescent who scored low seemed less likely to be at risk for depression as he expressed considerable optimism about continuing to receive help for reading and schoolwork from his friends and parents to meet university and career goals. This boy appeared to be quite popular and enjoyed a vibrant social life. However, his reading level was one of the lowest in the study, necessitating overreliance on the support of others to meet school requirements. His depressed self-efficacy scores may reflect insecurity related to this dependence on others and a lack of confidence in his ability to achieve his goals.

The students who obtained high scores on both the Academic and Emotional Scales showed evidence of strong confidence in their abilities. These three boys all felt that their reading had improved considerably since the last interview four years ago even though they each rated the reading support obtained in school quite differently (i.e., poor, satisfactory and excellent). It should be noted that all three of these adolescents continue to experience reading problems, but each has learned to use special strategies to accommodate their problems and experience a measure of success at school. Perhaps this is why these adolescents also showed strong evidence of self-determination and perseverance. A keen desire to keep moving forward in spite of obstacles and to be successful in school and life was a recurring theme in their interviews.

Children's Hope Scale

Feeling hopeful and optimistic in spite of adversity can help children with dyslexia become more resilient and confident about their abilities. The theoretical construct of the Children's Hope Scale (Snyder et al., 1997) is rooted in the premise that obstacles to goals can cause negative emotions whereas the successful attainment of goals in spite of these impediments results in positive feelings about oneself. Snyder (2002) posited that children's hope involves the capability to find workable routes to goals in spite of obstacles. Those children who have high hope are more likely to find numerous ways to circumvent obstacles compared with those children with low hope who struggle to see how they can overcome these obstacles to move forward and secure goals. Although Snyder and his colleagues (1997) provided normative data for the Children's Hope Scale in their initial publication of the scale, a number of studies have since added normative data for this measure, the largest of which involved a clinical sample of 623 youths between the ages of 11 and 18 conducted by Bickman et al. (2007). Using the norms from this study, adolescents who scored greater than 4.67 (75th percentile) would be considered to have high hope and those who scored below 3.0 (25th percentile) would be considered to have low hope. In the current study, only one adolescent obtained a score that would be considered to be high (4.7), but there were two other students who had scores of 4.5, placing them at the 70th percentile. There were also two adolescents whose scores of 2.2 and 2.5 fell into the low hope range with another two students whose scores 3.3 placed them at the 33rd percentile. The remaining six adolescents had scores that fell in the midrange and would be considered to have average hope. Idan and Margalit (2014) studied the mediating role of hopeful thinking in interactions between risk and protective factors in high school students with and without learning disabilities. For this study, the mean from the Children's Hope Scale for the learning disability group (N = 327) was 4.35 compared to the mean of 4.5 for the typical peer group (N = 529), representing a statistically significant difference (p < .01). For our study, the mean of 3.75 for these adolescents with dyslexia suggests a lower level of hopeful thinking; differences could be related to the participants (i.e., Israel versus global sampling). However, the means are within the range of average hopeful thinking. Idan and Margalit concluded that hope was an important variable that mediated risk and protective factors as well as self-efficacy and promoted higher achievement and effort for both teens with and without learning disabilities.

In order to interpret the results on hopeful thinking, it is helpful to consider some of the comments of the boy with the highest hope score. First, it is important to note that this adolescent was the only boy in the study who described his reading support in school to be "excellent." He reported that all of his teachers with the exception of one understood his learning needs and the implications of dyslexia. So it could be said that this adolescent had good models who supported him, a strong predictor for high hope (Snyder et al., 1997). This adolescent also did not give way to goal-blocking ruminations, behavior that Snyder (1999) suggested can create anxiety and interfere with goal attainment. When this boy was asked the three wishes question, one of his wishes was he would like to "get rid of the dyslexia." However, when his interviewer asked if he thought about dyslexia a lot, he replied,

> No, I know that I can't do anything about it, so it feels like a waste to muse over it when there is no solution so I don't ponder a lot, but it happens that I think that it would be nice not to have it.

Even though this adolescent has not made significant reading progress, he had learned strong adaptive skills, was progressing well in school and on track to graduate with a positive outlook on his future. In contrast, the adolescent who had the lowest hope score rated his school support for reading as "poor" and complained about most of his teachers as being unkind and uninterested in his progress. Throughout his interview, he mentioned numerous times that he wanted to rid himself of dyslexia and was fixated on his plight. He ruminated on the problems imposed by dyslexia and his lack of help from teachers. Certainly, everything this adolescent said was true; he was not exaggerating the challenges that he faced, which were exacerbated by family financial problems and the harsh punitive parenting of his father. Yet resilience is often born from deplorable circumstances when an individual is able to rise above burdens imposed and move forward in spite of them. This can be very difficult for those with significant literacy problems, yet diminished hopeful thinking and depressive tendencies may limit an individual's motivation to invest the necessary effort to succeed (Lackaye et al., 2006) and without these hopeful thoughts, the pursuit of goals can become stymied (Idan & Margalit, 2014; Snyder et al., 1997; Snyder, 2002).

TABLE 16.3 Adolescents' Evaluation of Reading Skill Improvement and Support Received

Adolescent	Reading Skill 4 Years Ago (Scale of 1–5)	Current Reading Skill (Scale of 1–5)	Reason for Improvement or Lack of Improvement	Rating of School Support Received
Case 1	2.5	4	Motivated to improve	Poor
Case 2	3	1	Stopped reading because of loss of remedial support	Poor
Case 3	2	4	Tutoring support and working on improvement	Satisfactory
Case 4	2	4	Developed a special strategy	Poor
Case 5	2	1	No help at home or at school	Poor
Case 6	4	3	Missing data	Satisfactory
Case 7	2	3	Don't know	Satisfactory
Case 8	2	2.5	Uninterested in reading and don't like to read	Poor
Case 9	3	4	Started reading more	Satisfactory
Case 10	3	4	Started reading more	Satisfactory
Case 11	2	4	Devoted more time, not giving up	Satisfactory
Case 12	2	3–4	Reading more and faster	Excellent
Case 13	2	3	Showed more effort	Satisfactory

Perspectives on Reading

Reading Improvement

Table 16.3 provides a summary of reading skill improvement, reason for improvement or lack of improvement and rating of instructional support as perceived by the adolescents. The question "On a scale of 1 to 5 with 5 being the highest, how would you rate your reading skill at the time of our last interview four years ago?" was asked to obtain an estimate of former reading level. The mode for this response was a 2, suggesting below average performance. The second column of this table refers to the data from the question, "On a scale of 1 to 5 with 5 being highest, how would you rate your reading skills today?" Nine of the adolescents believed that their reading had improved while three students felt they had regressed and one student thought there had been negligible, if any, improvement. The comments the adolescents made in their interviews suggested that a rating of 3 was perceived as average, as one boy said, "I would say I'm about a 3 right now. I feel I'm pretty much average." Those adolescents who believed they had improved mainly attributed their progress to increased motivation and reading. For the four boys who felt they had regressed or not improved, two of the boys said their lack of progress was tied to a loss of remedial support and one boy indicated he had no interest in reading. The adolescents were also asked, "How would you rate the support you have received for your reading problem since you started school?" with the choices being excellent, satisfactory or poor. Of the five adolescents who rated their support as poor, two of these had regressed and one had made negligible progress. Only one adolescent in the entire group perceived his support as excellent, however; this may be somewhat misleading. While it is true that this adolescent had very good support, it mainly came by way of accommodations and technology assistance, such as audio books and software programs as opposed to direct instruction that might have improved his reading skills. Because he did not have intensive reading support, he is currently facing some serious school challenges related to his poor reading skills.

When the mothers were asked the question, "How much has your son improved in his reading in the last four years on a scale of 1 to 5 with 5 indicating the greatest improvement?," the majority of the mothers indicated 3 or 4 with two mothers identifying 1 and 2 on the scale, the latter of whom were the mothers of two of the adolescents who believed they had regressed in the past four years. Thus, the adolescents and their mothers were generally in agreement about the amount of improvement since the last interview. The mothers were also asked, "Do you feel that your son puts forth effort on improving his reading performance?" The majority of the mothers indicated that they did not perceive their sons were putting much effort into reading improvement. Some of these mothers felt that reading was simply too aversive, saying, "No effort, he does not like to read and doing so might diminish the time that he uses for playing" while other mothers felt that reading was disillusioning, saying, "It's too hard and even if he puts in effort, he is still not as good as the others" or, as another mother explained, her son did not work on his reading because it was devastating to his ego and he needed "to protect himself emotionally." One mother reported that her son did not work on his reading because he had decided that using technology was a good substitute for reading and his school was providing the necessary supports. She said, "I believe he is satisfied. He has found a way that works for him." The few mothers who believed their sons were extending effort to improve their reading explained this perception in reference to the increased reading they had observed. And one mother explained a very elaborate strategy that her child had developed to improve comprehension: "He has designed a reading system. He reads aloud, changes words, asks questions, writes principle ideas and reduces ideas to a concept in order to build a text. It is hard for him, but he does it."

As principal investigators, we believe that these children have certainly improved in the past four years, but the amount of progress is questionable as perceptions and actual growth are difficult to quantify. For example, the boy who said he was currently an average reader was actually reading well below grade level. Most of the schools in these 13 countries do not routinely test students' reading, even those who have been identified as dyslexic. Thus, we have recent standardized test scores for only three of these adolescents. For these three boys, the mothers all indicated reading improvement at a 3 or 3.5 when standardized scores for these adolescents ranged from the 3rd to 19th percentile rank for single word reading and the 3rd to 4th percentile rank for decoding, suggesting sluggish improvement in these areas. Other evidence of slow reading improvement was found in the mothers' interviews. One question asked the mothers to share their goals for their sons' reading for the next four years. The answers clearly indicated that the majority of mothers were cautious about expectations. One mother said, "I wish he could get through a text by himself," but added, "I do not know if it will be so and if he has the motivation or whether it is possible." Another said, "I want him to learn to read on his own, especially by the time he is in college"; however, this is the same child who does not believe he has made any improvement in the last four years and has very low reading scores. Some mothers wanted their children to read sufficiently well to graduate from high school while others hoped their children would have the necessary reading skill to pass a driver's license test. Additional evidence of slow reading growth for these adolescents was revealed by the amount of homework assistance that mothers were providing because of reading difficulties. Six of 13 mothers were helping their sons with reading on a regular basis. One mother said, "He is totally dependent on me for his reading. He does not make any effort. I have to read out everything to him." There was scant confirmation that the majority of these adolescents had made significant strides in reading in the past four years, which is consistent with research that has shown limited reading achievement gains for this population (Cortiella & Horowitz, 2014; Raskind et al., 1999; Spekman, et al., 1992; Swanson, 2008).

TABLE 16.4 Reading Challenges and Solutions

Adolescents	Most Difficult Aspect of Reading Problem	Special Strategies to Help Reading
Case 1	Reading aloud in class	Take it slow and avoid mistakes
Case 2	Reading aloud too slowly	Read silently
Case 3	Peers not understanding	No
Case 4	Reading aloud and not having enough time to finish reading assignments	Read silently and then aloud, ask questions and then summarize
Case 5	Cannot decode	Use computer to look up pronunciations and meanings
Case 6	Need so much more time to finish tasks	Get assistance from classmate and try to read faster
Case 7	Read too slowly	No
Case 8	Cannot decode	No, but if forced to read will break up words
Case 9	Reading aloud and not understanding text	No, have to read until succeed
Case 10	Lagging behind class	Read more for practice
Case 11	Reading aloud in class	Learning to breathe well and use pauses
Case 12	Cannot read words and slow reading	No
Case 13	Not understanding text and skipping over lines	Read materials with pictures and use a paper to keep place under lines

Yet, on the basis of the qualitative data, we can confidently say that there are three adolescents in this study who were reading close to grade level and have made significant improvement since their diagnoses. They have not "outgrown their dyslexia," but they have taken full advantage of tutoring and have worked very hard to reach a level that was previously thought to be unattainable, but they will continue to need accommodations to keep up with classmates because of slower rates of processing.

Reading Challenges

Table 16.4 provides a summary of the adolescents' perceptions of the most difficult aspect of their reading problems and special strategies that they had identified to help them with these challenges. The most often cited difficulty was the slowness of reading that was described as an impediment by almost half of the adolescents. This was not unexpected as reading speed deficits have previously been identified as a significant problem for children with dyslexia irrespective of language (Landerl, Wimmer & Frith, 1997; Landerl, 2001; Layes, Lalonde & Rebaï, 2015;

Tilanus, Segars & Verhoeven, 2013). Certainly deficits in speed hamper dyslexic children at all ages, but it becomes a greater problem as grade level advances because of the increasing demands of the curriculum and the painfully slow reading progress. Longitudinal studies of reading speed between first and eighth grades have revealed that there is little improvement during this period. Klicpera and Schabmann (1993) found that those students who were the weakest readers in second grade were six years behind typical readers by the time they reached eighth grade, which was consistent with Landerl and Wimmer's (2008) finding. Similarly, Tressoldi, Stella and Faggella (2001) reported that the reading speed gains of dyslexic students were less than half of what was achieved by students without this condition during this same time period. Rasinski (2000) noted that a growing number of studies are finding that reading fluency is a major concern for adolescents. Apparently speed is a factor that is taking its toll on adolescents with reading problems as it appears to be a pervasive problem that affects handwriting, coding, naming, spelling and math in addition to reading (Ackerman & Dykman, 1996). In summarizing her findings of the slow processing speed of dyslexics, Landerl (2001) concluded that this marked deficit in reading speed is a serious handicap as it puts children at a major disadvantage as they struggle to achieve in school tasks with extensive reading requirements.

After reading speed, the adolescents in this study identified reading aloud as the second most difficult aspect of a reading problem. It was appalling to find that at this age students are still being asked to read aloud in class in spite of all of the research documenting the emotional pain it has caused students with dyslexia (Glazzard, 2010; Humphrey & Mullins, 2002; McNulty, 2003). Certainly reading aloud in a remedial setting with fluency-related strategies would be expected, but not in a large general education classroom for secondary level students. One would have thought that by middle school teachers would understand that this is not the most appropriate classroom activity, particularly for those with reading problems. In addition to these adolescents with dyslexia, it is to be expected that there are at least several others in each classroom who are not reading on grade level and would also find this extremely uncomfortable. Oral reading is a source of anxiety for many children, as Jalongo and Hirsh (2010) noted, "Reading aloud is public speaking with the performance pressure of on-the-spot decoding accuracy coupled with the evaluation by teachers and peers" (p. 434). Allington (2014) recommended that oral reading should be used very selectively and by the middle of first grade most reading should be silent. He believes that teachers monitor good readers and poor readers differently when they read orally, interrupting struggling readers frequently for word correction while waiting for good readers to finish and then asking if their reading made sense. Consequently oral reading creates two groups of readers, one group of good readers who self-regulate and another group who frequently stop and look to their teachers for cues (Allington, 2012).

Decoding was identified as the major reading problem by several children. The majority of children who have dyslexia have problems with phoneme-grapheme correspondences, which explains why many definitions for this condition cite decoding as one of the major associated characteristics. However, it is important to remember that decoding problems are more persistent if the orthography of the language is opaque and there are fewer problems if it is shallow (Landerl et al., 2013). Fortunately, these problems are amenable to remediation if the child is provided with intensive instruction early on, but unfortunately, as the current research indicates, this remediation is often not forthcoming at the intensity and duration required for effectiveness (Swanson, 2008; Vaughn, Denton & Fletcher, 2010). The majority of the children in this study did not receive sufficient phonologically-based direct reading instruction at the intensity necessary to develop proficiency (Anderson & Meier-Hedde, 2011) and, therefore, it would be unlikely they will acquire these skills in the future. Also, even if they had received this intervention, the children with transparent orthographies may have improved their accuracy without gains in speed, a common characteristic of dyslexia in languages with consistent orthographies (Serrano & Defior, 2008; Share, 2008).

Although the adolescents could easily identify the most difficult aspect of their reading problems, they had problems figuring out how to address it. For those students who mentioned slowness as their most difficult problem, only two adolescents had strategies for helping; one adolescent said he "tries to read fast" and obtain help from classmates while the other adolescent said, "I try to read a lot for practice." Both of these strategies are defensible as ways of trying to improve: effort and practice potentially can lead to improvement. Horowitz-Kraus, Cicchino, Amiel, Holland and Breznitz (2014) found that use of a computerized fluency program requiring children to read at their "fastest self-paced rate" yielded improved speed and reading comprehension; however, there is concern that this type of practice does not generalize (Hintikka, Landerl, Aro & Lyytinen, 2008). For those who identified reading aloud as the great source of difficulty, two adolescents had general strategies for assistance, such as "take it slow and avoid mistakes," and "learning to breathe well and use pauses." Of the students who identified decoding problems as their great challenge, one indicated that he used the computer for assistance ("looking up pronunciations and meanings") while the other said he did not have any strategies, but if he was "forced to read" he would "break-up the words" and try to pronounce them. One adolescent who identified comprehension problems and difficulty keeping his place in reading had very practical strategies for his difficulties that included using reading materials with pictures and a place holder under lines of text. As a group, these adolescents seemed to struggle with these reading questions, their answers suggesting hesitation or confusion about possible solutions. For example, one boy said he did not have any strategies as "One just has to read till one succeeds," which would seem to be an unreliable plan of action. Conspicuously absent in this section of interviews was mention of teacher or tutor guidance with regard to reading strategies.

Reading Support

In the interest of investigating perceptions of reading support, these adolescents were asked, "Looking back over your school years, what was missing in your educational program?" In other words, "What did you need to help you with your reading that you did not receive?" Six of the adolescents indicated that they needed more intensive instructional support. For example, one boy stated, "I needed more support, extra classes and tutoring," while another said he needed additional "one to one instruction." One adolescent was concerned that he did not get the help he needed early on as his teachers were continually directing him to "Read this!" when he could not read and had no idea how to comply with their directions, resulting in enormous frustration. Three of the boys did not know if anything was missing and one adolescent seemed to have the impression that his school was under no obligation to provide this support as he said, "It's up to me," a disheartening perception as his very low level of reading suggested that he desperately needed assistance.

When the mothers were asked if they were satisfied with the reading support that teachers had provided, the majority indicated they were not. Several mothers expressed disappointment that there seemed to be ignorance of dyslexia among the content area teachers and a lack of well trained teachers to address this condition. One mother complained that actual reading instruction had ended after middle school and apparently the school held the opinion that there was no more instruction for those who had not learned to read at this point. She said the school was willing to provide a support teacher who "could help him and show him what to do and read aloud for him and explain more things. She did very well, but these small extra things were in fact stuff I, as a parent, could have done." Her disappointment with the school was related to the lack of reading support that would have helped her son learn how to read, but not with the support he was given in his content area curriculum. This sentiment was voiced by other mothers who mentioned a lack of actual reading instruction and less funding for such programs at the secondary level. One mother said, "It is very difficult for the children like M– who have a lot of potential. The children who have a lot of potential, but special problems like reading difficulties, don't have possibilities to make progress." Some of the mothers did not really know what kind of reading support their children were getting. One mother felt grateful that her son was excused from reading aloud in class and interpreted this to be a type of reading support. In addition, she noted that she knew her son was attending some remedial class at school, but she had never received a report from this teacher so she could not comment on that support.

Although most of the adolescents in this study were not receiving any remedial reading support from their schools, they were receiving accommodations for subject areas. The most common accommodation was extended time for examinations, typically 15 minutes extra. Some students also had their exams read to them, but this was not routine. Other accommodations included exemption from second language, reduction of homework, note-taking assistance, computer support and no penalty for spelling errors. Although this list of accommodations may seem sufficient, in reality this support fell far short of meeting the adolescents' needs. The extra 15 minutes for the exams was seldom enough time for the boys to finish, particularly if they did not have exam readers. The second language exemption should have been perfunctory as this allowance was usually mandated by the school/district/state policy but, instead, some parents had to vigorously fight for this accommodation, sometimes for years. Probably the most disappointing aspect of these accommodations was related to the routinized fashion with which they were provided, with little reflection on the actual needs of the adolescent. Thus, when a student failed an exam, he was told to "work harder" for the next one without any consideration of how the teachers or school could extend or modify support.

With regard to the computer assistance, the majority of the students did not have any digital textbooks. Only 4 of the 13 boys in this study had ever used a digital textbook, a finding that seems incredulous considering this technology has been available for many years now. It is routinely accepted that teachers in content areas in middle and high school rely heavily on textbooks that are largely inaccessible to students with print disabilities like dyslexia (Bruhn & Hasselbring, 2013). Digital textbooks have the potential to greatly increase learning opportunities and level the playing field for students with reading problems, but publishers have been reluctant to offer this option to schools. In the United States, the National Instructional Materials Accessibility Standard (NIMAS) mandates that school textbooks, kindergarten through twelfth grade, be produced in digital format, although in reality, many students with reading disabilities do not qualify for NIMAS textbooks because of the stringent criteria (i.e., certification by a medical doctor that the student has a physical dysfunction that prevents reading from text in a typical manner [Bruhn & Hasselbring, 2013]). It is frustrating to contemplate this lack of access to digital reading materials especially in light of the amount of effort that the mothers are putting forth at great sacrifice of personal and professional time as they are reading content so that these adolescents can do their homework and study. If the boys could read textbooks independently, both they and their mothers could enjoy more independence.

When these adolescents were asked if they had ever used a screen reader, widely available since the late 1990s, only one boy answered affirmatively. Screen readers, sometimes referred to as text-readers, provide an enormous source of reading support to struggling readers. According to Hasselbring and Bausch (2005/2006), these software tools can break down literacy barriers in two important ways: supporting achievement by providing access to grade level reading materials and strengthening reading skills. All students with dyslexia need access to the same materials their peers are using, but often this is not possible because the materials are written at a grade level well above that of their functioning and they are therefore excluded from acquiring valuable content, the result of which is they fall further and further behind. Text-readers such as Read & Write Gold (2015), one the most popular of its kind in the United States as well as other English speaking countries, has the capability of reading text in documents and web page formats regardless of the browser. In addition to the accessibility that text-reader software offers, we have known for some time that this technology provides a remedial component as it can offer specific instruction in phonemic awareness, phonological skill, word identification and passage comprehension (Olson & Wise, 2006; Torgesen & Barker, 1995) as well as practice opportunities that strengthen reading skills (Hall, Hughes & Filbert, 2000). Although these adolescents are not receiving the technological support that is widely available, most of them acknowledge that computers have helped them with their reading. They used computers to look up unknown words and find pronunciations as well as definitions. They also relied on computers for spelling and writing assistance. This is a group of adolescents who are interested in benefitting from assistive technology, but they appear to have a nascent awareness of the potential and applicability of this technology, which may be attributed to the lack of knowledge of their teachers due to inadequate training (Baek, Jung & Kim, 2008; Bausch & Hasselbring, 2004; Kazu, 2011) or the failure of schools to provide the necessary hardware and software.

Impact of Dyslexia on Mothers

Parenting a child with dyslexia can bring about a significant amount of stress (Dyson, 1996) and the mothers in this study had more than their share. When they were asked to rate the level of their stress on a scale of 1 to 5, with 5 indicating the highest level of stress, the average for these mothers was 4, with a range of 2 to 5+. We have known for some time now that parenting a child with a disability or a learning difference such as dyslexia can potentially create tension and pressure as families seek to support their children's progress through school and life (Snowling, Muter & Carroll, 2007). Although some research has shown increases in anxiety (Karande, Kumbhare, Kulkarni & Shah, 2009) others have not found this to be the case, but have suggested that parents have particular stress associated with the challenges of parenting a child with special needs and require assistance and understanding from teachers as they navigate the system (Bonifacci, Montuschi, Lami & Snowling, 2014; Earey, 2013).

When the mothers were asked if there had been specific times that were especially stressful, most mentioned the period when they first discovered their children had reading problems, usually in first or second grade. Karande and Kulkarni (2009) identified this as a time of parental risk because of stress associated with diagnosis. It was a shock for these mothers as all of the boys had clearly demonstrated that they were bright and alert children before they entered school. One of the mothers had a particularly difficult time as she had been told her son's reading difficulties were the result of an intellectual disability, which was clearly not the case. Other problems included school avoidance because a child was so upset about his reading difficulty, grade retention for reading underachievement that caused a child terrible emotional distress and removal from the school recommended by the principal and teachers because of a child's slow reading progress. These problems caused extreme tension for the child and the family as the mothers began to expend great amounts of effort trying to understand the true nature of the difficulty and deal with education professionals who were all too often ignorant or misinformed about dyslexia, the latter of which is a common occurrence (Bell, 2013; Sicherer, 2014). It would have made a huge difference to these children and their families if more teachers could have provided appropriate instruction and accurate information about the condition, but this was seldom the case as the lack of school support is often the primary complaint of parents (Rose, 2009). Overall the literature paints a dismal picture of parents struggling to support their children with dyslexia without assistance from teachers (Earey, 2013). At times, teachers inadvertently added to the stress by embarrassing the child and the mother. In one such case, a mother recounted a school meeting where the teacher was explaining the daily schedule and curriculum to all of the parents. As part of the presentation, this teacher used a projector to share some classroom pictures, but on the side of one particular slide there were specific notes about her son's performance and associated problems for all to see. All of the parents in the room began staring at the mother who wanted to cry from embarrassment. She said:

> And this was in the meeting and people started to look at me and I didn't know what to do. It wasn't a secret, but to be that odd person . . . and it is in an exposed situation to be the one who is different, and that is in a way a sorrow . . .

Fewer mothers identified the secondary level as being as stressful as the earlier years, but those who did referred to increasing amounts of homework, high stakes testing and even less teacher assistance. When asked if school was becoming easier or more difficult, five of the mothers felt it was becoming more difficult. One mother said:

> School is becoming more difficult for M–. The curriculum is very difficult and complex in the secondary school. There are so many tests and exams that he has to face. While he spends all his time on homework, he doesn't have room to review [what he has been previously taught]. I think he deserves a less demanding curriculum. School should think about designing a school-based curriculum for students with dyslexia.

Another mother voiced similar concerns:

> School is surely becoming more difficult for him. The syllabus and subjects are getting tougher. H– tends to forget what he has studied. Till now he had to remember only the first term portion for the first examination. There was a separate portion for the final examination. Now . . . he will have to remember the entire first and second term portion for his final board examinations. This is going to be a real challenge for him.

Additionally mothers who were concerned about the demands of the secondary school also noted more organization requirements, issues of slow reading in relation to curricular demands and need for increased attention and concentration.

The mothers had the greatest diversity of responses to the question "Are there specific aspects of your son's behavior related to his reading problem that caused stress for you on a daily basis?" Some mothers were concerned about the adolescents' behavior in terms of what it portends for the future. While one mother did not worry about her son on a daily basis, she said, "Occasionally I wonder how he will get on in the world and whether people are going to take advantage of him." And another mother said, "There is stress associated with your child not achieving a basic level of reading to exist in life." A major stressor that concerned the mothers on a daily basis was the need to provide assistance for homework. Some mothers could not help because they did not have the knowledge while others couldn't assist because of their work obligations. And at times the homework took so much of their personal time that they had nothing left for themselves. As one mother said: "It's time consuming. He refuses to read on his own, hence, I have to study his portion. For me, it's literally like going back to school. I don't have any time for myself." And as would be expected, some mothers were worried that they were not doing enough to support their sons. They wondered if they should be contacting the school more often, checking all of the homework and assignments or finding other tutors or better schools.

As can easily be seen, these mothers were extremely busy supporting their sons, which took a lot of time and effort. The question, "Have aspects of your son's reading problem influenced your professional or social life?" seemed to be difficult for the mothers because they were reluctant to admit that this was the case. Many of these mothers initially denied their son's dyslexia had exerted an influence on their professional or social lives, but then later on in the interview they would make reference to something that contradicted this. For example, the mother who was quoted above about not having any time for herself was one who said, "I have not allowed my child's problems to influence my personal or social life." Almost every mother, at some point in the interview, said something that indicated their children's reading difficulties had a negative impact on their lives. In most of the cases, the mothers talked about the toll on their professional lives including missed job opportunities, work absences, quitting their jobs to spend more time at home, or deciding not to go back into the work force because of the needs of the child. In terms of personal time, a few mothers indicated that they had less time for friends or themselves. One mother said, "I guess in a way because if C– needed help and he would come to me and not feel comfortable going to [father] and I would feel resentful because I had to be home and it was too frustrating." This lack of time for socialization has been noted in quality of life research focusing on parents of children with learning disabilities (Ginieri-Coccossis et al., 2012).

Approximately half of the mothers indicated that their sons' dyslexia had influenced their relationships with their husbands or significant others. One of these mothers reported that the challenges of having a child with dyslexia had actually made their marital relationship better, perhaps because their joint efforts on behalf of their son had made them closer. Those mothers who felt that dyslexia exerted a negative influence on their relationships voiced concerns for different reasons, such as husbands complaining that the wives spent too much time helping the child and mothers disappointed that the husbands did not contribute sufficiently. One mother spoke of her own dyslexia and associated inferiority complex being affected when her husband scolded their son for his problems that the father perceived as a weakness. When she tried to defend her son, her husband humiliated her and eventually they divorced because the stress was so great. The mother did not suggest that her son's problems caused the divorce, but the stress was a contributor. Another mother talked about stress associated with her husband's dyslexia and how this had at times caused friction and misunderstanding. The mother had anticipated that her husband would be more of a helpmate with the problems their son was having in school, but instead these difficulties brought back bad memories of his own school experience. So when their son has problems at school, the father "would be strongly reminded of how he didn't receive any help, which in turn means that he gets quite angry." Another mother spoke of the frequent fights that she and her husband had about her son's dyslexia. She said:

> I am the only person who rears my son. He always blames our son for being lazy. He always emphasizes that our son could perform better if he could work harder on reading. My husband blames me for not helping him with his reading. This is of course not the truth. I know how bad his reading problems have affected him. I have tried to explain how dyslexia has influenced him. It seems he doesn't understand this. Sometimes we have disputes.

Although these mothers disclosed their concerns and sources of stress, they also shared their hopes and dreams for their children. When they looked back and reflected on what they have learned about parenting and life in general as a result of having a child with a reading problem, many focused on the need for great amounts of patience and empathy. Another theme centered on the importance of being willing to fight for the assistance their sons needed and to trust their own instincts especially when professionals were making recommendations that they questioned. As one mother said, "We are all stronger than we think and I'm strong enough to make the tough decisions if I think they are the right decisions." These families have faced much adversity, but they have not lost hope and were guardedly optimistic about the future. As one mother philosophically noted: "Nothing is to be taken for granted. Many people struggle, but with different things. Life does not always turn out the way you expected it, but it can still be good."

Reflections

In summary, the most significant cross-case conclusion from this study is the finding that the majority of these adolescents with dyslexia, from all over the world, are demonstrating remarkable resilience in the face of dyslexia. This conclusion represents a departure from the historic case studies that represented a bleak portrayal of the lives of children with this condition. The adolescents in this study are showing excellent strength in important success markers such as self-awareness, effective use of support systems and goal setting. They also showed some evidence of emotional stability, proactivity and perseverance. These adolescents as a group are socially and emotionally stable and are enjoying rich social lives with their peers, families and communities. Most of these adolescents are conscientious and hard working with a hopeful outlook toward their future. They have faced all sorts of obstacles that they are successfully maneuvering as they seek to accomplish their goals. The remarkable finding that ten of these adolescents are doing very well is clouded by concerns for the three boys who appear to be at considerable risk as they showed less hopeful thinking, lower self-efficacy, insufficient evidence of important success markers (including social and emotional stability) and were struggling greatly at school. It is noteworthy that two of these boys had parents who were the least educated and from the lowest socioeconomic status when compared to other adolescents in the study. We think this is not a coincidence and points to a universal problem of lower school achievement associated with a lack of resources. Obviously, poor children do not fare as well as middle class children and they do even less well when challenged with dyslexia. The third adolescent who is struggling is in a middle class family that has extended considerable resources. All three of these boys are at risk of dropping out of school or failing to meet the requirements for graduation from secondary school. They not only need increased academic support, but assistance in the success attribute areas to bolster coping and self-determination. Without this assistance, they are likely to face a continuing downward spiral that will influence their chances for living productive independent lives.

 The second major finding of this study is that only three of these adolescents had made significant reading progress that placed them near grade level achievement and the rest were lagging significantly behind just as when they were originally diagnosed. This should not be considered news to anyone as we have come to accept that most children with dyslexia will not achieve skillful reading because they are not provided with the appropriate instruction at the age, intensity and duration necessary to close the gap between their reading level and grade level achievement. After elementary grades, few students with dyslexia are provided reading instruction unless their parents have the resources for private tutors, but this is still actually rare as the private tutoring for adolescents has shifted to focus on homework as opposed to the acquisition of basic reading skills. Thus, reading achievement in adolescence will likely predict reading achievement in adulthood. And this should be considered a discredit to teachers, schools and teacher training programs around the globe. We applaud the achievement of the three adolescents who "made it" through their own hard work and the diligence of their parents and teachers/tutors who provided the remedial programs, which is a great accomplishment on all sides, but we are also concerned about them becoming "victims of success," as one mother suggested, because they are in jeopardy of losing their accommodations as a result of increased achievement, without which they will surely suffer from adverse consequences as dyslexia has not been cured, but rather diminished. For the 10 adolescents who continue to have significantly depressed reading, it is likely that they will be struggling with decoding and largely dependent upon technological accommodations for the remainder of their lives, surely a disappointment for the boys and their families and a dishonor to the educational establishment.

The mothers of these adolescents continue to be heroic in their efforts to secure support for their sons. Their professional and personal lives have been greatly impacted by the stress of parenting a child with dyslexia. They have less time for spouses, other children, extended family, friends, hobbies and jobs, but there are few complaints. Their lives are very different than they would have been without their sons' dyslexia, but then again few parents can anticipate the revelation of parenthood with its parade of unanticipated events. Remarkably these mothers have channeled any disappointment or trepidation into purposeful energy to help these children live their best lives.

The voices of these adolescents and their mothers from around the globe, individually and collectively, are resounding as they echo familiar themes. This is not a distanced view of dyslexia in adolescence, but rather an upfront personal perspective of the lives of these individuals. These adolescents may be separated by geography, but they are connected by their similar stories irrespective of nationality and culture. This sharing of experiences closes some of the space that clouds our understanding and opens the dialogue for a world view of dyslexia.

References

Ackerman, P. T., & Dykman, R. A. (1996). The speed factor and learning disabilities: The toll of slowness in adolescents. *Dyslexia*, *2*, 1–21. doi:10.1002/(SICI)1099-0909(199602)2:1<1::AID-DYS33>3.0.CO;2-0

Alexander-Passe, N. (2006). How dyslexic teenagers cope: An investigation of self-esteem, coping and depression. *Dyslexia, 12,* 256–275. doi:10.1002/dys.318

Alexander-Passe, N. (2015). *Dyslexia and mental health.* London: Jessica Kingsley.

Allington, R. A. (2012). *What really matters for struggling readers: Designing research-based programs* (3rd ed.). Boston, MA: Pearson.

Allington, R. L. (2014). Reading moves: What not to do. *Educational Leadership, 72,* 16–21.

Anderson, P. L., & Meier-Hedde, R. (Eds.) (2011). *International case studies of dyslexia.* New York: Routledge.

Baek, Y., Jung, J., & Kim, B. (2008). What makes teachers use technology in the classroom? *Computers and Education, 50,* 224–234. doi:10.1016/j.compedu.2006.05.002

Bandura, A. (1997). *Self-efficacy: The exercise of control.* New York: Freeman.

Bausch, M. E., & Hasselbring, T. S. (2004). Assistive technology: Are the necessary skills and knowledge being developed at the preservice and inservice levels? *Teacher Education and Special Education, 27,* 97–104. doi: 10.1177/088840640402700202

Bell, S. (2013). Professional development for specialist teachers and assessors of students with literacy difficulties/dyslexia to learn how to assess and support children with dyslexia. *Journal of Research in Special Educational Needs, 13,* 104–113. doi:10.1111/1471-3802.12002

Bickman, L., Riemer, M., Lambert, E. W., Kelley, S. D., Breda, C., Dew, S. E., . . . Vides de Andrade, A. R. (Eds.). (2007). *Manual of the Peabody Treatment Progress Battery.* Retrieved from http://peabody.vanderbilt.edu/ptpb

Biddle, S. J., & Asare, M. (2011). Physical activity and mental health in children and adolescents: A review of reviews. *British Journal of Sports Medicine, 45,* 886–895. doi:10.1136/bjsports-2011-090185

Bonifacci, R., Montuschi, M., Lami, L., & Snowling, M. J. (2014). Parents of children with dyslexia: Cognitive, emotional, and behavioural profile. *Dyslexia, 20,* 175–190. doi:10.1002/dys.1469

Bouffard, T., Boisvert, J., Vezeau, C., & Larouche, C. (1995). The impact of goal orientation on self-regulation and performance among college students. *British Journal of Educational Psychology, 65,* 317–329. doi:10.1111/j.2044-8279.1995.tb01152.x

Bruhn, A. L., & Hasselbring, T. S. (2013). Increasing student access to content area textbooks. *Intervention in School and Clinic,* 49, 30–38. doi:10.1177/1053451213480030

Bryan, T. (2005). Science-based advances in the social domain of learning disabilities. *Learning Disability Quarterly, 28,* 119–121. doi:10.2307/1593608

Burden, R. L. (2005). *Dyslexia and self-concept: The search for dyslexic identity.* London: Wurr.

Burden, R. L., & Burdett, J. (2005). Factors associated with successful learning in pupils with dyslexia: A motivational analysis. *British Journal of Special Education, 32,* 100–104. doi:10.1111/j.0952-3383.2005.00378.x

Chung, K. K. H., & Ho, C. S. H. (2010). Second language learning difficulties: What are reading-related cognitive skills that contribute to English and Chinese word reading. *Journal of Learning Disabilities, 43,* 195–211.

Cortiella, C., & Horowitz, S. H. (2014). *The state of learning disabilities: Facts, trends and emerging issues.* New York: National Center for Learning Disabilities.

Diakogiori, K., & Tsiligirian, E. (2016). Parents and school career counsellors' evaluation of the occupational competence of children with dyslexia. *The European Journal of Counselling Psychology, 4,* 32–61. doi.10.5964/ejcop.v4i1.97

Dyson, L. L. (1996). The experience of families of children with learning disabilities: Parental stress, family functioning and sibling self-concept. *Journal of Learning Disabilities, 29,* 280–285. doi:10.1177/002221949602900306

Earey, A. (2013). Parental experiences of support for pupils with dyslexia: Ignoring the effect on parents. *British Journal of Learning, Support, 28*, 35–40. doi:10.1111/1467-9604. 12013

Edwards, J. (1994). *The scars of dyslexia*. London: Cassell.

Ginieri-Coccossis, M., Rotsika, V., Skevington, S., Papaevangelou, S., Malliori, M., Tomoras, V., & Kokevi, A. (2012). Quality of life in newly diagnosed children with specific learning disabilities (SpLD) and differences from typically developing children: A study of child and parent reports. *Child: Care Health and Development, 39*, 581–591.

Glazzard, J. (2010). The impact of dyslexia on pupils' self-esteem. *Support for Learning, 25*, 63–69. doi:10.1111/j.1467-9604.2010.01442.x

Goldberg, R. J., Higgins, E. L., Raskind, M. H., & Herman, K. L. (2003). Predictors of success in individuals with learning disabilities: A qualitative analysis of a 20-year longitudinal study. *Learning Disabilities Research and Practice, 18*, 222–236. doi:10.1111/1540-5826.00077

González-Pienda, J. A., Núñez, J. C., González-Pumariega, S., Alvarez, L., Roces, C., García, M., . . . Valle, A. (2000). Self-concept, causal attribution process and academic goals in children with and without learning disabilities. *Psicothema, 12*, 548–556.

Gwernan-Jones, R., & Burden, R. (2009). Are they just lazy? Student teachers' attitudes about dyslexia. *Dyslexia, 16*, 66–86. doi:10.1002/dys.393

Hall, T. E., Hughes, C. A., & Filbert, M. (2000). Computer assisted instruction in reading for students with learning disabilities: A research synthesis. *Education & Treatment of Children, 23*(2), 173–193.

Hasselbring, T. S., & Baush, M. E. (2005/2006). Assistive technologies for reading: Text reader programs, word-prediction software and other aids empower youth with learning disabilities. *Educational Leadership, 63*(4), 72–75.

Hayamizu, T., & Weiner, B. (1991). A test of Dweck's model of achievement goals as related to perceptions of ability. *Journal of Experimental Education, 59*, 226–234. doi:10.1080/00220973.1991.10806562

Helland, T., & Kaasa, R. (2005). Dyslexia in English as a second language. *Dyslexia, 11*, 41–60. doi:10.1002/dys.286

Hintikka, S., Landerl, K., Aro, M., & Lyytinen, H. (2008). Training reading fluency: Is it important to practice reading aloud and is generalization possible? *Annals of Dyslexia, 58*, 59–79. doi:10.1007/s11881-008-0012-7

Holopainen, L., Lappalainen, K., Junttila, N., & Savolainen, H. (2012). The role of social competence in the psychological well-being of adolescents in secondary education. *Scandinavian Journal of Educational Research, 56*, 199–212. doi:10.1080/00313831.2011.581683

Horowitz-Kraus, T., Cicchino, N., Amiel, M., Holland, S., & Breznitz, Z. (2014). Reading improvement in English- and Hebrew-speaking children with reading difficulties after reading acceleration training. *Annals of Dyslexia, 64*, 183–201. doi:10.1007/s11881-014-0093-4

Humphrey, N., & Mullins, P. M. (2002). Personal constructs and attribution for academic success and failure in dyslexia. *British Journal of Special Education, 29*(4), 196–203. doi:10.1111/1467-8527.00269

Idan, O., & Margalit, M. (2014). Socioemotional self-perceptions, family climate, and hopeful thinking among students with learning disabilities and typically achieving students from the same classes. *Journal of Learning Disabilities, 47*, 136–152. doi:1177/0022219412439608

Ingesson, S. G. (2007). Growing up with dyslexia: Interviews with teenagers and young adults. *School Psychology International, 28*, 574–591. doi:10.1177/0143034307085659

Jalongo, M. R., & Hirsh, R. A. (2010). Understanding reading anxiety: New insights from neuroscience. *Early Childhood Education Journal, 37*, 431–435. doi:10.1007/s10643-010-0381-5

Jenkins, J. R., Antil, L. R., Wayne, S. K., & Vadasy, P. F. (2003). How cooperative learning works for special education and remedial students. *Exceptional Children, 69*, 279–293. doi:10.1177/001440290306900302

Karande, S., & Kulkarni, S. (2009). Quality of life of parents of children with newly diagnosed specific learning disability. *Journal of Postgraduate Medicine, 55*, 97–103.

Karande, S., Kumbhare, N., Kulkarni, M., & Shah, N., (2009). Anxiety levels in mothers of children with specific learning disability. *Journal of Postgraduate Medicine, 55*, 165–170.

Karpicke, J. D., Butler, A. C., & Roediger, H. L. (2009). Metacognitive strategies in student learning: Do students practice retrieval when they study on their own? *Memory, 17*, 471–479. doi:10.1080/09658210802647009

Kavale, K. A., & Forness, S. R. (1996). Social skill deficits and learning disabilities: A meta-analysis. *Journal of Learning Disabilities, 29*, 226–237. doi:10.1177/002221949602900301

Kazu, I. Y. (2011). An investigation of factors affecting the use of educational technology in Turkish primary schools. *Education, 131*, 510–524.

Kemp, S. (2006) Dropout policies and trends for students with and without disabilities. *Adolescence, 41*, 235–250.

Klicpera, C., & Schabmann, A. (1993). Do German speaking children have a chance to overcome reading and spelling difficulties? A longitudinal survey from the second to the eighth grade. *European Journal of Psychology of Education, 8*, 307–323. doi:10.1007/BF03174084

Koulopoulou, A. (2010). Anxiety and depression symptoms in children—comorbidity with learning disabilities. *European Psychiatry, 25*, 432. doi:10.1016/S0924-9338(10)70427-2

Lackaye, T., Margalit, M., Ziv, O., & Ziman, T. (2006). Comparisons of self-efficacy, mood, effort, and hope between students with learning disabilities and their non-LD-matched peers. *Learning Disabilities Research & Practice, 21*, 111–121. doi:10.1111/j.1540-5826.2006.00211.x

Landerl, K. (2001) Word recognition deficits in German: More evidence from a representative sample. *Dyslexia, 7*, 183–196. doi:10.1002/dys.199

Landerl, K., Ramus, F., Moll, K., Lyytinen, H., Leppänen, P. H. T., Lohvansuu, K., ... Schulte-Körne, G. (2013). Predictors of developmental dyslexia in European orthographies with varying complexity. *Journal of Child Psychology and Psychiatry, 54*, 686–694. doi:10.1111/jcpp.12029

Landerl, K., & Wimmer, H. (2008). Development of word reading: Fluency and spelling in a consistent orthography: An 8-year follow-up. *Journal of Educational Psychology, 100*, 150–161. doi:10.1037/0022-0663.100.1.150

Landerl, K., Wimmer, H., & Frith, U. (1997). The impact of orthographic consistency on dyslexia: A German-English comparison. *Cognition, 63*, 315–334. doi:10.1016/S0010-0277(97)00005-X

Layes, S., Lalonde, R., & Rebaï, M. (2015). Reading speed and phonological awareness deficits among Arabic-speaking children with dyslexia. *Dyslexia, 21*, 80–95. doi: 10.1002/dys.1491

Lewis, S. K., & Lawrence-Patterson, E. (1989). Locus of control of children with learning disabilities and perceived locus of control by significant others. *Journal of Learning Disabilities, 22*, 255–257. doi: 10.1177/002221948902200410

Lindeblad, E., Svensson, I., & Gustafson, S. (2016). Self-concepts and psychological well-being assessed by Beck Youth Inventory among pupils with reading disabilities. *Reading Psychology, 37*, 449–469. doi:10.1080/08856250701650011

Liu, M., Wu, L., & Ming, Q. (2015). How does physical activity intervention improve self-esteem and self-concept in children and adolescents: Evidence from a meta-analysis. *PLOS ONE, 10*(8), 1–18. doi:10.1371/journal.pone.0134804

Mamlin, N., Harris, K. R., & Case, L. P. (2001). A methodological analysis of research on locus of control and learning disabilities: Rethinking a common assumption. *The Journal of Special Education, 34*, 214–225. doi:10.1177/002246690103400404

McMaster, K. N., & Fuchs, D. (2002). Effects of cooperative learning on the academic achievement of students with learning disabilities: An update of Tateyama-Sniezek's review. *Learning Disabilities Research & Practice, 17*, 107–117. doi:10.1111/1540-5826.00037

McNulty, M. A. (2003). Dyslexia and the life course. *Journal of Learning Disabilities, 36*, 363–381. doi:10.1177/00222194030360040701

Meyer, A., Rose, D. H., & Gordon, D. (2014). *Universal design for learning: Theory and practice.* Wakefield, MA: CAST Professional Publishing.

Milligan, K., Phillips, M., & Morgan, A. S. (2016). Tailoring social competence interventions for children with learning disabilities. *Journal of Child and Family Studies, 25*, 856–869. doi:10.1007/s10826-015-0278-4

Milsom, A., & Glanville, J. L. (2010). Factors mediating the relationship between academic and social skills and academic grades in a sample of students diagnosed with learning disabilities or emotional disturbance. *Remedial and Special Education, 31*, 241–251. doi:10.1177/0741932508327460

Muris, P. (2001). A brief questionnaire for measuring self-efficacy in youths. *Journal of Psychopathology and Behavioral Assessment, 23*, 145–149. doi:10.1023/A:1010961119608

Nelson, J. M., & Harwood, H. (2011). Learning disabilities and anxiety: A meta-analysis. *Journal of Learning Disabilities, 44*, 3–17. doi:10.1177/0022219409359939

Nielsen, C. (2011). The most important thing: Students with reading and writing difficulties talk about their experiences of teachers' treatment and guidance. *Scandinavian Journal of Educational Research, 55*, 551–565.

Núñez, J. C., González-Pienda, J. A., Rodríguez, C., Valle, A., Gonzalez-Cabanach, R., & Rosário, P. (2011). Multiple goals perspective in adolescent students with learning difficulties. *Learning Disability Quarterly, 34*, 273–286. doi: 10.1177/0731948711421763

Olson, R. K., & Wise, B. (2006). Computer-based remediation for reading and related phonological disabilities. In M. McKenna, L. Labbo, R. Kieffer, & D. Reinking (Eds.), *Handbook of literacy and technology*, Vol. 2 (pp. 57–74). Mahwah, NJ: Lawrence Erlbaum.

Palladino, P., Bellagamba, I., Ferrari, M., & Cornoldi, C. (2013). Italian children with dyslexia are also poor in reading English words, but accurate in reading English pseudowords. *Dyslexia, 19*, 169–177. doi:10.1002/dys.1456

Pham, Y. K., & Murray, C. (2016). Social relationships among adolescents with disabilities: Unique and cumulative associations with adjustment. *Exceptional Children, 82*, 234–250. doi:10.1177/0014402915585491

Rasinski, T. V. (2000). Speed does matter in reading. *The Reading Teacher, 54*, 146–151.

Raskind, M. H., Goldberg, R. J., Higgins, E. L., & Herman, K. L. (1999). Patterns of change and predictors of success in individuals with learning disabilities: Results from a twenty-year longitudinal study. *Learning Disabilities Research & Practice, 14,* 35–49.

Raskind, M. H., Goldberg, R. J., Higgins, E. L., & Herman, K. L. (2002). Teaching "life success" to students with LD: Lessons learned from a 20-year study. *Intervention in School and Clinic, 37,* 201–208.

Raskind, M. H., Margalit, M., & Higgins, E. L. (2006) "My LD": Children's voices on the internet. *Learning Disability Quarterly, 29,* 253–268. doi: 10.2307/30035553

Read &Write Gold (Version 11.5) (2015). Boston, MA: Texthelp.

Reiff, H. B., & Ofiesh, N. S. (2016). *Teaching for the lifespan: Successfully transitioning students with learning differences to adulthood.* Thousand Oaks, CA: Corwin.

Reis, S. M., McGuire, J. M., & Neu, T. W. (2000). Compensation strategies used by high ability students with learning disabilities who succeed in college. *Gifted Child Quarterly, 44,* 123–134. doi:10.1177/001698620004400205

Riddick, B. (2010). *Living with dyslexia* (2nd ed.). London: NASEN Routledge.

Roediger, H. L. (2013). Applying cognitive psychology to education: Translational educational science. *Psychological Science in the Public Interest, 14,* 1–3. doi: 10.1177/1529100612454415

Rogers, H., & Saklofske, D. H. (1985). Self-concepts, locus of control and performance expectations of learning disabled children. *Journal of Learning Disabilities, 18,* 273–278. doi:10.1177/002221948501800505

Rojewski, J. W., Lee, I. H., Gregg, N., & Gemici, S. (2012). Development patterns of occupational aspirations in adolescents with high-incidence disabilities. *Exceptional Children, 78,* 157–179. doi:10.1177/001440291207800202

Roll-Pettersson, L., & Heimdahl Mattson, E. (2007). Perspectives of children with dyslexic difficulties concerning their encounters with school: A Swedish example. *European Journal of Special Needs Education, 22,* 409–423. doi:10.1080/08856250701650011

Rose, J. (2009). *Identifying and teaching children and young people with dyslexia and literacy difficulties.* London: Department for Children, Schools and Families.

Sencibaugh, J. M., & Sencibaugh, A. M. (2016). An analysis of cooperative learning approaches for students with learning disabilities. *Education, 136,* 356–364.

Serrano, F., & Defior, S. (2008). Dyslexia speed problems in a transparent orthography. *Annals of Dyslexia, 58,* 81–95. doi:10.1007/s11881-008-0013-6

Share, D. L. (2008). On the Anglocentricities of current reading research and practice: The perils of overreliance on an "outlier" orthography. *Psychological Bulletin, 134,* 584–615. doi:10.1037/0033-2909.134.4.584

Sicherer, M. (2014). *Exploring teacher knowledge about dyslexia and teacher efficacy in the inclusive classroom: A multiple case study* (doctoral dissertation). ProQuest LLC (Accession No. 3620170).

Singer, E. (2005). The strategies adopted by Dutch children with dyslexia to maintain their self-esteem when teased at school. *Journal of Learning Disabilities, 38,* 411–423. doi:10.1177/00222194050380050401

Singer. E (2007). Coping with academic failure, a study of Dutch children with dyslexia. *Dyslexia, 14,* 314–333. doi:10.1002/dys.352

Smidt, M., Prah, A., & Čagran, B. (2014). Social skills of Slovenian primary school students with learning disabilities. *Educational Studies, 40,* 407–422.

Snowling, M., Muter, V., & Carroll, J. (2007). Children at risk of dyslexia: A follow-up in early adolescence. *Journal of Child Psychology and Psychiatry, 48,* 609–618. doi:10.1111/j.1469-7610.2006.01725.x

Snyder, C. R. (1999). Hope, goal-blocking thoughts, and test-related anxieties. *Psychological Reports, 84*, 206–208. doi:10.2466/pr0.1999.84.1.206

Snyder, C. R. (2002). Hope Theory: Rainbows in the mind. *Psychological Inquiry, 13*, 249–275.

Snyder, C. R., Hoza, B., Pelham, W. E., Rapoff, M., Ware, L., Danovsky, M., . . . Stahl, K. J. (1997). The development and validation of the Children's Hope Scale. *Journal of Pediatric Psychology, 22*, 399–442. doi:10.1093/jpepsy/22.3.399

Spekman, N. J., Goldberg, R. J., & Herman, K. L. (1992). Learning disabled children grow up: A search for factors related to success in the young adult years. *Learning Disabilities Research & Practice, 7*, 161–170.

Swanson, E. A. (2008). Observing reading instruction for students with learning disabilities: A synthesis. *Learning Disability Quarterly, 31*, 115–133. doi:10.2307/25474643

Terras, M. M., Thompson, L. C., & Minnis, H. (2009). Dyslexia and psycho-social functioning: An exploratory study of the role of self-esteem and understanding. *Dyslexia, 15*, 304–327. doi:10.1002/dys.386

Tilanus, E., Segars, E., & Verhoeven. L. (2013). Diagnostic profiles of children with developmental dyslexia in a transparent orthography. *Research in Developmental Disabilities, 34*, 4194–4202. doi:10.1016/j.ridd.2013.08.039

Torgesen, J. K., & Barker, T. A. (1995). Computers as aids in the prevention and remediation of reading disabilities. *Learning Disability Quarterly, 18*, 76–87. doi:10.2307/1511196

Tressoldi, P. E., Stella, G., & Faggella, M. (2001). The development of reading speed in Italians with dyslexia: A longitudinal study. *Journal of Learning Disabilities, 34*, 67–78. doi:10.1177/002221940103400503

Vaughn, S., Denton, C. A., & Fletcher, J. M. (2010). Why intensive interventions are necessary for students with severe reading difficulties. *Psychology in the Schools, 47*, 432–444. doi:10.1002/pits.20481

Wadlington, E., & Wadlington, P. (2005). What educators really believe about dyslexia. *Reading Improvement, 42*, 16–33.

Wang, M., & Eccles, J. S. (2012). Social support matters: Longitudinal effects of social support on three dimensions of school engagement from middle to high school. *Child Development, 83*, 877–895. doi:10.1111/j.1467-8624.2012.01745.x

Yale Center for Dyslexia and Creativity (2016). Artists, architects & designers. Retrieved from http://dyslexia.yale.edu/rogers.html

CONTRIBUTOR BIOGRAPHIES

Principal Investigators/Editors

Peggy L. Anderson, Ph.D., is Professor of Special Education in the School of Education at Metropolitan State University of Denver, Colorado, USA. Her research interests are dyslexia and curricular accessibility. Her publications include *International Case Studies of Dyslexia* (Routledge, 2011) co-edited with R. Meier-Hedde, *Case Studies for Inclusive Schools* (ProEd, 1997, 2005, 2013) and the *Streamlined Shakespeare Series* (Academic Therapy, 1999, 2000, 2004, 2006) co-authored with J. D. Anderson.

Regine Meier-Hedde, Dipl.Päd., M.Ed. (University of New Orleans, Louisiana, USA), is a dyslexia therapist in Hamburg, Germany with over 25 years of experience in private practice. Her research interests include case histories of dyslexia and outcome studies. Her publications include *International Case Studies of Dyslexia* (Routledge, 2011) co-edited with P. L. Anderson. For the past few years, as a wingwave (EMDR) coach, she has additionally specialized in treating dyslexic and other children with school-related anxiety.

International Researchers/Contributors

Australia

Christina (Christa) E. van Kraayenoord, Ph.D, is an associate professor in the School of Education at the University of Queensland, Brisbane, Queensland, Australia. Her research interests are related to literacy development and literacy education, learning difficulties and learning disabilities, especially in literacy, and whole school reform and teachers' pedagogical change in literacy. Her publications include journal articles and book chapters on literacy, learning difficulties, inclusive education and teachers' pedagogical practices. She is the President of the International Academy for Research in Learning Disabilities.

Brazil

Simone Aparecida Capellini, Speech Language Pathology, Ph.D. in Medical Sciences is Professor and Coordinator of the Investigation Learning Disabilities Laboratory (LIDA) at the Speech and Hearing Sciences Department, São Paulo State University "Júlio de Mesquita Filho" (UNESP), Marília, São Paulo, Brazil. Her research interests are reading disabilities, dyslexia, learning disorder, attention–deficit/hyperactivity disorder, assessment and intervention. Her publications include *Neuropsycholinguistic Perspectives on Dyslexia and Other Learning Disabilities* (Nova Publishers, 2007) as well as several chapters and books in Portuguese, English and Italian.

Giseli Donadon Germano, Speech Language Pathology, Ph.D. in Education, is a researcher of the Investigation Learning Disabilities Laboratory (LIDA) at the Speech and Hearing Sciences Department, São Paulo State University "Júlio de Mesquita Filho" (UNESP), Marília, São Paulo, Brazil. Her research interests are reading disabilities, dyslexia, learning disorder, attention–deficit/hyperactivity disorder, assessment and intervention. Her publications include several chapters, journal articles and books in Portuguese and English.

Canada

Brenda Linn, Ph.D., is a reading specialist who has worked with dyslexic children as a teacher, principal and psycho-educational consultant in urban settings and also in aboriginal communities in northern Canada. Her research interests include first and second language reading acquisition, dyslexia and giftedness. As a researcher at Oxford and McGill Universities, she investigated teachers' and teacher-educators' responses to the nationwide introduction of synthetic phonics in England and Wales, and explored teacher-educators' views of seminal cognitive reading research.

Barbara Bobrow, M.A., is a learning disabilities specialist who was one of the founders of the Learning Associates of Montreal, which was a non-profit center offering psycho-educational assessment, academic tutoring, remediation and unique after-school programs for children with learning disabilities. She has provided psycho-educational services to school districts in remote regions of Quebec and Nunavik. In private practice, she conducts psycho-educational assessments for child support agencies and private neuropsychological centers.

Ronald W. Stringer, Ph.D., is an associate professor in the School Psychology program of the Department of Educational & Counselling Psychology at McGill University in Montreal, Canada. His research interests include early reading acquisition and reading disabilities, as well as the experiences of students with learning difficulties, and Métis education. He is also a practicing psychologist in Montreal.

Chile

Arturo R. Pinto Guevara, Ed.D., is an academic and researcher in the Innovation Curricular Studies Department at the Universidad Playa Ancha, Valparaíso, Chile. He conducts research in the areas of cognition, language, special education needs and curriculum for teachers. He has developed undergraduate and graduate degree programs for national and international universities. He is a consultant to public and private schools that serve high achieving children and adolescents who have dyslexia and language disorders.

María Pomés, Ph.D., is a professor in the special education program of the Department of Diversity and Inclusive Education at the Universidad Católica del Maule, Talca, Chile. She has taught undergraduate students in the area of special education for 20 years. Her research interests are developmental screening, explicit vocabulary instruction and prevention of learning disabilities. Her recent publications include the examination of a developmental screening instrument for early childhood, the lexical availability process and explicit instruction for young children.

China

Steven S. W. Chu, Ed.D. Candidate, is Teaching Fellow of the Department of Special Education and Counselling at the Education University of Hong Kong, China. His research interests include developmental dyslexia, school bullying and adolescent mental health.

Kevin K. H. Chung, Ph.D., is Chair Professor in Special Education, Head of the Department of Early Childhood Education, and Director for the Centre of Child and Family Science, at the Education University of Hong Kong, China. His research interests are developmental dyslexia, learning difficulties, literacy assessment and instruction and social-emotional development. His publications include *Understanding Developmental Disorders of Auditory Processing, Language and Literacy across Languages: International Perspectives* (Information Age Publishing, 2014), co-edited with K. C. P. Yuen, and D. M. McInerney.

Hungary

Éva Gyarmathy, Ph.D, is Senior Researcher at the Institute of Cognitive Neuroscience and Psychology of the Research Centre for Natural Sciences of the Hungarian Academy. Her research interests focus on multiple exceptional gifted individuals such as talent associated with specific learning difficulties, attention-deficit/hyperactivity disorder, autism and/or social, cultural differences. She is university lecturer at University Budensis, Eötvös Lorand University in Budapest and University of Szeged. She is a consultant to private schools that serve gifted children and adolescents who could not be integrated in mainstream schools. She founded the Adolescent and Adult Dyslexia Centre and the Special Needs Talent Support Council. Her publications include *Holistic Learners* (Whurr Publishers, 2000) and *Diszlexia a digitális korszakban* [*Dyslexia in the Digital Age*] (Műszaki Könyvkiadó, 2012).

India

Sunil Karande received his M.D. (Pediatrics), FIAP from Seth Gordhandas Sunderdas Medical College & King Edward VII Memorial Hospital, Mumbai, India. Currently he is Professor of Pediatrics and In-Charge of the Learning Disability Clinic at his *alma mater*. He is a member of the Steering Committee that is developing the "International Classification of Functioning, Disability and Health (ICF) Core Set for attention-deficit/hyperactivity disorder (ADHD)," a research project being conducted at the Center of Neurodevelopmental Disorders at Karolinska Institutet (KIND), Stockholm in collaboration with the World Health Organization. He is the Editor of the *Journal of Postgraduate Medicine* (2016–2020).

Rukhshana F. Sholapurwala received her M.Ed. from Shreemati Nathibai Damodar Thackersey Women's University, Mumbai, India. Currently she is Special Educator at the Learning Disability Clinic, Department of Pediatrics, Seth Gordhandas Sunderdas Medical College & King Edward VII Memorial Hospital, Mumbai, India. Her research has included devising a screening tool to identify children with specific learning disabilities during their primary schooling years and she has published many articles on learning disabilities.

Israel

Talya Gur, Ph.D., is Head of the Special Education Department of Oranim Academic College of Education, Israel. Her research interests are reading and writing acquisition, and diagnosis and treatment of reading and writing disabilities. Her recent research investigates the self-regulation and writing strategies used by youth at risk.

Russia

Olga Inshakova, Ph.D., is Professor of the special education program of the Department of Speech Pathology at the Pedagogical State University of Moscow, Russia. Her research interests are reading and writing disabilities of students in grades 1–4 of comprehensive school, readiness of children for education, training students to work with pupils who have dysgraphia and dyslexia and who study not only in public schools, but also in special schools for children with serious speech problems. Her publications have focused on children with dysgraphia and dyslexia mastering reading and writing skills.

Spain

Rosa María González Seijas, Ph.D., is Professor in the Department of Developmental and Educational Psychology of the Faculty of Education Sciences at the University of A Coruña, Spain. Her research interests are prevention of and intervention for learning disabilities in reading and writing. She has published reading and writing curricula for early childhood including *Actividades para el aprendizaje de la lectura y la escritura* [*Activities to Learn Reading and Writing*] (CEPE, 2008) and *Javitor, the Reading Beaver and the Friends of the Letters* (CEPE, 2013).

Sweden

Eva Wennås Brante, Ph.D., is Postdoctoral Research Fellow in the Department of Education at Oslo University, Norway. Her research interests are in dyslexia, reading comprehension and critical reading. Her recent research focuses on dyslexic and non-dyslexic readers' comprehension of multimodal material and promoting upper-secondary school students' critical reading and learning in the 21st century information society.

INDEX

Note: Page numbers followed by 'f' refer to figures, followed by 'n' refer to notes and followed by 't' refer to tables.

accommodations: cross-case analysis 270–271; distress regarding 204; reluctance to accept 38; risk of losing right to 201, 277; in Russia 189; test 51, 55, 104, 123–124, 133–134, 189, 193; writing 102

Achievement Goal Disposition Survey 25; Alon 129, 135; Christian 219; cross-case analysis 259–260; Gwyn 59; Jacob 198–199; Jankó 174; Jim 237; João 146; Johan 43; Ka-Ho 77–78; Percy 111; Valeriy 185–186; Vicente 159; Xavi 93–94

acquired dyslexia 1

Al-Yagon, M. 63, 64, 133, 136

Alon, Israeli case study 121–138; Achievement Goal Disposition Survey 129, 135; background 121–123; careers and future goals 131–132; Children's Hope Scale 129; coping 130–131; diagnosis and treatment 121; educational perspectives 123–127; family and home life 122; friends 127–128; future goals and hopes 131–132; homework 127; learning style 126–127; medical and psychological aspects 122–123; mother, impact of dyslexia on 131; motivation for studying 129; private tuition 123, 124; reading achievement and progress 123–125; self-determination and coping 128–131; self-efficacy and motivation 128–129; Self-Efficacy Questionnaire for Children (S-EQC) 128–129; social development 127–128; teachers 126

anxiety disorder(s) 8, 231; diagnosis of a mild 229, 242; physical activity to reduce 247

assistive technologies 5–6, 7, 65, 178, 189, 196, 272; audio books 33, 34, 36, 40, 47; digital textbooks 271; screen readers 40, 271–272

attention deficit disorder (ADD) 71–72, 72–73, 148

attention deficit/hyperactivity disorder-combined type (ADHD-C) 103, 141, 153, 169, 231

audio books 33, 34, 36, 40, 47

Australian case study *see* Gwyn, Australian case study

awareness of dyslexia 2–3; teachers 64–65, 78, 82–83, 96, 98, 119, 257

background: Alon 121–123; Christian 210–212; Gwyn 50–52; Jacob

192–194; Jankó 167–169; Jim 227–231; João 139–141; Johan 33–35; Ka-Ho 68–72; Percy 101–103; Valeriy 180–182; Vicente 152–154; Xavi 87–89
bad grades, coping with 43, 94, 112, 125, 130, 146, 160, 174, 186, 199, 236; cross-case analysis 253
Bateriá de Aptitudes Diferenciales y Generales (BADYG) 88
Bateriá de Evaluación de los Procesos Lectores, Revisada (PROLEC-R) 87
behavior problems and dyslexia 229, 230, 238, 242
Bickman, L. 198, 263
Bonifacci, R. 44, 45, 272
Brazil: lack of policy and support for dyslexic students 147–148 *see also* João, Brazilian case study
bullying 57, 76, 78, 83–84, 145, 172, 184, 189, 217–218; cross-case analysis 255–256

Canada: avoidance of term "dyslexia" 203–204; "response to intervention model" 203; synthetic phonics programs 202–203 *see also* Jacob, Canadian case study
careers and future goals: Alon 131–132; Christian 222–223; cross-case analysis 258–259; Gwyn 61–62; Jacob 201; Jankó 176; Jim 239; João 147; Johan 46–47; Ka-Ho 80–81; Percy 105, 111, 115–116; Valeriy 188; Vicente 161–162; Xavi 93
Carroll, J. 44, 48, 97, 272
case study approach 16–19
categorical aggregation 27, 28
causes of dyslexia, research on 3
challenges, facing and dealing with 130, 160, 249, 250–251
characteristics of dyslexic adolescents 7–9
Children's Hope Scale 26; Alon 129; Christian 219; cross-case analysis of scores 262–264; Gwyn 59; Jacob 198; Jankó 173–174; Jim 236–237; João 146; Johan 43; Ka-Ho 77; Percy 110–111; Valeriy 186; Vicente 159; Xavi 93
children's voices 15–16
Chile *see* Vicente, Chilean case study

China: attitudes to dyslexia 81–82; Student Support Teams 82; teacher training in special education 83; Three-Tier Intervention Model 82 *see also* Ka-Ho, Chinese case study
Christian, German case study 210–226; Achievement Goal Disposition Survey 219; background 210–212; careers and future goals 222–223; Children's Hope Scale 219; coping 219–220; diagnosis and treatment 210–211; educational perspectives 212–217; family and home life 211–212; friends 217–218; future goals and hopes 222–223; homework 216–217; learning style 215–216; medical and psychological aspects 212; mother, impact of dyslexia on 220–222; motivation for studying 219; reading achievement and progress 212–214; self-determination and coping 218–220; self-efficacy and motivation 218–219; Self-Efficacy Questionnaire for Children (S-EQC) 218–219; social development 217–218; teachers 214–215
code-based reading programs 203
collective case studies 17, 19
compensatory strategies 135, 195, 205, 248–249; for learning 6–7, 47, 48
computer games 40–42, 57
computers, use of: cross-case analysis 271–272; leisure time 108, 122, 141, 153, 154, 155, 171, 211, 216; for school work 35, 40, 56, 65, 74, 92, 140, 153, 157, 178, 184, 193, 194, 196, 202, 234
content enhancement routines 6
control, research on locus of 251
coping: Alon 130–131; Christian 219–220; Gwyn 60; Jacob 199; Jankó 174–175; Jim 237–238; João 146; Johan 43–44; Ka-Ho 78; Percy 112–113; studies of patterns in 135; Valeriy 186; Vicente 159–160; Xavi 94
counseling, parental 38
Creswell, J. W. 17
cross-case analysis 28, 245–283; Achievement Goal Dispositions 259–260; Children's Hope Scale 262–264; impact of dyslexia on

mothers 272–276; reading, perspectives on 265–272; Self-Efficacy Questionnaire for Children (S-EQC) 260–262, 261t; success attributes 245–259
cross-case synthesis 28
Curriculum Based Test (CBT) 101

data analysis and interpretation 27–28
decoding 3, 241; cross-case analysis 268–269; PHAST Decoding Program 5; strategies to help with 269
defining dyslexia 1–3, 22
depression 8, 44, 110, 145, 231; and links with low SEQ scores 261–262
Deshler, D. D. 6
design, study 19–28; Achievement Goal Disposition Survey 25; adolescents' interviews 23–24; Children's Hope Scale 26; data analysis and interpretation 27–28; implementation of protocol 26–27; instrumentation 23–26; mothers' interviews 24; objective of study 19; participants 21–22; report guide 26–27; research questions 19–21; selection of researchers 22–23; Self-Efficacy Questionnaire for Children (S-EQC) 24–25
developmental dyslexia 1
diagnosis and treatment: Alon 121; Christian 210–211; Gwyn 50–51; Jacob 192–193; Jankó 167–168; Jim 227–228; João 139–140; Johan 33–34; Ka-Ho 68–70; Percy 101–102; research on scientific validity of 47; timing of 201; Valeriy 180–181, 187; Vicente 152–153; Xavi 87–89
Differential and General Aptitudes Battery (BADYG E2) 88
digital textbooks 271
Dweck, C.S. 25, 135

educational perspectives: Alon 123–127; Christian 212–217; cross-case analysis 265–272; Gwyn 52–57, 62–63; Jacob 194–197; Jankó 169–172; Jim 231–235; João 141–144; Johan 35–41; Ka-Ho 72–75; Percy 104–109; Valeriy 182–184; Vicente 154–158; Xavi 89–92

educational psychologist intervention program 50–51, 62
Elliott, J. G. 1, 3, 22, 25, 189, 203, 224
emotional stability 9–10, 246t, 254–256
ethnographies 17
Evaluación de los Procesos de Escritura (PROESC) 88
Evaluation of Writing Process (PROESC) 88
executive function 6–7, 164

Facebook 42, 58, 71, 78, 108, 141, 172–173, 216, 235
failure, reactions to message of school 9–10
family and home life 101–102; Alon 122; Christian 211–212; cross-case analysis 249–250; Gwyn 51; importance of 163; Jacob 193–194; Jankó 168; Jim 229–230; João 140–141; Johan 34–35; Ka-Ho 70–71; parenting a learning disabled child and impact on 136; Percy 102–103; Valeriy 181; Vicente 153; Xavi 89
F.A.S.T. Reading System 229
fathers: aggressive behavior of 70–71, 76, 79, 83, 168; disagreements with 79, 114, 172, 230; dyslexia affecting relationship with mother 60, 79, 175, 275; lack of empathy from dyslexic 45; supportive 60, 220
financial support for families, Sweden 45
Firth, N. 63, 135
Flyvbjerg, B. 17, 18
friends: Alon 127–128; Christian 217–218; Gwyn 57–58; Jacob 197; Jankó 172–173; Jim 235; João 144–145; Johan 41–42; Ka-Ho 75–76; Percy 109; Valeriy 184; Vicente 158; Xavi 92–93
Frostig Center study 23–24, 246, 256
future goals and hopes: Alon 131–132; Christian 222–223; cross-case analysis 246t, 258–259; Gwyn 61–62; Jacob 201; Jankó 176; Jim 239–240; João 147; Johan 46–47; Ka-Ho 80–81; Percy 114–116; Valeriy 188; Vicente 161–162; Xavi 95

Germany: training for dyslexia therapists 224 *see also* Christian, German case study
goals *see* future goals and hopes
Goldberg, R. J. 9, 10, 19, 20, 23, 246
Grigorenko, E. I. 1, 3, 22, 187, 189, 203, 224
grounded theory 17
group work 40, 56, 74, 92, 108, 144, 157, 234, 248
Gwyn, Australian case study 50–67; Achievement Goal Disposition Survey 59; background 50–52; careers and future goals 61–62; Children's Hope Scale 59; coping 60; diagnosis and treatment 50–51; educational perspectives 52–57, 62–63; family and home life 51; friends 57–58; future goals and hopes 61–62; homework 57; learning style 56; medical and psychological aspects 51–52; mother, impact of dyslexia on 60–61; motivation for studying 59; reading achievement and progress 52–55; self-determination and coping 58–60; self-efficacy and motivation 58–59; Self-Efficacy Questionnaire for Children (S-EQC) 58–59; social development 57–58; teachers 55–56
Gyarmathy-Smythe Cognitive Profile Test 167

Hayamizu, T. 23, 25, 43, 59, 77, 93, 111, 129, 146, 159, 174, 185, 198, 219, 237, 259, 260
Herman, K. L. 9, 10, 19, 20, 23, 24, 246
Higgins, E. L. 9, 10, 16, 19, 20, 23, 246
higher education, dyslexia and 47, 80, 95, 156–157; cross-case analysis 258, 259
home literacy environment 97–98
homework: Alon 127; Christian 216–217; cross-case analysis 252–253; Gwyn 57; Jacob 196–197; Jankó 171–172; Jim 234–235; João 144; Johan 40–41; Ka-Ho 75, 80; Percy 103, 108–109; a stressor for mothers 274; Valeriy 184; Vicente 154, 157–158; Xavi 92
Hong Kong, Test of Specific Learning Difficulties in Reading and Writing for Primary School Students 68
Humphrey, N. 84, 177, 268

Hungary: understanding of dyslexia in 177 *see also* Jankó, Hungarian case study
Idan, O. 263, 264
Ildkó Meixner Test 167
India: adolescent school experience studies 117; awareness of dyslexia 119 *see also* Percy, Indian case study
Ingesson, S. G. 20, 33, 34, 42, 48, 242, 256, 259
instrumental case studies 17
instrumentation 23–26
International Dyslexia Association (IDA), definition of dyslexia 2, 3
interviews, semi-structured: adolescents 23–24; mothers 24
intrinsic case studies 17
Iowa Tests of Basic Skills 232
Israel: army service 132, 136; support for learning disabled pupils 133, 136 *see also* Alon, Israeli case study

Jacob, Canadian case study 192–209; Achievement Goal Disposition Survey 198–199; background 192–194; careers and future goals 201; Children's Hope Scale 198; coping 199; diagnosis and treatment 192–193; educational perspectives 194–197; family and home life 193–194; friends 197; future goals and hopes 201; homework 196–197; learning style 195–196; medical and psychological aspects 194; mother, impact of dyslexia on 199–201; motivation for studying 198–199; reading achievement and progress 194–195; self-determination and coping 197–199; self-efficacy and motivation 197–199; Self-Efficacy Questionnaire for Children (S-EQC) 197–198; social development 197; teachers 195
Jankó, Hungarian case study 167–179; Achievement Goal Disposition Survey 174; background 167–169; careers and future goals 176; Children's Hope Scale 173–174; coping 174–175; diagnosis and treatment 167–168; educational perspectives 169–172; family and home life 168; friends 172–173; future goals

and hopes 176; homework 171–172; learning style 171; medical and psychological aspects 168–169; mother, impact of dyslexia on 175–176; motivation for studying 174; private tuition 170; reading achievement and progress 169–170; self-determination and coping 173–175; self-efficacy and motivation 173–174; Self-Efficacy Questionnaire for Children (S-EQC) 173; social development 172–173; teachers 170–171

Jensen, F.E. 8

Jim, American case study 227–243; Achievement Goal Disposition Survey 237; background 227–231; careers and future goals 239; Children's Hope Scale 236–237; coping 237–238; diagnosis and treatment 227–228; educational perspectives 231–235; family and home life 229–230; friends 235; future goals and hopes 239–240; homework 234–235; learning style 234; medical and psychological aspects 230–231; mother, impact of dyslexia on 238–239; motivation for studying 235–236, 237; reading achievement and progress 231–233; self-determination and coping 235–238; self-efficacy and motivation 235–237; Self-Efficacy Questionnaire for Children (S-EQC) 236; social development 235; teachers 233–234

João, Brazilian case study 139–151; Achievement Goal Disposition Survey 146; background 139–141; careers and future goals 147; Children's Hope Scale 146; coping 146; diagnosis and treatment 139–140; educational perspectives 141–144; family and home life 140–141; friends 144–145; future goals and hopes 147; homework 144; learning style 144; medical and psychological aspects 141; mother, impact of dyslexia on 146–147; motivation for studying 146; reading achievement and progress 141–142; self-determination and coping 145–146; self-efficacy and motivation 145–146; Self-Efficacy Questionnaire for Children (S-EQC) 145; social development 144–145; teachers 141–142, 142–143

Johan, Swedish case study 33–49; Achievement Goal Disposition Survey 43; background 33–35; careers and future goals 46–47; Children's Hope Scale 43; coping 43–44; diagnosis and treatment 33–34; educational perspectives 35–41; family and home life 34–35; friends 41–42; future goals and hopes 46–47; homework 40–41; Johan 33–49; learning style 40; medical and psychological aspects 35; mother, impact of dyslexia on 44–46; motivation for studying 43; reading achievement and progress 35–39, 47; self-determination and coping 42–44; self-efficacy and motivation 42–43; Self-Efficacy Questionnaire for Children (S-EQC) 42; social development 41–42; teachers 36–37, 39–40

Jolly Phonics 203

Ka-Ho, Chinese case study 68–86; Achievement Goal Disposition Survey 77–78; background 68–72; careers and future goals 80–81; Children's Hope Scale 77; coping 78; diagnosis and treatment 68–70; educational perspectives 72–75; family and home life 70–71; friends 75–76; future goals and hopes 80–81; homework 75, 80; learning style 74–75; medical and psychological aspects 71–72; mother, impact of dyslexia on 79–80; motivation for studying 77–78; private tuition 75, 78, 79; reading achievement and progress 72–73; self-determination and coping 77–78; self-efficacy and motivation 77–78; Self-Efficacy Questionnaire for Children (S-EQC) 77; social development 75–76; teachers 73–74, 82–83

Kaufman Test of Educational Achievement - Second Edition 231

Koschay, E. 212

Lami, L. 44, 272
Landerl, K. 4, 267, 268, 269
learned helplessness 8, 10, 251

learning style: Alon 126–127; Christian 215–216; cross-case analysis 247–248; Gwyn 56; Jacob 195–196; Jankó 171; Jim 234; João 144; Johan 40; Ka-Ho 74–75; Percy 107–108; Valeriy 184; Vicente 157; Xavi 91–92
life coach 122
lifespan, dyslexia affecting development across 20
listening to children 15–16
longitudinal research: as distinct from outcome studies 19; Frostig Center 23–24; reading speed 268; study design 19–28
Lory Rechtschreibrest 210

Margalit, M. 16, 26, 133, 135, 262, 263, 264
McKendree, J. 47
McNulty, M. A. 20, 225, 247, 255, 258, 268
medical and psychological aspects: Alon 122–123; Christian 212; Gwyn 51–52; Jacob 194; Jankó 168–169; Jim 230–231; João 141; Johan 35; Ka-Ho 71–72; Percy 103; Valeriy 181–182; Vicente 154; Xavi 89
medical school study 47
Meeting Street School Screening Test (MSSST) 167
Mentes Unicas (Unique Minds) 88–89
metacognition 6–7
Montuschi, M. 44, 272
Morgan, P. 16
mothers, impact of dyslexia on: affecting relationship with fathers 60, 79, 175, 275; Alon 131; Christian 220–222; cross-case analysis 272–276; Gwyn 60–61; Jacob 199–201; Jankó 175–176; Jim 238–239; João 146–147; Johan 44–46; Ka-Ho 79–80; Percy 113–114; Valeriy 187; Vicente 160–161; Xavi 94–95
motivation for studying: Alon 129; Christian 219; cross-case analysis 259–260; Gwyn 59; Jacob 198–199; Jankó 174; Jim 235–236, 237; João 146; Johan 43; Ka-Ho 77–78; Percy 111–112; Valeriy 185–186; Vicente 159; Xavi 93–94
multisensory phonological approaches 4–5

Muris, P. 23, 24, 42, 43, 58, 63, 77, 93, 109, 110, 111, 128, 129, 145, 158, 173, 185, 197, 198, 218, 236, 257, 260, 261
Muter, V. 44, 63, 97, 272

narrative research 17
National Reading Panel (NICHD) 2, 4
Nitzan 134
note taking 38

Orton-Gillingham remedial method 4
outcome studies, as distinct from longitudinal studies 19

parenting practices, study of 118
participants in study 21–22
Peer Assisted Learning Strategies (PALS) 6
Percy, 19th century case study 16
Percy, Indian case study 101–120; Achievement Goal Disposition Survey 111; background 101–103; careers and future goals 105, 111, 115–116; Children's Hope Scale 110–111; coping 112–113; diagnosis and treatment 101–102; educational perspectives 104–109; family and home life 102–103; friends 109; future goals and hopes 114–116; homework 103, 108–109; learning style 107–108; medical and psychological aspects 103; mother, impact of dyslexia on 113–114; motivation for studying 111–112; private tuition 101–102, 104, 113, 117; reading achievement and progress 104–106; self-determination and coping 109–112; self-efficacy and motivation 109–112; Self-Efficacy Questionnaire for Children (S-EQC) 109–110; social development 109; teachers 105–106, 107
Perseverance 10, 23, 246t, 251–254
PHAST decoding program 5
phenomenology 17
phonics instruction 4, 193, 202–203, 229
Play-On Software 140
private tuition: Alon 123, 124; Jankó 170; Ka-Ho 75, 78, 79; Percy 101–102, 104, 113, 117; Vicente 154, 157, 161; Xavi 88
proactivity 10, 23, 246t, 249–251
Prueba de Dyslexia Específica 152

qualitative research methods 15, 16, 27; case study approach 16–19; distinction between quantitative and 18
quantitative research methods 18–19
questions, research 19–21; flexibility in asking 27

Raskind, M. H. 7, 9, 10, 16, 19, 20, 23, 24, 246, 249, 251, 254, 256, 258, 266
Raven's Matrices 33, 68
reading achievement and progress: academic development and implications 4–6; Alon 123–125; challenges 267–269, 267t; Christian 212–214; cross-case analysis 265–272, 276–277; Gwyn 52–55; improvement 264t, 265–267; Jacob 194–195; Jankó 169–170; Jim 231–233; João 141–142; Johan 35–39, 47; Ka-Ho 72–73; Percy 104–106; support 264t, 265, 270–272; Valeriy 182–183; Vicente 154–155; Xavi 89–90
reading aloud 52, 90, 127, 268; strategies to help with 269
reading disability, terminology 3–4
Reading Processes Assessment Battery, Revised (PROLEC-R) 87
reading programs 4–6, 50, 52–53, 62, 163, 193, 202, 213; in Canada 202–203; computerized fluency 269; F.A.S.T. Reading System 229; *Jolly Phonics* 203; Play-On Software 140; problems despite 240–241; in secondary school 5–6; *Understanding Words* 50; *Words in Colour* 193
reading, shared 97
reading speed 3, 267–268, 269; strategies to help with 269
Reiff, H. B. 5, 8, 9, 247, 248
remedial lessons: declining 123, 182, 193; group size 240; variables affecting progress rate for pupils 240–241
researchers: as listeners 15–16; selection of 22–23
retaining students 139, 146, 152, 160–161, 170, 210–211, 261
retesting for dyslexia, problems with 204
Riddick, B. 4, 9, 16, 20, 21, 81, 189, 190, 255
Rogers, R. 259

Rose Report 4
Rosetti, C. W. 10, 20
Russia: accommodations 189; awareness of dyslexia 190 *see also* Valeriy, Russian case study

Sätze nach Bauer 210
Schulte-Koerne, G. 224
scientific validity of tests and teaching methods for children with dyslexia 47
screen readers 40, 271–272
second languages, learning 36, 90, 102, 104–105, 123, 193, 204, 247; exemptions from 271; overlap in reading and language disabilities 133
self-awareness 10–11, 246–249, 246t
self-determination and coping: Alon 128–131; Christian 218–220; Gwyn 58–60; Jacob 197–199; Jankó 173–175; Jim 235–238; João 145–146; Johan 42–44; Ka-Ho 77–78; Percy 109–112; Valeriy 185–187; Vicente 158–160; Xavi 93–94
self-efficacy and motivation: Alon 128–129; Christian 218–219; cross-case analysis 260–262; family environment and links to 135; Gwyn 58–59; Jacob 197–199; Jankó 173–174; Jim 235–237; João 145–146; Johan 42–43; Ka-Ho 77–78; Percy 109–112; Valeriy 185–186; Vicente 158–160; Xavi 93–94
Self-Efficacy Questionnaire for Children (S-EQC) 24–25; Alon 128–129; Christian 218–219; cross-case analysis of scores 260–262, 261t; Gwyn 58–59; Jacob 197–198; Jankó 173; Jim 236; João 145; Johan 42; Ka-Ho 77; Percy 109–110; Valeriy 185; Vicente 158–159; Xavi 93
self-esteem: issues 8, 9, 58, 63, 84, 163, 176, 225, 254, 255, 256; sport as a boost to 117, 135, 194, 247
shared reading and writing activities 97
Shaywitz, S. E. 2, 4, 8, 240
siblings: with dyslexia 34, 70; impact of dyslexia on 131, 187, 200, 230, 238
Siegel, L. S. 3, 202, 204
Snowling, M. J. 3, 5, 44, 47, 48, 63, 97, 204, 272

Snyder, C. R. 23, 26, 43, 59, 63, 77, 93, 110, 129, 146, 159, 173, 186, 198, 219, 236, 249, 252, 254, 262, 263, 264
social development 9–10, 249, 250; Alon 127–128; Christian 217–218; Gwyn 57–58; Jacob 197; Jankó 172–173; Jim 235; João 144–145; Johan 41–42; Ka-Ho 75–76; Nitzan study of learning disabled students and 134; Percy 109; Valeriy 184; Vicente 158; Xavi 92–93
social media 42, 58, 71, 78, 172–173, 216
socioeconomic class and dyslexia 21–22, 97, 276
Spain: accessing special needs support 96, 98; awareness of dyslexia 98; Orientation Departments 98 *see also* Xavi, Spanish case study
specific learning difficulties 2
specific learning disability (SLD) 2
speech and language therapy 140, 147, 180–181
Spekman, N. J. 9, 23, 246, 266
Spelling Mastery 50
spelling programs 40, 50
sports: boost to self-esteem 117, 135, 194, 247; goal of success in 117, 132, 176, 205
Stake, R. E. 17, 18, 19, 20, 27, 28
stress: management research-based program 206; parental 44–45, 79, 131, 136, 187, 220, 238, 272–273, 274, 275; strategies for dealing with school 43, 64, 94, 237, 247, 252, 255
success attributes for dyslexia 10–11, 23–24, 246–249, 246t; appropriate goal setting 258–259; emotional stability 254–256; perseverance 246t, 251–254; proactivity 246t, 249–251; self-awareness 246–249, 246t; support systems 246t, 256–257
support: financial 45; groups for parents 161, 164; lack of school 273–274; and parental control 136; protective function of family 64, 163; reading 264t, 265, 270–272; social-emotional school 213, 214; use of effective systems 246t, 256–257
Sweden: eligibility for support in secondary school 34; financial support, special needs 45; investigation of methods and tests for children with dyslexia 47; shortcomings in teaching children with dyslexia 47–48 *see also* Johan, Swedish case study
synthetic phonics instruction 4, 193, 202–203

teachers: Alon 126; awareness of dyslexia 64–65, 78, 82–83, 96, 98, 119, 257; Christian 214–215; frequent changes of 36–37; Gwyn 55–56; insensitivity and lack of understanding 45–46, 74, 75, 251, 255, 256; Jacob 195; Jankó 170–171; Jim 233–234; João 141–142, 142–143; Johan 36–37, 39–40; Ka-Ho 73–74, 82–83; lack of support from 273; Percy 105–106, 107; -student relationships 250; students' ability to obtain support from 257; Valeriy 183; Vicente 156–157; Xavi 90–91
teasing 145, 235, 255–256
terminology 2–4
test accommodations 51, 55, 104, 123–124, 133–134, 189, 193; cross-case analysis 270–271; distress regarding 204; reluctance to accept 38; risk of losing right to 201, 277
Test of Early Reading Ability Third Edition 228

Understanding Words 50
Unique Minds (Mentes Unicas) 88–89
United States of America: ambiguous terminology 3–4; definitions of dyslexia 2–3 *see also* Jim, American case study

Valeriy, Russian case study 180–191; Achievement Goal Disposition Survey 185–186; background 180–182; careers and future goals 188; Children's Hope Scale 186; coping 186; diagnosis and treatment 180–181, 187; educational perspectives 182–184; family and home life 181; friends 184; future goals and hopes 188; homework 184; learning style 184; medical and psychological aspects 181–182; mother, impact of dyslexia on 187; motivation for studying 185–186; reading achievement and progress 182–183;

self-determination and coping 185–187; self-efficacy and motivation 185–186; Self-Efficacy Questionnaire for Children (S-EQC) 185; social development 184; teachers 183
Vicente, Chilean case study 152–166; Achievement Goal Disposition Survey 159; background 152–154; careers and future goals 161–162; Children's Hope Scale 159; coping 159–160; diagnosis and treatment 152–153; educational perspectives 154–158; family and home life 153; friends 158; future goals and hopes 161–162; homework 154, 157–158; learning style 157; medical and psychological aspects 154; mother, impact of dyslexia on 160–161; motivation for studying 159; private tuition 154, 157, 161; reading achievement and progress 154–155; self-determination and coping 158–160; self-efficacy and motivation 158–160; Self-Efficacy Questionnaire for Children (S-EQC) 158–159; social development 158; teachers 156–157
video games 60, 78, 147
videos, learning with 40, 108, 234, 248
visual processing speed 3

Wechsler Individual Achievement Test 51, 229, 231–232
Wechsler Intelligence Test for Children 33, 101, 121, 140, 210, 229
Wechsler Preschool and Primary Scales of Intelligence 228

Weiner, B. 23, 25, 43, 59, 77, 93, 111, 129, 146, 159, 174, 185, 198, 219, 237, 259
Wide Range Achievement Test 101, 104
Wilson Reading Method 4
Wimmer, H. 4, 267, 268
Woodcock Johnson-III Tests of Achievement 104, 228
Words in Colour 193
writing: accommodations 102; assessment test 88; mother's assistance with 56, 57; shared reading and 97; software programs 7, 213; using computers for 65, 196

Xavi, Spanish case study 87–100; Achievement Goal Disposition Survey 93–94; background 87–89; careers and future goals 93; Children's Hope Scale 93; coping 94; diagnosis and treatment 87–89; educational perspectives 89–92; family and home life 89; friends 92–93; future goals and hopes 95; homework 92; learning style 91–92; medical and psychological aspects 89; mother, impact of dyslexia on 94–95; motivation for studying 93–94; private tuition 88; reading achievement and progress 89–90; self-determination and coping 93–94; self-efficacy and motivation 93–94; Self-Efficacy Questionnaire for Children (S-EQC) 93; social development 92–93; teachers 90–91

Züricher Lesetest 210

Taylor & Francis eBooks

Helping you to choose the right eBooks for your Library

Add Routledge titles to your library's digital collection today. Taylor and Francis ebooks contains over 50,000 titles in the Humanities, Social Sciences, Behavioural Sciences, Built Environment and Law.

Choose from a range of subject packages or create your own!

Benefits for you
- Free MARC records
- COUNTER-compliant usage statistics
- Flexible purchase and pricing options
- All titles DRM-free.

Benefits for your user
- Off-site, anytime access via Athens or referring URL
- Print or copy pages or chapters
- Full content search
- Bookmark, highlight and annotate text
- Access to thousands of pages of quality research at the click of a button.

REQUEST YOUR **FREE** INSTITUTIONAL TRIAL TODAY

Free Trials Available
We offer free trials to qualifying academic, corporate and government customers.

eCollections – Choose from over 30 subject eCollections, including:

Archaeology	Language Learning
Architecture	Law
Asian Studies	Literature
Business & Management	Media & Communication
Classical Studies	Middle East Studies
Construction	Music
Creative & Media Arts	Philosophy
Criminology & Criminal Justice	Planning
Economics	Politics
Education	Psychology & Mental Health
Energy	Religion
Engineering	Security
English Language & Linguistics	Social Work
Environment & Sustainability	Sociology
Geography	Sport
Health Studies	Theatre & Performance
History	Tourism, Hospitality & Events

For more information, pricing enquiries or to order a free trial, please contact your local sales team:
www.tandfebooks.com/page/sales

The home of
Routledge books

www.tandfebooks.com